About the editors

Chris Saunders is an emeritus professor at the University of Cape Town and a research associate at the Centre for Conflict Resolution.

Gwinyayi A. Dzinesa is a former senior researcher at the Centre for Conflict Resolution in Cape Town.

Dawn Nagar is a researcher at the Centre for Conflict Resolution in Cape Town.

Region-building in southern Africa

Progress, problems and prospects

edited by Chris Saunders, Gwinyayi A. Dzinesa
and Dawn Nagar

Zed Books

LONDON | NEW YORK

Region-building in southern Africa: Progress, problems and prospects was first published in 2012 by Zed Books Ltd, 7 Cynthia Street, London N1 9JF, UK and Room 400, 175 Fifth Avenue, New York, NY 10010, USA

www.zedbooks.co.uk

Set in OurType Arnhem, Monotype Gill Sans Heavy by Ewan Smith, London
Index: ed.emery@thefreeuniversity.net
Cover designed by Rogue Four Design
Printed and bound by CPI (UK) Ltd, Croydon, CRO 4YY

FSC
www.fsc.org
MIX
Paper from responsible sources
FSC® C013604

Distributed in the USA exclusively by Palgrave Macmillan, a division of St Martin's Press, LLC, 175 Fifth Avenue, New York, NY 10010, USA

A catalogue record for this book is available from the British Library
Library of Congress Cataloging in Publication Data available

ISBN 978 1 78032 179 0 hb
ISBN 978 1 78032 178 3 pb

Contents

Illustrations

Tables

Figures

Map

Boxes

Abbreviations and acronyms

ACP	African, Caribbean and Pacific
AFRICOM	Africa Command (United States)
AGOA	Africa Growth and Opportunity Act (United States)
AIDS	Acquired Immune Deficiency Syndrome
ANC	African National Congress
APRM	African Peer Review Mechanism
ASF	African Stand-by Force
AU	African Union
BLNS	Botswana, Lesotho, Namibia and Swaziland
BNC	Bi-National Commission
BRIC	Brazil, Russia, India, China
CAADP	Comprehensive Africa Agriculture Development Programme
CCI	Climate Change Initiative
CCR	Centre for Conflict Resolution
CDM	Clean Development Mechanism
COMESA	Common Market for Eastern and Southern Africa
CRP	common revenue pool
DBSA	Development Bank of Southern Africa
DFI	development finance institution
DRC	Democratic Republic of the Congo
EAC	East African Community
EC	European Commission
ECCAS	Economic Community of Central African States
ECF	Electoral Commissions' Forum
ECOWAS	Economic Community of West African States
EEC	European Economic Community
EISA	Electoral Institute of Southern Africa
EMB	electoral management body
EPA	economic partnership agreement
EU	European Union
FAFS	Framework for African Food Security
FAO	Food and Agricultural Organization (United Nations)
FDI	foreign direct investment
FLS	Frontline States
FOCAC	Forum on China–Africa Cooperation
FRELIMO	Mozambique Liberation Front

FTA	free trade area/agreement
GAD	Declaration on Gender and Development (SADC)
GDP	gross domestic product
GEC	global environmental change
GHG	greenhouse gas
HIV	Human Immunodeficiency Virus
IDC	Industrial Development Corporation
IEPA	interim economic partnership agreement
IFPRI	International Food Policy Research Institute
IGAD	Intergovernmental Authority on Development
IMF	International Monetary Fund
IPCC	Intergovernmental Panel on Climate Change
MDC	Movement for Democratic Change (Zimbabwe)/Maputo Development Corridor
MDG	United Nations Millennium Development Goal
MFN	most favoured nation
MONUC	United Nations Organization Mission in the Congo (later MONUSCO, UN Stabilization Mission in the Congo)
MPLA	Popular Liberation Movement (Angola)
MW	megawatt
NEPAD	New Partnership for Africa's Development
NGO	non-governmental organization
OAU	Organization of African Unity
OPDSC	Organ on Politics, Defence and Security Cooperation (SADC)
PEMMO	Principles for Election Management, Monitoring and Observation
PEPFAR	President's Emergency Plan for AIDS Relief (George W. Bush, Jr)
PRC	People's Republic of China
PSC	Peace and Security Council (African Union)
RDF	revenue distribution formula
RDP	Reconstruction and Development Programme (South Africa)
REC	regional economic community
RISDP	Regional Indicative Strategic Development Plan (SADC)
RPTC	Regional Peacekeeping Training Centre
SACU	Southern African Customs Union
SADC	Southern African Development Community
SADCBRIG	SADC Stand-by Brigade
SADCC	Southern African Development Coordination Conference
SADC-PF	SADC Parliamentary Forum
SADCSF	SADC Stand-by Force
SAMP	Southern African Migration Project
SADF	South African Defence Force
SAPP	Southern African Power Pool

SDI	Spatial Development Initiative
SHIRBRIG	Standby High-Readiness Brigade (UN)
SIPO	Strategic Indicative Plan of the Organ (SADC)
SPA	SADC Programme of Action
SWAPO	South West Africa People's Organization
TB	tuberculosis
TDCA	Trade, Development and Cooperation Agreement
UN	United Nations
UNAVEM	United Nations Angola Verification Mission
UNCTAD	United Nations Conference on Trade and Development
UNDP	United Nations Development Programme
UNFCCC	United Nations Framework Convention on Climate Change
UNITA	National Union for the Total Independence of Angola
UNSCR	United Nations Security Council Resolution
UNTAG	United Nations Transitional Assistance Group
WFP	World Food Programme (United Nations)
WTO	World Trade Organization
ZANU-PF	Zimbabwe African National Union–Patriotic Front

Acknowledgements

This volume is one of the products of a four-year project on 'Peace-building in Africa' undertaken by the Centre for Conflict Resolution (CCR), in Cape Town, South Africa. Most of the chapters are based on papers presented at a policy seminar organized by CCR in Cape Town in February 2010, which explored the various processes involved in region-building in southern Africa, from organizations and institutions to issues of regional integration and human and military security. We would like to thank all those who participated at the seminar; their comments were tremendously helpful in shaping this publication. One of the sessions at the seminar, on how to turn the papers delivered there into a book, was chaired by the former publisher of the University of KwaZulu-Natal Press, Glenn Cowley. His lively interest in all of CCR's work made his sudden death in May 2011 the more shocking for those of us who knew him. We are certain that he would have welcomed the publication of this volume.

This is not the first book to be published on region-building in southern Africa, but it is perhaps the most wide-ranging in terms of the topics it addresses, as well as in its pan-African approach, with authors from South Africa, Lesotho, Namibia and Zimbabwe, along with two British scholars. We thank them all for responding to our queries so promptly and efficiently.

We would like to convey particular thanks to Adekeye Adebajo, Executive Director of CCR, for his guidance, enthusiasm and perseverance throughout the time it took to prepare this publication. We would also like to thank Jason Cook for his help in copy-editing the book, and our colleagues at CCR for their support and administrative assistance. Margie Struthers, the Centre's librarian, was always helpful in acquiring necessary source material.

We are grateful to all the contributors for their commitment to this project, and we thank Zed Books, and Ken Barlow in particular, for agreeing to publish this volume. We hope it may promote a lively debate on how region-building can be furthered in southern Africa and beyond.

Chris Saunders, Gwinyayi A. Dzinesa and Dawn Nagar
August 2011

Foreword

The Centre for Conflict Resolution (CCR), in Cape Town, South Africa, is pleased to be publishing this unique volume on *Region-building in Southern Africa.* The book is based largely on strong and diverse pan-African perspectives, involving both scholars and a few scholar-practitioners, including a former Executive Secretary of the Southern African Development Community (SADC), Kaire Mbuende.

Region-building is commonly defined as the effort by states in a common region to cooperate in ways that enhance their political, socio-economic, security and cultural integration. South Africa's role is central to any debates on region-building in southern Africa. Apartheid South Africa used its military strength aggressively to subdue its neighbours through a destructive policy of military destabilization that resulted in about a million deaths and cost southern Africa an estimated $60 billion in damages in the 1980s alone. The country currently accounts for about 80 per cent of the region's economic strength, and its corporations and franchises are ubiquitous across southern Africa. South Africa is potentially the dominant actor in both SADC and the Southern African Customs Union (SACU). Its Development Bank of Southern Africa (DBSA) and the Industrial Development Corporation (IDC) – historically used to support South African firms investing abroad – can, however, now play a potentially developmental role in the subregion, as can initiatives such as the Maputo Trade Corridor with Mozambique and the Southern Africa Power Pool. South Africa has contributed to peacemaking efforts in Lesotho, Zimbabwe and the Democratic Republic of the Congo (DRC) – a SADC member since 1997 – and is expected to play a leading role in the Southern African Brigade of an evolving African Stand-by Force (ASF). The country's past history of aggressive hegemonic dominance has, however, made its post-apartheid leaders cautious about appearing to impose their will on weaker neighbours.

The Southern African Customs Union, established in 1910 between South Africa, Botswana, Lesotho and Swaziland (and now involving Namibia), symbolized Pretoria's mercantilist approach towards its neighbours. Through SACU, South Africa promoted one-sided trade deals while restricting access to its own markets. This was a customs union that distributed its rewards unevenly. Agricultural products, vital for other SACU members, were excluded from tariff-free trade.

Pretoria unilaterally determined the union's tariffs and was responsible for administering all duties. Far from promoting industrial development within SACU, South Africa often obstructed the industrialization efforts of other members. For over a century, South Africa's mines, farms and industry also attracted hundreds of thousands of workers from neighbouring countries, becoming a major source of revenue for Mozambique, Malawi and Lesotho. Xenophobic attacks in South Africa against foreigners, largely from southern Africa, in May 2008, resulted in sixty-two deaths and about 100,000 displaced persons, again underlining the need for genuine region-building in southern Africa.

More positively, South Africa agreed to restructure SACU to render greater benefits to its other members, and to democratize decision-making. By 2004, the SACU headquarters was moved from South Africa's Department of Trade and Industry to an independent secretariat in Namibia. Policy-makers in Tshwane (formerly Pretoria) are now increasingly conscious of the need to promote investment and industrialization policies that benefit their neighbours. However, the divisions that occurred within SACU in 2008/09 over the European Union's (EU) economic partnership agreements (EPAs) are a clear sign that all is not well with the region-building project in southern Africa. The political and economic roles of China and the United States in the broader southern African region will also need to be closely watched. Prospects for a wider free trade area have, however, been boosted by an agreement in 2011 between SADC, the Common Market for Eastern and Southern Africa (COMESA) and the East African Community (EAC) which seeks to accelerate the establishment of a free trade area.

Governance and electoral challenges also remain in southern African countries such as Zimbabwe, Swaziland and Madagascar (suspended from SADC in March 2009 after an unconstitutional change of government), which will need to be urgently addressed if the region is to be stable. Southern Africa is the region of the world most badly affected by the HIV/AIDS pandemic; it continues to suffer droughts – linked also to issues of climate change – that have threatened food security; and despite some progress, the region continues to experience violence against women and challenges of gender inequality that must be addressed if region-building efforts are to progress in southern Africa. All the issues raised in this foreword are discussed in greater detail in this rich volume.

The Cape Town-based Centre for Conflict Resolution has established itself as one of the most internationally recognized think tanks in Africa. Having published ten previous books on topics as diverse as South Africa in Africa; Nigeria's foreign policy; China in Africa; the African Union and its institutions; the United Nations and Africa; Africa's human rights architecture; transitional justice in Africa; and HIV/AIDS and society in South Africa, the Centre is pleased to be publishing this unique collection on *Region-building in Southern Africa*, which builds on the Centre's well-received 2007 publication, *South Africa in Africa: The Post-Apartheid Era*, as well as a 2012 publication, *The EU and Africa: From Eurafrique to Afro-Europa*.

Between 2004 and 2011, CCR held ten policy seminars in South Africa, Namibia, Lesotho and Tanzania, which focused on: South Africa's role in Africa; the South African, Namibian and Tanzanian chairs of the SADC Security Organ; HIV/AIDS and militaries in southern Africa; strengthening the SADC Secretariat; civil society's contribution to security and governance in southern Africa; security and development in southern Africa; governments, traditional leaders and civil society in southern Africa; building peace in the Democratic Republic of the Congo; region-building in southern Africa; and state-building in Zimbabwe. Ten policy reports and three books (on South Africa in Africa, HIV/AIDS and society in South Africa, as well as this volume) have been produced from this work. I would like to thank all my colleagues at CCR who worked tirelessly on these projects, particularly Dawn Nagar, Elizabeth Otitodun and Angela Ndinga-Muvumba. I would also like to thank the three co-editors of this book, Chris Saunders, Gwinyayi Dzinesa and Dawn Nagar, for their tireless efforts in coordinating the nineteen pan-African authors of these sixteen chapters.

The current SADC Executive Secretary, Tomaz Augusto Salomão; former SADC Executive Secretaries Kaire Mbuende and Simba Makoni; director of the SADC Organ on Politics, Defence and Security Cooperation (OPDSC), Tanki Mothae; head of the SADC gender unit, Magdeline Mathiba-Madibela; head of the SADC HIV/AIDS unit, Antonica Hembe; head of the Planning Element of the SADC Brigade, General Lancaster Bottoman; Namibia's defence minister, General Charles 'Ho Chi Minh' Namoloh; chief of staff of Namibia's Defence Force, General Charles Shalumbu; HIV/AIDS Coordinator at the Namibian defence ministry, Colonel Marianne Muvangua; professor at the University of Namibia, André du Pisani; South Africa's Special Representative to the Great Lakes region, Welile Nhlapo; director-general in South Africa's Department of Military Veterans, Tsepe Motumi; former Director-General of Human Resources Management in the South African National Defence Force (SANDF), General Solly Mollo; former chief of the Botswana Defence Force, General Louis Fischer; and chief of Mozambique's Defence Force, General Paulino Macaringue – all contributed substantially to these efforts, and we are grateful for their time. We also thank all the scholars, policy-makers and civil society activists who have worked with us in seeking to build a more peaceful southern Africa over the last decade. In the same period, CCR's regional training programme has also worked to strengthen the conflict management capacity of government and civil society actors in Lesotho and Swaziland, and we are thankful for its rich practical insights into this research project.

This book thus builds on vast research, policy development and capacity-building experiences. It assesses southern Africa's contemporary region-building challenges, highlighting cases and actors such as South Africa, Angola, Namibia, Mozambique, Lesotho, Swaziland, Zimbabwe and the DRC. Attention is also paid to the four key priorities of the SADC Secretariat: military security; food security; HIV/AIDS; and governance. Though much literature exists on southern Africa's regional challenges, few comprehensive studies have yet addressed the broad spectrum of region-building challenges in post-apartheid southern Africa. We are particularly proud that a diverse team of scholars and policy intellectuals, including three southern African co-editors, have produced this volume.

Finally, I wish to thank the main funders of CCR's Africa Programme – the governments of Denmark, the Netherlands and Sweden – who provided the support for the publication of this book, and for supporting all the policy seminars, reports and policy briefs on southern Africa's region-building and peace-building challenges that we have produced over the last decade. I also thank the Swiss Agency for Development and Cooperation (SDC) for supporting the Centre's work in Lesotho and Swaziland.

Dr Adekeye Adebajo, Executive Director, Centre for Conflict Resolution, Cape Town, South Africa

Introduction

Gwinyayi A. Dzinesa, Dawn Nagar
and Chris Saunders

Region-building, which takes many different forms, may be defined in different ways. While some see it as 'the adoption of a regional project by a formal regional economic organization designed to enhance the political, economic, social, cultural, and security integration and/or cooperation of member states',[1] it is, more broadly, a process in which states and/or non-state actors cooperate in some way in a given region. Since the Second World War there have been many experiments in regional integration in different parts of the world, in which attempts have been made to harmonize policies among states and align state activities to accelerate regional development and to deal with regional challenges, whether political, economic or concerning security in one form or other.[2] This volume considers experiments of this kind carried out in southern Africa, the reasons for them, and why success has been so limited. Most of the sixteen chapters that follow were first presented as papers at a research and policy seminar held by the Centre for Conflict Resolution in Cape Town, South Africa, in February 2010.[3] They were subsequently revised and updated, and further papers were commissioned to expand the scope of this volume, whose authors are mostly African-based specialists.

Relatively little has been published to date on region-building in southern Africa. The single most substantial volume, Margaret C. Lee's *The Political Economy of Regionalism in Southern Africa*, was published in 2003. Gabriel Oosthuizen's *The Southern African Development Community: The Organisation, Its Policies and Prospects* is a useful factual compilation of material about SADC, but was published in 2006.[4] A number of Nordic scholars have written about the region; their books include Bertil Oden, *Southern Africa After Apartheid*; Lennart Petersson, *Post-Apartheid Southern Africa*; and Fredrik Soderbaum's sociological account entitled *The Political Economy of Regionalism: The Case of Southern Africa*.[5] Other work focuses not on region-building as such but on South Africa and the region: David Simon (ed.), *South Africa in Southern Africa: Reconfiguring the Region*; Mwesiga Baregu and Christopher Landsberg (eds), *From Cape to Congo: Southern Africa's Evolving Security Challenges*; and Adekeye Adebajo, Adebayo Adedeji and Chris Landsberg (eds), *South Africa in Africa: The Post-Apartheid Era*.[6] *From Cape to Congo*, which is perhaps the closest to the present book, grew out of a seminar held in 2000; the present book not only presents an update, a decade later, but addresses many new topics, such as the impact of food security, migration and climate change on the region and the role of development financial institutions in southern African region-building efforts.

Regionalism: a conceptual and empirical assessment

Theories relating to regional integration in Europe, and experience there, may provide lessons for region-building in southern Africa, if carefully applied to a very different context. In Europe, regional integration evolved from the European Coal and Steel Community (ECSC) of 1951 into the European Economic Community (EEC) in 1957, and then into the Maastricht Treaty of 1992, which formally inaugurated the European Union (EU).[7] The initial aim was merely to provide a framework within which to produce and market coal and steel across Europe, prevent competition and ultimately jointly regulate and end tariffs and border controls. In fostering transnational interdependence in one area, the ECSC in turn created the possibility of interdependence in others.[8]

Between 1958 and 1964, the European integration experience provided Ernst Haas with the framework for his theory of 'neo-functionalism', which rejected the artificial separation of politics from economics and argued that transborder exchanges and cooperation in technical areas would increase transnational interdependence, in turn creating functional spillovers and leading to a free trade area, a customs union, a single market, a common currency and an economic and political union.[9] As we will see in this volume, in southern Africa the spillover effects of regional cooperation have been limited, owing to lack of adequate economic and political government structures, institutions and policies. An audit report of the African Union (AU) in 2007, chaired by Adebayo Adedeji, executive secretary of the United Nations Economic Commission for Africa (UNECA) between 1975 and 1991, highlighted the many capacity challenges that African states still face, including funding and human resource problems, as well as inadequate planning. In general, regional integration requires strengthening the capacity of states to fulfil their core functions.

In southern Africa, market integration efforts have attempted to expand the region's 'periphery' by strengthening weaker economies through robust trade and market integration efforts. These have been relatively unsuccessful to date, as evidenced by South Africa's outward-looking trading patterns – though the country accounts for 70 per cent of overall trade in the Southern African Development Community (SADC), about 90 per cent of South Africa's trade is conducted outside the region.[10] As Andre Gunder Frank suggests, the core can be a major obstacle to regional integration when it begins feeding off the periphery in its imbalance of trade.[11] Yet South Africa should provide leadership in region-building efforts in southern Africa. Charles Kindleberger defines hegemonic stability as strong leadership and responsibility by a single dominant state, and Robert Keohane's theory of 'hegemonic power' asserts that a single state can be dominant yet simultaneously and freely establishing and maintaining the norms and rules of a liberal economic order.[12]

Before the advent of African independence, such leaders as Côte d'Ivoire's Félix Houphouët-Boigny, Kenya's Jomo Kenyatta and Senegal's Léopold Senghor believed that economic integration should precede political integration.[13] Other leaders, most notably Ghana's Kwame Nkrumah, pushed for federalist political integration in the form of a 'United States of Africa'. During the struggle for political independence, African continental unity and regional cooperation was a strategy for combating foreign dependence and underdevelopment. In the late 1950s, scholars of regionalism identified six key stages critical to integration: a preferential trade area, a free trade area, a customs union, a common market, an economic union and a common monetary zone. (See Khadiagala in this volume.) When African states became independent, however, their leaders wanted to preserve their independence and adopt an incremental process to regional integration as a stepping stone towards eventual continental unity.[14] The Ghana–Guinea–Mali Union, formed in 1958, lasted only three years,[15] and as the number of independent African states grew from 1960, leaders found it difficult to implement economic and political integration. The UN's Economic Commission for Africa (ECA), founded in 1958 to support Africa's regional integration efforts, helped to establish several regional economic communities (RECs).[16] These, it was hoped, would boost trade and investment and provide greater economies of scale, while allowing for freer movement of resources and people, greater cooperation, peace and security, and improved bargaining power. These regional groupings included the Economic Community of West African States (ECOWAS), the Economic Community of Central African States (ECCAS), the Economic Community of the Great Lakes, the East African Community (EAC), and the Eastern and Southern African Preferential Trade Area (PTA), which later became the Common Market for Eastern and Southern Africa (COMESA).[17]

Though the Organization of African Unity (OAU) had been created in May 1963 primarily to accelerate political liberation, particularly in southern Africa, in 1991 it took on the challenge of regional integration by adopting the Abuja Treaty, which recognized the coordination, harmonization and integration of Africa's RECs as a prerequisite to their serving as building blocks for the creation of an African Common Market by 2028. Similar to Europe's 1957 Treaty of Rome, the Abuja Treaty followed the gradualist approach to integration adopted by the UN's ECA, and regarded the subregional bodies as the building blocks for the functional integration of the continent. The 2007 audit report of the AU, the successor to the OAU in 2002, reaffirmed the Abuja Treaty as the blueprint for regional economic cooperation and the road map for integration efforts on the continent.[18]

The AU's Assembly of Heads of State and Government meeting in Banjul, Gambia, in July 2006 officially recognized eight RECs: the Arab Maghreb Union (AMU), COMESA, the Community of Sahel-Saharan States (CEN-SAD), the East African Community, the Economic Community of Central African States, the Economic Community of West African States, the Intergovernmental Authority on Development (IGAD) and SADC.[19] While regional integration seeks to strengthen the capacity of states to fulfil their core functions, each of Africa's RECs has its own interests and agendas, which obstruct effective cooperation within and between these bodies. The fact that most African states belong to more than one regional economic grouping continues to hinder the implementation of key political and economic processes, such as trade agreements, at the subregional level.[20]

Regional integration: the case of southern Africa

Southern Africa has a long history of regional cooperation, though there have been many different ideas about what the region should comprise. Though southern Africa has never been united politically, certain commonalities underpin its region-building project. One is a history of colonialism, for though different European colonial powers were involved – Britain, Germany and Portugal – the entire region was subject to a form of colonial rule until the 1960s. Struggles against colonialism and white settler rule were to some extent interlinked across the region. Because of its relatively advanced economy, what is now South Africa has long attracted migrant workers from elsewhere in the region, and, since the gold and diamond revolution in the late nineteenth century, which attracted colonial buccaneers such as Cecil Rhodes, arguments for region-building have been advanced based on ideas of having a larger market, integrating means of transport and imposing common tariffs and customs. The creation of the Union of South Africa from four territories in 1910 was, in a sense, a region-building project, and the makers of the Union expected at the time that the new entity would in time come to embrace other parts of southern Africa. Certainly it was anticipated that the three British High Commission territories of Basutoland, Bechuanaland and Swaziland would be incorporated into the Union of South Africa. In 1910 these three states, together with South Africa, formed the Southern African Customs Union (SACU), now the oldest such union in the developing world. The incorporation of the British territories into the Union never happened, because of the racist policies of the Union government, and because, for the same reason, what had been German South West Africa, which South Africa seized in 1915 and then occupied, was never formally incorporated into South Africa.[21] When South African occupation of that de facto colony finally ended

4

in March 1990, and it became the independent country of Namibia, the country joined SACU as its fifth member. (See Gibb in this volume.)

A number of other attempts at region-building have been made. The British formed the Central African Federation in the early 1950s as a counterweight to apartheid South Africa, and thirty years later, in 1979, the apartheid government of Pieter Willem Botha in South Africa, then in the process of granting nominal 'independence' to four South African Bantustans (Transkei, Ciskei, Bophuthatswana and Venda), proposed the idea of a Constellation of Southern African States (CONSAS), an idea that never came to fruition because of its apartheid origins. Much more significant, the independent southern African states that were opposed to apartheid South Africa came together as the Frontline States (FLS) from the mid-1970s. After the independence of Zimbabwe in 1980, the FLS formed with that country the more formal Southern African Development Coordination Conference (SADCC), composed of nine states: Angola, Botswana, Lesotho, Malawi, Mozambique, Swaziland, Tanzania, Zambia and Zimbabwe. (See Khadiagala and Mbuende in this volume.) SADCC aimed to coordinate action against the apartheid regime, then destabilizing the region through attacks on neighbouring countries, which the Botha government claimed were harbouring guerrillas of the region's liberation movements. An estimated one million deaths and $60 billion of damages resulted from these policies in the 1980s.[22]

The era of destabilization ended in the late 1980s. As South Africa, which had the largest and most industrialized economy in the region, moved from apartheid to democracy beginning in 1990, SADCC restructured itself and, in August 1992 in Windhoek, established SADC, which South Africa joined after its first democratic election in 1994. (South Africa might also have joined the larger Common Market for Eastern and Southern Africa, but chose not to, in part because of its debt to the former FLS and in part because there was a perception at the time that COMESA was too large and unwieldy.)[23] Under President Nelson Mandela (1994–99) and his successors Thabo Mbeki (1999–2008) and Jacob Zuma (2009–), South Africa has played an active role in promoting subregional stability and development. Meanwhile, SADC was greatly enlarged in size with the addition to its membership of the sprawling Democratic Republic of the Congo (DRC) in 1997. Though endowed with great mineral wealth, the Congo remains both extremely poor and conflict-prone. Other SADC states – Angola, Namibia, South Africa and Zimbabwe – have been involved in the DRC, both militarily and as peacemakers, aided in the latter role by a 20,000-strong UN mission.

Unlike the EU, SADC has added new members without imposing any tests of readiness for membership. It has grown to fifteen states, though at the time of writing in 2011, Madagascar was suspended from the organization because of the unconstitutional way in which the military-dominated government there, under President Andry Rajoelina, came to power. But SADC essentially encompasses the entire southern half of the African continent, as well as island-states off the East African coast: Mauritius has played a leading role in SADC, while Seychelles rejoined the organization in 2008. One of the major tasks of the organization has been to bring stability to the region as a whole, but the autocratic regimes in a number of its member states, such as Zimbabwe and Swaziland, have not been effectively challenged, and SADC has failed to link development, its main goal, with democracy. (See especially Matlosa in this volume.)

SADC's developmental framework

With an expanded mandate for greater economic and political integration of the subregion, SADC was committed to the creation of 'a framework and mechanisms to strengthen regional solidarity and provide for mutual peace and security'.[24] (See Landsberg in this volume.) SADC placed great emphasis on integrating markets within the subregion and strengthening economic ties between SADC member states and external actors. This 'new regionalism' meant the removal of some trade barriers and greater movement of goods, people and capital across national borders. A range of multinational corporations – mainly South African-based – were able to develop new markets. But open or 'neoliberal regionalism' differs from 'development regionalism', which speaks to the role of the state and its intervention in markets to promote national development agendas, yet at the same time can serve as a vehicle to achieve global competitiveness. As a number of chapters in this volume show, developmental integration still has a long way to go in southern Africa. The economies of most of the states in the region remain weak, and there are inherited divisions that work against united action, while institutional capacity is lacking for both national and supranational entities. And the benefits of regionalism have come at a price: increased migration has, for example, created new challenges, such as the wave of xenophobic attacks in South Africa in 2008, which resulted in sixty-two deaths and over 100,000 displaced persons.[25] (See Nyamnjoh and Mususa in this volume.)

Effective regional integration requires democratic governance, political will and visionary leadership. National political and economic policies have to be aligned with regional agendas.[26] SADC's fifteen members have instead seen limited results in generating internal wealth and in tackling poverty and diseases such as HIV/AIDS. (See Dzinesa and Drimie and Gandure in this volume.) Though a regional free trade area (FTA) was established in 2008, southern Africa's 'periphery' remains heavily dependent on the 'core'. As mentioned earlier, South Africa, the regional hegemon, is responsible for 70 per cent of southern Africa's overall trade.[27] While the 'new regionalism' agenda emphasizes the need to build intra-regional trade in order to compete in the global marketplace, unilateral actions have worked against that agenda, such as the bilateral preferential trade agreement between Namibia and Zimbabwe that entered into force in 1992, the Europe–South Africa Trade, Development and Cooperation Agreement (TDCA) of 1999, and the recent interim economic partnership agreements (IEPAs) signed with the European Union by Botswana, Lesotho, Swaziland and Mozambique, but not South Africa and Namibia, in June 2009.[28] The TDCA, which offered trade and tariff preferences for EU goods entering South Africa, was seen by other SADC countries as a major threat to regional development and the chances of success for a SADC free trade area.[29]

SADC aims at both production integration – based on what particular countries can best produce, and under what conditions – and market integration. But three of its members (Angola, the DRC and Seychelles) are not yet part of the free trade area, introduced in 2008, while eight SADC member states – the DRC, Madagascar, Malawi, Mauritius, Seychelles, Swaziland, Zambia and Zimbabwe – also belong to COMESA. Angola and the DRC are members of the Economic Community of Central African States, Mauritius is part of the Indian Ocean Commission (IOC), and Tanzania belongs to the EAC. The SADC member states that belong to other RECs are subject to various negotiation protocols, which makes implementing such protocols difficult.[30]

SADC countries plan to eliminate barriers to trade in goods and services, establish a common external system of tariffs, and redistribute tariff revenues among themselves. A monetary union could bring real advantages to the southern African subregion and would, among other things, reduce the transaction costs associated with trading goods and services between countries using different currencies. In 1986 a common monetary area (CMA) agreement was signed by Lesotho, South Africa and Swaziland, while Namibia joined the CMA after it became independent in 1990.[31] But SADC still needs to create both the institutional capacity and the conditions for currency convergence among its fifteen members. The customs union, which was to begin in 2010, has not been achieved, and now the plan is that a common market for SADC's 257 million people is to be created by 2015, a monetary union by 2016, and a common currency by 2018. And southern Africa's regional integration efforts have to date produced little real trade liberalization within SADC. Where strong trade links exist, they have generally been created by strong bilateral deals with South Africa, such as those agreed by Mozambique, Zambia and Zimbabwe in 2000.[32] Though in February 2010 SADC urged its members to strengthen the free trade area, talks had begun in October 2008 between SADC, COMESA and the EAC, in Kampala, Uganda, on forming a tripartite free trade area, and the idea was pushed strongly by President Zuma of South Africa in 2011. Such a tripartite free trade area would cover twenty-six states and more than half of the entire continent, but whether the three regional organizations will be able to work together effectively remains to be seen.

While South Africa's economy continues to dominate the subregion, this is not reflected in a comparable level of trade with southern Africa. In 2010, South Africa's exports to Asia were R19.5 billion; to the European Union more than R16 billion, and to China and America more than R7 billion. But South Africa's total trade with other SADC countries amounted to less than R6 billion, and its imports from SADC countries were worth only R2.3 billion.[33] South Africa accounted for 70 per cent of all foreign direct investment in southern Africa, although external investment in Angola and the DRC has risen rapidly as a result of trade with China. (See Nagar, le Pere in this volume.) South Africa's trade patterns therefore provide little relative benefit to other SADC member states. Other factors that have hindered regional integration in southern Africa have included conflicts, such as those in Angola and Mozambique from the 1970s, apartheid South Africa's military destabilization of the region, especially in the 1980s, and the war in the DRC from 1996, which has constrained that country from joining SADC's free trade area. High levels of crime in South Africa have also deterred foreign direct investment into the country and neighbouring states. It is abundantly clear that SADC's economic goals can be realized only when the southern African subregion achieves peace and security.

Politics, security and governance

As Africa's RECs have evolved, they have begun to tackle such issues as 'good governance', peace and security, gender, food security, HIV/AIDS and climate change. Democratic governance, for example, plays a critical role in economic development and region-building, and southern Africa is confronted with ongoing governance challenges that include the need to consolidate democracy, weak electoral and oversight processes, and tensions around political power-sharing. (See Matlosa in this volume.) The absence of peace, security and stability has had deleterious consequences for region-building in Africa. For example, the conflict in the Great Lakes brought region-building in ECCAS to a standstill. The civil war in the DRC in the late 1990s was particularly divisive, as were conflicts in Rwanda and Burundi in the same period. Wars in Liberia, Sierra Leone, Guinea-Bissau and Côte d'Ivoire slowed region-building in the ECOWAS region. Sudan's protracted north–south wars, the destructive conflict in the country's western Darfur region, the Ethiopia–Eritrea war of 1998–2000 and persistent conflict in Somalia have also had adverse impacts on region-building in eastern Africa.[34] In SADC, instability during the apartheid era, prolonged conflict in Angola and the DRC, and an attempted coup d'état in Lesotho in 1998, followed by a military intervention by South Africa and Botswana, adversely impacted regional integration.

Against such a background, most RECs have incorporated peace and security into their constitutive instruments and have a clear mandate to resolve conflicts and keep the peace in their regions. This is in line with Chapter VIII of the United Nations Charter of 1945, which encourages the peaceful settlement of local disputes through regional arrangements. The AU's fifteen-member Peace and Security Council (PSC) also seeks to build a continental peace and security architecture that not only focuses on military deployment, but also involves preventive deployment of effective mediation strategies as well as early response systems. Africa's five subregions (Southern, Central, Eastern, North and West) are currently engaged in establishing stand-by brigades as part of the AU's 15,000-strong Standby Force. (The AU seems to think it is ready!) The force will consist of stand-by brigades from all five African subregions, and will undertake traditional peacekeeping operations as well as observer missions and peace-building activities. SADC is in the process of creating a Southern Africa Stand-by Brigade (SADCBRIG) to engage in multidimensional UN and AU peacekeeping operations.[35] (See Saunders in this volume.)

Gender issues play a significant role within the frameworks of the RECs, which recognize how gender inequality adversely impacts region-building efforts. The Abuja Treaty of 1991 requires member states to establish and harmonize policies and mechanisms for the full participation of African women in development by improving their economic, social and cultural conditions.[36] Achieving gender equality is enshrined in the treaties, protocols and constitutions of Africa's RECs. Several RECs, such as SADC and ECOWAS, have also established gender units to promote gender equality and ensure implementation of the various international, continental and regional conventions on gender equality. For example, the COMESA Treaty has an entire chapter dedicated to women's issues,[37] and the organization adopted a gender policy in 2005. The ECOWAS Treaty calls upon member states to establish and harmonize policies and mechanisms for enhancing women's economic, social and cultural conditions. The treaties that established the EAC and IGAD also provide for regional cooperation on gender matters. SADC recognizes that the mainstreaming of gender issues into its legal framework is important for sustainable regional development. (See Otitodun and Porter in this volume.) It established a gender unit in 1998 and has adopted instruments such as the 2008 Protocol on Gender and Development.

The devastating HIV/AIDS pandemic is one of the pervasive threats to region-building in southern Africa, the worst-affected region in the world and home to 35 per cent of all people living with HIV/AIDS worldwide and 32 per cent of new HIV infections and AIDS-related deaths worldwide. (See Dzinesa in this volume.) Region-building initiatives can have a twofold impact on HIV/AIDS. First, since the pandemic transcends borders, it can be accelerated by the population mobility facilitated by regional integration. Secondly, and conversely, region-building can also contribute to controlling HIV/AIDS through the coordination of policies across countries, harmonization of responses, and pooling and scaling of resources. Global resources in the fight against HIV/AIDS have supported regional initiatives, and Africa's RECs have mainstreamed health issues into their priority programmes. SADC was the first organization to adopt a protocol on health and formulate a substantive, normative HIV/AIDS framework. These initiatives and protocols have resonated with continental and global instruments and mechanisms to combat the impact of HIV/AIDS, such as the 2001 Abuja framework to combat HIV/AIDS and related opportunistic infections; the SADC HIV/AIDS Strategic Framework and Plan of Action: 2003–2007, adopted in Maseru, Lesotho, in July 2003;[38] and the 2006 Brazzaville commitment to upscale universal access to HIV/AIDS prevention, treatment, care and support.

There is a growing recognition that climate change will negatively affect all of Africa's economic sectors and will therefore present unique challenges for region-building and sustainable development on the continent.[39] This has made it imperative for Africa's RECs, such as SADC, to integrate strategies to combat the negative impacts of climate change on their resources, livelihoods and economies into national decision-making processes. African countries are promoting the 2009 'African Common Position on Climate Change', which seeks predictable and reliable funding to fight development challenges posed by the impacts of climate change.[40] Some RECs have developed policy frameworks to combat climate change and its adverse impact. (See Simon in this volume.) African countries have also increasingly recognized that efficient and effective region-building cannot be exclusively driven by governments and non-governmental organizations (NGOs). Private sector and development finance institutions (DFIs), such as the Development Bank of Southern Africa (DBSA) and the Industrial Development Corporation (IDC), have been constructive partners in strengthening development and region-building. DFIs, for example, have been important providers of human capital as well as technical and financial support for the implementation of projects that promote regional development and region-building, such as construction of infrastructure. (See Monyae in this volume.) Some RECs, such as the East African Community, have specific protocols on the role of the private sector in region-building. In West Africa, Ecobank Transnational Incorporated (ETI) has funded region-building schemes and currently has a presence in eighteen countries, with a network of over 320 branches and offices established between 2000 and 2010.[41]

International links and key trade partners

External actors, such as the United States, China and the EU, have played important roles in supporting, or sometimes undermining, region-building in Africa through security, political and trade relationships with the RECs. The US Africa Growth and Opportunity Act (AGOA) of 2000 aimed to boost trade between Africa and the USA,[42] but has been criticized for being too focused on oil exports from African countries. External actors such as the USA can potentially play a critical role in supporting efforts towards development, and Washington stands to gain from engagement with SADC, with which it has been negotiating a free trade accord. The USA believes that investing in African national armies and subregional organizations would help prevent, manage and resolve conflicts and thereby 'reduce pressure on US forces to conduct reactive combatant evacuation and humanitarian relief operations'.[43] Building partnership capacity is a key goal of American military strategy in Africa, and is consequently a key mandate for the US Africa Command (AFRICOM).[44] The USA supports development of the African Stand-by Force (ASF), but its anti-terrorism activities have been criticized for violating civil liberties in African countries, such as in Djibouti, where 1,200 US troops have been deployed. While AFRICOM is perceived, in some American quarters, as building partnership capacity, some key SADC states and civil society activists see it as an example of American military expansionism in the name of the 'war on terror' waged under the administration of George W. Bush between 2001 and 2008. It is important, therefore, to monitor the development of AFRICOM in order to safeguard the interests of Africa's subregions, including southern Africa. (See Ngwenya in this volume.)

China proposed creation of the Forum on China–Africa Cooperation (FOCAC),[45] which was established in October 2000 and began as a triennial ministerial conference that aimed to provide a mechanism for collective consultation, dialogue and pragmatic cooperation between China and African countries. While Beijing has a structured, long-term view of engaging Africa at FOCAC, Africa has yet to develop a coherent multilateral response to the initiative. Analysts have stressed the need for the AU and Africa's RECs to adopt appropriate policies, strategies and responses to engaging China more effectively, in order to ensure that this partnership promotes effective region-building on the continent.[46] (See le Pere in this volume.)

The EU has sought to devise a comprehensive, integrated and long-term framework for its relations with Africa, including the continent's regional organizations. In December 2005, Brussels adopted a strategic document entitled 'The EU and Africa: towards a strategic partnership'.[47] This document – based on the four pillars of 'good governance'; peace and security; trade; and health, education and a safe environment – sought to support Africa's efforts to achieve the UN Millennium Development Goal of halving poverty by 2015, and to establish the practical modalities for an ongoing partnership between Africa and Europe. The policy was one-sided, however, having been developed and refined within the EU Commission in Brussels with little or no input from partner states in Africa.[48] In consultation with the AU, this document was later amended into a joint strategy and action plan, with substantial follow-up and monitoring mechanisms duly approved at the EU–Africa summit in Lisbon, Portugal, in December 2007. Central to the debates on EU–southern Africa relations is the fate of SACU. In 2011, this relationship hung in the balance as a result of the IEPAs. (See Gibb, Qobo in this volume.) SACU members remain divided on the question: South Africa and Namibia oppose IEPAs with the EU, while Botswana, Swaziland and Lesotho have signed them for fear of losing out on EU aid and market access. Such divisions could have negative and pernicious implications for region-building in southern Africa.[49]

Structure of the book

Historical legacy Part One of this book provides background to current issues in region-building in southern Africa. Kenyan scholar Gilbert Khadiagala provides a historical overview of the Frontline States and then the Southern African Development Coordination Conference, and identifies two legacies of the latter – first a state-centric and highly individualized regionalism, and secondly a sector-led coordination approach defined as 'decolonization-driven regionalism' that promotes infrastructural development through Spatial Development Initiatives (SDIs). An example of the latter is the transport corridors used as a means of promoting regional integration to mitigate the effects of economic dependence on apartheid South Africa. Khadiagala discusses the impact of these legacies on SADC and its efforts to build autonomous institutions, and concludes with recommendations for a new phase of regionalism, involving both market and economic integration and security efforts, that can forge a common identity and help in peace-building, peacemaking and conflict resolution efforts in southern Africa.

Kaire Mbuende, a Namibian technocrat who was SADC Executive Secretary between 1994 and 1999, provides an insider perspective on the creation of SADC and its *raison d'être*, including mediation processes and shuttle diplomacy practices. Mbuende analyses the genesis of regional integration in southern Africa and the development of an agenda of three pillars: political cooperation, functional cooperation and market integration. This made southern Africa's regional integration agenda complex and difficult to manage. The author discusses the importance of a peaceful and secure state for creating viable markets and attracting foreign direct investment, which is critical to achieving regional development in southern Africa. He elaborates on SADC's institutional architecture as its economic and security practices evolved. Mbuende claims that southern Africa's regional integration efforts are unique, for SADC has embarked on a complex regional integration process that includes political, economic, social and cultural aspects. Successful integration will depend on the contributions of governments, institutions and non-state actors, but the multiplicity of commitments under the various multiple trade integration schemes have worked against a SADC trade regime. Mbuende concludes by suggesting that SADC should take bold steps to advance its market integration strategy and become less dependent on external donor support.

Governance and military security In Part Two we turn to governance and military security perspectives. South African scholar Chris Landsberg shows the key role of the heads of state summits and the Organ on Politics, Defence and Security Cooperation (OPDSC), but finds the SADC Secretariat to be overwhelmed and therefore not as effective as it might be. He advances suggestions as to how the SADC Tribunal could be strengthened, and argues for civil society to play a more important role in region-building and outlines the institutional architecture of SADC. In the next chapter, Lesotho academic Khabele Matlosa is concerned mainly with governance and electoral issues. As Matlosa points out, the holding of elections does not necessarily mean that a democratic regime is in place; few SADC countries are effective liberal democracies. South African historian Chris Saunders then discusses the UN's peacekeeping involvement in four SADC countries – Namibia, Angola, Mozambique and the DRC – traces the development of the idea of creating a SADC Stand-by Force, as part of a continental African Stand-by Force, and considers how the SADC force might be used. Elizabeth Otitodun and Antonia Porter, a South African and a British analyst respectively, then highlight in their joint chapter the importance of mainstreaming gender into peace-building and region-building processes. They outline the evolving regional and international gender architecture, and specifically the problems and progress of and prospects for promoting gender equality in the region through the implementation of SADC, continental and international gender instruments. They argue that, while progress has been made, greater political will is required if the gaps in implementing the region's gender instruments are to be filled. Employing the cases of Angola and the DRC – countries that have recently experienced prolonged conflict – they demonstrate how women have played important peace-building roles.

Economic integration Part Three of the volume considers economic integration. Dawn Nagar, a South African analyst, first discusses SADC's resource-led development strategy, which involves SDIs and the Southern African Power Pool (SAPP). Through a detailed analysis of SAPP, the author identifies a number of areas of concern, such as the profound imbalance between supply and demand in the region's electricity grid for its twelve SADC member states; the hegemonic position of South Africa as the largest consumer of electricity and the dominance of its parastatal power utility, Eskom; and the DRC's abandonment of an electricity project that could have benefited the region but which failed to secure a partnership owing to South Africa's hegemonic position and a multibillion-dollar agreement with China. Nagar further assesses SADC's free trade area, the hegemonic position of South Africa and its skewed trade patterns within the region, and the role of powerful multinational corporations. The author discusses SADC's Regional Indicative Strategic Development Plan (RISDP) of 2003, which seeks economic growth and development within the region but has been unable to address how members with relatively large manufacturing sectors, such as South Africa and Mauritius, can use their comparative advantage effectively for region-building.

British academic Richard Gibb then discusses the Southern African Customs Union and the pressure exerted by South Africa on the four other SACU members – Botswana, Lesotho, Namibia and Swaziland – in wanting to restructure several strategic elements underpinning the arrangement. He explains the importance of regionalism as a mechanism to integrate smaller markets by creating larger ones that are more successful within the global economy. He believes that regionalism should be viewed in terms of both security and politics as much as economics and trade. SACU's asymmetrical imbalance of trade leaves South Africa with a multibillion-dollar regional trading surplus, and Gibb notes that South Africa now wants to renegotiate SACU's distribution formula, which would seriously disadvantage its poorer members. This poses a threat to the continued existence of SACU itself, though South Africa has said that it aims to enlarge SACU by bringing other SADC countries into the Union. South Africa's trade with its SACU partners remains a relatively minor component of its overall trade, however: in 2007/08, SACU imports constituted only 2 per cent of South Africa's total imports, and over 91 per cent of SACU's gross domestic product was produced in South Africa. By contrast, SACU payments accounted for over 60 per cent of Lesotho's government revenue in 2008. SACU therefore raises the question of how a semi-developed state, South Africa, can best be integrated with relatively poor and much less economically developed countries. Gibb notes, however, that SACU should not be seen as only an economic and technical issue, for regionalism is as much a political and social process as an economic one. SACU forms a core to the building of a larger regionalism in southern Africa, since all its member states belong to SADC.

Finally, David Monyae, a South African scholar, focuses on institutions that are rarely explored in region-building debates. He considers development finance institutions as important actors in region-building in southern Africa through infrastructure development. Lack of infrastructure has hindered economic growth and development in the region and can fuel conflicts and tensions. Monyae focuses on the roles of two South African DFIs, the Development Bank of Southern Africa and the Industrial Development Corporation, in promoting infrastructure development in southern Africa and the rest of Africa. He argues that South African DFIs could potentially become key vehicles in the implementation of the country's foreign policy objectives to contribute to economic development and integration in southern Africa.

Human security Part Four of the volume is concerned with human security issues. Scott Drimie, a South African scholar, and Sithabiso Gandure, a Zimbabwean analyst, together assess southern Africa's chronic food and nutrition insecurity and SADC's response to this situation. They maintain that food security is the cornerstone of human security and suggest that food insecurity presents a major threat to peace and security efforts in southern Africa. They conclude that SADC's responses to food insecurity have remained static, making it critical for southern African governments to deliver on their commitments to implement declarations in various SADC protocols and agreements in order to address this crisis. Zimbabwean scholar Gwinyayi Dzinesa then provides in his chapter a critical assessment of the nexus between the HIV/AIDS pandemic and human security. He observes that southern Africa remains the 'global epicentre of HIV/AIDS' and that the pandemic has wrought devastation on human security in the region. He observes that while SADC's evolving harmonized policy and institutional framework for HIV/AIDS is commendable, its effective implementation at the national level remains uneven. Dzinesa contends that other SADC sectors can draw lessons from the progress made by SADC militaries – a sector particularly vulnerable to the pandemic, with estimates of 20–60 per cent infection rates – in developing regional minimum standards for the harmonized control of HIV/AIDS among security sectors. The chapter commends the growing engagement of civil society in the region's human security agenda and fight against the pandemic.

The joint chapter by Cameroonian scholar Francis Nyamnjoh and South African Patience Mususa scrutinizes the causes of the xenophobic attacks in South Africa in May 2008, which resulted in sixty-two deaths and over 100,000 displaced, and the discourse of the 'foreigner' in relation to the experiences of migrants in southern Africa. The authors suggest that the major political and economic transitions that southern Africa has experienced in the past are likely to recur and create similar conflicts in contemporary patterns and trends of migration. They assess the different responses by governments to xenophobia in the region, particularly in South Africa, and contend that SADC's official discourse of deeper integration through regional free movement of people is undercut by calls for tighter immigration controls by its member states. Finally, David Simon, a United Kingdom-based South African scholar, examines the challenges for region-building in southern Africa posed by climate or global environmental change. He evaluates the engagement of both SADC and COMESA with such issues and concludes that they are in the early stages of addressing climate change challenges and must necessarily mainstream their responses effectively into their integration and region-building agendas.

External actors Part Five of the book concerns external actors. South African economist Mzukisi Qobo contends that the EU's economic hegemony, entrenched through massive financial assistance, has effectively locked SADC into Brussels' sphere of influence. He argues that the changing global geopolitical landscape, including the rise of emerging powers such as China, India and Brazil, has prompted the EU to consolidate its sphere of influence to gain competitive advantage and increase its global market share relative to these rising powers. Finalizing an economic partnership agreement (EPA) with southern Africa is a key part of this calculation. EPAs are therefore not instruments for deepening regional integration and delivering development outcomes, but rather commercial strategies that address the EU's internal constraints and respond to the new wave of globalization driven in part by the emerging powers. Nomfundo Ngwenya, a South African international relations specialist, argues in her chapter that US policy towards southern Africa has been consistent across various administrations since the end of the Cold War in 1991, though George W. Bush had a special input in providing funds to tackle HIV/AIDS between 2001 and 2008. The Africa Growth and Opportunity Act of 2000 has helped boost trade with the region, but in future the USA is likely to focus attention on the two leading economic powers in the region, South Africa and Angola, the latter being the source of about 7 per cent of US oil. Finally, South African scholar Garth le Pere considers the role of China in relation to region-building in southern Africa. He traces the development of links between an economically resurgent China and a number of SADC states, especially Angola, which supplies China with a significant share of its oil requirements, but also including such mineral-rich countries as South Africa, Zambia and Zimbabwe. In 2000 the China–South Africa Bi-National Commission was established, by 2010 China had become South Africa's largest bilateral trading partner, and in 2011 South Africa formally joined the BRIC (Brazil, Russia, India, China) group of countries, in large part because of its role in SADC.

Problems and challenges

From its inception, SADC has been the most important regional organization in southern Africa. It has constructed an elaborate structure to deal with economic, political and security issues (see Landsberg, Mbuende in this volume) and is recognized by the African Union as one of its eight constituent regional economic communities. Regional economic integration is seen as essential for economic growth in an era of ever-increasing globalization. Many of the chapters in this book concern aspects of the work of SADC, which aims at a regional free trade area, customs union and monetary union (see Nagar in this volume) and has organized a stand-by military force, one of five that are to constitute a continental African force. (See Saunders in this volume.) SADC's Secretariat is now housed in a large new building in Gaborone, Botswana, which formally opened in November 2010, but many of

SADC's ambitious plans and goals remain unimplemented. The organization drew up its Principles and Guidelines for Governing Democratic Elections in 2004, for example, but failed to ensure they were followed in Zimbabwe during polls in 2008. SADC's mediation efforts have had only limited success. While South Africa's Thabo Mbeki helped produce a Global Political Agreement in Zimbabwe in 2008, providing for a coalition government, the mediation efforts of the former president of Mozambique, Joaquim Chissano, to try to restore constitutional normality in Madagascar, had by April 2011 achieved nothing, for the government of Andry Rajoelina remained in power. In 2010, SADC's Tribunal was in effect suspended, after it had handed down judgments that the government of Zimbabwe did not like.[50]

It is relatively easy to be critical of the region-building attempts that have been made to date in southern Africa. Some will argue that, to be effective, region-building should begin with a relatively small unit and work outward, and that an organization such as SADC cannot deal with the vast problems of poverty, underdevelopment and gross inequalities that plague so much of the region, whose peoples remain divided. New problems are looming, such as the impact of climate change (see Simon in this volume), which will likely add to food insecurity and may also produce further conflicts. SADC remains very dependent on donor support (over 70 per cent of its funds), especially from the EU, and if this is cut back severely, the entire region-building project may be placed in jeopardy. The member states of SADC have not yet shown any appetite for surrendering any sovereignty to the regional body, which has proved unable to deal successfully with crises in Madagascar and Zimbabwe. Many of the key states in the SADC region are, in 2011, still governed by parties that led armed struggles against colonialism and apartheid, and their leaders remain united in part because of that past history of solidarity. But, in time, a new post-liberation-struggle leadership will emerge, one without these past ties. South Africa remains the regional hegemon, with vast wealth relative to many of its neighbours. And region-building is inevitably shaped in part by outside forces and agents. (See Ngwenya, Qobo, le Pere in this volume.) An estimated 77 per cent of SADC's trade continues to take place with countries from outside the region.[51]

There is ample evidence in the chapters that follow, however, that it would be wrong to be too pessimistic about the prospects for region-building in southern Africa. Numerous organizations in both civil society and government are working to bring the peoples of the region together – ranging from SADC and the SADC Parliamentary Forum, to SACU, the Development Bank of Southern Africa and the Industrial Development Corporation. As this process continues, a sense of regional identity among the peoples of southern Africa will develop. SADC's Spatial Development Initiatives, such as the cross-border transport corridors it has promoted, and its Power Pool (see Nagar in this volume), have brought significant economic benefits to its 257 million inhabitants, and the organization has aided the creation of trans-frontier conservation areas to preserve wildlife and prevent environmental degradation.[52] South Africa's DBSA and IDC continue to finance developmental projects in many countries of the region. (See Monyae in this volume.)

This book, then, written mostly by African authors, reflects the state of play regarding regionalism in southern Africa in early 2011. It analyses both the challenges that face the region-building project in southern Africa and how the region is responding to these challenges, and suggests lessons not only for other regions of Africa, but also for region-building elsewhere in the world.

Notes

1 Margaret C. Lee, *The Political Economy of Regionalism in Southern Africa* (Boulder, CO: Lynne Rienner, 2003), p. 8.

2 John Akokpari, 'Dilemmas of regional integration and development in Africa', in John Akokpari, Angela Ndinga-Muvumba and Tim Murithi (eds), *The African Union and Its Institutions* (Johannesburg: Jacana, 2008), p. 87.

3 See Centre for Conflict Resolution (CCR), 'Building peace in southern Africa', Seminar report, Cape Town, 25–26 February 2010.

4 Lee, *Political Economy*; Gabriel Oosthuizen, *The Southern African Development Community: The Organisation, Its policies and Prospects* (Institute for Global Dialogue, 2006). Other relevant publications, produced by institutions in South Africa, include Christopher Clapham et al., *Regional Integration in Southern Africa: Comparative International Perspectives* (Johannesburg: South African Institute of International Affairs, 2001); Talitha Bertelsman-Scott and Peter Draper, *Regional Integration and Economic Partnership Agreements. Southern Africa at the Crossroads* (Johannesburg: SAIIA, 2006); and W. Carlsnaes and Philip Nel (eds), *In Full Flight: South African Foreign Policy After Apartheid* (Midrand, South Africa: Institute for Global Dialogue, 2006). Jörgen Vogt, *Die regionale Integration des südlichen Afrikas: unter besonderer Betrachtung der Southern African development community (SADC)* (*Schriften zur Europäischen Integration und internationalen Wirtschaftsordnung*, Baden-Baden: Nomos, 2007) is not available anywhere in southern Africa.

5 Bertil Oden, *Southern Africa after Apartheid* (Uppsala: Nordic Africa Institute, 1993); Lennart Petersson, *Post-Apartheid Southern Africa* (Routledge, 1998); Fredrik Soderbaum, *The Political Economy of Regionalism: The Case of Southern Africa* (London: Palgrave, 2004).

6 David Simon (ed.), *South Africa in Southern Africa: Reconfiguring the Region* (Oxford: James Currey, 1998); Mwesiga Baregu and Christopher Landsberg (eds), *From Cape to Congo: Southern Africa's Evolving Security Challenges* (Boulder, CO: Lynne Rienner, 2003); Adekeye Adebajo, Adebayo Adedeji and Chris Landsberg (eds), *South Africa in Africa: The Post-Apartheid Era* (Scottsville: University of KwaZulu-Natal Press, 2007); W. Carlsnaes and Philip Nel (eds), *In Full Flight: South African Foreign Policy After Apartheid* (Midrand, South Africa: Institute for Global Dialogue, 2006).

7 John Pinder and Simon Usherwood, *The European Union: A Very Short Introduction* (Oxford: Oxford University Press, 2007). See also Anne Deighton, 'The Remaking of Europe', in Michael Howard and William Roger Louis (eds), *The Oxford History of the Twentieth Century* (Oxford: Oxford University Press, 1998); Chris Hill and Michael Smith, *International Relations and the European Union* (Oxford: Oxford University Press, 2005); Anand Menon,

Europe: The State of the Union (London: Atlantic, 2008).

8 Harry Stephan and Angus Fane Hervey, 'New regionalism in southern Africa: functional developmentalism and the southern African power pool', *Politeia*, 27(3), 2008.

9 Ibid.

10 South African Department of Trade and Industry (DTI), 'A South African trade policy and strategy framework', May 2010, pp. 69–71, www.dti.gov.za/TPSF.pdf.

11 See the discussion on modern world systems in Robert Gilpin, *The Political Economy of International Relations* (Princeton, NJ: Princeton University Press, 1987), pp. 67–9.

12 See the discussion of hegemonic stability in Gilpin, *The Political Economy of International Relations*, p. 72. See also the discussion on Robert Keohane and Robert Gilpin in Harry Stephan et al., 'Two-level games and the Africa dilemma', in Stephan et al., *The Scramble for Africa in the 21st Century: A View from the South* (Cape Town: Renaissance), p. 225.

13 John Akokpari, 'Dilemmas of regional integration and development in Africa', in Akokpari, Ndinga-Muvumba, and Murithi, *The African Union and Its Institutions*, p. 87; Guy Martin, *African World Politics: A Pan-African Perspective* (Trenton, NJ: Africa World Press, 2002), pp. 125–7.

14 Immanuel Wallerstein, *Africa: The Politics of Independence and Unity* (Lincoln: University of Nebraska Press, 2005).

15 Samuel Kingsley Botwe Asante in collaboration with David Chanaiwa, 'Pan-Africanism and regional integration', in Ali A. Mazrui and C. Wondji (eds), *General History of Africa*, vol. 8: *Africa Since 1935* (Oxford: James Currey, 1999), pp. 725–7.

16 United Nations Economic Commission for Africa, 'Institutions and regional integration in Africa', 2005, www.uneca.org/aria2/chap2.pdf.

17 Adebayo Adedeji, 'Comparative strategies of economic decolonization in Africa', in Mazrui and Wondji, *General History of Africa*, vol. 8, p. 413.

18 African Union (AU), 'Audit report', 2010, europafrica.net/key-documents.

19 CCR, 'Adedeji at 80: moving Africa from rhetoric to action', Policy brief, Ijebu-Ode, Nigeria, 18–20 December 2007, p. 3.

20 In AU terminology the southern African region is a subregion. Here the term subregion is used interchangeably with region.

21 The boundaries of South Africa today therefore remain virtually the same as those of 1910. On the attempts at enlarging South Africa, and the failure of those attempts, see especially Ronald Hyam, *The Failure of South African Expansion, 1908–1948* (London: Macmillan, 1972). See also Martin Chanock, *Unconsummated Union* (Manchester: Manchester University Press, 1997).

22 Adebayo Adedeji, 'Within or apart?', in Adedeji (ed.), *South Africa in Africa: Within or Apart?* (London: Zed Books, 1996), p. 9.

23 Cecilia Hull and Markus Derblom, *Abandoning Frontline Trenches? Capabilities for Peace and Security in the SADC Region* (Stockholm: Swedish Defence Research Agency, 2009), p. 28.

24 SADC was established under Article 2 of the SADC Treaty by member states represented by their respective heads of state and government. See www.sadc.int/index/browse/page/119.

25 Patrick Bond, 'First class failure', *BBC Focus on Africa*, October–December 2010, p. 26.

26 Gilpin, *The Political Economy of International Relations*, p. 11. Gilpin concludes that markets are a means to achieve and exercise power, and that the state can be used, or is used, to obtain wealth; hence 'the state and the market interact to influence the distribution of power and wealth in international relations'.

27 John Friedmann, *A General Theory of Polarized Development*, 1972, cited in Gilpin, *The Political Economy of International Relations*, p. 21. See also the discussion on modern world systems in Gilpin, ibid., pp. 67–9.

28 See Qobo in this volume. See also Brendan Vickers, 'SADC's international trade relations', in Charles Harvey (ed.), *Proceedings of the 2009 FOPRISA Annual Conference* (Gaborone: Botswana Institute for Development Policy Analysis, 2010), p. 143.

29 Guy Martin, 'African regional cooperation and integration' in Martin, *African World Politics.*

30 Jonathan Mayuyuka Kaunda and Farai Zizhou, 'Furthering southern African integration', in *Proceedings of the 2008 FOPRISA Annual Conference* (Gaborone: Botswana Institute for Development Policy Analysis, 2009), pp. 33–4.

31 The CMA agreement provides fixed exchange rates among its members, a common bloc for intra-regional capital accounts and financial transfers, and use of the South African rand as a common currency. The South African Reserve Bank sets interest rates for the CMA.

32 Lee, *Political Economy of Regionalism*, pp. 114–35.

33 South African Department of Trade and Industry (DTI), 'A South African trade policy and strategy framework', May 2010, pp. 69–71, www.dti.gov.za/TPSF.pdf. See also www.thedti.gov.za/econdb/raportt/rapcont.html; and www.thedti.gov.za/econdb/raportt/rapregi.html.

34 See CCR, 'Stabilising Sudan: domestic, sub-regional, and extra-regional challenges', Seminar report, Cape Town, 23/24 August 2010.

35 AU, 'Roadmap for the operationalisation of the African Standby Force', Experts' Meeting on the Relationship Between the AU and the Regional Mechanisms for Conflict Prevention, Management, and Resolution, EXP/AU-Recs/ASF/4(I), Addis Ababa, 22/23 March 2005.

36 Adebayo Adedeji, 'ECOWAS: a retrospective journey', in Adekeye Adebajo and Ismail Rashid (eds), *West Africa's Security Challenges: Building Peace in a Troubled Region* (Boulder, CO: Lynne Rienner, 2004), p. 40.

37 See about.comesa.int/attachments/comesa_treaty_en.pdf.

38 CCR, 'HIV/AIDS and militaries in Africa', Seminar report, Addis Ababa, Ethiopia, November 2007, p. 9.

39 United Nations and AU Commission, 'Report on climate change and development in Africa', 2010, www.uneca.org/cfm/2010/documents/English/Report-onClimateChange-andDevelopment-inAfrica.pdf.

40 See AU, 'AU Assembly decision on the African Common Position on Climate Change', Assembly/AU/Dec.236(XII), 2009, www.africa-union.org/root/ua/conferences/2009/jan/summit_jan_2009/doc/conference/assembly%20au%20dec%20%20208-240%20(xii).pdf.

41 The eighteen countries are Benin, Burkina Faso, Cameroon, Cape Verde, Central Africa, Chad, Côte d'Ivoire, Ghana, Guinea, Guinea Bissau, Liberia, Mali, Niger, Nigeria, São Tomé, Senegal, Sierra Leone and Togo, and there are plans to establish a presence in East and southern Africa. See the Ecobank website, www.firstglobalselect.com/scripts/cgiip.wsc/globalone/htm/quote_and_news.r?pisharetype-id=17780.

42 The Africa Growth and Opportunity Act was signed into law on 18 May 2000. See the AGOA website, www.agoa.gov.

43 Jendayi Frazer, 'The United States', in Baregu and Landsberg, *From Cape to Congo*, p. 278.

44 According to AFRICOM's mission statement: 'United States Africa Command, in concert with other US government agencies and international partners, conducts sustained security engagement through military-to-military programs, military-sponsored activities, and other military operations as directed to promote a stable and secure African environment in support of US foreign policy.' See www.africom.mil/About AFRICOM.asp.

45 See Kweku Ampiah and Sanusha Naidu (eds), *Crouching Tiger, Hidden Dragon? Africa and China* (Scottsville: University of KwaZulu-Natal Press, 2008).

46 See Ampiah and Naidu, *Crouching Tiger, Hidden Dragon?*

47 Council of the European Union, 'The EU and Africa: towards a strategic partnership', Brussels, December 2005, www.consilium.europa.eu/ueDocs/cms_Data/docs/pressData/en/er/87673.pdf. See also Daniel Bach, 'The AU and the EU', in Akokpari, Ndinga-Muvumba and Murithi, *The African Union and Its Institutions.*

48 CCR, 'Africa and Europe in a new century', Seminar report, Cape Town, 31 October–1 November 2007; CCR, 'From Eurafrique to Afro-Europa', Seminar report, Stellenbosch, 11–13 September 2008.

49 Talitha Bertelmann-Scott, 'The European Union', in Baregu and Landsberg, *From Cape to Congo*, p. 314.

50 See, for example, *Southern Africa Today*, 12(6), October 2010, p. 4.

51 Fantu Cheru, *African Renaissance: Roadmaps to the Challenge of Globalization* (London: Zed Books, 2002), p. 132. It has even been suggested that the region may 'dissolve' as a result of Chinese involvement and other alternatives to regional integration presenting themselves. William G. Martin, 'South Africa's imperial futures: Washington Consensus, Bandung Consensus, or People's Consensus', *African Sociological Review*, 12(1), 2008, p. 131.

52 See Tsitsi Effie Mutambara, 'Regional transport challenges within the Southern African Development Community and their implications for economic integration and development', *Journal of Contemporary African Studies*, 27(4), October 2009. The Maputo Corridor project, for example, links South Africa and Mozambique.

PART ONE

Historical legacy

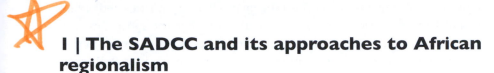

1 | The SADCC and its approaches to African regionalism

Gilbert M. Khadiagala

The Southern African Development Coordination Conference (SADCC) emerged in 1980, at the height of the decolonization and struggles against settler regimes in southern Africa, to promote integration and mitigate the effects of economic dependence of these regimes on apartheid South Africa. This chapter addresses the origins of SADCC against the backdrop of the concerted efforts made by its predecessor organization, the Frontline States (FLS) of 1975, to promote integration among weak and vulnerable states. Through its sector-led coordination approach to integration, SADCC was an attempt to transcend the post-colonial approaches to regionalism by emphasizing trade and market integration. The analysis will suggest that SADCC's integration efforts have bequeathed two contrasting legacies of a sector-coordinated approach to integration that also inform the current trajectories of regionalism and security in southern Africa. The legacy of sector coordination was institutionalized by promoting infrastructural development through the Spatial Development Initiatives (SDIs). Also recognized as the 'corridor approach to integration', SDIs were created to deepen integration by drawing on the comparative advantages inherent in existing transport corridors. The second legacy adopted by SADCC was that of state-centric and highly individualized regionalism, owing to the circumstances surrounding southern Africa's decolonization processes. The legacy of strong individuals was evident in the creation of the successor organization, the Southern African Development Community (SADC) of 1992, and its integration efforts as it sought to build autonomous institutions.

Background to SADCC and FLS

Regional integration in Africa stemmed from the realities of colonialism to create functional economic and political linkages among the various colonial territories. On the eve of Africa's independence, Europe, through its newly formed European Economic Community (EEC) of 1957, influenced the pattern of regionalism in Africa by inducing former French colonies into an association that grew into the Yaoundé Conventions of 1963 and 1969 and subsequent Lomé Conventions of the 1970s, 1980s and 1990s. Europe's integration schemes tried to manage Africa's economically and politically fragile post-independence states through bilateral and multilateral arrangements among Africa's individual states and between Africa and the rest of Europe.[1] For the most part, the thinking behind these schemes was that regionalism in Africa would mirror the gradualist orientation adopted by the EEC, in which cooperation proceeded in functional stages from lower to higher forms of integration. In the late 1950s, scholars of regionalism identified six key stages critical to integration: a preferential trade area, a free trade area, a customs union, a common market, an economic union and a common monetary zone. Through these stages, increased trade and market cooperation was viewed as the core foundation for substantive integration to occur. Within the phases of integration, the penultimate stage is the creation of an economic union, in which states lose some autonomy and sovereignty over economic policy and experience the beginning stages of political integration.[2]

Throughout eastern, central, southern and western Africa, regional integration schemes proliferated to foster trade, industrial development, infrastructural cooperation and shared services. Earlier integration processes were marked by the implosion of federations crafted by colonial powers that exploited Africa's geographical proximities, laying the foundation for trade, monetary, industrial and infrastructural cooperation.[3]

During the early years of Africa's independence, the centrifugal forces of sovereignty and nationalism placed significant strain on the regionalism pattern by engendering the adoption of a more functionalist and economically coordinated approach. The major issue was that newly independent African states opted for a more gradual approach and placed a premium on narrower and more elastic versions of regionalism and economic collaboration than on the grandiose vision of regionalism that required elaborate steps of ceding some forms of sovereignty. It was therefore difficult for most African countries to balance nationalism and supranationalism. Such difficulties confronted the East African Community (EAC) (Kenya, Tanganyika – later Tanzania) – and Uganda) during its earlier experiments at integration. During the mid-1970s, problems of ideological distinctiveness, leadership contests and sharing of gains derived from integration dominated the debates concerning the meaning of regional integration, and profoundly weakened the EAC – an institution that some observers had regarded as the most developed common market and monetary union in the world.[4]

The weakening of the EAC and its eventual collapse in 1977 coincided with the shift in Tanzania's foreign policy from eastern to southern Africa. Tanzania had, since the 1960s, assumed the pivotal role in Africa's decolonization efforts and also hosted the Liberation Committee of the Organization of African Unity (OAU) during that period. Dar es Salaam's efforts were strengthened by the overtures of its former president, Julius Nyerere, to Zambia's president at the time, Kenneth Kaunda. Together, both leaders launched a more vigorous policy framework for coordinating liberation activities under the informal structure of the Mulungushi Club. In implementing the broad mandate of the OAU towards southern Africa's liberation struggle, the Mulungushi Club was spurred on by the collapse of the fascist regime in Portugal in April 1974, which allowed for the independence of Angola and Mozambique. In 1975, Tanzania and Zambia expanded the Mulungushi Club and formed the Frontline States, which included Botswana, Mozambique and later Angola.[5]

As the epitome of the liberation-based infrastructure for regionalism, the major objectives of the FLS were to end the apartheid regime of South Africa and the settler governments in South Africa, Rhodesia (Zimbabwe), South West Africa (Namibia) and elsewhere in the region, through either a negotiated settlement or an armed struggle with support from the various national liberation movements: South Africa's African National Congress (ANC), Namibia's South West Africa People's Organization (SWAPO), Angola's Popular Liberation Movement (MPLA), Mozambique's Liberation Front (FRELIMO), and Zimbabwe's African National Union (ZANU) and African People's Union (ZAPU).

I have described elsewhere the FLS as an alliance in adversity that permitted weak states the opportunity to coalesce around a narrow but significant objective, at considerable cost to their economic and political security.[6] The huge commitment to the decolonization process, and the considerable sacrifices made by the FLS, allowed for a wide range of external actors to become pertinent players in assisting the FLS to realize its objectives more fully. The violent end to the decolonization of Angola during the period 1974–76 was an initial test, assessing the FLS's ability to maintain a measure of coherence despite obstacles to the coordination of diplomatic efforts. The triumph of the MPLA against military pressures from apartheid South Africa and Western-leaning Zaire (now the Democratic Republic of the Congo – DRC) strengthened the FLS in its efforts to liberate southern Africa. The persistence and tact of the FLS during Zimbabwe's protracted conflict, in combining both armed pressure and negotiated diplomacy, bore fruit and led to the end of Zimbabwe's liberation struggle in 1980. Zimbabwe's independence in turn allowed the FLS to begin to coordinate economic integration efforts and reduce dependence on South Africa.

Formation of SADCC

When SADCC was formed in 1980, the Southern African Customs Union (SACU), established in 1910, was the dominant regional institution. Under South Africa's tutelage, SACU comprised, besides South Africa itself, Botswana, Lesotho and Swaziland (BLS). SACU demonstrated the umbilical economic ties that apartheid South Africa exerted over the region through an elaborate system of revenue-sharing and other economic exchanges with its BLS partners. (See Gibb in this volume.) In response to attempts made by the FLS to broaden its economic reach and in its fight against settler rule, increased pressure from South Africa under former president P. W. Botha brought about the formation of a new organization, the Constellation of Southern African States (CONSAS) in the latter half of the 1970s. The successful attempts by the FLS to institutionalize its successor organization, SADCC, in 1980 as a new regional economic bloc presented a major challenge to South Africa's hegemonic position, provoking the apartheid apparatus to adopt a policy of regional destabilization that intimidated the region.

In conceptualizing SADCC's regional efforts, this clearly was a decolonization-driven regionalism that departed from the gradualism of previous integration schemes, emphasizing and harnessing the gains from political collaboration through economic liberation. More important, instead of adopting and erecting weak intergovernmental institutions that concealed the commitment to sovereignty, SADCC's attempts at regionalism were based on a realistic framework of several functional roles as states became decolonized and independent.[7]

Before the formal independence of Zimbabwe in April 1980, the FLS had already begun to seek ways of transforming its informal political alliance into an economic grouping designed to foster economic liberation. As in the case of the independence of Angola and Mozambique in 1975, Zimbabwe's independence changed the pattern of relations for southern Africa, presenting the region with new possibilities and options for addressing South Africa's dominant role.

In addition, in alleviating the burdens of war, Zimbabwe's independence brought about an independent transport network that provided options for an improved economic regionalism within the reach of the FLS. Zimbabwe was viewed as the hub of the transportation network, north of the Limpopo river, and was key to the endeavours of the FLS in reducing the region's transport dependence on South Africa. Furthermore, the creation of SADCC dovetailed with the vision of Zambia's Kenneth Kaunda and Tanzania's Julius Nyerere to build a transcontinental belt of independent and economically powerful states stretching from Dar es Salaam and Maputo on the Indian Ocean to Luanda and Walvis Bay on the Atlantic.[8]

In May 1979 the formal conception of SADCC originated at a meeting of foreign affairs ministers of the FLS in Gaborone, where Botswana's former president Seretse Khama expressed the need to consolidate and expand areas of cooperation among the FLS group. In his address at the meeting, Khama noted:

> The strength and effectiveness of coordinated action in the political liberation encourages us to believe that a similar dynamic of coordination is attainable on the economic front. This is not to gloss over the national interest or differ-

ences of opinion ... There must be a perception of common regional interests, but the pursuit of these common interests must provide for the real and immediate needs of each cooperating state.[9]

A few months later, at a meeting in Arusha, Tanzania, in July 1979, the FLS finance ministers adopted the broad parameters of SADCC's agenda. Four main development objectives were identified: reducing economic dependence, particularly on South Africa; forging stronger links to create genuine and equitable regional integration; mobilizing resources that promoted national interstate and regional policies; and making a concerted effort to secure international cooperation within the framework of a regionally determined strategy for economic liberation.

Following the Arusha conference, the FLS offered SADCC membership to other majority-ruled states of southern Africa. As a political alliance, the FLS maintained a separate identity, inviting Lesotho, Malawi and Swaziland to join SADCC owing to their economic links to the rest of their independent neighbours. This was a calculated invitation on the part of the FLS to wean these countries from their economic ties and avoid deeper economic relations with South Africa.[10]

The FLS initiative formally adopted the Lusaka Declaration for Economic Liberation in April 1980, forming the Southern African Development Coordination Conference of nine states: Angola, Botswana, Lesotho, Malawi, Mozambique, Swaziland, Tanzania, Zambia and Zimbabwe. At this meeting, SADCC's role was described as a short- and long-term vehicle for fostering development in the region. The consensus among the nine member states was to create a regional economic organization that would bind members together, harmonize policies, minimize the impact of South Africa's hegemony on the region, and, more importantly, reject Botha's Constellation of Southern African States grouping. According to SADC's first executive secretary, Zimbabwe's Simba Makoni:

> The basic issue of dependence and domination, although a function of politics, is also very strongly economic. It would be equally unacceptable tomorrow, when the ANC is in power in South Africa, for the nine states which constitute SADCC at the moment to be as dependent on South Africa as they are today. We have made it clear that the relevance and validity of SADCC will not end the day a people's flag is raised in Pretoria.[11]

Furthermore, Botswana's President Khama noted that 'only in coordinated action can small independent states of Southern Africa achieve the economic strength and power necessary to resist those who are tempted to exploit us and to perpetuate our economic fragmentation and dependence'.[12]

In seeking to meet the goals of economic development and disengagement from South Africa, the 'founding fathers' of SADCC sought to avoid the shortcomings of the previous functionalist integration schemes in Africa, which had been characterized by a fixation on sovereignty, a lack of political will, overambitious development programmes, and an inequitable distribution of benefits. SADCC deliberately established a limited and flexible organization identified by two distinctive features: an emphasis on sector coordination, and primacy conceded to national decision-making.

Eschewing the grandiose schemes of integrating diverse national economies under a supranational economic body, SADCC emphasized a step-by-step approach to sector development, with each member state overseeing a specific sector: Angola, energy coordination; Botswana, the Secretariat, crop research and animal control; Lesotho, soil conservation and land utilization; Malawi, fisheries, wildlife and forests; Mozambique, transport and communications; Swaziland, manpower; Tanzania, industrial development; Zambia, mining; and Zimbabwe, food security.[13] The sector coordination formula that SADCC agreed upon in Blantyre, Malawi, in 1981 was viewed as a flexible and voluntary approach to regional harmonization that sought to accommodate the diversities among member states. As Makoni stated:

> This mode of operation guaranteed us a direct involvement by our govern-
> ments and their functionaries in the activities of the organization. It places
> primary responsibility and accountability for the organization's policies,
> programs, and projects on the member Government rather than on a distant,
> faceless, and impersonal bureaucracy. Such a decentralized system demands
> of its members maximum political commitment to the ideals and objectives
> being pursued, as well as maximum confidence and trust in each other. These
> attributes ... are the hallmarks of SADCC: the explanation and vindication of
> how Marxist Mozambique and capitalist Malawi or Republican Tanzania and
> traditional monarchist Swaziland can work so well and effectively together.[14]

SADCC's achievements and shortcomings

Despite the elaborate division of labour across coordinating sectors, SADCC's main priority was reducing dependence on the South African Transport Services (SATS) – recognized as a broader regional problem. During the 1970s and into the 1980s, South Africa's policy of regional destabilization reached its peak with the invasion of, and determination to fight, the Marxist MPLA government of Angola, which resulted in the South African Defence Force (SADF) illegally occupying southern Angola. External actors played both productive and counterproductive roles, with Cuban president Fidel Castro assisting Angola's struggle through deployment of 50,000 troops in 1976, and apartheid South Africa's attempt to prevent the MPLA government from controlling the entire country involving support for the US-backed National Union for the Total Independence of Angola (UNITA) to gain victory.[15] Through direct military attacks and indirect attrition, South Africa progressively continued its policy of regional destabilization and fought the Marxist government in Mozambique, while strongly supporting the Mozambique National Resistance (RENAMO) against the FRELIMO government.

This insurgency invariably refocused regional and international attention on transport as a strategic sector within SADCC. The galvanization of international attention and resources was decisive in muting some of the worst aspects of South African destabilization, which gave SADCC a renewed determination in its commitment and in support of the liberation movements – South Africa's ANC and Namibia's SWAPO.[16] Moreover, SADCC's new focus on transport provoked the wrath of South Africa, which through its policy of regional destabilization sabotaged key transport infrastructures in Angola, Mozambique and Namibia, resulting in estimated damages of US$60.5 billion between 1980 and 1988 and the deaths of a million people and displacement of millions more.[17]

In fostering the goal of transport coordination, SADCC established the Southern Africa Transport and Communications Commission (SATCC), based in Maputo. SATCC's objectives were fourfold: improve transport communication in the region; provide economic and efficient means of transport and communications; achieve self-sufficiency in the maintenance of equipment and plant; and encourage the efficient utilization of available resources for the improvement of transport and communications. SADCC's overall strategy was to integrate all transport systems connected with the regional ports of Dar es Salaam, Lobito and Benguela in Angola, and Beira, Maputo and Nacala in Mozambique. In November 1980, external donors pledged $650 million to SADCC for projects in the transport sector.[18]

Although SADCC attempted to improve the entire transport sector, priority was given to development of alternative transport routes through Mozambican ports. SADCC viewed Beira, Maputo and Nacala as critical in restoring regional self-sufficiency in transport in order to expand trade. At the centre of these efforts was the rehabilitation of the 170-mile Beira Corridor – a vital road, rail and oil pipeline that stretched from eastern Zimbabwe to Beira. SADCC assisted in the rehabilitation of the corridor, and established the Beira Corridor Group (BCG) – a consortium of private and public companies from Botswana, Malawi, Zambia and Zimbabwe. Besides improving the physical infrastructure of the Beira Corridor, the BCG presented an opportunity for coordinating interests in the business sector by executing strategic projects along the corridor. By 1987 the BCG had organized 246 business ventures with $147 million in investment deals made from the corridor.[19]

Because of the strategic significance of transport and the important role played by Mozambique, SADCC did not make considerable progress in the coordination of other sectors. The emphasis on securing Mozambique within the overall framework of improving the economic opportunities of SADCC allowed these countries to play a dominant role in attracting Western actors who were supportive of the broader objectives of decolonization.[20] SADCC was able to seek Western assistance to boost its objective of infrastructural development through a strategy of presenting itself as an anti-apartheid organization.

Whether the organization was able to develop African ownership is critical, as earlier suggested by Makoni. SADCC members relied heavily on the support of external donors during the Cold War era. Southern Africa received US aid of $53.7 million in the period 1975–79, and $154.4 million in the period 1980–84. The 1974 *coup d'état* in Lisbon that brought about independence for Angola and Mozambique raised concerns for the United States. Washington thought that the new communist movements and self-proclaimed Marxist regimes in Angola and Mozambique would infiltrate into Namibia as well as South Africa. The collapse of the Soviet empire in 1989 and subsequent end of the Cold War resulted in a further increase in US aid, which was amended to $58.4 million for Malawi, $41.7 million for Zambia and $29.4 million and $102 million for Angola and Mozambique, respectively, with the ending of their civil wars.[21] In drawing on the resources of Western countries, SADCC was able to mobilize both its strategic partners – the Scandinavian countries as well as South Africa's sympathetic allies, particularly the United States and the United Kingdom. As Makoni stated:

> I regret to say that a large part of this [Western] support has really not come to us on our own account. It has come to us as sympathy support against apartheid. People saw our countries being destabilized, being aggressed, being attacked by South Africa and this was their response. It was not their response to SADCC, and that is going to be our next major challenge in terms of our international relations. People have to accept SADCC for what it is, and we have a lot of positive things in our own right – SADCC as SADCC, with or without South Africa. ... We have to generate support with or without apartheid. ... That is both a challenge and a disappointment because there are a lot of people who have read us in the opposite image of apartheid.[22]

The FLS's main aim was to secure the region and establish a base from which to strengthen weak states through a collaborative effort to achieve and to maximize limited objectives. The FLS's successor organization, SADCC marked the beginning of efforts to foster greater regional economic independence. SADCC's main shortcomings were its singular focus on transport at the expense of other sectors, its one-sided dependence on the West, and its failure to make meaningful progress on reducing dependence on South Africa. However, these criticisms belie the decolonization pressures that SADCC faced amid pushing an economic agenda. SADCC ought to be evaluated more modestly and realistically. Evaluations of SADCC should also take into account the decolonization pressures with which it was confronted. Furthermore, the political imperatives of finding an arrangement that would accommodate the diverse interests of actors subsumed SADCC's vital goal of reducing dependence on South Africa and the heavy reliance on Western donors. SADCC evolved from the FLS into a regional institution that was limited in its economic objectives, depending heavily on the success of the decolonization process through the liberation of South Africa and Namibia. At the 1992 summit in Windhoek, Namibia, that launched the Southern African Development Community (SADC), SADC regional governments recognized the importance of SADCC's main developmental role amid many obstacles in 'forging a regional identity and a sense of common destiny among countries and the peoples of Southern Africa'.[23]

Beyond SADCC: legacies for SADC

The FLS and SADCC epitomized a decolonization-driven regionalism that combined both a security and an economic dimension. Since the demise of apartheid, southern Africa has been presented with opportunities for deepening the avenues of both economic and security regionalism within the new structures of SADC. In pursuit of these objectives, southern Africa has been able to build on the limited experiences of SADCC in historical trade, infrastructural development and investment links unique to the region. The wide array of economic interdependence ties had contributed significantly to the region's distinctiveness, but apartheid and racial discrimination had impeded the translation of these economic links into political institutions that legitimized and stabilized the regional order. The 're-emergence' of South Africa within SADC marked a decisive transformation from a decolonization-driven regionalism to a functional integration that exploits existing regional comparative advantages. In the transition to the new regional order, some of the questions that SADC's founders faced centred on effective ways to manage the two legacies of sectoral coordination and state-centric, highly individualized regionalism.

SADCC's sectoral coordination in transport and the Beira Corridor Group remains a model for SADC's key initiatives, such as Spatial Development. The broadening of the integration mandates to include negotiations for a common market and free trade area has not eclipsed the increased significance of transport corridors as a means for regional integration. SDIs, however, seek to unlock the inherent economic potential of a specific geographic location through investment in infrastructure (through private–public partnerships), investment in anchor projects (through the private sector), removal of barriers to investment (administrative and legal), and political focus (by a political champion).[24] (See Nagar in this volume.) At the SADC summit in August 2007, member states addressed the importance of regional coordination and project development by drawing on the private sector through public and private partnerships in the provision and operation of transport systems. The key to the SDIs is regional cross-border infrastructure, especially transport, energy and water, which SADC perceives as contributing to regional integration and poverty alleviation. Thus far, there are eighteen regional SDIs that have tried to exploit development opportunities along major transport corridors. In an assessment of one of the most successful SDIs, the Maputo Development Corridor (MDC), Rosalind Thomas notes:

> In Southern Africa the Maputo Development Corridor was the first SDI to be implemented at the regional level. It involved a partnership between Mozambique and South Africa and at the same time presented an unprecedented level of economic cooperation between the two countries. ... MDC has provided a demonstration effect for other corridors and SDIs in Africa. The corridor links South Africa's industrialized, but effectively land-locked northern and eastern regions of Gauteng and Mpumalanga provinces to the Mozambican port of Maputo, and centres on a system of road, rail, and border posts, port, and terminal facilities. It has created a host of industrial and commercial opportunities along the 590km route from Johannesburg to Maputo, which now is populated with steel mills, petrochemical plants, quarries, mines and smelters, sugar cane and forestry plantations, and manufacturing facilities.[25]

To strengthen the SDI approach, SADC has also adopted a Regional Infrastructure Development Master Plan, whose key components are the Road Truck Route Network (RTRN), the Southern African Power Pool (SAPP) and the Regional Strategic Water Infrastructure Development Programme (RSWIDP). The most prominent corridors are the Lesotho Highlands Water Project (LHWP); the Trans-Kalahari Highway, linking South Africa, Botswana and Namibia; the Unity Bridge, between Mozambique and Tanzania; and the MDC. These developments have helped transform a low-growth area of Africa into a region of high-growth potential. The countries involved have since experienced new investment streams attracted by these corridors. Since the mid-2000s the Development Bank of Southern Africa (DBSA) has channelled funds to the region to assist in the development of regional infrastructure projects.[26] (See Monyae in this volume.)

The functionalism embedded in the development of corridors was critical in placing the SADC integration project on the same 'classical' European institutional footing that had initially propelled collaboration in the arenas of coal and steel. But European functionalism had also evolved against the backdrop of the emergence of autonomous regional institutions coexisting with national institutions. SADC, however, faced the legacy of close links between national and regional institutions, captured in the centrality of national leadership in the propagation of regionalism. From the Mulungushi Club to the FLS and then SADCC, regionalism has been animated by the convergence of interests and decisions among a core elite leadership. This also helped in elite socialization, which was important in building consensus and reducing conflicts. At the height of the decolonization process, strong personal relationships among the leaders also assisted in creating a wider camaraderie that insulated the FLS and SADCC from the debilitating fissures of sovereignty.

In the post-apartheid era, dependence on strong leaders to determine the contours of regional integration has stunted the evolution of collective institutions. In the earlier period of SADC's formation, a gulf emerged between the security and economic components of integration, illustrated by the debates between the old guard (FLS security-oriented elites) versus the economic-leaning technocrats of the new order. Rightly or wrongly, by the end of the 1990s these differences had turned into competition between Zimbabwe's Robert Mugabe, symbolizing the continuity of FLS collaborative traditions, and South Africa's Nelson Mandela, representing the new priorities of strengthening SADC as a vehicle for economic collaboration and market integration. These differences hinged partly on contrasting visions of leadership and chasms in the definition of governance, but they also spoke to how SADC states defined their post-apartheid priorities.[27] The internal conflicts were resolved gradually by the creation of the SADC Organ on Politics, Defence and Security (OPDS) in June 1996; the Interstate Politics and Diplomacy Committee (ISPDC), comprising subregional foreign ministers, in August 1999; and the Interstate Defence and Security Committee (ISDCS), retained from the FLS and comprising ministers of foreign affairs, defence, public security and state security, also in August 1999. All these institutions sought to map out a division of labour between security and economic cooperation. In conceding that economic integration cannot proceed without sound security architecture, SADC has tried to accommodate the statist and security orientation that drove previous patterns of integration with growing pressures for the diminution of sovereignty.

More lasting, however, has been the legacy of elite camaraderie in the evolution of a strong institutional base for SADC. There has been a growing perception that the continuity of strong leaders in national contexts has contributed to the slow movement towards supranational institutions that are autonomous and governed on professional lines. Some critics have indicated that the weakness of the SADC Secretariat, based in Gaborone, Botswana, is attributable to the failure of member states to cede meaningful power to an institution that is able to enforce agreed decisions and programmes, but which lacks the political authority to formulate a regional agenda. (See Mbuende, Landsberg in this volume.) The SADC Secretariat remains hostage to the competitive interests of member states, exemplified by the reluctance to ratify a range of protocols and projects.[28] For this reason, the tension between narrow nationalisms and supranationalism will continue to affect the future course of regionalism in Southern Africa.

Conclusion

Post-independence patterns of regional integration in Africa can be characterized as cheap forms of regionalism that have assumed an almost magical linear progression from lower to higher forms of economic cooperation. These experiments were frustrated through the allegiance to sovereignty and have over the years weakened African states as the providers of order, security and development. SADCC departed from this African norm by trying to build collaboration around an existing security challenge – decolonization. Security regionalism sought to create a common frame of reference that would propel functionalism around economic and market integration. But SADCC accomplished very little in terms of strengthening economic integration other than promoting the rehabilitation of Mozambique's transport routes. For the most part, SADCC remained a security organization with unfulfilled economic ambitions, yet this framework provided a solid grounding for subsequent efforts to construct more profound economic integration.

A new phase of regionalism has been inaugurated by the emergence of SADC's attempts to reconcile the functionalist goals of market and economic integration with the security collaboration necessary for peace-building, peacemaking and conflict resolution. These roles are frequently difficult to manage in the face of constrained resources, the absence of common value systems, and continued disagreements over the meaning of sovereignty. Through SADCC, southern Africa demonstrated the importance of forging a common identity and political infrastructure that can sustain deeper forms of economic integration. For this reason, SADCC marked the first essential step in the search for a regional identity, unity and integration.

Notes

1 For analyses of these regional schemes, see William I. Zartman, *The Politics of Trade Negotiations Between Africa the Economic Community: The Weak Confront the Strong* (Princeton, NJ: Princeton University Press, 1971).

2 See, for instance, Bella Balassa, *The Theory of Economic Integration* (Baltimore, MD: Johns Hopkins University Press, 1961); Jacob Viner, *The Customs Union Issue* (New York: Carnegie Endowment for International Peace, 1950); and Peter Robson, *The Economics of International Integration* (London: Routledge, 1998).

3 For wide-ranging discussions on colonial schemes, see Reginald Green and Krishna Green, *Economic Cooperation in Africa: Retrospect and Prospects*

(London: Oxford University Press, 1967); Peter Robson, 'Economic integration in southern Africa', *Journal of Modern African Studies*, 5(4), 1967; and Julienne Roland, 'The experience of integration in French-Speaking Africa', in Arthur Hazelwood (ed.), *African Integration and Disintegration* (New York: Oxford University Press, 1967).

4 For analyses of the East African Community, see Donald C. Mead, 'Economic cooperation in East Africa', *Journal of Modern African Studies*, 7(2), 1969; and Aggripah T. Mugomba, 'Regional organizations and African underdevelopment: the collapse of the East African Community', *Journal of Modern African Studies*, 2(2), 1978.

5 On the origins of the Mulungushi

Club, see Carol Thompson, *Challenge to Imperialism: The Frontline States in the Liberation of Zimbabwe* (Harare: Zimbabwe Publishing House, 1985); and B. Z. Osei-Hwedie, 'The Frontline States: cooperation for the liberation of southern Africa', *Journal of African Studies*, 10(4), 1983.

6 Gilbert M. Khadiagala, *Allies in Adversity: The Frontline States in Southern African Security, 1975–1993* (Athens: University of Ohio Press, 1994).

7 Margaret C. Lee, *SADCC: The Political Economy of Development in Southern Africa* (Nashville, TN: Winston-Derek, 1989); Mwesiga Baregu and Christopher Landsberg (eds), *From Cape to Congo: Southern Africa's Evolving Security Challenges* Boulder, CO: Lynne Rienner, 2003).

8 Amon Nsekela, *Southern Africa: Toward Economic Liberation* (London: Rex Collings, 1981); Julius Nyerere, 'North–South dialogue', *Third World Quarterly*, 6(4), 1984, p. 836.

9 Cited in 'Southern African Development Coordination Conference: Toward Economic Liberation – Declaration by the Frontline States Made at Gaborone, Botswana, 15 May 1979', in Colin Legum (ed.), *Africa Contemporary Record: Annual Survey and Documents, 1979–1980* (New York: Africana Publishing House, 1981), p. C118.

10 Cited in ibid.

11 Simba Makoni, 'SADCC's new strategies', *Africa Report*, 32(3), 1981, pp. 31–2.

12 Cited in 'Southern African Development Coordination Conference: Toward Economic Liberation', p. C118.

13 Lee, *SADCC*.

14 Cited in Ibbo Mandaza, 'Perspectives on economic cooperation and autonomous development in southern Africa', in Samir Amin, Derrick Chitala and Ibbo Mandaza (eds), *SADCC: Prospects for Disengagement and Development in Southern Africa* (London: Zed Books, 1987).

15 Dawn I. Nagar, 'Towards a Pax Africana: Southern Africa's Development Community's architecture and evolving peacekeeping efforts, 1996–2010', Master's thesis, University of Cape Town, South Africa, 2010. See also Margaret C. Lee,

The Political Economy of Regionalism in Southern Africa (Lansdowne, South Africa: University of Cape Town Press, 2003), p. 45.

16 For comprehensive analyses of SADCC and South Africa's destabilization, see Phyllis Johnson and David Martin (eds), *Destructive Engagement: Southern Africa at War* (Harare: Zimbabwe Publishing House, 1986); and Thomas Ohlson and Stephen John Stedman, *The New is Not Yet Born: Conflict Resolution in Southern Africa* (Washington, DC: Brookings Institution, 1994).

17 Assis Malaquias, 'Dysfunctional foreign policy: Angola's unsuccessful quest for security since independence', in Korwa Gombe Adar and Rok Ajulu (eds), *Globalization and Emerging Trends in African States' Foreign Policy-making Process: A Comparative Perspective of Southern Africa* (Aldershot: Ashgate, 2002), pp. 19–31.

18 'Southern African Development Coordination Conference: Toward Economic Liberation', p. C32.

19 Reginald H. Green, 'The SADCC on the frontline: breakdown or breakthrough?', in Colin Legum (ed.), *Africa Contemporary Record: Annual Survey and Documents, 1986–1987* (New York: Africana Publishing House, 1988), pp. A33–4; Vaughn O'Grady, 'Corridors of commerce', *African Review of Commerce and Technology*, 1, March 1987, p. 8357.

20 Reginald H. Green and Carol B. Thompson, 'Political economies in conflict: SADCC, South Africa, and sanctions', in Johnson and Martin, *Destructive Engagement*, pp. 245–80.

21 Adar and Ajulu, *Globalization and Emerging Trends*, pp. 332–3.

22 Simba Makoni, 'SADDC in a post-Apartheid environment', *Africa Report*, 35(5), 1990, p. 35.

23 Cited in Siphamandla Zondi, 'The state of Southern African Development Community: a critical assessment', Paper prepared for the Development Bank of Southern Africa project 'Regionalism in Africa', Midrand, 2008, p. 24.

24 Trudi Hartzenberg, 'South African

regional industrial policy: from border industries to Spatial Development Initiatives', *Journal of International Development*, 13, 2001, p. 771; and Grant de Beer, 'Regional development corridors and Spatial Development Initiatives: some current perspectives and potentials on progress', Paper presented at the conference 'Transport Challenges in Southern Africa', July 2001, repository.up.ac.za/upspace/bitstream/2263/8129/1/3a11.pdf.

25 Rosalind H. Thomas, 'SDIs in southern Africa as a strategy for attracting FDIS into the SADC region: origins and future prospects', (Gaborone: SADC, 2002). See also Christian M. Rogerson, 'Spatial Development Initiatives in southern Africa: the Maputo Development Corridor', *Tijdschrift voor economische en Sociale Geografie*, 92(3), 2000, pp. 324–46.

26 Rosalind H. Thomas, 'Development corridors and Spatial Development Initiatives in Africa', Mintek Research Report, Johannesburg, January 2009.

27 Some of these debates are captured in Baregu and Landsberg, *From Cape to Congo*; York Bradshaw and Stephen N. Ndegwa (eds), *The Uncertain Promise of Southern Africa* (Bloomington: Indiana University Press, 2000); and James J. Henz, *South Africa and the Logic of Regional Cooperation* (Bloomington: Indiana University Press, 2005).

28 See, for instance, Zondi, 'The state of Southern African Development Community'.

2 | The SADC: between cooperation and development – an insider perspective

Kaire M. Mbuende

Regional integration under the aegis of the Southern African Development Community (SADC), formed in 1992, has defied theorists and well-wishers and has not conformed to conventional approaches. Southern Africa's integration efforts are unique to the region, having evolved from specific historical circumstances in the 1980s to strengthen economic structures and lessen the dependency of SADC member states on the apartheid regime of South Africa. This chapter is based on both academic research and my own practical insights from serving as SADC Executive Secretary between 1994 and 1999.

Conventional methods of regional integration can be conceptualized as a gradualist approach adopted through systematic phases and stages of integration. According to some theorists, the conventional approach defines the initial stage of regional integration as the formation of a preferential trade area in which members of a group of neighbouring states coordinate trade policies, such as applying lower tariff rates to each other than to third parties and facilitating the free movement of goods within the area.[1] The second stage is creating a free trade area, by removing artificial trade barriers and restrictions to trade and reducing tariff rates among participating members, though members are allowed to maintain their own external tariffs with respect to third parties. The process then proceeds to formation of a customs union, which includes a free trade area for member states as well as a common external tariff for non-members. Once the customs union is in place, the next stage is creation of a common market, encapsulating the free movement of capital, labour, goods and services and complemented by the harmonization of macroeconomic policies. This is followed by formation of an economic union, in which either a single currency is established or monetary policies are jointly managed. The final stage is creation of a political union, in which the political institutions are unified through supranational institutions.[2]

No regional integration process could follow such a linear scheme in sequence, of course. However, regional integration organizations have attempted to conceptualize the process in terms of deepening or scaling up integration. For example, the North American Free Trade Agreement (NAFTA) (a regional trade grouping consisting of Canada, Mexico and the United States, formed in

January 1994) defined an integration process in more narrow but precise terms. NAFTA was a process mainly driven by the USA to liberalize regional trade as a prelude to liberalizing global trade, and as a response to the slow pace of the latter owing to the drawn-out 1986–93 Uruguay round of the General Agreement on Tariffs and Trade (GATT) and the final Uruguay round, which was ratified only in 1994. The US government became anxious about the emerging regional blocs in Asia and the European Union's (EU) move towards a monetary union – hence Washington's move to embrace regionalism.[3] Like NAFTA, such regional agreements were to serve as a precursor to global trade liberalization.[4]

There have been other regional integration schemes that are partially inward-looking whose objectives include more than trade liberalization. The EU is probably the best example. The integration schemes in Africa and the developing world are similar to the EU's open regionalism strategy.[5] The Europeans have over the years gone through various distinct phases in their integration process. In southern Africa, the Common Market for Eastern and Southern Africa (COMESA) of 1994 started off as a preferential trade area in 1981 and was subsequently transformed into a common market, denoting a change from one level of ambitions to another.

Generally, regional organizations follow a market integration principle that leads to other areas of cooperation as initiators for trade facilitation. But for SADC, the process of regional integration was completely different. From the outset, a holistic approach to integration, known as 'development integration', was adopted.[6] Thus the agenda for economic cooperation was transformed into a regional integration agenda and became the basis of integration instead of being its mere precursor. SADC's regional integration agenda rested on three pillars: political cooperation, functional cooperation, and market integration. This made the organization's regional integration agenda ambitious, complex, difficult to manage, and more difficult to measure in terms of progress.

Earlier attempts at regional economic integration

Although SADC's official documents talk about 'deeper integration', the initial planning and thinking processes concerning the various stages of integration were absent.[7] This could be due to the specific history of the organization, which began with a programme of economic cooperation to assist member states with specific problems, constraints and dependencies. The SADC Programme of Action (SPA), adopted by SADC's predecessor – the Southern African Development Coordination Conference (SADCC) of 1980 – was seen as a practical way for the organization to help southern Africa as a whole achieve specific development objectives through sector coordination.[8] In mid-1993, the SPA had 464 projects that required funding of US$9 billion, with only 22 per cent of these projects being truly regional. By the late 1990s, there were nineteen sectors and the SPA had 380 projects and had secured

49 per cent of its funding. Member states were unable to provide adequate resources and sufficient staffing for the Secretariat, which limited the capacity of SADCC and later SADC to deliver effectively on its mandate.[9] (See Landsberg in this volume.)

The transition from SADCC to SADC was supposed to be a transition from economic cooperation to regional integration. Instead, for a considerable period of time, the process focused on formalization of cooperation through legally binding instruments and protocols. The protocols contained elements of integration such as harmonization of policies in the various sectors. However, the sectoral cooperation project mainly focused on the mobilization of external resources for projects that benefited individual member states. Not all projects, however, benefited all member states. Some projects benefited some member states more than others. On the whole, all the member states derived benefits from the sectoral cooperation projects one way or another without necessarily advancing regional integration.[10]

SADC's development integration was not only ambitious, but also required greater technical capability, better and streamlined rules of procedures, and competent institutions. But instead, the organization relied too heavily on the varied capacity of its member states to deliver a regional programme, which became both its strength, because it anchored the regional programme squarely within member states' anticipation of commitment by governments, and also its weakness, because, in the end, no true regional capacity was created.

It is easy to measure trade integration by the existing trade regime on the one hand and its results on the other. Economists would ask whether the trade arrangements are trade-diverting, or trade-creating. In short, they will have a set of indicators and benchmarks by which trade activity is measured. This may include volume of intra-regional trade and harmonization of practices. Unfortunately, the SADC experiment cannot be measured by such criteria as the basis for any single economic activity or sector. What, then, are the indicators for the southern African region that mark its integration as a community?

It is generally believed that apart from a clearly identifiable geographic space, southern Africa is also identified by its peoples, who broadly share common cultures and languages. Furthermore, the geopolitical entities created through British, German and Portuguese colonialism buttressed the southern African region as a loose social, political and economic entity. Present-day Malawi, Zambia and Zimbabwe were initially part of the Federation of Nyasaland and Rhodesia from 1953 to 1963,[11] where there was free movement of people, goods and services between the three countries. Most of the leaders who led southern African countries to independence have developed close relationships with each other. The people of Angola and Mozambique were part of the Portuguese overseas territories and quite a number of them went to study in Portugal and developed close relations there. Botswana, Lesotho and Swaziland were part of the British High Commission territories and shared many institutions that were run from South Africa. Namibia was administered as part of South Africa after World War I ended in 1918. In short, settler regimes in southern Africa imposed close relations between the countries of the region and South Africa through joint institutions and dependency on its infrastructure, such as roads and railways.

In addition, the settler regimes created an environment that helped to solidify the affinities established among the peoples of the region. The most decisive fact that made a conscious process of integration possible was the cooperation of the peoples of the region in the struggle against colonialism. Leaders of the national liberation movements worked closely with the leaders of the independent states through the Organization of African Unity's (OAU) Liberation Committee and the Frontline States (FLS), which contributed to southern Africa's efforts to integrate the region.[12]

History and geography are an advantage but are not sufficient for the construction of a regional community. There must be a favourable environment, but also the political will and commitment to the project. Southern African countries had initially set out to create a community that would evolve common political values, systems and institutions, promote and defend peace and security, and achieve economic growth and development. But this can only be achieved when a number of principles are in place, such as sovereign equality of member states; human rights, democracy and the rule of law; and equality, balance and mutual benefit.

Political cooperation and development of a shared value system

In theory and practice, regional integration takes place within a political context where member states come together to define an agenda for cooperation and integration within a political framework. Countries with greater affinities, including similarities in political system and adherence to the rule of law, tend to be more successful at integrating their economies, instead of merely cooperating, compared to those without shared values. The SADC Treaty of 1992 rightly observed this principle of mutual understanding and good neighbourliness as indispensable for successful integration. Political cooperation for SADC was about not only providing a framework to deal with economic cooperation, but also evolving common political values, systems and institutions; promoting and defending peace and security; and promoting coordination and harmonization of the international relations of member states.[13]

The Southern African Development Coordination Conference of 1980 represented an agenda for economic cooperation, while the Frontline States of 1975 had focused on political cooperation. The SADC Treaty brought these two elements of political and economic cooperation together under one roof, even though there had always been a dimension of political cooperation in the economic cooperation agenda, as well as an element of economic cooperation within the political agenda. Yet the short-term objectives of both sides varied in terms of attaining certain economic and political goals.[14]

Successful efforts at regional integration require a peaceful and secure state in order to create the viable markets and foreign direct investment (FDI) necessary to achieve economic development. On the whole, peace and security are viewed as constituting a human right for all citizens. In southern Africa, widespread instability reigned for decades owing to the intransigency of the settler regimes and the struggle for national independence. Once national independence was attained, citizens felt that it should be maintained through conscious and deliberate efforts.

The 1992 SADC Declaration of Heads of State commits southern Africa to strengthen 'regional solidarity, and peace and security, in order for the people of the region to work together in peace and harmony'.[15] The region had for decades been embroiled in conflict. In the 1990s, the majority of SADC member states made a transition from one-party to multiparty systems. (See Matlosa in this volume.) There was a 'democracy fever' similar to the atmosphere in the independence period of the 1960s. In fact, the lack of democracy was blamed for all the ills that the region was experiencing. SADC was to play a catalytic role in deepening the process of democratization through the development of common values and systems and strong institutions. Between 7 and 11 February 1994, the SADC Sector for Culture and Information, in collaboration with the United Nations Educational, Scientific and Cultural Organization (UNESCO) and the International Commission of Jurists (ICJ), held a conference in Maputo, Mozambique, on promoting democracy and human rights in southern Africa.[16]

Furthermore, the SADC Secretariat organized a historic workshop in Windhoek from 11 to 16 July 1994 on promoting democracy, peace and security in order to design a programme of cooperation under SADC. Consistent with the framework and strategy for building the Community, this meeting brought together chiefs of defence forces, ministers of defence, intelligence, home affairs and foreign affairs, and members of parliament, academia, professional associations and non-governmental organizations (NGOs).[17]

SADC's process of defining common values and institutions took place within the context of commitments to popular participation in building a community and brought non-state actors into the security debate. However, the challenges facing the organization were further compounded by the SADC institutional structures and processes in which specific areas of cooperation were coordinated by a member state. Some member states expressed the divergent view that politics, defence and security did not lend themselves to coordination in the same manner as other areas of cooperation. Members of the Frontline States, with the exception of Botswana, wanted to use the model of the FLS in cooperating in the areas of politics, defence and security.

At the same time that the SADC Secretariat was spearheading the process of implementing the treaty provisions pertaining to cooperation in the areas of politics, defence and security, members of the FLS were considering the future, following the 1994 democratization of South Africa. Some members of the FLS wanted to see peace and security issues handled by a separate successor organization to the Frontline States. It was argued that the FLS had been successful in dealing with past conflicts, and its experience should not be lost to the region. As such, there was an attempt to reconstitute the Frontline States to include all member states of SADC and to operate as a separate organization, apart from SADC. The example of the Organization for Security and Cooperation in Europe (OSCE) being a separate entity from the EU was given at the time. The name 'Association of Southern African States' (ASAS) was proposed. However, other member states (primarily those that were not members of the FLS) argued that the region could not dissipate resources between two organizations, particularly when the SADC Treaty of 1992 had already made provisions for cooperation in those areas within the Community. In the interest of finding a compromise, the Summit of Heads of State and Government decided to harmonize the two processes: the one that was spearheaded by ministers of foreign affairs under the chairmanship of Zimbabwe to establish a successor organization to the FLS, and the one that was managed by the Executive Secretary of SADC to establish an appropriate mechanism for cooperation in the areas of politics, defence and security as provided for by the SADC Treaty.

After a series of meetings, differences still persisted and the creation of a hybrid structure was proposed, one that would satisfy member states that wanted to have an organization independent from SADC, and those that wanted to establish a mechanism within SADC. The SADC Organ on Politics, Defence and Security Cooperation (OPDSC) was thus created in June 1996 as a compromise, with the structure of the Organ initially characterized by 'constructive ambiguity'. It was to be an SADC mechanism as the name denoted but would operate independently from the Secretariat, even though the Executive Secretary was to attend all the meetings of the Organ.

It is important to note that, contrary to popular perceptions that have been reinforced by some studies, the difference in terms regarding how cooperation in the areas of politics, defence and security was to be organized was not between Zimbabwe and South Africa. Rather, it was between FLS and non-FLS members. The only exception to the rule was Botswana. Zimbabwe and South Africa were on the same side during those negotiations until a compromise was reached. The differences occurred in subsequent developments owing to operational difficulties.

It did not take long before the 'constructive ambiguity' that was created could be put to the test, which happened at the first meeting of the Organ at the level of heads of state, which took place in Angola on 2 October 1996 to discuss the situation in that country. The summit was called by the chairman of the Organ, President Robert Mugabe of Zimbabwe. The chairman of SADC, President Nelson Mandela of South Africa, went to Luanda on the understanding that he would be chairing the meeting, as it was essentially a SADC summit in all but name. After an initial stand-off and behind-the-scenes consultations, it was resolved that the meeting be chaired by the chairman of the Organ: Mugabe. This led President Mandela to demand that the relationship between the two bodies, SADC and its Organ, be clarified. Essentially this signalled the end of the period of 'constructive ambiguity' during which tough decisions had been avoided because of differences of opinion among member states. The Luanda summit was the first and the last of its kind. Thereafter the Community embarked on the process of drafting a protocol for cooperation on politics, defence and security.

These institutional challenges notwithstanding, the SADC Organ has been responsive in dealing with threats to peace and stability in the region. SADC has been engaged in trying to find a lasting solution to the situations in Angola, Lesotho, the Democratic Republic of the Congo (DRC) and Zimbabwe. SADC was for a long time engaged with the situation in Lesotho through diplomatic means. Two of its members – South Africa and Botswana – were instrumental in restoring the democratically elected government through a military intervention in September 1998 after what was termed a 'palace coup'.[18] Attempts had earlier been made to facilitate national dialogue through public debates within Lesotho with a view to ensuring commitment by all sides to holding free and fair elections, and respecting the outcome of such elections.[19]

Almost immediately after the DRC joined SADC, in 1997, the Great Lakes region was plunged into conflict. The governments of Rwanda and Uganda, which had earlier propelled President Laurent Kabila to power in the Congo in 1997, turned against him and backed his ouster from power. A year later, President Kabila appealed for assistance from SADC member states to repel what he called an invasion by Rwanda and Uganda. At a meeting of ministers of defence that took place in Harare in August 1998, the possibility of deploying troops to the DRC was discussed. The majority of member states felt that they were not in a position to commit troops to the DRC. Three member states – Angola, Namibia and Zimbabwe – however, declared their readiness to deploy troops in support of the DRC government, which eventually prevented its ouster from power.[20] The violence persisted and, after months of fighting, civil society organizations requested that I, as SADC's Executive Secretary, consult the SADC leadership with a view to initiating dialogue between the rebel factions and the DRC government. I was authorized to talk to the rebels, and the first meeting took place in Zambia in 1998. I then submitted a report to the chairman of SADC, Nelson Mandela, about the willingness of the rebels to talk to the DRC government.

A mediation process under the chairmanship of Zambian president Frederick Chiluba was authorized at the SADC summit in Mauritius in September 1998. The Kabila government initially refused to sit in the same room with the rebels, and proximity discussions or 'shuttle diplomacy' were conducted by a committee consisting of South Africa, Tanzania, Zambia, the SADC secretariat, the OAU and the United Nations. It was with the facilitation of this group that the Lusaka Accord was signed on 10 July 1999 by the DRC government and the rebels, as well as the countries that had troops in the DRC – Rwanda and Uganda as well as Angola, Namibia and Zimbabwe. In addition, the accord was signed by President Chiluba, myself as SADC Executive Secretary, Salim Ahmed Salim as OAU secretary-general, and Ibrahim Fall, a representative of the UN secretary-general, as witnesses. The implementation of the accord brought new players on to the scene, and subsequently the UN assumed responsibility for the peace process.[21]

SADC was also instrumental in efforts to resolve the situation in Zimbabwe. Former South African president Thabo Mbeki was assigned by SADC to mediate between the different political parties – the Zimbabwe African National Union–Patriotic Front (ZANU-PF) and the two Movement for Democratic Change (MDC) formations – to resolve the political tensions in Zimbabwe in March 2007. Mbeki's mediation strategy was criticized in various quarters in light of the fact that it would have no immediate impact on the situation on the ground. However, this strategy has been credited with the formation of the government of national unity in February 2009, with all its ramifications and challenges.[22]

There has been a debate about the usefulness of the 'quiet diplomacy' approach pursued by Mbeki and other SADC member states. Western countries and some non-state actors in the region believed that South Africa had the capacity to force the government of Zimbabwe into a desired course of action through public condemnations and sanctions. But SADC member states believed that public condemnation could harden rather than soften the position of the government in question. Furthermore, one cannot obtain cooperation from a government that one has condemned publicly. The situation in Zimbabwe also affected the relationship of SADC with its largely Western cooperating partners. They were reluctant to support regional projects from which Zimbabwe would benefit because of the sanctions against the leaders of that country. SADC has thus on a number of occasions decided to forgo assistance because of solidarity with Zimbabwe.[23]

Political instability in the region has had a negative impact on the effectiveness of the Community, since substantial time and resources must be allocated to peace and security efforts, at the neglect of areas of economic cooperation. This has also undoubtedly affected operations in other areas. At the same time, economic cooperation depends on political stability. Experience has shown that there is causal relationship between peace and security and development. The absence of peace and security impacts negatively on poverty reduction strategies, economic growth and development, and creates widespread poverty, with the potential to cause regional instability.

Developmental integration

It is generally recognized that the threat to peace and security in southern Africa will primarily come from non-traditional sources such as poverty and unemployment, natural disasters and environmental degradation. Political cooperation and good neighbourliness require a mechanism for economic co-operation to ensure that stability is sustained. It is therefore not surprising that the history of economic cooperation in southern Africa was linked to a political agenda. It was a matter not only of providing resources for the struggle for independence, but also of sustaining peace through economic reconstruction and development in the rest of the region. In fact, SADC was viewed in these terms. A number of donors who committed themselves to supporting SADCC viewed it as some sort of 'Marshall Plan' for reconstructing post-apartheid southern Africa, even though their strategies changed after the end of the Cold War.

It has been generally recognized that national development strategies in Africa were adversely affected by a number of fundamental structural weaknesses, including small economies, low incomes and wages, and inadequate infrastructure and the high costs of providing it. To some extent this situation prevented African countries from increasing their share of international trade and foreign direct investment. In a bid to overcome the structural weaknesses of individual countries, regional integration was embraced to complement national development efforts. SADC adopted a twofold strategy for economic development through regional integration as outlined in the Framework and Strategy for Building the Community of 1993. Functional cooperation was initiated under SADCC to address the bottlenecks in production and infrastructure development. Secondly, a market integration component sought to reduce barriers to trade and cross-border investments in order to create an integrated regional market. These two strategies are interrelated and mutually reinforcing. Functional cooperation contributes to the development of infrastructure and enhancement of production capacities, especially in agriculture through research and training and access to seed technology. Regional trade promotion also stimulates production activity, contributes to a competitive environment, and improves productivity. These two aspects together constitute what is referred to as 'development integration'. In fact, the name 'Southern African *Development* Community' comes from this theoretical underpinning.

Functional cooperation

Functional cooperation has allowed the peoples of southern Africa to feel that they are part of a broader community. SADC has attracted substantial funding from donors that invest in infrastructure, transport and communication, energy, and agriculture and food security among other areas. Infrastructure development has been the primary concern of SADC, with member states working together to overcome the challenges of landlocked countries by providing export and import routes. Infrastructure development started as part of the struggle for liberation to reduce the dependency of the countries of the region on apartheid South Africa's transport system. In this regard, the ports of Dar es Salaam in Tanzania and Beira in Mozambique were rehabilitated to manage greater cargo loads from neighbouring countries. Roads were also rehabilitated and new ones were constructed to link the different countries to each other. Today, all the countries of the region are interconnected through all-weather roads or railways or both. It is now possible to move goods and services throughout the SADC region, from east to west and from south to north, because of the subregional body's extensive infrastructure development. (See Khadiagala in this volume.)

Genuine integration in this area has also taken place, as the development of infrastructure was accompanied by the adoption and implementation of common policies and standards. The Protocol on Transport, Communications and Meteorology, which entered into force on 6 July 1998, was important in this regard. Integration in the transport sector went beyond functional cooperation to encompass the adoption of common policies and standards, such as for railways and road loads. A SADC driver's licence was also created. Furthermore, the transport corridors, which were initially designed to facilitate the free movement of persons, goods and services, have been transformed into investment opportunities. The Maputo Corridor, created in August 1995 to increase trade between South Africa and Mozambique, is a good example of such an initiative. (See Khadiagala in this volume.)

The energy sector is another area where integration of physical infrastructure was accompanied by adoption and implementation of common policies. Electrical interconnectivity has allowed the region to draw power from the most efficient source at a given time. During the rainy season the region can rely more on hydroelectric power, and during the dry season it can increase the use of fossil fuels. The Southern African Power Pool (SAPP), established in September 1995, brought together twelve different national utilities and ministries. Through the power pool, utilities have been working together to set standards, trade in power, and identify projects for investment. (See Nagar in this volume.)

An area of functional cooperation that has had a direct impact on the life of the citizens of the region is agriculture and food security. Agriculture is the backbone of most of the region's economies, with 70–80 per cent of SADC's 257 million population and labour force dependent on agriculture for subsistence, employment and income.[24] While agricultural production takes place at the level of individual countries, there has been significant exchange of information about new production techniques. Drought mitigation to safeguard food security is one of the major achievements of the programme. An early warning system was established that provides information about rainfall patterns and allows stakeholders to take preventive measures and to identify potential sources for imports. (See Simon in this volume.) There has also been regular regional crop assessment to determine the amount of cereals produced in the SADC region in a particular season and how much of SADC's crop harvest is sourced from within the region as well as from outside. This is important for transport coordination to keep SADC ports free from congestion, which can cause food insecurity because of delays in delivery. (See Drimie and Gandure in this volume.)

Trade and investment

Trade is considered by integration theorists to be key to successful regional integration. The word 'integration' has virtually become synonymous with the terms 'trade liberalization' and 'market integration'. Regional trade agreements facilitate the movement of goods and services within SADC and thereby create a competitive market that helps to enhance the global competitiveness of member states. Furthermore, the existence of a large market allows for the development of economies of scale that attract domestic and foreign direct investment. It is investment within domestic markets which transforms the economy, rather than the classic colonial investment of extracting raw materials for external markets.

While SADC did not adopt a market integration approach per se, trade and the desire to create a larger market have been important aspects of economic cooperation and regional integration in southern Africa. From the very outset, a sector on trade and industry was created. Though progress has been slow in creating a unified regional trade regime, member states have relied on arrangements other than the SADC regime to trade with each other. There have been a number of important bilateral trade agreements between the different countries of the region, some of which pre-dated SADC. These bilateral trade agreements are more advanced than the regional trade regime. They contribute to the development of local businesses and take advantage of neighbouring markets that can become building blocks for a common regional trade regime. The problem, however, is that they are so different. The Southern African Customs Union (SACU) involves five SADC member states, a free trade area exists between Malawi, Zambia and Zimbabwe, and a free trade agreement has been established between Namibia and Zimbabwe. Furthermore, some members of SADC are also members of COMESA and thus participate in the latter's trade liberalization scheme. In fact, trade in the region has been more greatly facilitated by these bilateral and multilateral subsets rather than by the regionwide instrument.

In addition, some SADC member states have individually undertaken commitments to trade liberalization in the context of other initiatives. Some SADC members implemented structural adjustment programmes of the World Bank and International Monetary Fund (IMF), as well as trade liberalization policies, disregarding the regional situation. This in effect reduced their own tariffs significantly below what their counterparts in the region were prepared to offer each other. Some of these countries urged other members of the Community to synchronize their tariffs. The response was that trade liberalization must be induced internally rather than externally. In short, there was a rejection of, as one minister of trade called it during a heated debate, implementation of structural adjustment programmes 'through the back door'.

The result is that SADC states have unequal access to each other's markets. Some countries have accessed the liberalized markets of their neighbours while applying non-liberal policies to the region, further buttressing trade imbalances in southern Africa. There was an attempt to reverse this situation through a cross-border initiative sponsored by the World Bank, the IMF, the African Development Bank (AfDB) and the European Union. This initiative provided financial incentives to countries that liberalized their trade. It was hoped that this would not only accelerate the process of trade liberalization but also create a level playing field. Countries such as Malawi, Tanzania, Zambia, Uganda and Mauritius which had liberalized their trade under structural adjustment programmes and other unilateral or bilateral initiatives were willing to take further liberalization measures under the cross-border initiative. These countries had nothing to lose, as they had already opened up their markets significantly. While this initiative accelerated open regionalism, it did not help the management of common regional programmes.

There was no common trade regime covering all member states until the adoption of SADC trade protocols in 1996 and 2000, which aimed to create a free trade area within eight years. A forum was also established through which member states could conduct detailed trade negotiations. The signing of the trade protocols involved many behind-the-scenes consultations to allay the fears of some member states. A decade and a half later, SADC has yet to establish the free trade area envisaged in 1996. Instead, its member states have greater ambitions, such as creation of a customs union.

The slow pace of trade negotiations in the context of SADC has been in stark contrast to a more dynamic global environment that promotes freer trade. There was a risk that the SADC process would be overtaken by developments elsewhere, thereby rendering the entire process redundant. Regional trading blocs are to be precursors to global trade liberalization and competitiveness. Through regional integration, the SADC region should prepare itself for global competition. The competition at the regional level should lead to enhanced productivity and competitiveness. The slow pace of the conclusion of the

World Trade Organization's (WTO) Doha round, which began in 2001, has given regional arrangements a second chance. SADC should speedily implement the commitments of member states under its trade protocols. Cooperation between SADC, the East African Community (EAC) and COMESA should also be implemented with vigour in order to create a vibrant common economic space. Trade liberalization in itself cannot bring about economic development. It is investments which create wealth through the production of various goods and services and creation of employment. In fact, trade is an effect of production, while production is made possible by investment.

Africa's share of investment flows is very low. Investment flows are far from a level that can reduce poverty. A number of reasons have been cited as to why Africa, including southern Africa, has not attracted sufficient FDI, including political stability, risk of policy reversals, inefficient physical and technological infrastructure, and the small size of most markets. SADC member states have taken measures to create favourable environments for domestic and foreign investment. Most states have promulgated investment laws and special incentives for foreign investors, such as repatriation of profits, borrowing on local markets, grants for training of local workers, and arbitration mechanisms in case of dispute between investors and governments. Most SADC countries have also signed investment protection treaties with a number of industrialized countries. SADC member states are also members of the World Bank's Multilateral Investments Guarantee Agency (MIGA).

It is argued, however, that creating larger markets based on comparative advantage, while potentially attracting investment, can also create economies of scale. Furthermore, responses to the individual and collective efforts of SADC members to create favourable investment climates have not been commensurate with the actual flows of investment. Despite favourable ratings in terms of the business environment, the flow of FDI to the SADC region has been erratic. Between 1992 and 1997 the average annual flow of FDI into the region was a mere US$1.8 billion, and between 1998 and 2003 it was US$4.9 billion, the bulk of which was invested in Angola and South Africa.[25] On the whole, Africa's share of global FDI was no more than 4 per cent by 2007. Most SADC members have undertaken policy reforms to address some of these impediments. The region has also tried to complement the efforts of member states in specific areas and has introduced a system by which the SADC summit is tasked to focus on areas in which progress is needed.

The SADC Secretariat has actively engaged in investment promotions. An important initiative was the co-organization of the Southern African Economic Summits with the World Economic Forum from 1996 to 1999. I was co-chairperson of the summits, along with Klaus Schwab of the World Economic Forum. The participation of the Secretariat in the design of the programme was important in ensuring that future summits focused on the region's needs.

These summits provided a platform for a meeting between southern African and international political and business leaders. They also provided an opportunity for regional businesses to meet potential investors and to create joint-venture partnerships. The SADC Secretariat has also organized meetings between regional leaders in other localities, such as New York, on the fringes of the United Nations General Assembly. In short, no opportunity has been lost to promote investment, whether through activities organized by SADC member states, the Secretariat or any other organization.

While the SADC region has attracted investment in the extractive sectors and in production of raw materials for export to the industrialized countries, there is further need for investment to create more jobs, in order to transform the economies of the region.

Management of regional integration

Southern Africa has embarked on a complex regional integration process that consists of political, economic, social and cultural aspects. This is quite different from the regional integration schemes that are simply concerned with integration of markets. Successful integration will thus depend on the contribution of various stakeholders, including governments, southern African institutions and non-state actors at large.

The role of governments The success of any integration scheme depends on the willingness of participating countries to harmonize their policies and practices and the pace at which they want to integrate. Equally important is the amount of resources that they are prepared to expend on regional integration. Regional integration is conceived, designed, driven and to a large extent managed by member states. They play an important role in the management of regional integration through sectoral committees of ministers that take decisions in respect of their areas of responsibility. Once these decisions are endorsed by the Council of Ministers or the summit, they go back to the same ministers for implementation. The frequency of these meetings leaves much to be desired. The changing regional and global situation requires closer interaction among member states than what the current structure and practice of the organization permits. Other stakeholders can aid the process only by taking advantage of the policy space created by governments for them to establish cross-border relations with their counterparts. The role of governments is particularly crucial when it comes to policy harmonization. The emergence of a larger economic and political space can be achieved only through policy convergence in various fields. The domestication of regional policies is of cardinal importance in this regard.

Inasmuch as governments are committed to regional integration, line ministers are preoccupied with the day-to-day operations of government business and national priorities. They have little time for regional issues except in cases where there are projects to be implemented in their respective countries. The degree of involvement of governments and ministers differs from country to country. Some ministers prioritize the regional agenda, whereas others think about SADC only just before the next meeting. There is a need for mechanisms through which member states can remain engaged with the issues of the Community on a continuous basis. The model of the African Union (AU) and the United Nations, where representatives of member states are continuously engaged in the affairs of the organization, is worth considering. Such an arrangement would not only ensure the input of member states on a continuous basis, but also enhance the effectiveness of SADC.

Regional institutions The presence of strong regional institutions is a prerequisite for the success of regional integration. At the time of its creation, SADC did not seriously consider creation of the institutions necessary to achieve the ambitions set out in its founding treaty. Instead, it continued with the sector system, whereby each member state was designated a sector or sectors to coordinate. The sectors were part of the ministries where they were located, and sector coordinators were supervised by and reported to their permanent secretaries. However, permanent secretaries were often too busy running ministries and attending to national priorities. The sector coordinators were meeting twice a year under the chairmanship of the SADC Executive Secretary to report on implementation of Council of Ministers decisions for their respective sectors as well as on new initiatives that they intended to take to the Council, which invariably had already been submitted to the sectoral ministerial committees.

The advantage of this system was that it ensured the active involvement of governments in SADC's work. The pitfall was the lack of regular interaction with other SADC institutions. Furthermore, the capacity of some of the sector coordination units was weak. On the other hand, some sector coordinators were creative and brought stakeholders into the planning and implementation of decisions as well as finance. A case in point was the mining sector coordination unit, which established subcommittees through which regional chambers of mines participated. It took ten years following the adoption of the 1992 SADC Treaty before the sector-coordinating system was ultimately abolished.

The restructuring of SADC institutions to bring the Community's structure into line with treaty ambitions went a long way towards creating coherence among SADC's institutions. It was important to bring all institutions responsible for the management of the process of regional integration under the same authority. The Secretariat has an important role to play in the process of regional integration, in its planning and strategic management mandate, and in identifying key strategic projects to be approved by the Council of

Ministers and the Summit of Heads of State. The challenge that remains is to build adequate capacity to manage implementation of the Regional Indicative Strategic Development Plan (RISDP) of 2003 and the Strategic Indicative Plan of the Organ on Politics, Defence and Security Cooperation (SIPO) of 2004.

The SADC Secretariat The Executive Secretary, as head of the SADC Secretariat in Gaborone, apart from being responsible for the strategic management of the institution and the servicing of the meetings of Council and Summit, must maintain close relations with the member states and provide periodic briefings and exchanges of views on matters of interest to SADC with senior officials, ministers and heads of state, as well as non-state actors. This requires that the participation of the Executive Secretary in public debates on SADC-related matters and shared values, such as the independence of the media, must be ensured. The Executive Secretary, as chief diplomat of the Community, is responsible for publicizing the activities of SADC, regionally as well as internationally, and representing the body at meetings of major international forums, such as the World Trade Organization, the World Bank and International Monetary Fund, the United Nations General Assembly, the African Development Bank and the African Union.

The Executive Secretary is also the chief spokesperson of the Community, charged with public diplomacy in articulating the policies and decisions of SADC and promoting and defending its common values through advocacy and other efforts. Furthermore, the Executive Secretary has important outreach responsibilities to the constituencies, governments, NGOs, the private sector, cooperating partners and the international community at large.

As head of the SADC Secretariat with its meagre resources and ambitious agenda, the Executive Secretary must be creative in harnessing the resources of all the citizens and institutions of the region and taking advantage of international goodwill towards southern Africa. In this regard, during my term in office (1994–99), I practised an open-door policy that allowed NGOs, academia and the private sector to contribute to regional integration and development. I will mention three examples of how the harnessing of the resources of the constituencies helped to advance regional integration in specific areas. The first area was that of gender and the empowerment of women, the second involved cooperation with the private sector, and the third focused on harnessing international goodwill towards the region.

After the SADC Secretariat was mandated by its Council to explore the most effective ways to integrate gender issues into the SADC Programme of Action, a number of activities were undertaken, including the incorporation of gender in project selection criteria. An Eminent Persons Group was constituted to undertake a study on this matter. Though this issue was kept on the agenda, no significant progress was made. Substantial progress on gender was made years later when key stakeholders approached me, as SADC Executive Secretary, to facilitate the creation of an institutional mechanism for cooperation in the area of gender. I viewed this as an opportune moment and challenged the stakeholders to become involved in the process of establishing the appropriate institutional framework. The regional advisory committee that was established to follow up on the Beijing Women's Conference of 1995 worked closely with the SADC Secretariat and contributed significantly to the decision of the Council of Ministers of February 1997 to create a gender unit within the Secretariat. (See Otitodun and Porter in this volume.)

During my tenure I also created a thriving partnership with the Geneva-based World Economic Forum to organize the Southern African Economic Summits. As mentioned earlier, I co-chaired these meetings with the president of the World Economic Forum, Klaus Schwab, between 1996 and 1999. This partnership resulted from the outreach functions of the Executive Secretary to those various constituencies.

With regard to harnessing international goodwill towards the region, I took a number of initiatives in conjunction with cooperating partners. The most important was the one that resulted in the adoption of the declaration known as the Berlin Initiative of September 1994. The SADC Council of Ministers agreed to the joint meeting between SADC foreign ministers and their EU counterparts after a protracted debate in 1994. Some member states felt that the meeting would undermine unity and solidarity within the seventy-nine-member African, Caribbean and Pacific (ACP) group of states. However, an institutional mechanism for political dialogue between the EU and SADC that involved a biannual meeting of ministers of foreign affairs was institutionalized without affecting ACP solidarity.

Another area in which I played an important role in harnessing international goodwill was in resource mobilization, to ensure the constant flow of resources from international cooperating partners despite the overall decline in official development assistance. In this regard, the Secretariat developed a cooperation framework for financing SADC activities with a number of governments. I negotiated with the government of Japan to second an adviser to the SADC Secretariat who would offer guidance about the best way to access Japanese resources for the Community. Similar arrangements were also made with the government of Germany.

The success of the SADC Secretariat in advancing the agenda for regional integration in future will depend on a number of factors. One such factor is its technical capacity: that is, the ability to prepare position papers on various policy initiatives for tabling before the various levels of decision-making within SADC. The ability to coordinate relations with regional institutions and associations, member states, SADC National Committees (SNCs) and the SADC Committees of Ambassadors and High Commissioners is of cardinal importance. The bottom line is the number of staff that member states are willing to finance within the Secretariat.

The role of non-state actors The success of regional integration depends not only on the commitments and capacity of government but on those of non-state actors as well. There has been a recognition that the legitimacy of regional integration depends on support from the peoples of the region. Regional integration by its very nature encroaches on the space of ordinary citizens in different ways and must therefore be acceptable to the citizens of member states. While decisions are taken by heads of state, implementation is mostly undertaken through the private sector and other institutions and individuals. In addition, the peoples of the region can make a significant contribution to the formulation of policies based on their experiences from their various walks of life. It was against this background that provisions were made for the participation of non-state actors in community-building. The 1992 Treaty makes provision that the Community 'shall seek to involve fully, the peoples of the region and Non-Governmental Organizations in the process of regional integration'. It also provides that SADC 'shall cooperate with and support the initiatives of the peoples of the region, and Non-Governmental Organizations, contributing to the objectives of this Treaty in the areas of cooperation in order to foster closer relations among communities, associations and peoples of the region'.[26]

The community-building process started with broad consultations with relevant stakeholders. Workshops were organized that brought together governments, professional associations, academia, NGOs and other relevant stakeholders on particular issues. The workshops resulted in policy recommendations presented to the sectoral ministerial committees and later to the Council of Ministers and the Summit. The involvement of non-state actors relates not only to their input into the SADC Programme of Action, but also to knowledge of their own areas of operations. Since integration is a multifaceted enterprise, NGOs can contribute to regional integration by working with their counterparts in other member states on a number of issues. Greater coherence of business practices across the region can also be facilitated by non-state actors. In fact, NGOs have formed a regional organization – the SADC Council of NGOs, established in 1998 – through which they can interact with SADC institutions and contribute to regional integration in their own right.

The provisions of the SADC Treaty for non-state actors to participate in regional integration have not always been translated into action. There has been apprehension among SADC governments about foreign-funded NGOs in a number of countries. NGOs are seen either as pursuing a foreign agenda or as opposition parties in disguise. One of the liveliest debates that I witnessed at SADC summits was when the Secretariat tabled a report on SADC cooperation with NGOs. Most of the heads of state who participated at the meeting expressed apprehension about the role of NGOs.

There is no doubt that various non-state actors can add value to the process of regional integration in southern Africa. It is important to underscore the differential roles of NGOs and governments. NGOs cannot be a substitute for governments even in areas where government institutions are weak. The challenge is to work towards strengthening such institutions. There are functions that can be carried out effectively by civil society, while others remain the preserve of the state. What is of cardinal importance, however, is to design appropriate mechanisms to institutionalize the involvement of non-state actors in the process of regional integration. Thus far, this involvement has been sporadic and unpredictable.

A successful regional integration scheme must be rules-based, and the involvement of non-state actors cannot be an exception. An institution must be created through which NGOs can systematically, and continuously, provide their input into regional integration efforts. One possibility is to establish an SADC 'Economic and Social Council', which could meet twice a year. Such a council could be attended by representatives of governments, business organizations, labour, research institutions and NGOs and could serve as a forum for exchange of views among its various stakeholders. Debates in this council could lead to policy initiatives and programmes for identification of SADC projects. It is important to note that the proposed council would be an SADC institution in the same fashion as the United Nations Economic and Social Council (ECOSOC) and the African Union's Economic, Social and Cultural Council (ECOSOCC).

Conclusion

Regional integration as espoused by SADC is a product of southern Africa's specific historical circumstances and has not conformed to conventional approaches. Whereas most regional organizations followed a market integration approach and other areas of cooperation were initially seen as trade facilitations, SADC adopted from the outset a holistic approach to integration known as 'development integration'. Uniquely to Africa, SADC combined political cooperation, functional cooperation and market integration. This made the agenda for regional integration under SADC ambitious, complex and difficult to manage, and progress difficult to measure.

SADC has made considerable progress in the areas of political cooperation and functional cooperation, but little progress in the area of market integration. Political cooperation had a long-standing tradition in the Frontline States, serving as a basis for progress even though the context and form of cooperation were different. The FLS dealt with interstate conflicts, while the SADC Organ on Politics, Defence and Security has been dealing primarily with intrastate conflicts.[27]

There have been two cases of interstate conflict in the SADC region since the formation of the Community. One was a dispute between Botswana and Namibia over an island on the Chobe river, Sidudu/Kasikile, that erupted in 1996. This matter was not resolved through a regional mechanism but was referred to the Hague-based International Court of Justice (ICJ), which led to the signing of the 1999 agreement between the two countries.[28] The other case was a 1998 dispute between Angola and Zambia in which Luanda accused Lusaka of supporting the rebel movement, the National Union for the Total Independence of Angola (UNITA). This matter was dealt with on a bilateral basis, and the two countries asked Swaziland to mediate. I was co-opted partially because of my personal relations with the two countries. The matter was resolved amicably in 1999.

The success in the area of functional cooperation builds on the progress of SADCC, which is why the transition from economic cooperation to economic integration proved to be so difficult for southern Africa. SADC as an entity had no tradition of market integration to rely on at the time when it embarked on that path. The existence of multiple trade integration schemes with which SADC countries were associated has not assisted in advancing the creation of a unified regional market. Some SADC member states (Botswana, Lesotho, Namibia, South Africa and Swaziland) have commitments under the Southern African Customs Union, which, with its own external tariff and mechanisms for revenue-sharing from trade proceeds, represents the most advanced form of integration in the region. (See Gibb, Qobo in this volume.)

In practice, there are very few barriers to trade among the countries of southern Africa. However, there exists a multiplicity of commitments under different initiatives that sometimes work against the SADC trade regime. As such, it is difficult to deal with balance-of-payment issues and competition policies. If SADC is to make progress in the area of market integration and to project itself as an emerging market, it must use the most advanced basis of integration in the region, which is SACU, with all its implications.

Finally, the construction of an integrated community in southern Africa has relied on the region's political capital of a long history of solidarity and donor support for economic cooperation. There is now a need to take bold measures that can advance market integration and generate the investment and regional resources necessary for SADC to finance its own development. SADC should also make available substantial resources to build the technical capability of its institutions, which is essential to managing the complex agenda on which the Community has embarked.

Notes

1 African Development Bank (AfDB), 'Economic integration in southern Africa', Oxford, 1993; Samuel Kingsley Botwe Asante, *Regionalism and Africa's Development*

(London: Macmillan, 1997), pp. 21–44; Ibbo Mandaza and Arne Tostensen, *Southern Africa: In Search of a Common Future* (Gaborone: Southern African Development Community, 1994).

2 Ali M. El-Agraa (ed.), *Economic Integration Worldwide* (New York: St Martin's, 1997), discussed in Margaret C. Lee, *The Political Economy of Regionalism in Southern Africa* (Lansdowne: University of Cape Town Press, 2003), p. 20.

3 Lee, *The Political Economy of Regionalism*, p. 30.

4 Ibid., p. 176.

5 Open regionalism is based on neoclassical and/or neoliberal economic theory, which emphasizes that markets should drive the integration process with a strategy that is designed to be outward-looking, avoiding high levels of protection, and that regionalization should become part of the economic globalization of the world economy. See Lee, *The Political Economy of Regionalism*, pp. 31–2. See also Charles Oman, *Globalization and Regionalization: The Challenge for Developing Countries* (Paris: Organization for Economic Co-operation and Development, 1994); Fredrik Söderbaum, *The New Regionalism and the Quest for Development Cooperation and Integration in Southern Africa*, Minor Field Study Series no. 73 (Lund: Department of Economics, Lund University, 1996).

6 For theories on development integration, see Lee, *The Political Economy of Regionalism*, pp. 22–3. See also Jens Haarlov, *Regional Cooperation and Integration within Industry and Trade in Southern Africa: General Approaches, SADCC, and the World Bank* (Aldershot: Averbury, 1997).

7 Southern African Development Community (SADC), 'Southern Africa: a framework and strategy for building the Community', Gaborone, 1993.

8 See Gabriël Oosthuizen, *The Southern African Development Community: The Organization, Its Policies, and Prospects* (Midrand, South Africa: Institute for Global Dialogue, 2006).

9 For related literature and research on the SPA, see Oosthuizen, *The Southern African Development Community*; Lee, *The Political Economy of Regionalism*, p. 51. See also Dawn I. Nagar, 'Towards a Pax-Africana: Southern African Development Community's architecture and evolving peacekeeping efforts, 1996–2009', Master's thesis, University of Cape Town, South Africa, 2010, pp. 15–16.

10 See Oosthuizen, *The Southern African Development Community*, pp. 81–2. See also Lee, *The Political Economy of Regionalism*, p. 50.

11 J. Mayuyuka Kaunda, 'Continuity and change in Malawi's foreign policy-making', in Korwa Adar and R. Ajulu (eds), *Globalisation and Emerging Trends in African States' Foreign Policy-making Process: A Comparative Perspective of Southern Africa*, (Aldershot: Ashgate, 2002) pp. 71–90.

12 SADC, *Declaration, Treaty, and Protocol of Southern African Development Community*, Art. 5, Gaborone.

13 Ibid., Art. 5.

14 See the discussion in Oosthuizen, *The Southern African Development Community*, pp. 68–9.

15 *A Declaration by the Heads of State or Governments of Southern Africa: Towards the Southern African Development Community*, Windhoek, 1992.

16 SADC Secretariat, 'SADC profile', Gaborone, 2010.

17 Ibid. See also Peter Meyns, 'Strengthening regional institutions: politics and governance in the SADC region', in Dirk Hansohm, Christian Peters-Berries, Willie Breyten Bach and Peter Meyns (eds), *Monitoring Regional Integration in Southern Africa* (Windhoek: Gamsberg Macmillan, 2002).

18 See Khabele Matlosa, 'Regional security in southern Africa', in Adekeye Adebajo, Adebayo Adedeji and Chris Landsberg (eds), *South Africa in Africa: The Post-Apartheid Era* (Scottsville: University of KwaZulu-Natal Press, 2007). See also Peter Vale, *Security and Politics in South Africa: The Regional Dimension* (Boulder, CO: Lynne Rienner, 2003).

19 See Leslie Gumbi, 'Instability in

Lesotho: a search for alternatives', *African Security Review*, 4(4), 1995.

20 Devon Curtis, 'South Africa: exporting peace to the Great Lakes region?', in Adebajo, Adedeji and Landsberg, *South Africa in Africa*.

21 Ibid., pp. 255–6.

22 Brittany Kesselman, 'Human security in the SADC region', *Pax-Africa: Africa Peace and Security Agenda*, 5(1), March 2009. See also Tongkeh Joseph Fowale, 'The Zimbabwe factor in Thabo Mbeki's fall: silent diplomacy', Suite 101.com, 19 July 2009; Celia W. Dugger, 'Mbeki's resignation risks Zimbabwe deal', *New York Times*, 23 September 2008.

23 Kesselman, 'Human security'.

24 Serigne T. Kandji and Louis Verchot, *Climate Change and Climate Variability in Southern Africa: Impacts and Adaptation in the Agricultural Sector* (Nairobi: United Nations Environment Programme and World Agro-Forestry Centre, 2006),

p. 3; M. Calcaterra, Johann Kirsten and Daneswar Poonyth, 'Is agricultural sector growth a precondition for economic growth? The case of South Africa', Working paper (Pretoria: Department of Agricultural Economics, Extension and Rural Development, University of Pretoria, 2001).

25 United Nations Conference on Trade and Development (UNCTAD), *World Investment Report 2004*.

26 See SADC, *Declaration, Treaty, and Protocol*, p. 19, www.sadc.

27 See Naison Ngoma, 'The Organ on Politics, Defence, and Security: the rise and fall of a security model?', in Ngoma, *Prospects for a Security Community in Southern Africa: An Analysis of Regional Security in the Southern African Development Community* (Pretoria: Institute for Security Studies, 2005).

28 Matlosa, 'Regional security in southern Africa'.

PART TWO

Governance and military security

3 | The Southern African Development Community's decision-making architecture

Chris Landsberg

How are decisions made in southern Africa's premier interstate body, the Southern African Development Community (SADC)? Which key structures and institutions are involved in decision-making at the regional level? This chapter explores the decision-making architecture and policy matrix of SADC, likening the overall style and approach of the body to what Charles Kegley refers to as 'governmental politics' – 'fighting among insiders within an administration and the formation of fractions to carry on battles over the direction of foreign policy decisions'.[1] Splits among key policy advisers and factions are commonplace. Students of governmental politics observe that politicians and diplomats favour diplomatic approaches to policy problems, as opposed to the military solutions preferred by militarists. We will test the propositions of the governmental politics model in relation to southern Africa and SADC.

Historical background

SADC was formed from a loose alliance of nine majority-ruled states in southern Africa known as the Southern African Development Coordination Conference (SADCC). (See Khadiagala in this volume.) The main aim of SADCC in the 1980s was to coordinate development projects and to lessen economic dependence on apartheid South Africa. Because the goals during the era of white minority domination were straightforward – to lessen black-ruled states' dependence on apartheid South Africa – decision-making was relatively clear cut. States banded together in solidarity and focused on strengthening cooperation with one another in order to reduce cooperation with apartheid South Africa. SADCC lacked a complex decision-making matrix or tapestry of structures and institutions. States came together at regular intervals and decisions were taken, and the Secretariat in Gaborone, Botswana, was expected to help operationalize and coordinate such decisions. Historical, economic, political, social and cultural factors created strong bonds of solidarity and unity among the leaderships of the region. These factors contributed to a 'distinct identity that underpins political and economic co-operation' pursued through SADCC.[2]

A treaty signed in Windhoek on 17 August 1992 transformed SADCC into SADC and 'a restructuring process was initiated which brought about new structures and mechanisms for the implementation of SADC's new regional integration mandate'.[3] The treaty 'redefined the basis of co-operation among member states from a loose association into a legally binding arrangement'.[4] SADC's vision is one of a common future in a regional community that will ensure economic well-being, improvement of standards of living and quality of life, and freedom, social justice, peace and security for the peoples of southern Africa. The vision, like the agenda, is explicitly developmental, as SADC sets out to 'promote sustainable equitable economic growth and socio-economic development through efficient productive systems, deeper co-operation and integration, good governance and durable peace and security, so that the region emerges as a competitive and effective player in continental and international relations'.[5]

As part of SADC's intergovernmental agenda, regional leaders have articulated a set of political and socio-economic strategic priorities at the core of the region's integration agenda, comprising unique protocols in various sectors that define the objectives, scope and institutional mechanisms for cooperation and integration. Protocols are approved by the Summit of Heads of State and Government on the recommendation of the Council of Ministers. Each protocol becomes a legal document, and states are expected to adjust their national laws in compliance. A protocol enters into force thirty days after the deposit of the instruments of ratification by two-thirds of SADC member states, and it is binding only on the member states that are party to it. Since 1992, some forty legal instruments, including sector protocols, declarations and charters, have been adopted by SADC. Three-quarters of these have been ratified by member states, giving them legal status. In theory this shows commitment by member states to cede some sovereignty to an interstate body, but there has been no concomitant domestication of protocols, nor adaptation of protocols to national laws.[6] SADC should move from rhetoric to implementation of these legal instruments.[7]

Policy agenda

SADC's core policy objectives are outlined in its 1992 Windhoek Treaty: promoting development, poverty reduction and economic growth through regional integration; consolidating, defending and maintaining democracy, peace, security and stability; promoting common political values and institutions that are democratic, legitimate and effective; strengthening links among the peoples of the region; and mobilizing regional and international private and public resources for the development of the region. Over the course of its nearly two-decade existence, SADC has developed a model of regional integration that, in broad terms, aims at the following goals:

1   Sustained and sustainable development of southern Africa.

2 Decreased unemployment, poverty and underdevelopment for the working people of the region.
3 Successful responses to the challenges of globalization, including strengthening of South–South relations and equitable and mutually beneficial co-operation.
4 Increased capacity for southern Africa to contribute as a region to the important project of African integration and unity.
5 Increased capacity for southern Africa to contribute to the emergence of a new world order that will fully restore Africa and the African diaspora to their rightful place on the international stage.[8]

This developmental integration model places emphasis on overcoming pervasive poverty, underdevelopment and uneven development.[9] Developmental integration is known as the 'new' regionalism and places emphasis on economic development, human security and social policy, resource governance, environmental protection and regional self-sufficiency.[10] Khabele Matlosa and Kebapetse Lotshwao say that 'SADC believes that regional economic integration may not succeed unless democracy and good governance as well as peace and security prevail in the region'.[11] What about integration in the political-security sphere?

Political, peace and security priorities

SADC's political, peace and security priorities are contained in the Strategic Indicative Plan of the Organ on Politics, Defence and Security Cooperation (SIPO), adopted by SADC leaders in 2004 as a strategic security framework for the region; this plan still constitutes the base for the region's political and security integration agenda.[12] SIPO was designed to provide guidelines for action (strategies and activities); shape the institutional framework for the day-to-day activities of the Organ on Politics, Defence and Security Cooperation (OPDSC), including operationalization of the Protocol of the OPDSC and the Mutual Defence Pact; and align the regional peace and security agenda with that of the African Union (AU), especially the AU's proposed Stand-by Force and aspects of good governance.[13] SIPO identifies four broad political integration priorities:

1 Promote democracy and rule of law, to safeguard human rights and basic freedoms, through development of democratic institutions and practices within territories of member states.
2 Develop common foreign policy approaches on issues of mutual concern, and advance such approaches collectively in continental and international forums.
3 Strengthen regional and continental capacity for conflict prevention, management and resolution in order to safeguard against instability arising from breakdown of law and order, intra- and interstate conflict, and aggression.

4 Develop enhanced regional and continental coordination and cooperation on matters related to security and law enforcement.[14]

However, there have been perennial problems with implementation and operationalization of SIPO and other regional plans. Between 2004 and 2009, for example, SIPO developed no fewer than 130 objectives, but never produced a proper implementation plan to accompany these ambitious goals.[15] The management of the Organ's affairs took place against the backdrop of a small administrative infrastructure and capacity. With limited staff, the Secretariat has long battled with effective implementation, monitoring and evaluation of policy. (See Mbuende in this volume.)

Socio-economic development and integration priorities

The socio-economic development priorities of the region are contained in SADC's Regional Indicative Strategic Development Plan (RISDP),[16] which spells out four broad integration plans:

1 Enhanced trade and financial liberalization as well as competitive and diversified industrial development to promote deeper regional and continental integration and poverty eradication through establishment of a number of organizations: SADC Free Trade Area (FTA) (2008), SADC Customs Union (2010), SADC Common Market (2015), SADC Monetary Union (2016), Continental Customs Union (2017–19), African Common Market (2019–23) and African Economic Community (2023–28).[17]
2 Sufficient, integrated, efficient and cost-effective infrastructure systems to support and sustain regional and continental economic development, trade, investment and agriculture, in order to eradicate poverty.
3 Efficient social infrastructure to address the regional and continental dimensions of emergencies, including HIV/AIDS epidemics (see Dzinesa in this volume), food insecurity (see Drimie and Gandure in this volume) and natural disasters.
4 Enhanced standard of living and quality of life for the peoples of southern Africa and greater support for the socially disadvantaged.

As with SIPO, the problem with the RISDP has been implementation. Former Executive Secretary of SADC Prega Ramsamy opined that 'the RISDP remains largely unimplemented as a result of resource and capacity constraints both at national and regional levels'.[18] An official perspective is that SADC has at times found itself in a 'state of paralysis' brought about by a 'combination of the organization's institutional transformation, weak political commitment from member states and inadequate technical capability'.[19] Because the SADC Secretariat and member states have been bogged down with policy-making and implementation issues, they have at times neglected the dominant challenges of governance, human development and human security.

Today, southern Africa faces a three-pronged crisis: a crisis of governance and in particular of the state; a crisis of development; and a crisis of human security. The potential for conflict in some of the states of the region, most notably Zimbabwe and the Democratic Republic of the Congo (DRC), threatens to reverse the gains they have achieved in terms of democratization. Even election disputes have become a cause for conflict in many states. Southern African politics and socio-economic developments remain contradictory and in a state of perpetual fluctuation. The global recession has had a major negative impact on the ability of the region to meet its development goals and to make inroads into tackling poverty and inequality. Shrinking levels of budgetary support over the years have been accompanied by increased human insecurity and deepening poverty. In 2009/10, for example, the SADC Council approved a budget for the Secretariat of US$54 million, of which international donors provided US$28 million, showing the reliance of SADC on external funding, even amid dwindling resources.[20] This has serious implications for policy ownership of the body's agenda by its own member states. If regional states fail to meet their financial obligations, how can they hope to be in full command of the security policy agenda?

While the RISDP provides the framework for implementation of the various strategies aimed at fulfilling the region's vision and socio-economic mission, the speed of implementation and the institutional and structural capacity constraints faced by SADC and its agencies remain matters of concern.

SADC's decision-making architecture

The AU has dubbed the regional economic communities (RECs) the 'building blocks' of continental union. With SADC constituting the premier integrating body in southern Africa, it is important to understand SADC's decision-making architecture and how the various units operate and interact within this architecture.

The Summit of Heads of State and Government is the ultimate decision-making institution, charged with responsibility for political direction and control of functions of the Community. The Summit meets at least once a year, usually in August. The chairperson and deputy are elected for one year on the basis of rotation from among the SADC member states. Heads of state and government at the summit level have personified SADC's governmental politics model of decision-making and shown strong political commitment towards the integration road map of SADC. Article 19 of the SADC Treaty stipulates that decision-making in SADC is 'by consensus'.[21] While this mode of decision-making has some advantages, it also has clear disadvantages. Because SADC decisions are taken by consensus as opposed to voting, the region and its leaders need to have a high degree of 'unity of purpose' for the bloc to meet its goals.[22] However, progress has often been retarded because decisions must be watered down to cater for all objections and opinions, sometimes to the critical detriment of the decision and its effectiveness.[23]

So, while the Summit is the highest decision-making structure, it typically resorts to lowest-common-denominator politics and frantic scrambles for consensus; different blocs and factions typically form around key issues, and over the years we have seen a bloc of countries ruled by liberation movements turned governing parties dominate regional politics. Issues of regional interest often come second to the narrow national interests of member states.[24] And the very ambitious policy decisions and plans adopted by heads of state have gone unimplemented; even at this level there is a problem with states not taking ownership and responsibility for implementing the regional agenda.[25]

There is little disputing the centrality and power of the Summit, the all-influential club of heads of state and government. This has major implications for all other SADC structures and actors. As Matlosa and Lotshwao put it, 'power to make decisions, even on democracy and governance matters, is centralised within the SADC Summit and this situation denudes the effectiveness of the SADC Secretariat as a whole and the Organ Directorate in particular'.[26] This observation brings us to two other powerful actors, also involving heads of state and government: the two 'troikas', one at the level of the Summit, and one for the OPDSC. Each comprises the preceding, current and forthcoming chairpersons, and enables the implementation of tasks and decisions as well as the provision of policy direction to SADC institutions between the regular Summits.[27] The two troikas exert much control and influence over SADC direction. Both are rotational, and decisions are taken through consultation and consensus as opposed to being dictated by one or a few states, no matter how powerful.[28] On issues of a political, military or security nature, SADC positions are driven by pan-African solidarity ideals.[29] In reality, however, some states are more active and energetic in nature, and drive the agenda more forcefully than others.

Troika members are entrusted with steering the SADC agenda as well as implementing decisions taken by the Summit. However, action at the level of the troika is dependent on the commitment of whoever presides over troika affairs for any given year. Some states are more committed than others, and are able to devote more resources and energy than others. Thus, because South Africa is more able to devote resources than other states, it has a greater influence on the agenda than do smaller SADC members.

A very influential actor or forum in SADC's intergovernmental system is the Council of Ministers, which comprises ministry representatives from each member state, usually from foreign affairs, economic development, planning and finance. The Council oversees the functioning of SADC and advises the Summit on policy matters and the development of SADC. It develops the organization's substantive agenda, sets its strategic priorities and targets, and ensures that policies are properly implemented. The Council meets before the regular Summit and at least one other time during the year. Most of its recommendations are accepted and endorsed by the heads of state at the Summit level.

Like the Council, the Integrated Committee of Ministers is pivotal in regional policy adoption, for it makes recommendations to the Summit. The Integrated Committee was created on 3 March 2003 to develop and oversee implementation of the RISDP through the coordination and harmonization of cross-sectoral activities, and to coordinate the work of different clusters, such as the peace and security cluster, the trade and economic development cluster, and the social development cluster.[30] Its responsibility is to direct the work of the four directorates at the SADC Secretariat charged with socio-economic issues. However, this has since been duplicated by sectoral ministerial committees tasked with the same functions. So, for example, finance ministers meet separately from defence ministers, and separately from home affairs ministers. Ministers responsible for political affairs have had more influence in setting SADC's agenda than ministers responsible for economic and social matters.[31] By extension, this means that the agendas of the Council and the Summit are dominated by political issues.

While the Council of Ministers and the Integrated Committee of Ministers are pivotal in regional policy adoption and SADC's governmental politics processes, the Standing Committee of Officials is key in regional policy formulation. It consists of a permanent secretary or director-general from each member state. The Standing Committee advises the Council of Ministers on technical matters, and meets in advance of Council meetings. In political terms, the Standing Committee can be likened to a policy gatekeeper. It acts under the direct instruction of ministers, usually ministers of foreign affairs, who often push agendas of national interest as defined by their political principals. As such, the Standing Committee enjoys significant influence in setting the agenda and mediates between the Council of Ministers and the Secretariat, as well as with the Integrated Committee, but the overall relationship between the Council and the Standing Committee does not function optimally.[32]

The SADC Secretariat, the principal executive institution of SADC, is responsible for the strategic planning, coordination and management of SADC programmes, implementation of the RISDP, management of the organization, and coordinating the policies and strategies of member states to ensure synergy with regional policy positions. By about 2003, the SADC Secretariat was starting to emphasize the need for 'restructuring' so as to 'increase the efficiency and effectiveness of SADC policies and programmes and to implement a more coherent and better co-ordinated strategy to eliminate poverty in the region'.[33] At the heart of the Secretariat is the Executive Secretary. Depending on the personality involved, the Executive Secretary can wield great influence in regional affairs. The

Executive Secretary manages consultations between governments and SADC, and is the interface between SADC and other regional organizations. The Executive Secretary also organizes meetings of the Summit and the Council, and oversees the public administration machinery of the organization.

The Secretariat is only as strong as SADC member states allow it to be, and SADC states (like SADCC states before them) have generally been loath to give the Secretariat the necessary political weight to play a role beyond mere political coordination and administration in carrying out the wishes of individual member states and serving international donors. On the other hand, there has been a tendency for SADC states to expect the Secretariat to initiate policy and agenda items. This means that SADC must constantly walk a political tightrope. Matlosa and Lotshwao, two close observers of SADC, put it bluntly: the 'Secretariat remains weak without the requisite political gravitas to implement the regional integration mandate of the regional economic community ... [P]ower is centralised in the hands of the heads of state and government [and this] undermines the supra-nationality that SADC requires in order to make headway in pursuing political integration'.[34] This again corroborates the view that the Secretariat is dependent on the whims and wishes of governments in the region to empower it to become more effective.

Under trying circumstances the Secretariat is doing a relatively good job in coordinating and managing strategic planning in the region. Though in 2003 the Department of Strategic Planning, Gender and Policy Harmonization was established within the Secretariat, as the core of SADC's programmes and projects,[35] the Secretariat continues to be both understaffed and overwhelmed, and spends a great deal of time serving the interests and concerns of member states, while also serving and accounting to donors. The Secretariat lacks the permanent management capacity to clearly articulate and monitor common goals, strategies and time-frames, remaining institutionally weak and ineffective in carrying out its mandate. Indeed, the Secretariat lacks the capacity to drive the development and integration agenda from a technical perspective, and has been unable to steer the implementation of the RISDP and provide well-researched political and economic integration policy options.[36] For years it has suffered from weak strategic management, poor administrative systems and weak technical competencies.

Today the Secretariat comprises four functional directorates:

- Trade, Industry, Finance, Investment and Mining
- Food, Agriculture and National Resources
- Infrastructure and Services
- Human and Social Development

Though the Secretariat is typically overwhelmed with political administration and project management, it continues to play an important role in the region. It is the one actor that can bring states together in pursuit of common regional and Community interests; no other actor is as focused on SADC's interests. Each SADC member state has a national contact point (NCP) for communicating with the Secretariat, as well as a national secretariat for coordinating the SADC agenda. Despite this litany of weaknesses, the Secretariat, the Executive Secretary and the NCPs continue to create opportunities to influence the agenda in the direction of integration. To date, the NCPs have not been very functional or effective, and governments and civil society actors in many member states have been equally inactive and poorly organized in getting these structures off the ground.

The major challenges faced by the southern African region are not interstate conflicts or war, but regional development and integration, consolidation of peace and security, and consolidation of democratic governance. Because the challenge of consolidating democratic governance remains crucial, there is a need to prioritize issues of institutional development in the region, placing the nature and quality of decision-making firmly on the agenda. By 2008, SADC had itself recognized that there was a need to strengthen the Secretariat's capacities, systems and management processes; sharpen the region's integration agenda and regional governance and management structures; strengthen regional SADC subsidiary bodies, such as the SADC Tribunal; and support regional Centres of Excellence.[37] Not even SADC is prepared to turn a blind eye to its decision-making challenges. Yet the issue of strengthening the institutional edifice of SADC has received scant attention over the course of the first three decades of the Community.

The Organ on Politics, Defence and Security Cooperation The Organ on Politics, Defence and Security Cooperation is arguably the most powerful organ of SADC. It seeks to promote peace and security in the region. Strategies and programmes are elaborated through SIPO. One of the changes being mooted is that of minimizing the role and influence of foreign donors and governments over the region's security agenda, and for member states to take greater ownership and responsibility for this sector. While in theory this is a noble objective, member states may find it tough to make the necessary investments in regional peace and security. The burden may fall disproportionately on countries such as South Africa to make resources available. Also, a distinct possibility is that SADC may continue to rely on the resources of donor partners but may insist on greater control and appropriation of such resources. They may, for example, punt the idea of a regional security trust fund through which resources would be channelled.

Within the OPDSC are two powerful committees, both established in August 1999: the Interstate Defence and Security Committee (ISDSC), a successor institution to the disbanded Frontline States (FLS), and the Interstate Politics and Diplomacy Committee (ISPDC).[38] Both committees are tasked with regional preventive peace and security, and the latter also with diplomacy and conflict mediation. This structure has not yet been properly established, and faces many serious institutional and political challenges, thereby robbing the region of a real preventive diplomacy mechanism. Some of these challenges include inadequate financial resources and lack of human and technological resources.[39] The OPDSC's secretariat and directorate lack the wherewithal to implement the various declarations, conventions and decisions of SADC.[40] The region is especially in need of a mechanism that could promote a conflict resolution paradigm that links preventive diplomacy, peacekeeping and peace-building. As the Centre for Conflict Resolution recently stated, '... the SADC secretariat should be better capacitated, in the area of peace and security, in terms of its staffing and absorption and use of funds'.[41]

The Tribunal The SADC Tribunal was established on 14 August 2001 to ensure adherence to, and proper interpretation of, the provisions of the SADC Treaty and subsidiary instruments, and to adjudicate disputes referred to it. It is located in Windhoek, Namibia. The Tribunal has jurisdiction over all disputes between member states; disputes between SADC and Tribunal staff over conditions of employment; disputes between SADC and legal persons such as companies; and disputes between member states and natural legal persons.

Southern Africa lacks an oversight and compliance mechanism. The absence of an enforcement mechanism, in the form of an interstate or supranational authority, has resulted in SADC member states failing to honour decisions of the Tribunal.[42] The mandate of the Tribunal could be increased to strengthen its role as guardian of the Community's interests, so it can monitor adherence to the letter and spirit of those interests as defined in the SADC Treaty and other instruments. Indeed, one of the major contributions the Tribunal could make would be to define a regional jurisprudence and community law. One of the issues member states might consider is the possibility in the short term for the Tribunal to receive and consider matters regarding non-implementation of, and non-compliance with, agreements and decisions, and what penalties and corrective measures should be put in place.

National Committees To democratize regional policy-making processes, SADC leaders created National Committees to create space for governmental and non-governmental organizations (NGOs) to come together. These committees have been established as part of the transformation of SADC, and have replaced the national-level sectoral coordination units (SCUs), which existed as national structures of the old SADCC.[43] These structures are responsible for the initiation of projects and commission issue papers as discussion documents, which serve as inputs to help with the implementation of the RISDP.[44] The National

Committees comprise key stakeholders from government, the private sector and civil society, including NGOs and worker and employer organizations in SADC member states,[45] and each National Committee is supposed to reflect the core areas of integration and national coordination in its composition. The responsibilities of SADC National Committees are threefold: provide inputs at the national level into the formulation of regional policies, strategies and planning; coordinate and guide the implementation of such policies at national level; and serve as a platform for closer cooperation between SADC and its member states as a key step towards deepening integration.[46]

The National Committee is one of the most important structures, yet one of the least effective, within the SADC architecture. Garth le Pere has likened National Committees to mere 'bureaucratic shells' and argues that 'most are yet to define their proper role and function, including how they should relate to stakeholders outside government'.[47] While SADC decision-makers envisioned National Committees becoming 'networks of excellence',[48] to date there is hardly any SADC state that can claim to have a functioning National Committee. So decisions taken at the regional level are not translated into national ownership. In fact, most states are preoccupied with narrow national interests, and do not have a strong sense of regional interests. The lack of seriousness about National Committees also reflects the dominance of states and the weaknesses of civil society, which is unable to organize itself effectively within states and across borders so as to influence the regional policy agenda. As a result, National Committees have remained state-directed,[49] with some observers characterizing them as paralysed, dysfunctional or even non-existent.[50] They must be overhauled, bolstered and provided with the necessary resources to drive SADC's regional mandates.

Regional civil society and SADC's Council of Non-governmental Organizations The 1992 SADC Treaty identifies a special place for civil society organizations in regional agenda-setting and policy formulation. Chapter 7, Article 23 of the treaty stipulates that 'SADC shall co-operate with and support the initiatives of the peoples of the region in the process of regional integration'.[51] However, an assessment of the past two decades or so reveals that regional civil society actors have not made serious inroads into the regional agenda. Engaging SADC has been the prerogative of specialist think tanks and research organizations, with few or no grassroots organizations being afforded the opportunity for policy influence. At the national level, there is a distinct lack of integration portfolios, with parliaments and NGOs feeling that they have been left in the dark and kept at arm's length on regional integration matters, and that they do not have claims on integration mandates. SADC bills and protocols are shrouded in secrecy, and national parliaments receive bills very late in the legislation process.

NGOs have been shown to be their own worst enemies, given how poorly networked they are across borders. Even nationally there is much infighting and competition among NGOs, and they have displayed no culture of working together at home.[52] The result of this dynamic has been to ensure the continued dominance of states and governments in determining the integration trajectory of the region, and the continued underperformance of SADC. While 'civil society groups [may] command a comparative advantage in their knowledge and experience of a number of areas', including 'agriculture and food security; community-based natural resource management and conservation; education and vocational training; gender issues; combating HIV/AIDS; and cross-border trade and small scale enterprise development',[53] they need to realize the limits of their influence.

There are examples of civil society showing that it can be effective in influencing the regional agenda. For example, regional women's lobbies have been highly effective in mobilizing around SADC's Gender and Development Protocol and ensuring that it is on the regional agenda.[54] This protocol deals with a number of issues that affect women: constitutional and legal rights, governance, education, productive resources, gender-based violence, health and HIV/AIDS, peace-building and conflict resolution, and the media. The actions of the regional women's movement have ensured that governments make commitments in favour of gender empowerment. The challenge now is to ensure that states live up to these commitments. Progress on implementing them has been slow, as has progress on implementing the third Millennium Development Goal, pertaining to gender equality.

In order to democratize this prevailing state- and elite-driven status quo, SADC civil society actors assembled in 1998 to create a coordinating structure in the form of the SADC Council of NGOs (SADC-CNGO). Comprising national umbrellas of NGOs in all member states, SADC-CNGO set out to engage the Community and influence political and economic integration agendas. SADC-CNGO has experienced major challenges to its functionality and effectiveness, including political infighting among civil society actors, both within states and among states, and financial crises. This has rendered it too weak to challenge governments and play an important countervailing role in the region, thereby making it easier for governments to set policy agendas. So, we face a double-edged sword as far as decision-making in the region is concerned: on the one hand, states dominate policy-making processes in SADC, yet remain poorly organized and divided among themselves. On the other hand, there is a tendency to overstate the capacities of regional civil society to both serve as a counterweight to governments and to engage them in an effective and robust manner. Regional civil society remains for all practical purposes demobilized and highly ineffective.

Conclusion

SADC's Secretariat is imbued with inferior decision-making powers, and has a poorly constructed decision-making edifice. One cannot emphasize enough the urgent need for improvements in the organization, management and functioning of the regional organization and its substructures. The southern African region has over the past three decades taken key decisions, but its premier integration body is fragmented and scarcely acts as a rational, unitary whole. The governance and interstate institutions put in place nationally and regionally in the SADC region are weak, and SADC states have been reluctant to render to them the necessary political powers to function optimally. The SADC Secretariat remains essentially an administrative body, serving the wishes of heads of state and the international donor community. Unlike the Economic Community of West African States (ECOWAS), SADC plays little role even in mediating conflicts. At best, SADC is an implementation body, but it is the heads of state and government that call the proverbial shots in the region. The states in the two troikas set the agenda and determine progress in the region. Significantly, not all members of the troikas show the same commitment to advancing the region's policy agendas. Some states are more committed than others, and some are better resourced to play activist roles. South Africa has both the resources and the will to influence the regional agenda, whereas Angola has the resources but lacks the political will to play an activist role.

SADC is facing an implementation crisis. While it has over the years developed laudable programmes and projects, many such initiatives remain unimplemented and even unimplementable because they are so highly ambitious; by 2004 the peace and security programme alone contained no fewer than 130 objectives, yet lacked a clear execution plan to operationalize them. Many of these programmes and projects remain dependent on donor funding and technical support, and even more programmes remain short-term and narrow in nature. It is often difficult to discern where exactly the policy-making epicentre in SADC really is. There is thus lack of capacity in terms of adequate institutional arrangements, ineffective engagements and an insufficient number of professionals to supervise partnerships and policy decisions. It is not always clear who takes ownership of decisions in the region, so matters drift and an overwhelmed Secretariat often finds itself having to pick up the pieces. In the end, SADC politics are driven by a governmental style in which a number of deeply politicized modes of operation prevail: tensions between various regional governmental delegations, coalition and bloc formations, at times infighting and jealousies, and the pushing of crude national-interest agendas. Ultimately, the decision-making architecture of SADC reveals a culture in which interstate politics and perpetual vying for influence and prominence trump implementation and execution.

It seems fair to insist on a reform process within SADC that would strengthen both the strategic capacities of SADC and its institutions, most notably the Secretariat, as well as the policy-making and management practices, and in a manner that would ensure that the region realizes its policy objectives as set out in SADC's integration agenda. SADC needs a more structured approach to decision-making, and a commitment to building meritocratic regional institutions. Emphasis should be placed on SADC's regional ancillary structures, as well as on the revival of weak national structures. Regional integration, we should remember, begins at home.

Notes

1 Charles W. Kegley Jr, *World Politics: Trend and Transformation*, 11th edn (Belmont, CA: Wadsworth Publishing, 2007), p. 79.

2 Munetsi Madakufamba, 'SADC in the 21st century', *Open Space*, 2(1), November 2007, p. 90.

3 President Benjamin Mkapa, Foreword to Southern African Development Community (SADC), *Regional Indicative Strategic Plan*, Gaborone, 2004; Khabele Matlosa and Kebapetse Lotshwao, *Political Integration and Democratization in Southern Africa: Progress, Problems, and Prospects* (Johannesburg: Electoral Institute of Southern Africa, 18 December 2009), p. 8.

4 Madakufamba, 'SADC in the 21st century', p. 91.

5 Siphamandla Zondi, 'The State of the Southern African Development Community: A Critical Assessment – State of Regional Integration Project of the Development of Southern Africa', Paper prepared for the Southern African Development Bank, Midrand, 2008, p. 15.

6 Madakufamba, 'SADC in the 21st century', p. 91.

7. Centre for Conflict Resolution, *Building Peace in Southern Africa*, policy seminar report, Vineyard Hotel, Cape Town, South Africa, 25–26 February 2010, p. 10.

8 SADC, *Amended Declaration and Treaty*, Gaborone, 1992; Department of Foreign Affairs (DFA), 'Developments in the SADC region', Briefing to the diplomatic trainees (Pretoria: Foreign Service Institute, 16 April 2008).

9 Zondi, *The State of the Southern African Development Community*, p. 4.

10 Ibid., p. 6.

11 Matlosa and Lotshwao, *Political Integration and Democratization in Southern Africa*, p. 7.

12 For an assessment of SIPO, see Khabele Matlosa, 'Regional integration and civil society engagement in southern Africa: can SADC-CNGO make a difference?', *Open Space*, 2(1), November 2007, p. 97.

13 Anthoni van Nieuwkerk, 'Overview of the SADC Strategic Indicative Plan for the Organ (SIPO): achievements and challenges', *Pax-Africa*, 5(1), March 2009, p. 9.

14 Ibid.

15 Ibid.

16 P. A. Mohamudally, *Regional Indicative Strategic Development Plan (RISDP)*, Mauritius, 2005.

17 DFA, 'Developments in the SADC region'.

18 Prega Ramsamy, 'African regional integration', Paper presented at the Department of International Relations and Cooperation conference 'Closing the Gap Between Domestic and Foreign Policies', Pretoria, 5/6 November 2009.

19 DFA, 'Revitalising the SADC economic development and integration agenda', Draft discussion paper prepared by the Inter-Departmental Task Team, Pretoria, June 2006.

20 See 'Post-Council media briefing' by Nkosasana Dlamini-Zuma, South African minister of foreign affairs and chair of the SADC Council of Ministers, Cape Town, 27 February 2009.

21 H. W. Short, 'Revitalizing the SADC economic development and integration agenda', Commandant's research paper, South African National Defence College, 31 October 2006, p. 17.

22 Madakufamba, 'SADC in the 21st century', p. 93.

23 Short, 'Revitalizing the SADC economic development and integration agenda', p. 17.

24 Ibid.

25 DFA, 'Developments in the SADC region'.

26 Cited in Matlosa and Lotshwao, *Political Integration and Democratization in Southern Africa*, p. 10.

27 For a perspective on the troikas and the Organ, see International Peace Academy (IPA), 'Southern Africa's evolving security architecture: problems and prospects', Seminar report, Gaborone, December 2000.

28 Madakufamba, 'SADC in the 21st century', p. 93.

29 Ibid.

30 DFA, 'Developments relating to SADC, African Union, and NEPAD', Pretoria, 31 March 2003.

31 DFA, 'Revitalizing the SADC economic development and integration agenda'.

32 AfDevInfo, 'SADC Standing Committee of Officials, SADC Council of Ministers', 28 April 2008, www.sadc.int/ English/about/struct...; www.afdevinfo. com/htmlreports/org/org_48953.html.

33 DFA, 'Developments relating to SADC, African Union, and NEPAD'.

34 Matlosa and Lotshwao, *Political Integration and Democratization in Southern Africa*, p. 34.

35 DFA, 'Developments relating to SADC, African Union, and NEPAD'.

36 IPA, 'Southern Africa's evolving security architecture'.

37 SADC, 'SADC Secretariat Capacity Development Framework', SADC/CM/2/ 2008/3.5, Gaborone, March 2008, p. 4.

38 Ibid.

39 Matlosa and Lotshwao, *Political Integration and Democratization in Southern Africa*, p. 34.

40 Ibid.

41 Centre for Conflict Resolution, *Building Peace in Southern Africa*, Policy seminar report, Vineyard Hotel, Cape Town, South Africa, 25/26 February 2010, p. 48.

42 Short, 'Revitalizing the SADC economic development and integration agenda', p. 15.

43 Cited in Matlosa and Lotshwao, *Political Integration and Democratization in Southern Africa*, p. 13.

44 DFA, 'Developments in the SADC region'.

45 Ibid., p. 25.

46 Ibid.

47 Quoted in Madakufamba, 'SADC in the 21st century', p. 93.

48 Short, 'Revitalizing the SADC economic development and integration agenda', pp. 15, 26.

49 Matlosa and Lotshwao, *Political Integration and Democratization in Southern Africa*, p. 13.

50 Ibid., p. 14.

51 Matlosa, 'Regional integration and civil society engagement', p. 99.

52 Centre for Civil Society, 'Civil society guide: deliberative policy, civil society, and Africa's continental mechanisms and programmes', Durban, November 2006, p. 2.

53 See South African Institute of International Affairs, *SADC Barometer*, 5, April 2004, p. 1.

54 Sheila Bunwaree, 'Achieving human security in insecure southern Africa: a gender perspective', *New Agenda*, 4th Quarter 2008, pp. 68–71. See also Otitodun and Porter in this volume.

4 | Elections and conflict management

Khabele Matlosa

Elections are supposed to build democratic governance, peace and political stability. A recent handbook produced by the United Nations Development Programme (UNDP) observes aptly that elections that are credibly conducted can imbue the government with legitimacy through popular consent, creating a stable government and a peaceful post-election environment.[1] However, elections can also ignite political tension and instability in situations where violent conflict has not been fully terminated through a durable and sustainable peace.[2] Precisely because they are high-stakes contests for retention, control and capturing of state power, elections can 'often generate vulnerabilities for escalation of conflict into violence'.[3]

Context

One of the major concerns in the democracy literature in Africa continues to be the extent to which democracy and elections help or facilitate peace, security and political stability, as these are considered a *sine qua non* for sustainable human development. The current democratic 'moment' in Africa as a whole, and southern Africa in particular, has profound implications for contemporary conflicts and the manner in which they are managed, as well as for the sustainability of peace in post-conflict societies.[4] In order to make sense of the election–conflict interface in southern Africa, the political landscape of the region and its contemporary governance trajectory must be put into perspective.

The prevailing governance model in southern Africa is predicated on electoral democracy marked by the dominant-party syndrome, with the political elite emphasizing regular elections irrespective of their imperfections. Despite a multiplicity of political parties contesting each successive election, more often than not one party emerges as a victor and controls state power for ages. An example is Botswana, where the ruling Democratic Party has been in power for more than four decades. Between elections, the institutional architecture for democratic governance still leaves a lot to be desired, and this has dire consequences for sustainability of constitutionalism, rule of law, peace and security. Consequently, democratic governance and sustainable human development remain elusive goals, and elections become merely ritualistic plebiscites meant to satisfy the political egos of the elite. In this way, elections tend to make little sense to ordinary voters, as they do not bring about meaningful change to their daily lives. As the political fortunes of the elites are enhanced through elections, the socio-economic conditions of ordinary people hardly change for the better. As poverty becomes more and more entrenched, citizens are becoming increasingly disenchanted with politics, including with the institutions of democracy themselves. Citizens are mobilized during elections to elevate a small coterie of the political elite to echelons of state power on the basis of empty political promises that are hardly ever realized after elections. This trend reduces politics and democracy in the region to simple elite games for political power, which in turn detaches the citizenry from the pursuit of democracy.

Not all Southern Africa Development Community (SADC) countries are advancing towards sustainable democratic governance. As Table 4.1 illustrates, some are making 'democratic progress'; others have not even undergone the 'democratic transition'; some are stuck in a 'democratic standstill'; while others are doomed to 'democratic backsliding'. The worst governance model in southern Africa is Swaziland's closed authoritarian regime, for Swaziland has not yet experienced a democratic transition. SADC countries that can be classified as electoral authoritarian regimes are the Democratic Republic of the Congo (DRC), Madagascar and Zimbabwe. These countries hold regular elections, yet such elections hardly qualify as credible, democratic or peaceful. Over and above the democratic deficiencies of their elections, these countries

TABLE 4.1 Classification of regime types in SADC

Closed authoritarian	Electoral authoritarian	Electoral democratic	Liberal democratic
Swaziland	DRC	Angola	Botswana
	Madagascar	Lesotho	Mauritius
	Zimbabwe	Malawi	Namibia
		Mozambique	Seychelles
		Tanzania	South Africa
		Zambia	

Sources: Adapted from Jeff Haynes, 'Introduction', in Haynes (ed.), *Democracy and Political Change in the 'Third World'* (London: Routledge, 2001); Michael Bratton and Nicholas van de Walle, *Democratic Experiments in Africa* (New York: Cambridge University Press, 1997); Larry Diamond and Mark Plattner, *Democratisation in Africa: Progress and Retreat*, 2nd edn (Baltimore, MD: Johns Hopkins University Press, 2010).

also face profound limitations of their democratic order between elections, threatening rule of law and constitutionalism.

The majority of SADC member states are electoral democracies in which the governance system has undergone transition from dictatorial rule and the country has embraced a multiparty democratic dispensation, but the democracy in place is not a fully fledged liberal democracy as we know it in industrialized countries in Europe and North America. This narrow form of liberal democracy is confined primarily to the mere act of holding regular elections. Reduced to mere electioneering, democracy takes on a procedural form and remains devoid of substantive content. Under these circumstances, democracy is perceived by power elites as synonymous with electoralism. Countries that fall into this category include Angola, Lesotho, Malawi, Mozambique, Tanzania and Zambia. Although their political systems are occasionally marked by political turbulence, especially around election time, the political systems in these countries are stabilizing; if they manage to institutionalize their existing multiparty systems, they have the potential to transition to a relatively higher form of democracy, namely liberal democracy.

Few southern African countries are liberal democracies. In Botswana, Mauritius, Namibia, Seychelles and South Africa the governance realm is institutionalized through regular and credible multiparty elections, with a relatively fair amount of procedural certainty and substantive uncertainty. Constitutionalism and the rule of law are entrenched, and human rights are promoted and protected. These liberal democracies are stable and consolidating (but not yet consolidated), and have dominant-party systems (with the exception of Mauritius, whose system is marked by coalition politics).

Violent election-related conflicts are much more common in closed authoritarian and electoral authoritarian regimes. They occasionally occur in electoral democratic regimes, but rarely characterize liberal democratic regimes. This observation confirms the inextricable causal linkage between democracy and peace in Africa: more democracy will result in more peace. Put somewhat differently, the more democracy is deepened and institutionalized, the less the likelihood that election-related violence will lead to instability and war in a country. This is essentially what defines the peace dividend of democracy. The key question is whether, after the end of the Cold War and the demise of apartheid in South Africa, elections in southern Africa are facilitating this peace dividend.

The problematic nexus between elections and conflict: selected cases

At its heart, democracy is about negotiating, mediating and managing conflicts (whether violent or non-violent) at various layers of society. Although conflicts are inherent in all societies, the concept of 'conflict' remains both nebulous and elusive in social science discourse.[5] For the purposes of this chapter, the concept is used to denote incompatibility of interests, choices and goals with distribution of resources, ideological/identity orientation and distribution of power among various political actors. Conflict arises from an incompatible interaction between two or more actors in the political system in which the ability of one actor to gain depends to an important degree on some loss on the part of others. Politics is therefore a conflict-ridden game.

In and of itself, conflict is not necessarily a negative phenomenon. Conflict can be part of the social transformation of societies in a positive direction. What becomes a major problem, triggering various kinds of crises, is when conflict escalates into political violence and the conflicting parties attempt to resolve it by violent means through zero-sum strategies rather than resorting to constructive means involving positive-sum tactics. The constructive resolution of conflict means the political settlement of disputes through win-win and compromise solutions rather than the resort to violent means and other types of winner-take-all strategies. It is worth noting that, after protracted wars of liberation, followed in some countries (such as Angola and Mozambique) by internal wars among parties with external support in the context of the Cold War and apartheid, all the violent conflicts in the SADC region were resolved by way of political settlements involving multi-stakeholder dialogue and negotiation. For instance, in Angola the 1991 Bicesse Agreement played a crucial role in opening the political space for multiparty competition, and in Mozambique the 1992 General Peace Agreement, signed by the country's main political players in Rome, had a similar effect.[6]

Since the 1990s, there has been great variation in the region in the degree to which elections resolve or accentuate major conflicts. Three cases – South Africa, Zimbabwe and Lesotho – will help us make the point. These cases are interesting for a number of reasons. First, these three countries have different electoral systems: party-list proportional representation in South Africa, winner-take-all, first-past-the-post in Zimbabwe, and mixed-member proportional representation in Lesotho. Secondly, their political systems are also marked by vast differences: South Africa has an admixture of presidentialism and parliamentarianism; Zimbabwe's hyper-presidentialism has recently been tempered by a power-sharing agreement; and Lesotho has a constitutional monarchy. Thirdly, as Table 4.1 shows, the three countries are at different levels of democratic transition: Zimbabwe is an electoral authoritarian regime, Lesotho an electoral democratic regime, and South Africa a liberal democracy. Fourthly, of the three cases, only South Africa has not experienced major election-related violent conflict, with the exception of the transitional election of 1994. Even where elections have been marked by political violence in some parts of the country, especially the troublesome KwaZulu-Natal, constructive mechanisms for preventing this violence from triggering major instability and war have been put in place and to effective use. By contrast, in Zimbabwe and Lesotho, elections tend to take the form of war by other means as elites lock horns in tussles for control of state power. However, a caveat is needed here for Lesotho: the intensity of election-related violence in the country has been considerably reduced since the 2002 electoral reform, which witnessed the introduction of the mixed-member proportional system to replace the winner-take-all, first-past-the-post system that the country had been using since its political independence in 1966.

South Africa Quite clearly, elections helped in the process of political settlement of the South African conflict, ushering in the African National Congress (ANC) as the ruling party in 1994. The South African example is instructive in relation to how to institutionalize mechanisms for the constructive management of election-related disputes in post-conflict societies. In South Africa, various mechanisms are used in managing conflict, especially around elections, including an independent electoral commission, party liaison committees, conflict management panels, an electoral court, and a code of conduct for political parties. The electoral commission manages all aspects of elections, including disputes. It has the power to investigate and resolve disputes of an administrative nature and disputes that do not necessarily fall within the jurisdiction of the courts. Party liaison committees bring parties together in handling election disputes. Conflict management panels address electoral conflicts at their early stages in the provinces and at the national level. The electoral court adjudicates election disputes. The code of conduct commits political parties to agreed norms and ethical conduct during election campaigns. Partly as a result of the effectiveness of the established conflict management mechanisms and institutions, political stability has been achieved in South Africa and the country's proportional representation system allows broader inclusion of, and gives voice to, different key political actors in the legislature. In South Africa, therefore, elections have contributed to the wider peace and reconciliation process since 1994. Subsequent general elections held in 1999 and 2004 have helped nurture the country's democracy and peace. South Africa held its fourth election in April 2009, again under conditions of peace and tranquillity, with the ANC still the ruling party.

Zimbabwe Zimbabwe has been experiencing a deep-seated political crisis since the late 1990s, and this crisis manifests itself in the form of political tension and conflict among key political actors, especially the ruling Zimbabwe African National Union–Patriotic Front (ZANU-PF), led by President Robert Mugabe and opposition parties, notably the two factions of the Movement for Democratic Change (MDC): the majority faction, led by Morgan Tsvangirai (MDC-T), and the minority faction, led by Arthur Mutambara (MDC-M). As the political crisis in Zimbabwe deepened and the external position of the country became more and more precarious, a civil society electoral reform process was undertaken between 2003 and mid-2004. The Zimbabwe Election Support Network (ZESN) and the Electoral Institute of Southern Africa (EISA) collaborated with a variety of other stakeholders in Zimbabwe to recommend ways to address election-related conflict, focusing mainly on three areas: the institutional framework for elections (especially election management), the legal and regulatory framework for elections, and the electoral system itself.

On the basis of research and stakeholder consultations, appropriate recommendations were made regarding possible ways of levelling the political playing field in advance of Zimbabwe's 2005 parliamentary election, with a view specifically to addressing political tension and managing conflicts constructively. These recommendations included establishment of an independent electoral commission; reform of the legal arrangements for elections, including establishment of an electoral tribunal; and reform of the first-past-the-post electoral model and adoption of the mixed-member proportional system.

The ruling ZANU-PF announced in June 2004 that it would introduce electoral reforms that would conform to the SADC Principles and Guidelines Governing Democratic Elections, due to be adopted in August of that year at the annual Summit of Heads of State and Government. The proposed reforms included:

- Establishment of a five-person electoral commission.
- Establishment of an ad hoc electoral court or tribunal within six months of elections.
- Reduction of polling days from two to one.
- Increased number of polling stations and elimination of mobile polling stations.
- Use of visible, indelible ink for marking ballots.
- Replacement of wooden ballot boxes with translucent boxes.[7]

It was against this backdrop that the 2005 parliamentary election and the harmonized parliamentary, presidential, senatorial and local government elections of 29 March 2008 were held. Additional constitutional amendments were made as part of the negotiation process, involving ZANU-PF and MDC and facilitated by former South African president Thabo Mbeki as the SADC mediator tasked to deal with the Zimbabwe crisis. These included reconstitution of the electoral commission; harmonization of the parliamentary, presidential, senatorial and local government elections; and enlargement of the Senate and parliament. While less violent than the 2000, 2002 and 2005 general elections, the 2008 harmonized elections were still marked by deep-seated post-election violence, due in part to deep-seated polarization combined with an embedded culture of political intolerance. Of the total of 210 parliamentary seats, the opposition MDC-T won 109, ZANU-PF 97, and MDC-M 10, with Jonathan Moyo retaining the Tsholotsho constituency as an independent candidate and later rejoining ZANU-PF; in three constituencies, elections were postponed owing to the deaths of some of the candidates from natural causes. In the presidential election, Morgan Tsvangirai of MDC won 47.9 per cent of the votes and Robert Mugabe 43.2 per cent, with Simba Makoni, who stood as an independent candidate, winning 8.3 per cent and Langton Towungana, a fourth candidate, winning 0.6 per cent. Of 5,934,768 registered voters, 42.75 per cent participated in the presidential election. Given that no candidate won the necessary number of votes (50 per cent plus one) to be declared the outright winner, a run-off presidential election was to be held within twenty-one days of the announcement of the results of the first round of the race. But Morgan Tsvangirai pulled out of the run-off election, citing politically motivated violence and intimidation against his MDC supporters and alleging that the poll had been rigged to result inevitably in Mugabe's victory. After enormous internal pressure by organized civil society groups and external exhortation and cajoling, mainly by SADC, a compromise was reached by which MDC and ZANU-PF would share power and draft a new constitution that would be subjected to a referendum and lead to a general election.

Lesotho Another interesting case of elections being dogged by violence over the years is the small and landlocked mountain kingdom of Lesotho. A military coup in 1986 dislodged authoritarianism of a civilian type and replaced it with a military variety. Following some eight years of military rule, in 1993 Lesotho adopted a multiparty political system on the liberal democratic model, through a general election that was resoundingly won by the Basutoland Congress Party (BCP), which had previously been denied its legitimate victory by the then-ruling Basotho National Party (BNP) in the aborted 1970 election. Various types of violent and non-violent conflict marked Lesotho's young democracy between 1993 and the general election of 1998, which was immediately followed by a violent conflict in which the ruling Lesotho Congress for Democracy (LCD) locked horns in a fierce and bitter war with elements of opposition parties and sections of the security establishment. This caused enormous damage to the economy of the country, which witnessed external intervention by SADC. A group of SADC countries, including Botswana, Mozambique, South Africa and Zimbabwe, was then tasked to oversee and monitor democracy and peace in Lesotho.

A consensus emerged that many of Lesotho's problems stemmed from the nature of the electoral model, and the country took a deliberate decision to reform its electoral system to combine elements of first-past-the-post (80 parliamentary seats) and proportional representation (40 parliamentary seats). This was first put into effect in the May 2002 election, and the outcome has been quite impressive – for the first time, Lesotho boasts a highly inclusive multiparty parliament that is conducive to the political stability desirable for economic progress. The African Peer Review Mechanism (APRM), which assessed Lesotho's governance record under the stewardship of former APRM chairperson Adebayo Adedeji in 2009, noted that the new system 'was adopted after substantial consultations among political parties and other stakeholders. ... The negotiated compromise is highly regarded for having affirmed the maturity of Basotho in finding their own solutions to political conflict. The process has improved interparty dialogue, has encouraged inclusiveness and broader representation in the National Assembly, and has generally brought about relative peace.'[8] But the optimism that greeted the introduction of the mixed-member proportional system in Lesotho has been tempered by the post-election conflict that marked the 2007 parliamentary election, following manipulation of the electoral model by political parties. By establishing party coalitions and alliances (the Lesotho Congress for Democracy [LCD] and the National Independent Party [NIP] on the one hand, and the All Basotho Convention [ABC] and Lesotho Workers' Party [LWP] on the other), the model was distorted and the compensatory mechanism, meant specifically to benefit smaller parties, was severely compromised.

These three cases show that although elections are critical for building democracy and consolidation, they have posed enormous challenges in some SADC countries, especially in relation to peace, security and political stability. Elections have posed a much more serious political challenge in Zimbabwe and Lesotho than in South Africa.

Evolution of a normative framework for credible, peaceful and transparent elections in southern Africa

In recent years a regional normative framework for credible, peaceful and transparent elections in southern Africa has emerged. The three clearest examples of this are: the SADC–Parliamentary Forum (PF) Norms and Standards (2001) – an initiative of parliamentarians; the Electoral Institute of Southern Africa (EISA)/Electoral Commissions' Forum (ECF) (2003) – an initiative of civil society organizations; and the electoral management bodies (EMBs) together with the Principles and Guidelines Governing Democratic Elections (2004) – an initiative of SADC governments.

The SADC-PF Norms and Standards have since 2001 been used as guidelines in elections in the region. These guidelines cover: elections and individual rights; elections and government; and fostering transparency and integrity in the electoral process. Regarding elections and individual rights, the guidelines cover rights of citizens in electing their government of choice; voting and secrecy; and freedom of association and expression. Regarding elections and government, the guidelines cover commitment to pluralism and multiparty democracy; dates of elections; misuse of public resources and funding of political activities; government, political parties, non-governmental organizations, and the media; and electoral commissions.[9] Regarding freedom of association and expression, the guidelines cover registration of voters; voter education; boundary delimitation commissions; nomination processes; election campaigns; funding of political campaigns; role of the courts; the media; polling stations; ballot boxes; counting of votes; acceptance of election results; managing post-election conflicts; role of observers and SADC-PF; and reform of electoral laws.[10]

In 2000, EISA, jointly with the Electoral Commissions' Forum (ECF) of SADC countries, developed the Principles for Election Management, Monitoring and Observation in the SADC Region (PEMMO). These principles were adopted at a regional conference convened in Benoni, South Africa, in November 2003. In order to expand its utility throughout the region in terms of best electoral practices, the PEMMO principles are made available in English, French and Portuguese. EISA has used these principles in observing almost all general elections in the SADC region since 2004. Observation missions are coordinated by EISA's staff and comprise people from electoral commissions, civil society organizations, political parties, academia, parliament and faith-based organizations.

The PEMMO principles outline problems facing SADC countries in elections, recommend electoral best practices, and cover a wide gamut of the electoral process, including institutional framework; pre-election, election and post-election processes; and election observation and monitoring. The institutional framework covers the following areas: constitutional and legal framework, electoral systems, the election management body, and conflict management.[11] The pre-election principles cover challenges and best practices relating to constituency delimitation, voter registration, the nomination process, the campaign process, use of public resources, the role of security forces, political-party finance and voter education.[12] The election principles cover polling stations, secrecy of the ballot, ballot papers, ballot boxes and election materials, and counting. The post-election principles cover challenges and best practices relating to the announcement of overall results, acceptance of results, post-election review and post-election disputes.

While PEMMO is the most technically robust election management instrument in the region, it is less thorough when it comes to election monitoring and observation. What PEMMO is meant to do is to standardize election management systems; promote democratic culture and practice in between elections; suggest best election management and observation practices; provide technical nuts and bolts for electoral audits and electoral reforms in the region; and encourage peer review by electoral management bodies with a view to ensuring procedural certainty, while guarding against substantive uncertainty in electoral contests.

SADC heads of state and government adopted the Principles and Guidelines

Governing Democratic Elections at their August 2004 annual summit in Mauritius. These principles commit SADC member states to full participation of citizens in the political process; freedom of association and political tolerance; holding of elections at regular intervals; equal opportunity for all parties to access state media and for all to exercise the right to vote and be voted for; independence of the judiciary and impartiality of the electoral institutions; voter education; acceptance of and respect for election results proclaimed to have been free and fair by competent national authorities in accordance with national laws; and challenges to outcomes of elections in accordance with national laws.[13]

To ensure scrupulous implementation of the Principles and Guidelines Governing Democratic Elections, SADC member states are required to establish impartial, all-inclusive, competent and accountable national EMBs staffed by qualified personnel; safeguard the human rights and civil liberties of all citizens, including freedoms of movement, assembly, association and expression, and the right of all stakeholders to campaign and have access to the media during electoral processes; provide adequate logistics and resources for democratic elections; ensure provision of adequate security to all parties participating in elections; encourage the participation of women, the disabled and youth in all aspects of the electoral process; and ensure the transparency and integrity of the entire electoral process by facilitating the deployment of representatives of political parties and individual candidates at polling and counting stations and by accrediting national and other observers and monitors.[14] Adoption of the Principles and Guidelines was the first public declaration by the regional states of adherence to certain best practices in conducting elections. However, SADC has proved itself over the years to be extremely good at making progressive declarations that are hardly ever given the political commitment necessary to translate them into implementable policies and political reforms. Further, assessing whether or not the elections of a SADC country comply with the Principles and Guidelines has proved problematic.

While the SADC Principles and Guidelines constitute an important initiative that commits governments to credible, democratic and peaceful elections, PEMMO is a noble initiative by both civil society and election management bodies to achieve the same goal. There are major complementary areas among the three normative framework instruments. The SADC Principles and Guidelines constitute a public commitment by governments to strive towards best practices in election management and observation to which civil society and other non-state actors are better able to hold them accountable, and define clearly the obligations and responsibilities of governments of countries holding elections. While the SADC-PF Norms and Standards constitute a comprehensive guide for election *observation*, providing a crucial political lobby strategy for electoral reform, the EISA/ECF initiative is a comprehensive guide for election *management*, providing crucial technical know-how for electoral reform. Taken together, the three present a comprehensive guide for commitment to institutionalized democratic governance and sustainable peace and security through promotion of best practices in the conduct of elections. However, it is one thing to have a plethora of commitments to democratization through credible, democratic and peaceful election, and it is quite another to translate these into democratic culture and practice on the ground in SADC member states. One of the key actors that has the responsibility of holding the political elite accountable by, among other things, lobbying for and advocating adherence to existing normative frameworks is civil society. Does civil society have a role in democratization and peacebuilding in the SADC region?

The role of civil society

With the onset of the political transition from one-party to multiparty rule on the African continent since the early 1990s, democracy discourse has been marked by a critical probe into the state and role of civil society organizations (CSOs) in democratization and peace-building.[15] This is as it should be, for the building of sustainable democratic governance, peace and security is not the preserve of the state and the political elite alone. CSOs can play an important role in the governance process and have been and continue to be influential in both democratization and peace-building processes in Africa. As Emmanuel Gyimah-Boadi writes: 'among the forces that dislodged entrenched authoritarianism in Africa and brought about the beginnings of formal democracy in the early 1990s, the continent's nascent civil societies were in the forefront'.[16]

Almost all accounts of civil society's role in democratization and peace-building in Africa in general, and southern Africa in particular, bemoan the serious weaknesses of civil society.[17] For instance, Udaya Wagle observes lack of coordination and duplication of programmes as among the weaknesses facing civil society, leading to cut-throat rivalry in some instances. He thus notes that 'because of these rivalries, many activities are duplicated by different organisations, causing a waste of resources'.[18] The stronger the civil society, the more effective it is in influencing democratization and peace-building processes through lobbying and advocacy. But the reverse is also true: the weaker civil society is, the less effective it is in influencing state-dominated democracy and peace-building initiatives.

Depending on the country's context and stage of development, CSOs play either a tangential or a central role in the prevention, management and resolution of election-related conflicts in southern Africa. The tendency in a majority of SADC countries is to reserve the management of election-related conflicts to institutions such as security forces (especially the police), the EMBs, the judiciary and political parties, and in few countries are CSOs provided with space in which to proactively prevent, manage and resolve election-related conflicts and in the process complement the efforts of these institutions. Of all the SADC countries, it is South Africa which has the best-organized and best-poised CSOs with respect to democratization and peace-building, particularly in relation to dealing with violent election-related conflicts. The strategies and mechanisms that South Africa has put in place since the 1994 transition have brought together both state and non-state actors in a joint effort to nurture the country's new democracy and consolidate its post-apartheid peace. These include an EMB that enjoys public trust and integrity, party liaison committees, conflict management and peace panels, an enforceable and justiciable code of conduct, an electoral court, and a constitutional court.

Every time an election is held, these various institutions work closely together, constantly liaising with CSOs with a view to making sure that elections are credible, democratic and peaceful. Strategies for prevention, management and resolution of election-related conflicts include litigation where necessary, but with a heavy dose of arbitration, mediation and alternative dispute resolution (ADR) as well. While litigation in matters of electoral disputes cannot be wished away, it is important that southern African countries also give pride of place to ADR mechanisms in order to anchor sustainable democracy and peace on a firmer political foundation.

Conclusion

This chapter has assessed the state of democratization in southern Africa and probed the role of elections in peace-building. In the interests of best practices and institutionalizing a political culture of credible, democratic and peaceful elections, a plethora of normative frameworks have been developed in the SADC region. But the region's democracy glass seems half full rather than half empty. The region needs to move beyond rhetoric and translate its normative frameworks into policies and political practice.

While democracy cannot survive in southern Africa, or anywhere else for that matter, without peace, the reverse is also true: peace may not be sustainable without democracy. Elections are supposed to be an institutional mechanism for peacefully managing competition over state power. In some cases they do promote peaceful competition for the capture and control of state power, but in others they trigger conflicts that lead to political instability and in the process threaten peace and security. Policy-makers and civil society actors need to appreciate this paradox if democracy and peace are to be nurtured, sustained and consolidated. Although elections may in certain contexts help to heal the wounds of old conflicts, in others they have reopened them. Combined with the winner-take-all electoral systems in some SADC member states, this has created an inclement political environment for sustainable peace and democracy. In Lesotho (1998) and Zimbabwe (2000, 2002, 2005, 2008), winner-take-all systems have stirred electoral violence.

Yet elections, combined with a complex array of other factors, have helped heal the wounds of old conflicts in Namibia (1989), Mozambique (1994) and South Africa (1994). In these countries, appreciable progress has been made towards nurturing democracy and peace, although serious challenges still remain. That in these countries party-list proportional representation has been adopted as the preferred electoral model since their political transitions has helped facilitate a more inclusive political culture and a more broadly representative political system amenable to sustainable peace and democracy.

The critical challenge facing electoral management bodies, political parties, civil society organizations and the electorate alike is how to ensure that an election does not worsen insecurity and instability, but rather adds value to existing institutional mechanisms for democratization and peace-building. Management of violent election-related conflicts should not be confined to the state and the political elite alone. Civil society actors should be actively involved, so that the process of resolving conflicts is not merely elite-driven and state-centric in both form and content. While recognizing the significance of litigation in election disputes, it is important to emphasize the need for institutionalizing alternative dispute resolution mechanisms in dealing with violent electoral conflicts. In this area, civil society organizations can make a meaningful and sustainable contribution to democratization and peace-building in southern Africa.

Notes

1 UNDP, 'Elections and conflict prevention: a guide to analysis, planning, and programming', Mimeo, New York, 2010.

2 See Paul Collier, *Wars, Guns, and Votes: Democracy in Dangerous Places* (London: Bodley Head, 2009); Khabele Matlosa, 'Elections and conflict in southern Africa', in Alfred Nhema and Paul Zeleza (eds), *The Resolution of African Conflicts: The Management of Conflict Resolution & Post-Conflict Reconstruction* (Oxford: James Currey, 2008); Khabele Matlosa, Gilbert Khadiagala and Victor Shale (eds), *When Elephants Fight: Preventing and Resolving Election-related Conflicts in Africa* (Johannesburg: EISA Books, 2010).

3 UNDP, 'Elections and conflict prevention'.

4 Ho-won Jeong, *Peacebuilding in Postconflict Societies: Strategies and Process* (London: Lynne Rienner, 2005).

5 Thomas Ohlson and Stephen Stedman, *The New is Not Yet Born: Conflict Resolution in Southern Africa* (Washington, DC: Brookings Institution, 1994); Timothy Sisk and Andrew Reynolds (eds), *Elections and Conflict Management in Africa* (Washington, DC: US Institute of Peace Press, 1998); Jeong, *Peacebuilding*.

6 Khabele Matlosa, 'Elections and conflict in southern Africa', in Nhema and Zeleza, *The Resolution of African Conflicts*.

7 Khabele Matlosa, 'The role of the Southern African Development Community in mediating post-election conflicts: case studies of Lesotho and Zimbabwe', in Matlosa, Khadiagala and Shale, *When Elephants Fight*.

8 APRM Secretariat, 'Country review report no. 12: Kingdom of Lesotho, Midrand, South Africa', Mimeo, 2010.

9 SADC-PF, 'Norms and standards for elections in the SADC region', Mimeo, Windhoek, Namibia, 2001.

10 Ibid.

11 EISA, 'The 2003 EISA/ECF Principles for Election Management, Monitoring, and Observation (PEMMO) in the SADC region', Mimeo, Johannesburg, South Africa, 2003.

12 Ibid.

13 SADC Secretariat, 'Principles and guidelines governing democratic elections in the SADC region', Mimeo, Gaborone, 2004.

14 Ibid.

15 Lloyd Sachikonye, 'Civil society, social movements, and democracy in southern Africa', *Innovation*, 8(4), 1995.

16 Emmanuel Gyimah-Boadi, 'Civil society in Africa', *Journal of Democracy*, 7(2), April 1996, p. 118.

17 Sachikonye, 'Civil society, social movements, and democracy'; Gyimah-Boadi, 'Civil society in Africa'; Udaya Wagle, 'The civil society sector in the developing world', *Public Administration and Management: An Interactive Journal*, 4(4), 1999.

18 Wagle, 'The civil society sector'.

5 | Peacekeeping: from the United Nations to the SADC Stand-by Force

Chris Saunders

Within a few years, beginning in 1989, the United Nations (UN) sent missions to three southern African countries emerging from long years of conflict. In two of those countries, the UN helped usher in a new era of peace, while in a third it was unsuccessful in achieving that goal. After admitting failure in Angola and withdrawing from that country in 1999, the UN began another mission, later in the same year, in the Democratic Republic of the Congo (DRC) to help in stabilizing the situation there after much internal strife and military intervention by neighbouring countries. Over a decade later, that UN mission remained in place, though its presence was little acknowledged by the leaders of the Southern African Development Community (SADC).[1] SADC and, since its establishment in 2002, the African Union (AU) believed that a regional military force should be developed, in part so that, in future, UN intervention, or any other kind of external involvement,[2] might not be necessary. Though in some cases African countries had sought UN assistance, in general African problems, so the thinking went, should be solved by Africans, not outsiders. An SADC force could, in theory at least, be used to meet a possible external threat to the region or to act where necessary in the interests of peace and stability within the region. The establishment of such a force was seen as an important element in regional integration.

UN peacekeeping missions

UN involvement in peace processes in southern Africa began in July 1960, when Secretary-General Dag Hammarskjöld told the Security Council that the situation in the newly independent Congo constituted a threat to international peace and security and the Council then passed a resolution mandating him to take the necessary steps to provide military assistance to the new state. The following February, the Council increased the number of UN personnel in the UN Operation in the Congo (ONUC) to 20,000 and allowed it to use force if necessary as a last resort. But by the time ONUC withdrew from the Congo three years later, only a measure of stability and peace had been restored, and the mission had long been bedevilled by Cold War politics.[3]

The problems the UN encountered in the Congo in the early 1960s did not encourage further UN attempts at peacemaking in Africa. Nevertheless, in September 1978 the Security Council authorized the creation of the military and civilian UN Transitional Assistance Group (UNTAG) to intervene in South African-occupied Namibia to take that country to independence. The Soviet Union did not veto Security Council Resolution 435 of 1978, because the idea of UN intervention in Namibia was supported by the African countries at the UN, which saw intervention as the only way to bring about a transition in that country from South African rule to independence. However, implementation of Resolution 435 was blocked by South Africa for over a decade, and Washington insisted on Cuban troop withdrawal from Angola as a quid pro quo for Namibian independence. After further delays caused in part by a dispute over its size and mandate, UNTAG finally began from April 1989 to police the ceasefire between the South West Africa People's Organization (SWAPO) guerrillas and the South African Defence Force (SADF), to monitor SWAPO military bases in neighbouring countries, to supervise the phased withdrawal of the South African military forces from Namibia, and to organize and supervise Namibia's first democratic election, which took place in November 1989. As UNTAG's mission ended, after it had successfully assisted the transition to independence, the UN secretary-general, Javier Pérez de Cuéllar, was master of ceremonies at Namibia's celebration of independence on 21 March 1990.[4]

In the same year that UNTAG became operational, another UN mission was established to verify the withdrawal of all Cuban troops from Angola, as agreed in the December 1988 New York Accords signed between Cuba, Angola and South Africa.[5] The UN Angola Verification Mission (UNAVEM), which comprised seventy military observers and twenty civilians, completed its mandate ahead of schedule. Then, in 1992, the UN sent a mission, similar in size to UNTAG, to Mozambique, to stabilize that country in the aftermath of a long and bitter post-independence conflict and assist in the holding of a democratic election. A significant measure of demobilization was achieved before the election took place; both parties wished to see the conflict end, and the rebel group did not have the means to return to war. As in Namibia, the UN Operation in Mozambique (ONUMOZ) went off remarkably smoothly, given the prior conflict. UN involvement in Mozambique lasted twice as long as in Namibia, but the outcome, as in Namibia, was a peaceful election that ushered in a new democratic order.[6]

Whereas UN missions were successful in Namibia and Mozambique, those that aimed at restoring peace in Angola were not. After the warring movements – the ruling Popular Liberation Movement (MPLA) and the rebel National Union for the Total Independence of Angola (UNITA) – concluded an agreement in Bicesse in May 1991 to end sixteen years of hostilities, the UN was asked to help implement the accord.[7] The Security Council would not approve a large mission, however, and the second UN Angola Verification Mission (UNAVEM II), only a few hundreds strong, did not have the means to verify the ceasefire or to disarm and demobilize existing armies and form them into a new national army before the election took place. When UNITA did not accept the result and returned to war, the UN Security Council first reduced the size of the mission, then withdrew all its military personnel. After the warring parties were persuaded to come together at Lusaka, Zambia, in November 1994, the Security Council in February 1995 authorized the deployment of UNAVEM III in another attempt to bring peace to Angola.[8] This time, the UN force was over ten times larger than UNAVEM II, with 7,000 men and women – but it could not force UNITA to disarm and, when its mandate expired in June 1997, the Security Council would approve of continuation of United Nations involvement only through establishment of the UN Observer Mission in Angola (MONUA), which comprised 1,500 troops. As the two armies continued to fight, even MONUA was eventually shut down, in February 1999. But Angola remained at war. The UN had failed to bring about peace because the conditions were not conducive for it to play a constructive role.[9] The conflict ended only with the assassination of UNITA leader Jonas Savimbi by government troops in 2002.

By then the UN had returned to neighbouring Congo. After the collapse of the dictatorship of the former president of Zaire (DRC), Mobutu Sese Seko, Angola, Namibia and Zimbabwe sent forces to the Congo, following an earlier intervention by Rwanda and Uganda, and a regional war ensued until a ceasefire agreement was reached in July 1999. The UN Security Council then authorized the deployment of UN military liaison personnel to what was now called the DRC to help ensure the agreement stuck, and in November 1999 these personnel were organized into the UN Mission in the Congo. After the assassination of President Laurent Kabila in January 2001 heightened the conflict, the Security Council formalized the deployment of MONUC and gave it a mandate to continue to monitor the withdrawal of foreign forces and disarm armed formations. MONUC grew to 10,800 personnel in 2003, and by 2008 there were 20,000 UN peacekeepers in the DRC tasked to deter the use of force, protect civilians, assist pacification, and contribute to general security in the country.[10] Though the UN helped organize the first ever presidential and legislative elections held in the DRC, in July 2006 MONUC found it difficult to deal with security in Kivu and Orientale provinces, where foreign troops, armed groups, militias and rebel groups continued to be active.[11] MONUC could neither negotiate with the leadership of the foreign armed groups nor offer them any kind of immunity.[12] In July 2010 MONUC's name was changed to the UN Stabilization Mission in the Congo (MONUSCO), with the mission comprising some twenty thousand peacekeepers, and in 2011 it was still working to protect civilians and help bring lasting peace to the DRC,[13] as SADC did not have the financial means or the political will to undertake the tasks the UN continued to perform.[14] Despite this, the idea had been mooted long before 2011 that SADC should acquire the capacity to act militarily to bring peace to the region, and perhaps even to other parts of Africa. South Africa and Mozambique had deployed many of the troops for the AU, then UN, peacekeeping force in Burundi between 2001 and the final withdrawal of those troops eight years later in September 2009.[15]

Towards a regional military force

Regional integration can, of course, take many different forms and must always remain a work in progress (as complete integration would mean that the region as such no longer existed). (See Khadiagala, Mbuende, Nagar in this volume.) Military integration may be an important aspect of regional integration, but neither the Southern African Development Coordination Conference (SADCC) nor SADC was formed primarily with any military purpose in mind. Though regional integration was a stated objective of SADCC, that body was established in 1980 chiefly to oppose apartheid South Africa, and it was not envisaged that SADCC would do more than coordinate activity towards this end.[16] (See Khadiagala in this volume.) SADC, as its name suggests, placed its prime emphasis on development, for which peace and stability were, of course, essentials, but there was initially no idea of a regional military force being formed to help secure this. The original SADC Treaty, signed in Windhoek in 1992, merely spoke in vague terms of the regional organization having the 'peaceful settlement of disputes' as one of its five basic principles, and then provided for the promotion of defence, peace and security.[17] In 1993, however, the idea of regional cooperation on military matters began to be raised, and the establishment of a Regional Peacekeeping Training Centre (RPTC) was mooted at a seminar for battalion commanders held in Zimbabwe.[18] Most work at this time went into forming a regional mutual defence pact. There were strong disagreements over such a pact, particularly between Nelson Mandela's South Africa, after it became a member of SADC in 1994, and Zimbabwe under Robert Mugabe, and it was not until 2003 that such a defence pact was eventually signed, and even then it was a loose one that did not commit states in the region to come to the aid of each other.[19]

Early in the history of the UN the idea surfaced that a rapidly deployable multinational stand-by force should be formed to aid peace and stability, but during the Cold War it was impossible to establish one. In 1992, however, UN secretary-general Boutros Boutros-Ghali called on governments to commit themselves to hold ready, at an agreed period of notice, specially trained units for peacekeeping service, and in 1996 the UN established the Stand-by High-Readiness Brigade (SHIRBRIG), which had its headquarters outside Copenhagen in Denmark.[20] In the aftermath of the genocide in Rwanda in 1994, when the UN reduced its 2,500-strong peacekeeping force and about 800,000 people were killed, the Organization of African Unity (OAU) summit in

Addis Ababa in 1995 endorsed the idea that 'ready contingents' from African armies should be available for deployment for peacekeeping purposes, but the organization did not translate this into practice and instead left the responsibility for peacekeeping to the UN.[21] Farther afield, the Nigerian-led Economic Community of West African States (ECOWAS) launched peacekeeping missions into Liberia and Sierra Leone in the 1990s,[22] and by the late 1990s SADC countries were beginning to cooperate militarily. In 1997, eight of them participated in a field training exercise at the battalion level, called Exercise Blue Hungwe, in Zimbabwe. The following year, SADC ministers of defence and foreign affairs and high-level military officials visited Denmark and Bosnia to evaluate the feasibility of forming a SADC Stand-by Brigade (SADCBRIG) along the lines of SHIRBRIG, and they returned enthusiastic that one could and should be established.[23]

When in 1998 the Lesotho government called on SADC to send a military force to help it deal with a situation of instability that had arisen in the mountain kingdom, South Africa and Botswana responded and sent a joint force composed primarily of troops from the South African National Defence Force (SANDF) together with a smaller number of troops from the Botswana Defence Force. This was a model – two or more national defence forces working together on a particular mission – that might have been built upon by SADC, but was not, for various reasons. Though the intervention – Operation Boleas – achieved its goal of maintaining the Lesotho government in power, the mission was botched and caused regional tensions, for it was not clear that the correct SADC procedures had been followed in authorizing it, and it received an official SADC imprimatur only *ex post facto*.[24] (See Mbuende in this volume.)

Also in 1998, units from the national armies of three SADC countries – Zimbabwe, Angola and Namibia – intervened in the DRC in support of Laurent Kabila, but in an uncoordinated fashion, and this intervention too was given SADC sanction only after the event. Other countries in SADC, including South Africa, opposed the intervention, further increasing tensions within the region. Both the Lesotho and DRC interventions, then, suggested the need for much greater coordination and joint planning within SADC, and that instead of ad hoc uncoordinated interventions, there should instead be an SADC force available on permanent stand-by, drawn from all the countries in the region, or at least from as many as could offer useful components of such a force. In 1999, SADC held a brigade-level peacekeeping exercise, Blue Crane, in South Africa to enhance the capacity of SADC forces in joint operations. Yet the move towards greater regional military cooperation, which to some extent drew on the West African example of the force that ECOWAS sent to Liberia and Sierra Leone in the 1990s, the ECOWAS Ceasefire Monitoring Group (ECOMOG), was hampered by the fact that the SADC Organ on Politics, Defence and Security

Cooperation (OPDSC) (see Landsberg in this volume), established in 1996, was riven with division and did not become fully operational until after the SADC summit of August 2001 because of disagreements over its nature and form and the extent to which it should be autonomous of SADC itself.[25]

The AU and the continental drive for an African army

Though the idea of a 'great Pan-African army' goes back at least to Marcus Garvey in 1922, the concept of a continental military force was revived by Ghana's founding president, Kwame Nkrumah, who even before the establishment of the OAU in 1963 proposed the idea of an African High Command through which a continental army would be established to prevent external intervention and to undertake liberation wars.[26] Nkrumah was not able to persuade other sovereignty-protecting African leaders to support the idea, which faded away during the life of the OAU, and it was only with the creation of the AU in place of the OAU by 2002 that the idea of creating a continental African Stand-by Force (ASF) came to the fore. With the Rwanda genocide of 1994 still very much in mind, the AU's Constitutive Act of 2000 envisaged, as the OAU had not, military intervention in 'grave circumstances, namely war crimes, genocide and crimes against humanity'.[27] Fifteen AU member states were elected on a rotational basis to serve on a Peace and Security Council (PSC), whose mandate included overseeing the establishment of an ASF.[28] Since 2004 the PSC has imposed sanctions on various regimes, and authorized peace operations in Burundi, Sudan, the Comoros and Somalia.[29] Alongside the development of the use of African militaries for peacekeeping on the continent – in which South Africa played a leading role, sending troops to Burundi, Sudan's Darfur region and elsewhere, under AU auspices[30] – came the development of the idea that it was wrong for Africa to rely on foreign forces when military assistance was needed in peacekeeping operations. As Africans saw UN military forces playing increasingly important roles on the continent, British forces intervening in Sierra Leone, and French forces in francophone Côte d'Ivoire, DRC and Chad/Central African Republic, the perception grew that such foreign forces were able to pull strings and undermine African independence. An ASF should therefore be created so that such interventions would not happen. The SADC Stand-by Force (SADCSF) was to be one of the five components of this ASF. In this case, the regions would truly be the building blocks for, and pillars of, the envisaged continental structure. In its 2005 road-map document, the AU set the end of June 2010 as the deadline for establishing an ASF composed of five regional stand-by forces.[31]

In 2003, planning for the SADCSF got under way at SADC headquarters in Gaborone, Botswana, in the context of the Strategic Indicative Plan of the Organ (SIPO) (see Landsberg in this volume), though SIPO was so vague and general – with over 130 non-prioritized objectives and no provision for effective implementation or monitoring – that it was of little practical assistance.[32] Military cooperation in SADC continued – for example, in Exercise Airborne Africa, a skills competition that rotated within SADC: the first took place in South Africa in 2001, the second in Botswana in 2002, and the third again in South Africa in 2004.[33] However, political crisis in Zimbabwe delayed matters (see Matlosa in this volume), for it led, among other things, to the withdrawal of donor support for the RPTC which had been established in Harare.[34] But in August 2007 the SADCBRIG was launched with a parade and considerable fanfare at the time of a SADC summit in Lusaka, Zambia.

It was nevertheless clear that much still needed to be done in terms of joint training and ironing out problems of interoperability. In 2009 a map exercise was held in Angola in February, a command-post exercise in Mozambique in April, and a major field training exercise named Golfinho (Portuguese for 'Dolphin') in September at the Combat Training Centre at Lohatla in South Africa's Northern Cape province. This brought together components from twelve SADC countries. Madagascar, which had been suspended from AU and SADC membership after the de facto military coup there, was not involved, and neither were Mauritius or the Seychelles, which seemed to prefer to work with the East African stand-by arrangements[35] and did not provide any military component to SADC. An accompanying naval exercise was held at Walvis Bay in Namibia and off the Namibian coast. This was the first time that large parts of the proposed SADCSF – the name was adopted in 2009 to align SADC with the AU's security architecture and to suggest that this force was more than an infantry brigade[36] – had exercised together. The chief of staff of the SADCSF, General Lancaster Bottoman, who has been seconded to that post from the South African army, then said that the SADCSF was on track to meet the AU's deadline of full operationability by the end of June 2010, but the meaning of 'full operationability' was far from clear. In theory, the SADCSF was supposed to be ready for deployment within thirty days of its use being authorized. All that could be said with any certainty was that SADC was at least as far advanced as any other subregion, with the possible exception of ECOWAS, in moving towards having an ASF fully operational, while in terms of integrating police and civilian components it was ahead of any other.[37] In March 2010 a combined exercise was organized by the South African National War College, with support from a British Peace Support team,[38] and in October of that year the SADCSF was involved in a ten-day exercise in Ethiopia, which brought together the five stand-by forces for the first time.[39] In his speech that opened the exercise, the AU Commission chairman, Jean Ping, stressed that the regional stand-by forces gave Africa greater ownership of peace and security on the continent, and that the need for an ASF had been underscored by the world's inadequate response to crises in places like Rwanda and Somalia: 'The international community could not always be relied on to address all the threats to peace and security on the African continent. Indeed, Somalia and Rwanda were painful lessons for us all.'[40]

The SADCSF: issues of capacity, operability and usage

South Africa remains the regional hegemon, with by far the largest economy in the region and the best-equipped military force. Yet South Africa is aware that residual distrust remains owing to the 'destabilization' wrought by the highly destructive SADF military interventions in the 1980s. Though Angola had by 2011 become an increasingly important player militarily in the region, South Africa remained the provider of the bulk of the resources and funding for the SADCSF and had the greatest relevant experience, having supplied almost all the troops for the AU mission in Burundi and two operations in the Comoros, as well as troops for the AU and UN missions in Darfur and the DRC. Yet South Africa's resources were constrained by the many domestic demands on the budget of the state. How a domestic decision might have potentially major negative repercussions for the SADCSF was shown in November 2009 when the South African government cancelled the orders it had placed for eight Airbus A400M transport aircraft, with an option on a further six, because, it was claimed, the cost of these aircraft had escalated to R47 billion. Only South Africa could supply the necessary airlift capacity for a major intervention by the SADCSF, and its existing planes were not able to transport, say, Rooivalk attack helicopters or heavy vehicles or equipment for earth-moving and bridge-building. The orders it cancelled were for planes that were to have formed an important part of South Africa's contribution to the logistics of the SADCBRIG.[41]

The most successful examples of military intervention to stop mass killing in recent years – by the North Atlantic Treaty Organization (NATO) in Bosnia in 1995 and Kosovo in 1999 – required highly sophisticated aerial bombing. Not only was the aerial capacity of the SADCSF very limited, but it was also difficult to envisage the South African Air Force providing any of its extremely costly Gripen fighters to an SADC force under any but South African command. Problems of command, control and support are likely to bedevil any future SADCSF deployment. And lack of resources is likely to continue to curtail what is possible. The countries involved in Exercise Golfinho paid for their troops to attend it, and there is an understandable reluctance to accept donor money for such purposes, but the hard fact is that any substantial development of the SADCSF is dependent on donor support. By far the largest donor to African security in general is the European Union, and it remains to be seen, given the continuing economic crisis in Europe in 2011, whether it will be able to continue its past levels of support.

The countries of southern Africa have come together because they are in the same geographical space; they do not yet have a set of either common interests or common values.[42] All under colonial or apartheid rule only six decades ago, they were subject to different colonizers who spoke different languages. Whatever nominal commitment to democracy there may be, and whatever pleasantries may be exchanged by SADC heads of state at their regular summit meetings, these states have very different political practices, ranging from absolute monarchy and highly authoritarian rule to at least the semblance of constitutional democracy. (See Matlosa in this volume.) Though there has been a long history of disputes between them, significant efforts have been made to paper over such differences. The 2008 SADC Protocol on Politics, Defence and Security Cooperation provides for a summit of heads of state, on the advice of the chairperson, resorting to 'enforcement action ... against one or more of the disputant parties ... as a matter of last resort and ... with the authorisation of the United Nations Security Council',[43] but SADC summits have been reluctant to interpret conflicts as threats to 'peace and security in the region' and instead have strongly supported the principles of sovereignty and non-interference in domestic affairs. There would need to be consensus in SADC before the ASF could be authorized to act. What might give rise to such authorization, other than a 'grave circumstance' such as genocide? If the AU or UN were to authorize use of the SADCSF, would SADC need to agree? It seems unlikely that SADC would authorize the use of the stand-by force in the region unless there were a clear consensus and a belief in the appropriateness of its use.[44]

When called upon, the SADCSF is supposed to be assembled rapidly from the earmarked components in the constituent countries to form a well-trained force capable of carrying out a joint operation effectively. This would require regular ongoing training if the ASF is to be ready to act whenever necessary, yet regular joint exercises are expensive and beyond the resources of most SADC countries. There remains, therefore, a large question mark over whether SADC as a region has the resources and capacity to sustain an ASF in the necessary state of readiness and interoperability. Beyond training – and how effectively the revived RPTC is operating in Harare also remains unclear – a multinational force requires common systems, tactics, techniques and procedures. To what extent these have been achieved is not known, for there has been no independent review of the 2009 training exercises, nor of the SADCSF's present state of readiness. We do not know whether, say, the different countries' walkie-talkies are talking to each other, or whether the problems arising from language differences have all been dealt with. The SADCSF has military, police and civilian components, and it is not clear how well they would work together if required to do so.

The SADCSF would presumably be called into action either by the Organ (under a troika comprising the rotating chair and the incoming and outgoing chairs) or a summit of heads of state and government, which would seek UN

Security Council approval. But what if the Organ thought that the SADCSF should intervene, say, in eastern DRC, yet the DRC government opposed such an intervention? In the absence of mutual trust and a shared vision among the SADC member countries, would the concept of 'sufficient consensus' on deployment apply if the SADC member country in question did not invite the intervention?[45] If as a result of climate change, say, a resource such as water becomes very scarce, one can envisage a situation in which two or more countries in the region might engage in a war to control water resources. Namibia, Angola and Botswana might come into conflict, say, over access to the water of the Kavango river. How would SADC reach agreement on an intervention to end such a conflict?

There are, of course, other possible scenarios in which the SADCSF might act. An oppressive regime, civilian or military (for while there are no military regimes in the region now, one or more may emerge in the future), may seem to be moving towards using genocidal measures against its people. But while some have argued that the Zimbabwe African National Union–Patriotic Front (ZANU-PF) government has on occasion been moving in this direction in recent years, and others have predicted that in the event of the Zimbabwean military taking power, there is likely to be a move in this direction, the evidence of the decade of the 2000s suggests that SADC would do nothing effective in such a situation and would not authorize an SADCSF to take on the Zimbabwean military. What if, as the result, say, of a natural disaster or the overthrow of a leader, an SADC country collapsed into something approaching the kind of anarchy seen in Somalia after 1995? Intervention by a small SADCSF might help to stabilize a failed state for a time, but surely could not be expected to rebuild it, though 'returning normalcy to a failed state' is one of the potential tasks of an SADCSF.[46] As conceived, the SADCSF would be employed for relatively brief rapid-response missions, whereas peacekeeping can be a lengthy business, as the UN has discovered in the DRC. And the SADCSF, with 4,000 personnel in all, could hardly replace MONUSCO, which, as mentioned, had 20,000 personnel on the ground in the DRC in 2011.

Ideally the ASF would know what might be required of it ahead of time, to help determine the necessary standards, systems and procedures, yet if an SADCSF were ever called into action, as part of the ASF, under an AU or perhaps even a UN mandate elsewhere in Africa, it would probably not know the terrain or environment in which it would be operating. Scepticism about how an SADCSF might be used effectively is surely justified, given the inability of the AU force to operate on its own in Darfur successfully, and the very limited success AU forces have had in Rwanda and Somalia. An effective division of labour is surely needed between SADC, the AU and the UN, with provision being made for the UN to take over from a rapidly deployed SADC force if necessary, given the region's relative lack of the resources and logistics to conduct a long-term mission. While an SADCSF could play a potentially useful role in a humanitarian disaster situation, such as in the aftermath of a devastating earthquake or large-scale flooding, the planning so far done for the use of the force – and a planning element has been in place in Gaborone for some years – seems rather to envisage its use in a situation of conflict.

The culture of secrecy in militaries is often justified in terms of not wanting potential enemies to know one's defence capacity. Such reasoning hardly applies when a regional peacekeeping force is concerned, yet there is little attempt to make information about the SADCSF readily available. SADC's own website provides very little relevant information, while if, for example, one enters 'SADCBRIG' into the search function of the South African Department of Defence website, one finds nothing at all. A search in South African media files revealed only one substantial article on the SADCBRIG/SADCSF in the whole of 2010, and no other SADC country provided any greater coverage. SADC's failure to communicate about the SADCSF with civil society within the region via the media means there is little public buy-in to the project.[47] There appears no provision for, say, reporting regularly to the legislatures or executives of the respective countries from which the components of the SADCSF are drawn, yet without such reporting national parliaments may well begin to baulk at voting the necessary funding for the force. Much greater transparency and accountability are needed if the SADCSF is to become a key element in future regional integration in southern Africa.

Conclusion

The SADCSF is potentially an important element in region-building. Though there has been considerable progress in its development, in 2011 it still faced enormous challenges, given the resource constraints and the difficulties of operationalizing the new structures, which include cooperating across linguistic and other divisions. Many question marks remain over the possible circumstances under which such a force might be used. Relations between the SADCSF and the ASF have still to be clarified.[48] An evaluation of what was called Exercise Carana, held by the AU at the end of October 2010 as the first test of the ASF, may throw some light on this.[49] Lessons should be learned for the SADCSF from UN peacekeeping missions in Namibia, Angola, Mozambique and the DRC. Is there sufficient political will within SADC to drive the process of establishing a fully operational SADCSF and sustaining it? SADC lacks a common position on security issues, and includes countries that are not politically stable, such as Zimbabwe, the DRC and Swaziland. The circumstances in which an SADCSF might be deployed should be decided, and it may be that the UN should continue to take the lead in peacekeeping in the region. However the role of the SADCSF is defined, the security aspects of region-building will remain important. Once there is sustainable peace in the region, it may be possible to divert scarce resources from security to other forms of region-building.

Notes

1 The communiqués from annual SADC summits in recent years have almost entirely ignored the presence of the UN in the region.

2 By 2011 the most potent possible external military involvement in Africa was the very well-resourced Africa Command (AFRICOM) established by the United States in 2008, on which see www. africom.mil. Much criticized within Africa, AFRICOM was unable to find anywhere in Africa for its headquarters.

3 See, for example, Georges Abi-Saab, *The United Nations Operation in the Congo, 1960–1964* (Oxford: Oxford University Press, 1978); David Gibb, 'The United Nations: international peacekeeping and the question of "impartiality" – revisiting the Congo operation of 1960', *Journal of Modern African Studies*, 38(3), 2000.

4 The fullest accounts of UNTAG are Roger Hearn, *UN Peacekeeping in Action: The Namibian Experience* (Commack, NY: Nova Science, 1999); and Cedric Thornberry, *A Nation is Born: The Inside Story of Namibia's Independence* (Windhoek: Gamsberg Macmillan, 2004).

5 For full details, see www.un.org/depts /DPKO/Missions/unavem1/unavemi.htm.

6 The best account is Richard Synge, *Mozambique: UN Peacekeeping in Action, 1992–1994* (Washington, DC: United States Institute for Peace, 1997).

7 The most detailed account is Margaret Anstee, *Orphan of the Cold War: The Inside Story of the Collapse of the Angolan Peace Process, 1992–93* (Basingstoke: Macmillan, 1996).

8 See www.un.org/Depts/DPKO/Missions/unavem3.htm.

9 For an overview, see Manuel J. Paulo, 'The role of the United Nations in the Angolan peace process', 2004, www.c-r. org/our-work/accord/angola/un-role.php. For comparative analyses, see Gwinyayi Dzinesa, 'A comparative perspective of UN peacekeeping in Angola and Namibia', *International Peacekeeping*, 11(4), 2004; and Chris Saunders, 'UN peacekeeping in southern Africa: Namibia, Angola, and Mozambique', in Adekeye Adebajo (ed.), *From Global Apartheid to Global Village: Africa and the United Nations* (Pietermaritzburg: University of KwaZulu-Natal Press, 2009). Compare also Ibrahim A. Gambari, 'The United Nations', in Mwesiga Baregu and Chris Landsberg (eds), *From Cape to Congo: Southern Africa's Evolving Security Challenges* (Boulder, CO: Lynne Rienner, 2003); and Philip Sibanda, 'Lessons from UN peacekeeping in Africa: from UNAVEM to MONUA', in Jackie Cilliers and Greg Mills (eds), *From Peacekeeping to Complex Emergencies* (Johannesburg: South African Institute of International Affairs, 1999).

10 Filip Reyntiens, *The Great African War: Congo and Regional Geopolitics, 1996–2006* (Cambridge: Cambridge University Press, 2009); Eric Miller, *The Inability of Peacekeeping to Address the Security Dilemma: A Case Study of the Rwandan–Congolese Security Dilemma and the United Nation's Mission in the Congo* (Saarbrucken: Lambert Academic, 2009).

11 See, for example, United Nations, *Twenty-third Report of the Secretary-General on the United Nations Organization Mission in the Democratic Republic of the Congo*, S/2007/156, 20 March 2007.

12 Mwesiga Baregu, 'Congo in the Great Lakes region', in Gilbert Khadiagala (ed.), *Security Dynamics in Africa's Great Lakes Region* (New York: International Peace Academy, 2006).

13 See monusco.unmissions.org.

14 In June 2003, South African president Thabo Mbeki told parliament that South Africa's peacekeeping effort in the DRC was costing South Africans R819.6 million over a twelve-month period.

15 Buanews, 'SA's Burundi mission accomplished', 31 July 2009,

www.southafrica.info/news/international/burundi-310709.htm.

16 Gabriel H. Oosthuizen, *The Southern African Development Community: The Organisation, Its Policies, and Prospects* (Midrand: Institute for Global Dialogue, 2006), p. 69.

17 Articles 4 and 5.

18 M. C. Chirwa and C. A. D. Namangale, 'SADC training needs for peace support operations: the case for wider future role of the RPTC', Paper prepared for the Foprisa conference, Centurion, South Africa, November 2008.

19 Article 6: 'An armed attack against a State Party shall be considered a threat to regional peace and security and ... shall be met with immediate collective action', but '[e]ach State Party shall participate in such collective action in any manner it deems appropriate'.

20 See Joachim Koops and Johannes Varwick, *Ten Years of SHIRBRIG: Lessons Learned, Development Prospects, and Strategic Opportunities for Germany* (Berlin: Global Public Policy Institute, 2008). It was deployed to the Horn of Africa in 2000 as part of a UN mission there.

21 OAU discussions of the early 1990s on military security envisaged mechanisms to anticipate and prevent conflicts, not to deal with them once they had broken out.

22 See, for example, Charles Dokubo, 'Nigeria's international peacekeeping and peacebuilding efforts in Africa, 1960–2005', in Bola Akinterinwa (ed.), *Nigeria and the United Nations Security Council* (Ibadan: Vantage, 2005).

23 Robert Rotberg, *Peacekeeping and Peace Enforcement in Africa* (Washington, DC: Brookings Institution, 2000), p. 89.

24 See, for example, Khabele Matlosa, 'The Lesotho conflict: major causes and management', in Kato Lambrechts (ed.), *Crisis in Lesotho: The Challenge of Managing Conflict in Southern Africa* (Johannesburg: Foundation for Global Dialogue, 1999), pp. 6–10; Katharina P. Coleman, *International Organisations and Peace Enforcement: The Politics of International Legitimacy* (Cambridge: Cambridge University Press, 2007), pp. 160–93.

25 Laurie Nathan, 'The failure of the SADC Organ: regional security arrangements in southern Africa, 1992–2003', Unpublished PhD thesis, University of Cape Town, 2009; Willie Breytenbach, 'Failure of security cooperation in SADC: the suspension of the Organ for Politics, Defence, and Security', *South African Journal of International Affairs*, 7(1), 2007, p. 7.

26 Benedict Franke, 'Africa's evolving security architecture and the concept of multilayered security communities', *Cooperation and Conflict*, 43, 2008, p. 317, quoting *Communist Review*, 1922; Adekeye Adebajo, 'Rethinking a continent: from Kwame Nkrumah to Thabo Mbeki', *Mail and Guardian*, 30 April–6 May 2004, www.ccr.org.za.

27 African Union (AU), *Constitutive Act*, 2000, Articles 4(h) and 4(j).

28 AU Commission, *Protocol relating to the Establishment of the Peace and Security Council of the African Union*, Durban, 2002, Article 13. This came into force in December 2003 when ratified by twenty-seven of the fifty-three members of the AU.

29 Paul D. Williams, 'The Peace and Security Council of the African Union: evaluating an embryonic international institution', *Journal of Modern African Studies*, 47(41), 2009, pp. 604, 618. However, the PSC has dealt with issues after they have arisen, and failed to take on lawless authoritarian regimes, such as Mugabe's in Zimbabwe.

30 South African troops were sent to Burundi before the AU mission there began, and they stayed on after it ended.

31 AU, *Roadmap for the Operationalization of the African Standby Force*, 2005. Compare Louis Matswengeyo Fisher, 'Peace support operations: UN/AU implications for SADC', 2008, www.foprisa.net/publications/documents/PeaceSupportOperations-UN-AU.pdf; Louis Matswengeyo Fisher, 'The Southern African Development Community in the continental security architecture', Unpublished paper,

n.d. I thank General Fisher for giving me a copy of the unpublished paper.

32 See especially Anthoni van Nieuwkerk, 'Overview of the SADC Strategic Indicative Plan of the Organ (SIPO): achievements and challenges', *PaxAfrica*, March 2009. Though a new SIPO for 2010–15 has been drafted, it is little different from the previous plan, according to the Organ director. Telephone interview with Lieutenant Colonel T. Mothae, 4 February 2010.

33 South African Department of Defence, *Bulletin*, 71, 15 September 2004, www.dcc.mil.za/bulletins/Files/2004/71bulletin2004.htm.

34 The United Kingdom and Denmark were the two main funders until 2001, when the SADC Secretariat took over funding for the RPTC. Chirwa and Namangale, 'SADC training needs', p. 9.

35 Thomas Mandrup, 'South Africa and the SADC Stand-by Force', *Scientia Militaria: South African Journal of Military Studies*, 37(2), 2009, pp. 4, 10. The East African Brigade (EASBRIG) does not correspond to a regional organization in the way that the SADCSF does to SADC. Compare also Jackie Cilliers and Johann Potgieter, 'The African Standby Force', in Ulf Engel and João Gomes Porto (eds), *Africa's New Peace and Security Architecture: Promoting Norms, Institutionalizing Solutions* (Farnham, Surrey: Ashgate Publishing, 2010); Benedickt Franke, 'Steady but uneven progress: the operationalization of the African Standby Force', in Hany Besada (ed.), *Crafting an African Security Architecture* (Farnham, Surrey: Ashgate Publishing, 2010).

36 Anton Bosl et al. (eds), *Monitoring Regional Integration in Southern Africa*, vol. 9 (Stellenbosch: Trade Law Centre for Southern Africa, 2009), p. 4. See also Dawn Isabel Nagar, 'Towards a *Pax Africana*: Southern African Development Community's architecture and evolving peacekeeping efforts, 1996–2009', Unpublished Master's thesis in international relations, University of Cape Town, 2010, esp. pp. 32–5.

37 Lancaster Bottoman, email to the author, 14 December 2009, and telephone conversation, 1 February 2010. However, the West African Stand-by Force, based on ECOMOG, has much greater operational experience, and in developing an early warning system SADC lags behind both ECOWAS and IGAD. Adekeye Adebajo, *The Curse of Berlin* (London: Hurst, 2010), p. 43.

38 This was held under the auspices of the African Conference of (Staff College) Commandants, established in 2007. See www.acoc-Africa.org/docs/28JuneCJACInstruction.pdf.

39 The Amani Africa exercise involved the Vrai Mouvement Patriotique de Carana (VMPC), a group opposed to the AU Mission in Carana (AMICA) and seeking to gain a foothold in a province of Carana, the fictitious name of a republic in a subregion of Africa called Kisiwa. The concept of Carana was originally developed as a training tool within the UN Department of Peacekeeping Operations. The 2010 exercise was planned by Captain Kobus Maasdorp of the South African navy.

40 AU Press Release no. 150 of 2010. See also www.globalsecurity.org/military/library/news/2010/10/mil-101022-voa05.htm.

41 Helmut Rohmer-Heitman, 'A400M – R30 billion saved? Not really', *Weekend Argus*, 11 November 2009. The only other options, Rohmer-Heitman suggests, would be chartering old ex-Soviet Air Force transport planes or calling on the United States to assist.

42 Naison Ngoma, 'SADC: towards a security community?', *African Studies Review*, 12(3), 2003; Laurie Nathan, 'The AU and regional organisations in Africa: security communities or communities of insecurity?', *African Studies Review*, December 2009.

43 SADC, *Protocol on Politics, Defence, and Security Cooperation*, 2008, Article 11, paras 3(c) and 3(d). The AU is not mentioned, strangely.

44 The range of possible circum-

stances in which the SADCSF might be used appears highly limited. The idea of the SADCSF intervening in Madagascar to oust the regime there, for example, is hardly realistic, even if it were thought desirable.

45 For a sceptical view, see Deane-Peter Baker and Sadiki Maeresera, 'SADCBRIG intervention in SADC member states: reasons to doubt', *African Security Review*, 18(1), 2009.

46 See Mandrup, 'South Africa and the SADC Stand-by Force', p. 12.

47 While the AU did provide a media day for Exercise Carana, no news of the exercise appeared in the southern African media.

48 The case for clarification is argued in Thandisizwe Myataza, 'Towards security co-operation between African sub-regional organisations and the African Union: the case of Southern African Development Community and the AU', Unpublished paper, Grahamstown, November 2009.

49 Aleksandra Dier, 'The African Standby Force put to the test', *CSS Analysis in Security Policy*, 84, November 2010, p. 3; 'New African Standby Force faces first test', VOA News.com, 22 October 2010.

6 | Gender and peace-building

Elizabeth Otitodun and
Antonia Porter[1]

The relationship between gender and peace is densely complex, sometimes mutually exclusive and certainly crucial. A highly gendered society, in which the oppression of women is often explained or at least justified in terms of culture, cannot be a peaceful society.[2] Peace requires the transformation of gender relations – the removal of the 'costume, [the] mask, [the] straitjacket in which men and women dance their unequal dance'.[3] Why? Our conception and usage of the term 'peace' accord with Johan Galtung's 'positive peace' – a vision that includes not only sustained restoration of relations between adversaries, but also addressing structural inequalities across long-standing societal fault-lines, such as gender, race and class.[4] Galtung differentiates such a setting from 'negative peace', which he describes as being merely the end of widespread violent conflict associated with war, such as the enactment of a ceasefire. Unfortunately, among governments and international agencies, there is still a commonly held view of 'negative peace' as peace. Adding gender[5] equality to the long list of peace-building challenges[6] facing countries emerging from conflict has historically not been a consideration, let alone a priority. However, given that gender is a central fault-line in *all* societies, gender equality must form a foundational brick if positive and, consequently, sustainable peace is to be built.[7] As violent conflict tends to bear roots in structural and other forms of inequality, so peace-building must include measures that challenge, and assist in the elimination of, such forms of inequality. These should include gender inequality, and the system of patriarchy, from which gender inequality derives.[8]

Gender equality must be treated as a peace-building issue not only because it is an integral element of sustainable and positive peace, but for two further reasons: first, women are disproportionately targets of violent conflict, and constitute the majority of all victims of contemporary armed conflicts;[9] and secondly, women are largely excluded from the processes of building and keeping peace. These are unfortunate realities for women globally, and certainly across the southern African region. In a region that has experienced a great deal of armed conflict over recent decades,[10] with conflicts of various types currently unfolding in the Democratic Republic of the Congo (DRC), Madagascar,

Swaziland and Zimbabwe[11] (see Matlosa, Saunders in this volume), several of the principal challenges for women pertain directly to violent conflict and its consequences. Women constitute the majority of southern Africa's estimated 470,000 refugees, internally displaced persons (IDPs) and asylum seekers, and are increasingly subject to xenophobia and discrimination in their host countries.[12] Furthermore, as in many patriarchal and conservative post-conflict settings, women in Mozambique, Namibia and Zimbabwe have experienced rejection of their wartime freedoms from both governments and communities, and have usually been compelled to return to the domestic arena. Women compose the majority of the poor in the region,[13] and have limited access to resources such as credit finance, land and livestock. (See Drimie and Gandure in this volume.) They lack access to justice, and are generally under-represented in governance structures. Trafficking of women and children is also on the increase in southern Africa,[14] and traditional law and customary practices often take precedence over formal law to oppress women's rights, such as guardianship over children and the right to own property.[15] Child soldiers were part of combat forces in Mozambique and the DRC, which has subsequently posed a particular challenge for women in these countries. Child soldiers tend to grow up without respect for elders, in part given their access to light weapons, which allows them power over unarmed people of any age. After conflicts, this loss of respect for elders is particularly experienced by women, as levels of rape perpetrated by young boys on older women rise.[16] Even in the absence of armed conflict, physical violence and rape of women, often accompanied by psychological abuse, are pervasive across the region.[17] Against this background, effective peace-building aimed at creating a society that functions at optimum levels requires gender analysis at each step of the way.

As mentioned earlier, the injustice is double: women are also excluded from processes of peace-building. The African Union (AU), in its 2008 Gender Policy, set its member states a target to achieve 50/50 representation of women and men in politics and decision-making by 2020, in line with Article 9 of the 2003 AU Protocol on the Rights of Women in Africa, Commitment 5 of the 2004 Solemn Declaration on Gender Equality in Africa (SDGEA), and United Nations Security Council Resolution (UNSCR) 1325 of 2000.[18] Although the proportion of women in parliaments in the Southern African Development Community (SADC) region increased from 17.5 per cent at the time of the Solemn Declaration in 2004 to more than 25 per cent by the end of 2009, and although progress has been significant in some areas of the region, as we will explore later, recent elections in certain countries of the region have shown regression of women's representation in parliament.[19] For example, elections in 2009 saw female representation in Botswana fall from 18 per cent to 6.6 per cent. Polls in Namibia in the same year saw the number of women elected reduce from 30 per cent to 22 per cent.[20] Peace settlements usually include only leaders of political organizations: when women are not in political leadership positions, they are excluded from these crucial processes of peacemaking.

Women's needs are especially neglected in the area of justice and security sector reform (SSR). African-American gender analyst Jennifer Klot has focused attention on the need to address more effectively the neglect of women's needs in this area. She highlights the fact that women's protection, especially in the aftermath of conflict, receives far less attention than street crimes, homicides, political corruption, gangs, and disarmament, demobilization and reintegration (DDR) initiatives. Klot believes that the failure to prioritize women's protection is rooted in the fact that most often 'women's security is considered a human rights or women's issue rather than a security sector imperative'.[21] This is particularly an issue for southern Africa, where six countries have undergone DDR processes; namely, Angola, Mozambique, South Africa, the DRC, Namibia and Zimbabwe. DDR processes notoriously exclude women and women's issues, focusing primarily on assisting male ex-combatants. To compound this injustice, levels of domestic violence by male ex-combatants against women tend to increase during DDR processes.[22] Every element of reconstruction, such as DDR processes, rebuilding shattered infrastructure, both physical and human, promoting social and economic development, providing basic social services, and planning for return of refugees and IDPs,[23] has a gendered impact as women and men are affected differently.

While current peace-building processes do not change existing gender hierarchies, which are at the root of ongoing gender discrimination during armed conflict, the process of peace-building presents a unique opportunity to do this: women's roles often undergo changes during times of conflict, and the recovery phase has the potential to be a period of positive transformation for gender relations. Gender-sensitive peace-building, however, requires much more than merely the inclusion of women in peace-building processes, and too often these processes have mistakenly been reduced to politicians seeking to meet their gender equity quotas. They require a broader transformation of patriarchal structures, policies, perceptions, attitudes, beliefs, norms and relationships.[24] As will be explored further, it is therefore misleading to measure gender equality in terms of mere numbers of women occupying positions of power. Quotas 'should not overshadow long-term strategies that address women's socio-economic marginalization'.[25] Neither are current popular 'gender mainstreaming' SSR processes adequate. They tend to instrumentalize women as 'overlooked beneficiaries' in DDR processes, which, according to Zambian gender activist Yaliwe Clarke, falls far short of a feminist approach, which would tackle issues of hierarchy and masculinity and seek to undertake a thorough transformation of the gender relations that typify security institutions and systems.[26]

An evolving gender architecture

A growing recognition of the significant role of women in peace-building[27] is evident in the evolving international and regional gender architecture. At an international level, this includes the 1979 Convention on the Elimination of All Forms of Discrimination Against Women (CEDAW), which calls for quotas and other measures to increase the number of women in political decision-making positions; the 1994 Dakar Platform for Action; the 1995 Beijing Platform for Action, which is broadly seen as a turning point in the advancement of the rights of women; and UN Security Council Resolutions 1325 (2000), 1820 (2008), 1888 (2009) and 1889 (2009), on women, peace and security. UNSCR 1888 specifically recognizes sexual violence against women during conflict as a global security concern, and in 2009 Sweden's Margot Wallström was appointed Special Representative to the UN's secretary-general on Sexual Violence in Conflict. In addition to the gender- and security-focused UNSCRs, the third UN Millennium Development Goal (MDG) (2000), aimed at promoting gender equality and empowering women, also prioritizes the essential importance of addressing women's needs around the world. Some analysts perceive that if this third MDG is not achieved before the 2015 deadline, none of the MDGs will in fact be achieved, since all the MDGs bear a special relevance to women.[28]

In July 2010 the UN General Assembly established the Entity for Gender Equality and the Empowerment of Women (UN Women) as part of a broader reform process under way at the world body, which seeks to combine mandates and resources for greater impact. UN Women is thus a merger of four UN entities that had focused on gender equality and women's empowerment – the well-known United Nations Development Fund for Women (UNIFEM), the Division for the Advancement of Women (DAW), the International Research and Training Institute for the Advancement of Women (INSTRAW), and the Office of the Special Adviser on Gender Issues and Advancement of Women (OSAGI). The growing importance of creating gender equality is reiterated in UN secretary-general Ban Ki-moon's July 2010 report to the UN General Assembly, in which he states that 'gender issues are at the core of the United Nations mandate. Peace, security, development and human rights will find no application and success unless women are an integral, equal and participatory part of those processes.'[29] The importance of gender equality to peace-building is also underlined by its adoption as the only thematic area of the UN Peace-building Commission created in December 2005.[30]

At a regional level, the principle of gender equality is enshrined in Article 4(l) of the Constitutive Act of the AU of 2000.[31] The 2001 New Partnership for Africa's Development (NEPAD) also pays some attention to women in its provisions, such as 'promoting the role of women in social and economic development by reinforcing their capacity in the domains of education and training; by developing revenue generating activities through access to credit;

and by assuring their participation in political and economic life in African countries'.[32] Some of the key instruments that define Africa's gender architecture include the 2003 Protocol to the African Charter on Human and People's Rights on the Rights of Women in Africa, ratified by twenty-nine of the AU's fifty-three member states by 2010;[33] the SDGEA of 2004; the 2009 AU Gender Policy and its Action Plan; and the 2010 Fund for African Women, which is being implemented at the national level through the creation of National Gender Equality Funds.[34] Significantly, the AU has declared 2010 to 2020 to be the Decade of Women in Africa.[35] Launched officially in Nairobi, Kenya, on 15 October 2010, the declaration, which will be implemented in two five-year phases, seeks to 'reinvigorate commitments to accelerate implementation of agreed global and regional commitments of gender equality and women's empowerment'.[36] Spearheaded by the AU's Women, Gender and Development Directorate in Addis Ababa, Ethiopia, the declaration encourages a bottom-up approach, acknowledging the impact that grassroots stakeholders have at the community level.

Several campaigns have also been organized by the AU, such as the Africa UNiTE Campaign to End Violence Against Women – the regional component of the UN secretary-general's UNiTE campaign – which was launched during the AU Heads of State Summit held in Addis Ababa, in January 2010. The aims of the campaign are 'to mobilize and support governments to adopt and implement commitments to end violence against women, and to empower women and their communities to demand accountability'.[37] At an institutional level the AU has made some positive efforts. The continental body established the Women, Gender and Development Directorate in 2000 to coordinate activities on gender equality in the AU Commission, and gender balance is reflected in the 50 per cent representation of women on the ten-member Commission.[38] Women's organizations have lobbied that the quota for women serving in the Pan African Parliament, which currently makes provision for at least one woman to be included among the five members from each state who sit in the parliament, should be increased to two women per state.[39]

SADC's gender instruments

The SADC Protocol on Gender and Development of 2008 is generally viewed as the organization's 'roadmap to gender equality'.[40] Article 28 of the protocol focuses specifically on peace-building and conflict resolution, and calls for 'state parties to put in place measures to ensure that women have equal representation and participation in key decision-making positions in conflict resolution and peacebuilding processes by 2015 in accordance with United Nations Security Council Resolution 1325 on Women, Peace, and Security'. The protocol also urges state parties 'to take the necessary steps during armed and other forms of conflict to prevent and eliminate incidences of human rights abuses, especially of women and children, and ensure that the perpetrators of such abuses are brought to justice before a court of competent jurisdiction'.[41] The key objectives of the protocol are to provide for the empowerment of women; to eliminate discrimination and achieve gender equality and equity through development and implementation of gender-responsive legislation, policies, programmes and projects; to harmonize implementation of the various regional, continental and international instruments on gender equality and equity to which SADC member states have subscribed; and to deepen regional integration, attain sustainable development, and strengthen community building.[42]

SADC gender instruments that make up the overall framework for the achievement of gender equality at a regional level include Article 6(2) of the 1992 SADC Declaration and Treaty; the 1997 Declaration on Gender and Development (GAD) as well as its 1998 Addendum on the Prevention and Eradication of Violence Against Women and Children; and the 1999 Plan of Action for Gender in SADC. Article 5 of the SADC Treaty includes as one of its policies to 'mainstream gender in the process of community building'.[43] The 1997 GAD recognizes that gender equality is a fundamental human right, and that ensuring that gender issues are fully recognized by the SADC Programme of Action and Community Building Initiative is central to achieving sustainable development in the region. The 1998 addendum reaffirms the commitment of the organization's member states to the prevention and eradication of violence against women and children in the region. The 1999 action plan seeks to operationalize the commitments contained in the declaration and addendum.[44] The 2003 SADC Regional Indicative Strategic Development Plan (RISDP) identifies gender equality and development as one of several priority intervention areas.[45] These instruments address a wide range of issues that continue to affect women in the SADC region, including constitutional and legal rights, governance, education, productive resources, gender-based violence, health (particularly HIV/AIDS), peace-building and conflict resolution, and the media. The SADC Gender Unit, established in 1998, forms part of the SADC Secretariat in Gaborone, Botswana, and is responsible for working with national gender machineries that have been established in all fifteen SADC member states. The unit is also responsible for ensuring that a gender-sensitive approach permeates the SADC Programme of Action.

Technical progress and obstacles in SADC

The SADC Gender Protocol Campaign Programme, run by the Southern African Gender Protocol Alliance – a collective of over forty national and regional gender non-governmental organizations (NGOs) that has been conducting a campaign since 2005 for the adoption, ratification and implementation of the SADC Gender and Development Protocol – very usefully monitors progress towards achieving the twenty-eight targets set by this protocol. It produced the *SADC Gender Protocol 2010 Barometer*, a report that maintains that only limited progress has been achieved in increasing education on gender issues, increasing women's participation in political decision-making, and legal reform to eliminate discriminatory gender practices.[46] The 2010 report notes that while South Africa, Namibia and Malawi have good constitutional provisions for gender equality, other governments are lagging behind in their commitment to institute legal reform that would address discrimination against women. Some of the key areas for improvement that the report highlights are women's participation in economic decision-making; a need to reduce by 75 per cent the maternal mortality rate, which had increased from 171 deaths per 100,000 live births in 1990 to 381 in 2008;[47] and the provision of affordable quality healthcare. In relation to sexual and gender-based violence, the 2010 Barometer report highlights that only nine SADC countries currently have legislation on domestic violence,[48] and seven have specific legislation that relates to sexual offences.[49] But current policies and strategies are not able to address effectively challenges such as the mass rape that is occurring in the DRC despite national legislation against sexual violence, or the lack of participation of women in post-conflict and peace-building processes, which is particularly the case with Angola.

The non-legally binding nature of the GAD and its addendum on member states contributes to the delay in implementation of gender instruments in the region. Lack of ratification of the SADC Gender and Development Protocol was also initially cited as the biggest single technical obstacle to implementation. However, by March 2011 the protocol had been signed by thirteen of the fifteen SADC member states,[50] and ratified by eight.[51] Even so, implementation remains a long way out of sight. Only five of the member states to date have deposited ratification instruments with the SADC Secretariat.[52] One more country must ratify the protocol before it can come into force: this is anticipated to be either South Africa or Zambia, as both are moving forward with ratification.[53] It will be interesting to see how far implementation of the protocol advances as it becomes legally binding with the next ratification by a member state. Ratification of the protocol does not, however, seem to have significantly changed the pace at which it is being implemented, or to have assisted in overcoming some of the challenges of implementation. Certainly, ratification is a critical step, but raises the uneasy questions of the extent to which such policy instruments have affected the lives of southern African citizens, and of the potential for such instruments to effect change in the future.[54]

There is an increasing trend of peacekeeping forces perpetrating violence against women in their surrounding communities of deployment, both globally and across SADC. Graça Machel, the renowned Mozambican international advocate for the rights of women and children who produced the important

1996 *Impact of Armed Conflict on Children* report, stated that soldiers in the United Nations Operation in Mozambique (ONUMOZ) between 1992 and 1994 were recruiting teenage girls into prostitution.[55] Similar accusations followed against peacekeeping personnel in a number of African countries, including Somalia, the DRC, Eritrea, Liberia and Sierra Leone, between 1993 and 2011. Growing concern over this disturbing trend has led the UN to take stringent measures in the hope of curbing these incidents. A report and handbook were produced by the UN in 2005 aimed at eliminating sexual exploitation and abuse in its peacekeeping operations.[56]

African military structures have claimed to be concerned about the needs of women, as suggested by the growth of international and continental legislation on the issue.[57] But, as noted earlier, the willingness of SADC peacekeepers, militaries, mission leaders, negotiators and police officers to genuinely address gender issues in their operations and to take international and continental instruments and obligations seriously is insufficient. Is the answer to produce more training packages for peacekeepers which introduce gender issues and the relationship between gender and military structures? Or do these approaches simply amount to utilizing women to improve security operations? Yaliwe Clarke raises the controversial issue that such cooperation with military structures compromises feminism. She maintains that feminism should seek rather to deconstruct the militarized masculinities that are key to militarism, and perhaps the source of violent conflict to begin with.[58]

The protection of rights for sexual minorities also requires vast improvement in SADC countries and is an issue that is often omitted in discussions of human rights, peace-building and gender equality in the region. The 1981 African Charter of Human and People's Rights and the SADC Gender Protocol both protect against discrimination on the basis of sexual orientation. However, the enforcement of rights for gender and sexual minorities has been extremely limited to date, and domestic laws pertaining to homosexuality throughout the region remain largely discriminatory. The argument is often made by states that international charters do not override domestic legislation. In Malawi, the practice of homosexuality is outlawed, and incidents such as the infamous arrest of a gay Malawian couple who had held an engagement ceremony in 2009 are not isolated. On the Tanzanian island of Zanzibar, those convicted of practising homosexuality may receive prison sentences of up to twenty-five years. In Zimbabwe and Namibia, state-fuelled homophobia is also prevalent. In South Africa, where the Constitution protects gay rights, there has been a pandemic of 'corrective rape' violations against lesbian women.[59]

Members of civil society have often remained silent about such violations. Even organizations dedicated to the defence of human rights, such as the African Commission on Human and People's Rights (ACHPR), established in 1987,[60] was accused of discrimination against gay people following its refusal to award observer status to the Coalition of African Lesbians (CAL) so that it could attend the Commission's 48th ordinary session, held in November 2010. The Commission was also criticized for not being more vocal about the increasing violations against sexual and gender minorities across the continent over recent years. The protection of the rights of gender and sexual minorities belongs firmly within the discourse of human rights, and positive and sustainable peace requires their protection. Civil society, states and even regional instruments such as the ACHPR must therefore start taking the human rights violations of these minorities seriously.[61]

Another reason for slow progress in promoting gender issues is that insufficient funds have been allocated for women's empowerment. Promises made in international forums such as the Monterrey Consensus of 2002, where governments agreed to incorporate gender in all development policies, have not been fulfilled. The 2005 Paris Declaration on Aid Effectiveness also acknowledged the importance of financing gender development, and has the potential – if its principles are engendered – to advance gender equality.[62] The UN has estimated that US$25–28 billion will be required in 'dedicated external resources' in order to achieve the third MDG (promoting gender equality and empowering women) in low-income countries.[63]

The SADC Gender Unit also needs more funding, as it faces a huge challenge in its efforts to harmonize implementation of the various international and regional gender instruments.[64] Gender coordination at the national level continues to be weak, owing in part to the limited human and financial resources that are allocated to national gender machineries. It has also been difficult to track progress on the achievement of gender equality, and there is a need to strengthen monitoring and evaluation tools to gauge progress.[65] In this regard, it is important that the SADC Gender Unit continues to cooperate closely with the AU's Directorate for Gender, Women and Development and the gender units of other African regional economic communities. At the local level, there is a lack of information about gender instruments. Too often, even when distributed, information is not translated into local languages or is inaccessible to grassroots activists given the complicated, legalistic language in which the instruments are couched.[66]

Beyond policies: dealing with 'gender fatigue'?

While the growth of international and regional gender instruments is encouraging, the implementation of these instruments continues to be fraught with challenges, and progress has been slow. Some critics argue that the proliferation of instruments and the associated additional bureaucratic burden are causing 'instrument fatigue' among states, thereby hampering their compliance.[67] In southern Africa, as in much of the world, political will and enthusiasm for gender equality and gender-sensitive peace-building, within national governments and even within development and peace-building institutions, would seem to be lacking.[68] Some feminists maintain that this is because many large institutions and policy-making bodies worldwide, including those that are responsible for building peace, tend to be masculine rather than gender-neutral in culture and practice.[69] The argument follows that state bureaucracies and international bodies, and even the UN with its predominantly male leadership, operate according to norms of masculinity, with hierarchical structures, top-down leaderships and management styles, and encouragement of competitive behaviour between employees, regardless of the growing numbers of women in their midst.[70] 'Gender' and 'gender perspectives' are erroneously perceived as 'women' and 'women-specific' interventions. The popular strategy of 'gender mainstreaming',[71] which was designed to address such errors,[72] has on the whole not yielded real results, according to a growing consensus among many gender and development practitioners. Far too often, the 'mainstream' remains masculine.[73]

Is part of the problem also the 'professionalization' of feminism? Although hardly a well-funded field, gender equality work and women's rights are increasingly priorities for Western donors. Institutions sometimes adapt their focus to incorporate gender issues so that they may capture some of this funding, without necessarily understanding what feminism is all about, or employing feminists to implement these activities. South African gender activist Shamillah Wilson talks of the phenomenon of the 'professional feminist', who enters the feminist movement through academic women's and gender studies programmes at university, and who then may find paid employment in the field.[74] Feminists who are passionate about change may be left out of the organizations that purport to undertake gender equality work. Organizations and institutions with gender emphases should seek to recruit such activists and agents of change. For otherwise, as Indian theorist Aruna Rao posits, if institutional structures of peace-building, reconstruction and governance are characterized by norms of masculinity and are uncomfortable with conceptions of social transformation, then political will or initiative for the implementation of gender equality is unlikely to flourish.[75] The masculine mainstream must therefore be transformed.

Gender equality policies, including the SADC Gender Protocol, tend not to be adequately contextualized in terms of the larger feminist conceptual frameworks from which they originally emerged.[76] Nata Duvvury and Richard Strickland maintain that gender equality policies and approaches are often not framed in ways that allow the larger issues behind women's disenfranchisement in peace-building and post-conflict reconstruction to become clear.[77] This is unfortunate, for careful deconstructions of the widely held norms on which gender identities are based, and the relations between men and women, are crucial for shifting the power imbalance that leads to prejudicial attitudes and behaviour that deny women their human rights. The 'gender consciousness' that arises when these frameworks are made visible helps to illuminate how gender relations inform and create institutions such as the family and the military, and how power and oppression function through gender and other fault-lines such as class.[78] Moreover, making visible the histories and ongoing contexts of injustice and oppression of women, which the SADC Gender Protocol aims to address, may inspire in individuals and implementing bodies a greater investment and a greater sense of responsibility to use their positions to mobilize for change.

In sum, the argument here is that the individuals in policy bodies and governments who are responsible for implementation of the SADC Gender Protocol, if made aware of the nature and dynamics of patriarchal oppression, and such issues as gender socialization, may develop greater political will for gender equality. UNSCR 1325 provides an interesting entry point for the exploration of this issue. Articulation exists between UNSCR 1325 and the SADC Gender Protocol, in that the protocol identifies a target of gender parity by 2015. While, as earlier mentioned, it is acknowledged that women's political representation in the region is far from adequate, it is perceived that SADC has made positive strides in the implementation of UNSCR 1325, claiming second place globally after the Nordic region in the attainment of gender parity in political decision-making.[79]

South Africa's African National Congress (ANC) was the first political party in southern Africa to formally adopt and implement the SADC Gender Protocol's parity target, which it attained in the April 2009 elections, when 49.2 per cent of its members in the National Assembly were women.[80] In local government elections in 2006, South Africa adopted a legislated quota that resulted in 58 per cent representation by women. Malawi has also made progress in achieving gender parity in politics: the number of its female parliamentarians rose from only ten (6 per cent) in 1994 to forty (26.5 per cent) by 2009.[81] However, while the progress made in some countries should be recognized, there has been regression in women's representation in Botswana and Namibia, as indicated previously.[82] Other SADC states, such as the DRC, remain very much behind in this regard, with female representation in the Congolese parliament constituting only 8.4 per cent. Botswana, Lesotho, Mauritius, Namibia, Seychelles, Zambia and Zimbabwe have all yet to meet the 30 per cent minimum target for women's representation in public office.

Moreover, while southern Africa's efforts towards gender parity in politics must be acknowledged, activists within the region increasingly point out that gender equality in political decision-making requires far more than merely a greater numerical representation of women. Transforming the masculine mainstream will not be accomplished by the simple addition of women to decision-making bodies.[83] Ugandan analyst Joyce Laker cautions Africans against 'quota fever' and suggests that this preoccupation with numbers indicates a deployment of women as instruments for a political agenda.[84] Referring to Lourdes Beneria, she posits that this preoccupation is reducing gender equality to an 'add women and stir' approach: a technocratic liberal feminist approach.[85] Beneria identifies this approach as an attempt to conceptualize women's issues as a litmus test for analysis, rather than a strategic action to respond to essential concerns about the marginalization and exclusion of women.[86] This is deeply problematic: increasing women's political participation should at heart be about enhancing women's roles in decision-making. The persistently patriarchal environments of southern African governments, referred to earlier, and the 'masculinity model[s]' of democratic governance in Africa (and globally), tend to restrict this from happening. Admittedly, the SADC Gender Protocol does request campaigns to demonstrate the link between gender and governance.[87] But SADC's progress in attaining gender parity in political decision-making must not be conflated with progress in gender equality, and yet it sometimes is.[88] In part this conflation occurs because understandings of UNSCR 1325 and the SADC Gender Protocol are not sufficiently situated in the discourse of the politics of women's marginalization, and therefore the real purpose and intention of their implementation are somehow obscured.

A similar example could be made of affirmative action measures referring specifically to women, which the SADC Gender Protocol mandates national governments to implement. There are several instances of affirmative action being incorporated into laws and constitutions in SADC member states, and currently just over half of SADC countries have some sort of affirmative action provisions.[89] According to the protocol, all countries must put affirmative action programmes in place to generate greater participation of women throughout different levels of society. However, explanation and expression of this measure have not linked it adequately to historical economic oppression of women and the larger system of patriarchy, let alone in an accessible manner. Consequently, affirmative action for women is often viewed through a prism of negative attitudes about women's 'inferiority'.[90]

The importance of grassroots women's groups in the implementation of SADC's Gender Protocol

Political will is needed for progress towards the achievement of gender equality. One way to stimulate political will in policy bodies and governments is through more concentrated and sustained interaction between grassroots, higher-level women's groups and gender equality activists on the one hand, and policy-making bodies such as the AU Commission, peace-building institutions and national governments on the other. The principal agents of change for gender equality worldwide, and certainly across southern Africa, are women's rights NGOs, gender equality social movements and activists at the grass roots.

As the New York-based NGO Working Group on Women, Peace and Security[91] maintains, no matter how well articulated on paper, international instruments that promote women's rights can have little resonance unless grounded in the local and national realities of women, activists and organizations.[92]

Women's groups are able to achieve many of the goals of peace-building: they have demonstrated the ability to increase women's (and thereby household) income; to increase women's capacities to participate in public political processes and civil society more generally; to increase the number of women who become representatives and leaders (in accordance with UNSCR 1325); and to reinforce efforts to shift masculine cultures in society and in organizations.[93] As Yasmin Jusu-Sheriff, Sierra Leonean barrister and women's rights advocate, maintains, women in civil society have amalgamated new and traditional strategies and managed to create powerful coalitions across ethnic, class and geographical lines.[94] If gender equality is to be achieved, those who make and implement policy in regional institutions and governments will need to be guided by the priorities, experiences and best-practice strategies of grassroots women's organizations and gender equality social movements. This cannot be overemphasized. However, spaces and mechanisms for dialogue between gender equality grassroots NGOs and social movements on the one hand, and policy-making bodies on the other, must be created with care and sincerity. Policy bodies must recognize the asymmetry of power between themselves and the groups and social movements they are engaging with, and must assist them to express their views, priorities and experiences to the fullest extent.[95]

The creation of opportunities for sincere interaction between the grassroots and policy levels is not merely a one-way street. Grassroots women's groups often express a need to learn more about the legal instruments and rights that exist, so that they can deploy them to their full extent and can popularize and advocate among other organizations and communities, which training from policy-makers can provide. This is an important function that policy bodies and governments need to do more of; for, as is articulated by Ghanaian lawyer Evelyn Ankumah, 'if people are not aware of their rights they cannot ensure that they are protected'.[96]

In addition to engaging grassroots women's groups in dialogue in southern Africa, another effective means of bringing about implementation of the SADC Gender Protocol is for governments, other regional bodies and donors both regional and international to provide *financial support* directly to grassroots women's groups.[97] Women's groups in southern Africa are ultimately the drivers for implementation of the SADC Gender Protocol and other policies on gender equality. There would still seem to be considerable 'gender fatigue' within institutions and governments in this region and globally. Against this background, providing financial support to the chronically underfunded domain of grassroots women's groups and women activists[98] is a highly beneficial strategy that southern African governments, donors and other policy bodies can employ for implementation of the SADC Gender Protocol.

Conclusion

For perceptible shifts to occur in the power imbalance from which discriminatory attitudes and practices that oppress women in southern Africa arise, commonly held norms about gender identities and the relations between women and men must be recognized and transformed. This chapter has posited that contextualizing the SADC Gender Protocol and other gender equality policies within the system of patriarchy and the discourse of oppression, throughout both policy bodies and civil society, will assist with creating political will and an increased enthusiasm to address the subjugation of women. However, there are difficulties in making clear and meaningful the incredible complexities of the operations of the patriarchal system (such as socialization of gender norms, women internalizing their oppression, and so on). Gender norms are profoundly and acutely entrenched in all societies, even among institutions designed to promote gender equality. This is so much the case that, in a sense, cognitive and cerebral explanations of them and the structure that enables the oppression of women often fail to instigate in people a full understanding of the issues. These concepts need to be rethought in a more meaningful and engaging way, both at the policy level and in civil society. Psychosocial, transformational approaches that facilitate people's reflection on and awareness of the ways in which they themselves have been subject to gender conditioning may facilitate a fuller understanding of the oppression of women.[99] In this regard, providing forums in which people can enter into an experiential and insightful exploration of their own gender conditioning is one of the ways by which both men and women may be encouraged to challenge their personal assumptions and current socio-political conditions for women.[100] Incorporating men and boys into the struggle for gender equality is also increasingly recognized as a valuable strategy for reducing gender-based violence, and for tackling HIV/AIDS.[101] As the World Health Organization notes, to leave men and boys out of efforts to end violence separates them from the solutions to violence, and reaffirms gender norms around male violence.[102] The need to work with men and boys to achieve gender equality is also highlighted by African-American journalist and activist Jimmie Briggs, and American activist Andrew Levack,[103] who argues that gender socialization results in the development of complex masculinities whose damaging constructs need to be explored.[104]

Radically transformed power relations between women and men are clearly only possible when both sexes work together towards the goal of gender equality, and support each other when they behave differently from dominant gender roles or behaviours.[105] Instead of conceptualizing gender inequality as a struggle of men and boys against women and girls, it would be much more effective to conceptualize it in terms of a struggle of all men, women and children against inequality and oppression.[106] This chapter has highlighted the importance of integrating a gender-sensitive approach to peace-building efforts within the southern African region, and of taking gender equality as a peace-building priority seriously. A promising international and regional gender architecture is evolving, and efforts to promote gender equality in the SADC region are undeniably under way. During SADC's thirtieth-anniversary celebration in Windhoek, Namibia, in August 2010, member states delivered their first reports to the SADC Secretariat on progress in implementing the SADC Protocol on Gender and Development. While there are still major gaps to address in implementing the region's instruments, the gender architecture that is evolving on the continent clearly signals that peace and development will not be attained until women are treated as equal members of society. There has been some progress, but there is still a long way to go in reaching this goal. Increased political will, involving greater attention to and support for grassroots women's groups' priorities, is critical for success. Gender equality, which will benefit women, men and children, will only be possible through joint concerted efforts at international, regional and grassroots levels. Finally, achieving the goal of positive, and thereby sustainable, peace across the region will involve addressing *all* structural inequalities, including those of gender, race and class.

Notes

1 The authors wish to thank Patricia Daley and Adekeye Adebajo for their useful comments on an earlier version of this chapter.

2 Diana Francis, *Culture, Power Asymmetries, and Gender in Conflict Transformation* (Berlin: Berghof Research Centre for Constructive Conflict Management, 2004).

3 Gerda Lerner, *The Creation of Patriarchy* (New York: Oxford University Press, 1986), p. 238.

4 Johan Galtung, arguably the 'father' of the discipline of peace studies, often referred to a distinction between 'negative peace' and 'positive peace'. He spoke of 'negative peace' as referring to merely the absence of violence, such as the enactment of a ceasefire, and of 'positive peace' as referring to a context in which relationships between adversaries are restored, social systems that serve the needs of the whole population are established, and inequalities across long-standing societal fault-lines such as race, gender and class are addressed.

5 The term 'gender' denotes 'all the qualities of what it is to be a man or a woman which are socially and culturally, rather than biologically determined. Gender includes the way in which society differentiates appropriate behaviour and access to power for women and men, and, in practice, this refers to patterns in which women are generally disadvantaged over men.' Donna Pankhurst, 'Women, gender, and peacebuilding', Working Paper no. 5 (Bradford, UK: Centre for Conflict Resolution, University of Bradford, 2000), p. 10.

6 Countries emerging from conflict are faced with a gamut of peace-building challenges: shattered physical and human infrastructure, demobilization, disarmament and reintegration (DDR) processes, a dearth of social services, planning for return of refugees and internally

displaced persons (IDPs), volatile political situations, and so on.

7 We hold the view that the attainment of 'positive peace' is a requirement for sustained peace.

8 Pankhurst, 'Women, gender, and peacebuilding'.

9 United Nations (UN), *Report of the Secretary General on Women, Peace, and Security*, S/2002/1154, 16 October 2002.

10 Civil wars have occurred in Angola (1975–2002), Mozambique (1977–94), the Democratic Republic of the Congo (1996–2003) (with armed violence ongoing) and Zimbabwe, which has experienced violent conflict and oppression at various stages since its independence in 1980.

11 The DRC has been engulfed in conflicts and war since the fall of Mobutu Sese Seko; Zimbabwe has experienced severe political instability since the early 2000s, as have Swaziland and Madagascar, following the disputed elections of 2002 and even more recent coup attempts.

12 United Nations Refugee Agency, 'Southern Africa', 2011, www.unhcr.org/pages/49e45abb6.html.

13 Southern African Development Community (SADC), *Declaration on Gender and Development*, Preamble, www.sadc.int/index/browse/page/174.

14 Colleen Lowe Morna and Loveness Jambaya Nyakujarah (eds), *SADC Gender Protocol 2010 Barometer* (Johannesburg: Southern Africa Gender Protocol Alliance, 2010), p. 168. See also Carol Allais et al., *Tsireledzani: Understanding the Dimensions of Human Trafficking in Southern Africa* (Pretoria: National Prosecuting Authority of South Africa, 2010), www.hsrc.ac.za/Research_Publication-21609.phtml. See also Southern African Catholic Bishops Conference, 'Human trafficking in South Africa: 2010 and beyond', 2009, www.sacbc.org.za/Site/index.php?option=com_content&view=article&id=286&Itemid=111.

15 Morna and Walter, *SADC Gender Protocol Baseline Barometer*. See also 'Conflict transformation and peacebuilding in southern Africa', Seminar report, Johannesburg, 19/20 May 2008, p. 10.

16 Pankhurst, 'Women, gender, and peacebuilding'.

17 Romi Sigsworth, 'Gender-based violence in transition', Concept paper produced for the Centre for the Study of Violence and Reconciliation's 'Violence and Transition' project roundtable, Johannesburg, 7–9 May 2008.

18 Omer Redi, 'Women's Decade: greater attention to implementation', Inter Press Service News Online, 2010, ipsnews.net/news.asp?idnews=50419. See also African Union (AU), 'Gender policy', February 2009, www.africa- union.org/.../african%20union%20gender%20policy.doc.

19 'Elections in the region have shown regression with regard to women's representation in parliament.' United Nations Development Programme (UNDP) director Bo Asplund, speaking at a conference on women in politics in Johannesburg in 2010. 'Africa: African elections put fewer women in parliament', *Mail and Guardian Online*, 9 December 2010, mg.co.za/article/2010-12-09-un-african-elections-put-fewer-women-in-parliament.

20 Ibid.

21 Jennifer Klot, 'Women and peacebuilding', Independent expert paper commissioned by the United Nations Development Fund for Women (UNIFEM) and the UN's Peacebuilding Support Office (PBSO), 2007.

22 Pankhurst, 'Women, gender, and peacebuilding'.

23 Working Group on Women, Peace and Security, *Security Council Resolution 1325 on Women, Peace, and Security: Six Years On Report – SCR 1325 and the Peacebuilding Commission*, New York, 2006, p. 18.

24 Centre for Conflict Resolution, 'Peacebuilding in post-Cold War Africa: problems, progress, and prospects', Seminar report, Gaborone, 25–28 August 2009.

25 Heidi Hudson, 'When feminist theory meets peacebuilding policy: implications of gender mainstreaming and national action plans', Paper presented at the annual conference of the Inter-

national Studies Association, New York, 15–18 February 2009, p. 8.

26 Yaliwe Clarke, 'Security sector reform in Africa: a lost opportunity to deconstruct militarised masculinities?', *Feminist Africa*, 10, 2008, pp. 49–66.

27 Klot, 'Women and peacebuilding'.

28 Millennium Development Goals: MDG1: Eradicate extreme poverty and hunger; MDG 2: Achieve universal primary education; MDG 3: Promote gender equality and empower women; MDG 4: Reduce child mortality; MDG 5: Improve maternal health; MDG 6: Combat HIV/AIDS, malaria and other diseases; MDG 7: Ensure environmental sustainability; MDG 8: Develop a global partnership for development.

29 UN, *Implementation of the Recommendations Contained in the Report of the Secretary-General on the Causes of Conflict and the Promotion of Durable Peace and Sustainable Development in Africa*, A/65/152, 20 July 2010, p. 24. See also Josephine Odera and Irene Zirimwabagabo, 'The UN Development Fund for Women', in Adekeye Adebajo (ed.), *From Global Apartheid to Global Village* (Scottsville: University of KwaZulu-Natal Press, 2009).

30 Carolyn McAskie, 'Draft Statement for the Interactive Dialogue on the Review of the Implementation of the 2004 Agreed Conclusions on "Women's Equal Participation in Conflict Prevention, Management, and Conflict Resolution and in Post-Conflict Peacebuilding"', UN Commission on the Status of Women, 52nd session, 2008, www.un.org/peace/peacebuilding/Statements/ASG%20Carolyn% 20McAskie/ASG%20MCAskie%20CSW% 20SPEECH%2029.02.08.pdf.

31 Centre for Conflict Resolution, 'Women in post-conflict societies in Africa', Seminar report, Johannesburg, 6/7 November 2006.

32 Thapo Rapoo, *Gender and the New Africa Agenda: Examining Progress Towards Gender Equality in SADC*, Policy Brief no. 49 (Johannesburg: Centre for Policy Studies, 2007).

33 AU, 'Briefing Note: Mitigating vulnerabilities of women and children in armed conflict', PSC/PR/3 (CCXXIII), 2010. The 2003 protocol has been ratified by twenty-seven AU member states. A further twenty-one member states have signed the protocol but have not yet ratified it, and five member states have not yet signed the protocol.

34 Redi, 'Women's Decade'.

35 UN, *Implementation of the Recommendations*.

36 'African Women Decade promises greater gender parity', 2010, www.allvoices.com/contributed-news/7031937-african-women-decade-officially-launched.

37 PeaceWomen, 'Southern Africa: regional consultation on the Africa UNiTE Campaign', 2010, www.peacewomen.org/news_article.php?id=825&type=news.

38 Yetunde Teriba, 'The AU Solemn Declaration on Gender Equality in Africa', Paper presented at the conference 'Popularization and Implementation of the Solemn Declaration on Gender Equality in Africa: The Role of Parliament', Addis Ababa, Ethiopia, 10–12 October 2007. See also Rachel Murray, *Human Rights in Africa: From the OAU to the African Union* (Cambridge: Cambridge University Press, 2004), p. 137.

39 Murray, *Human Rights in Africa*.

40 Signature of the protocol by a member state indicates an initial endorsement. Article 41 demands that a majority of two-thirds should then ratify and deposit their instruments of ratification with the SADC Secretariat. Ratification is a formal act that legally binds a member state to the terms of the protocol. Sheila Bunwaree, 'Gender, human rights, and peacebuilding in Africa', Paper presented at the Centre for Conflict Resolution 'Peacebuilding in Africa' research and policy seminar, Gaborone, 25–28 August 2009.

41 SADC, *Protocol on Gender and Development*, 2008, www.genderlinks.org.za/page/sadc-protocol-policy.

42 Morna and Nyakujarah, *SADC Gender Protocol 2010 Barometer*.

43 SADC, *Regional Indicative Strategic Development Plan (RISDP)*, Gaborone.

44 Ibid., p. 45.

45 Ibid., p. 46.

46 Morna and Nyakujarah, *SADC Gender Protocol 2010 Barometer.*

47 United Nations Economic and Social Council (ECOSOC), 'Overview of economic and social conditions in Africa in 2010', E/ECA/COE/30/2 & AU/CAMEF/EXP/2(VI), March 2011, www.uneca.org/cfm/2011/documents/English/Overview-of-economic-and-social-conditions-inAfrica-in2010%20_11.pdf.

48 The nine countries are Botswana, Madagascar, Malawi, Mauritius, Mozambique, Namibia, Seychelles, South Africa and Zimbabwe. SADC, *Protocol on Gender and Development.*

49 The seven countries are Lesotho, Mauritius, Namibia, Seychelles, South Africa, Tanzania and Zimbabwe. SADC, *Protocol on Gender and Development.* See also Barbara Lopi, 'Is gender-based violence adequately addressed in SADC?', *Southern African News Features (SANF)*, www.sardc.net/editorial/newsfeature/gender.htm.

50 Botswana and Mauritius are the only SADC member states that had not signed the protocol by March 2011.

51 Angola, DRC, Lesotho, Mozambique, Namibia, Seychelles, Tanzania and Zimbabwe.

52 Lesotho, Mozambique, Namibia, Tanzania and Zimbabwe.

53 In the meantime, other countries that have ratified are under increasing pressure to deposit their ratification instruments with the SADC Secretariat. According to the Gender Protocol Alliance, this will signify that, as a region, SADC not only has committed to upscaling its effort to achieve gender equality, but also has become duty-bound to do so, and to report accordingly. See www.genderlinks.org.za/article/the-sadc-gender-protocol-ratification-process-status-and-updates-2011-03-02.

54 Centre for Conflict Resolution, 'Women in post-conflict societies in Africa'.

55 UN, *Promotion and Protection of the Rights of Children: Impact of Armed Conflict on Children*, A/51/306, 1996, www.unhchr.ch/huridocda/huridoca.nsf/(Symbol)/A.51.306.En?Opendocument.

56 This 2005 report was entitled 'A comprehensive strategy to eliminate future sexual exploitation and abuse in United Nations peacekeeping operations' and was further developed as a handbook on how to handle misconduct.

57 Clarke, 'Security sector reform in Africa'.

58 Ibid.

59 Voice of Africa's LGBTI Community, 'Is the African Commission dictated to by religious and political leaders on sexual minorities?', 2010, www.mask.org.za/is-the-african-commission-dictated-to-by-religious-and-political-leaders-on-sexual-minorities/#more-3076.

60 Scott Long, *More than a Name: State-sponsored Homophobia and Its Consequences in Southern Africa* (New York: Human Rights Watch and International Gay and Lesbian Human Rights Commission, 2003).

61 Ibid.

62 'The Paris Declaration on Aid Effectiveness in 2005 agreed on principles which, if engendered, could accelerate development in general and advance gender equality.' African Union Gender Policy, Rev 2/, 10 February 2009, p. 4. Available at www.africa-union.org/.../african%20union%20gender%20policy.doc.

63 Joyce Mulama, 'Women leaders ask where is our money', 2010, ipsnews.net/Africa/nota.asp?idnews=42914.

64 SADC, *RISDP*, p. 46.

65 Ibid.

66 Christi Van der Westhuizen (ed.), *Gender Instruments in Africa: Critical Perspectives, Future Strategies* (Midrand, South Africa: Institute for Global Dialogue, 2005), p. 165.

67 Ibid., p. 165.

68 For example, even within African Commission's Special Rapporteur mechanism (which includes a Special Rapporteur on the Rights of Women in Africa) a lack of initiative has been observed on the part of some Special Rapporteurs in implement-

ing their mandate. Centre for Conflict Resolution, 'Women in post-conflict societies in Africa'.

69 Cynthia Enloe, cited in Pankhurst, 'Women, gender, and peacebuilding'.

70 Pankhurst, 'Women, gender, and peacebuilding'.

71 The commonly accepted and most widely used definition of 'gender mainstreaming' is the one adopted by ECOSOC: 'Mainstreaming a gender perspective is the process of assessing the implications for women and men of any planned action, including legislation, policies or programmes, in all areas and at all levels. It is a strategy for making women's as well as men's concerns and experiences an integral dimension of the design, implementation, monitoring and evaluation of policies and programs in all political, economic and societal spheres so that women and men benefit equally and inequality is not perpetuated. The ultimate goal is to achieve gender equality.' UN Economic and Social Council (ECOSOC), *UN Economic and Social Council Resolution 1997/2: Agreed Conclusions*, 1997/2, 8 July 1997, www.unhcr.org/refworld/ docid/4652c9fc2.html (accessed 28 April 2011).

72 'Gender mainstreaming was adopted mainly to address the perceived failure of previous strategies such as women-specific projects to bring about significant changes in women's status.' Rekha Mehra and Geeta Rao Gupta, *Gender Mainstreaming: Making It Happen*, February 2006, siteresources. worldbank.org/INTGENDER/Resources/ Mehra GuptaGenderMainstreaming MakingItHappen.pdf.

73 Pamela Thomas, 'Women and gender mainstreaming', in *Women, Gender, and Development in the Pacific: Key Issues* (Canberra: Australian National University, Development Studies Network, 2008), pp. 1–7.

74 Shamillah Wilson, Anasuya Sengupta and Kristy Evans (eds), *Defending Our Dreams: Global Feminist Voices for a New Generation* (London: Zed Books in association with the Association for Women in Development, AWID, 2005).

75 Aruna Rao, cited in Jane Jaquette and Aruna Rao, 'Setting the context: approaches to promoting gender equity', in Elizabeth Bryan and Jessica Varat (eds), *Strategies for Promoting Equity in Developing Countries: Lessons, Challenges, and Opportunities* (Washington, DC: Woodrow Wilson International Center for Scholars, 2008).

76 Nata Duvvury and Richard Strickland, 'Gender equity and peacebuilding: from rhetoric to reality – finding the way', Discussion paper (Washington, DC: International Center for Research on Women, ICRW, 2003).

77 Ibid.

78 Cynthia Cockburn, 'Gender, armed conflict, and political violence', 2002, www.genderandpeacekeeping.com.

79 Morna and Nyakujarah, *SADC Gender Protocol 2010 Barometer*.

80 Electoral Institute of Southern Africa (EISA), 'South Africa: women's representation quotas', 2009, www.eisa. org.za/WEP/souquotas.htm.

81 Morna and Walter, *SADC Gender Protocol Baseline Barometer*.

82 'Elections in the region have shown regression with regard to women's representation in parliament.' UNDP director Bo Asplund, 'Africa', *Mail and Guardian Online*, 9 December 2010.

83 Lorraine Corner, cited in Thomas, 'Women and gender mainstreaming'.

84 Joyce Laker, 'Gender and democracy in Africa', Paper presented at the biannual conference of the South African Association of Political Studies (SAAPS), Stellenbosch, 1–4 September 2010.

85 Clarke, 'Security sector reform in Africa'.

86 Lourdes Beneria, cited in Laker, 'Gender and democracy in Africa'.

87 Morna and Walter, *SADC Gender Protocol Baseline Barometer*.

88 Laker, 'Gender and democracy in Africa'.

89 These countries include Botswana, Mozambique, Namibia, South Africa, Tanzania, Seychelles and Swaziland. Morna and Walter, *SADC Gender Protocol Baseline Barometer*. See also Aili Mari Tripp, 'The

changing face of Africa's legislatures: women and quotas', Paper presented at the Parliamentary Forum conference 'The Implementation of Quotas: African Experiences', International Institute for Democracy and Electoral Assistance (IDEA), Electoral Institute of Southern Africa (EISA) and Southern African Development Community (SADC), Pretoria, South Africa, 11/12 November 2003.

90 Another pertinent issue, which also suggests the importance of rooting policies more widely and accessibly in their *raison d'être,* is the ongoing practice of harmful traditional practices against women in certain SADC countries that, though outlawed by the Gender Protocol, have been known to persist in secret. Perhaps the protocol's demand for the ceasing of harmful practices against women could be framed in such a way that indicates such ceasing is not, as is likely anticipated, an ethnocentric and spurious injunction against tradition, but is based on the notion that gender socialization has allowed practices that have physically harmed, objectified and policed women's bodies.

91 The NGO Working Group on Women, Peace and Security, via its strategic positioning in New York at United Nations headquarters, plays an important global role in monitoring policy and practice on women, peace and security. Its mission is to collaborate with the United Nations, its member states and civil society towards full implementation of UNSCR 1325 and all other Security Council resolutions that address women, peace and security, including ensuring the equal and full participation of women in issues relating to peace and security.

92 Krista Lynes and Gina Torry (eds), *From Local to Global: Making Peace Work for Women* (New York: Working Group on Women, Peace and Security, 2005), p. 82.

93 Pankhurst, 'Women, Gender, and Peacebuilding'.

94 Yasmin Jusu-Sheriff, 'Civil society', in Adekeye Adebajo and Ismail Rashid (eds), *West Africa's Security Challenges:*

Building Peace in a Troubled Region (Boulder, CO: Lynne Rienner, 2004), p. 265.

95 Ranjita Mohanty, 'The infinite agenda of social justice: Dalit mobilization in the institutions of local governance', in Vera Schattan, P. Coelho and Bettina von Lieres (eds), *Mobilising for Democracy: Citizen Action and the Politics of Public Participation* (London: Zed Books, 2010), p. 97.

96 Quoted in Centre for Conflict Resolution, 'Women in post-conflict societies in Africa'.

97 'Nothing yields greater benefits than putting financial resources directly into the hands of women leaders on the ground.' Kavita Ramdas, 'It ain't what you do, it's the way that you do it', *Responsive Philanthropy: NCRP's Quarterly Journal,* Summer 2010, pp. 1, 11–14.

98 Urgent Action Fund, *Rising Up in Response: Women's Rights Activism in Conflict,* Urgent Action Fund summary by R. Jones, AWID, 4 March 2005.

99 Psychosocial approaches, in short, are aimed at addressing the well-being of individuals in relation to their environments.

100 See, for example, the US-based Satyana Institute, which has conducted collective gender reconciliation work globally over the past fifteen years, including in South Africa. Its workshops for male and female participants use a transformative, experiential methodology. The work aims less to analyse or theorize on the nature of gender differences, but rather to provide forums in which people of different genders can enter into an experiential and insightful exploration of their own gender conditioning. Participants at Satyana Institute workshops report that their model and approach generate a reflective understanding of gender conditioning and of the negative impacts of patriarchy on women and men, leading to positive attitudinal and behavioural shifts pertaining to gender equality. Will Keepin, *Divine Duality: The Power of Reconciliation between Women and Men* (Arizona: Hohm, 2007), p. 16.

101 Levack, cited in Jaquette and Aruna, 'Setting the context'.

102 An example that has been cited as a successful initiative in southern Africa is 'Men as Partners', which works with the military, unions and schools in South Africa to support men in developing alternative and more peaceful ways of being. There is also the global campaign 'Man Up', launched in South Africa in 2010, which works with young men and women to provide innovative training, resources and support to youth-informed initiatives against gender-based violence. The HIV-prevention project 'Young Men as Equal Partners' works in districts in Tanzania and Zambia. It strives to motivate young men to adopt responsible sexual behaviour, encouraged by teachers, church leaders, medical staff and young leaders.

Activities such as peer education and counselling, gender awareness workshops and drama performance are used and promoted. Current use of condoms among young men has apparently increased from 55 per cent to almost 78 per cent during the three-year project period.

103 Andrew Levack is a founding member of MenEngage, a global alliance of organizations that seeks to engage boys and men to achieve gender equality.

104 Andrew Levack, cited in Jaquette and Aruna, 'Setting the context'.

105 Emily Esplen, *Engaging Men in Gender Equality: Positive Strategies and Approaches – Overview and Annotated Bibliography*, BRIDGE Bibliography No. 15 (Brighton: Institute of Development Studies, 2006), p. 9.

106 Ibid., p. 15.4

PART THREE

Economic integration

7 | Regional economic integration

Dawn Nagar

From the 1950s onwards, as African states acquired sovereignty and developed autonomous structures, a strong sentiment grew among them to preserve their structures and adopt an incremental process to African unity. This gave rise to an understanding that regional integration should take on the form of a gradualist and functionalist approach. Neofunctionalism advocated that economic integration had to precede political integration.[1] In the 1960s and 1970s, regionalism in Africa was further inspired by European integration efforts and experiences. In Europe, regional integration evolved from the European Coal and Steel Community (ECSC). This was to provide a framework for its six members (Belgium, France, Germany, Italy, Luxembourg and the Netherlands) to cooperate peacefully to eliminate the possibility of war.[2] A second motive was for the European community to trade and barter in the production of coal and steel across Europe, preventing destructive competition as well as ending tariffs and border controls and, in turn, creating functional spillovers into other areas, with the integration process ultimately driving itself.[3] It is such efforts at integration that the fifteen-member Southern African Development Community (SADC) is currently pursuing. Europe's success was a model for African states, which believed that by adopting a similar regional integration path, the post-colonial ills plaguing their weak economies could be corrected.

However, in reality, Africa's socio-economic conditions, along generally with lack of technology and industrialization, prevented creation of the desired functional spillover and linkages envisaged. At the continental level, regional integration frameworks such as the Lagos Plan of Action (LPA) and the Final Act of Lagos (FAL) of 1980, the African Priority Programme for Economic Recovery of 1985, the African Alternative Framework to Structural Adjustment Programmme for Socio-Economic Recovery and Transformation (AAF-SAP) of 1989 and the African Charter for Popular Participation for Development of 1990 were agreed but not implemented.[4]

At the regional level, in 1975 the five Frontline States (Angola, Botswana, Mozambique, Tanzania and Zambia) of southern Africa formed an alliance to oppose apartheid South Africa, support the liberation of Zimbabwe and promote regional cooperation and development.[5] (See Khadiagala, Mbuende in this volume.) The further expansion of the Southern African Development

Coordination Conference (SADCC) – created in 1980 – into SADC, by 1992, has provided a multilateral platform for member states to achieve greater political and economic stability, with the goal of enabling successful regional integration. In reality, some member states are still seen to be operating in a vacuum and not fully aligning their domestic policies and practices to the SADC Treaty of 1992.[6] The democratic changes in his country from 1990 under former South Africa president Frederik Willem de Klerk allowed for South Africa's inclusion in the SADC community as a key member in 1994. Since its first democratic election, in 1994, South Africa has incorporated regional integration into its policies, viewing this effort as the primary building block for harnessing good political and economic ties with its neighbours in the region.[7]

For South Africa to be an effective player in southern Africa, it needs to take cognizance of the past, place less focus on current domestic economic policies, and shift its focus towards creating adequate policies that benefit the region's economic and political stability.

This history of regional integration in southern Africa – from the FLS to SADCC to SADC – has been covered in detail elsewhere in this volume (see Khadiagala, Mbuende). I will therefore focus more narrowly here on three key SADC initiatives that are critical to regional integration: the Southern African Power Pool (SAPP); the SADC Free Trade Area (FTA); and its Regional Indicative Strategic Development Plan (RISDP). This chapter assesses regional integration by examining the Southern African Power Pool, focusing particularly on the role of South Africa as the regional hegemon.

Spatial Development Initiatives: the Southern African Power Pool

SADC's four Spatial Development Initiatives (SDIs) – energy; oil and gas extraction; electrical power generation; and water and transport – were created between 1993 and 1996 to provide a platform for functional economic linkages within southern Africa.[8] Substantial efforts have been taken in the development of transport corridors: the Maputo Corridor, through Mozambique and South Africa, created in August 1995; and the Trans-Kalahari Corridor, connecting Namibia's port of Walvis Bay to South Africa, agreed in 1998. The September 2003 SADC Protocol on Shared Watercourses, ratified by two-thirds of SADC members, will be instrumental in managing the region's fifteen shared river basins.[9]

Electrical energy is an important social and economic development sector for the functioning of SADC states. In 1995, its members undertook their first initiative to combine major national utilities, creating the Southern African Power Pool.[10] SAPP's main aim is to optimize the use of available energy resources in the SADC region, as well as allowing member states to provide each other with necessary energy support by creating a common market for electricity. SAPP is guided by a 1995 intergovernmental memorandum of understanding (MOU) (revised in February 2006), an April 2007 inter-utility MOU that outlines its management of functions, and an April 2008 revised agreement that guides its operating principles, which are currently under review. SAPP has linked the major utilities of twelve SADC member states: Angola, Botswana, the Democratic Republic of the Congo (DRC), Lesotho, Malawi, Mozambique, Namibia, South Africa, Swaziland, Tanzania, Zambia and Zimbabwe. The 1995 SAPP agreement pledges full recovery of costs and equal sharing of profits.

During the late 1980s, 85 per cent of households in the southern African region had no electricity supply.[11] Only since the 1990s have national policies addressed a wider electricity supply for households in the region. This is evident in South Africa's Reconstruction and Development Programme (RDP) of 1994, which aimed to provide electricity to 70 per cent of households in the country.[12] To accelerate implementation of the regional power supply, the outstanding interconnectors for Angola, Malawi and Tanzania are to be installed by 2015. This will accelerate implementation of the regional power supply in other economic communities as well, and also build on the tripartite agreement between the Common Market for Eastern and Southern Africa (COMESA), the East African Community (EAC) and SADC. US$5.6 billion will be spent on regional transmission projects: Zimbabwe–Zambia–Botswana–Namibia (ZIZABONA) in 2010/11, Mozambique–Malawi in 2012, Zambia–Tanzania in 2014, DRC–Angola in 2015 and Mozambique–South Africa in 2015 – as well as strengthened transmission in South Africa and Botswana, between 2015 and 2025, and a 765-kilovolt strengthening project.[13]

Currently, there is a profound imbalance between supply and demand in the region's electricity grid. Statistics in 1996 indicated that South Africa, comprising 23 per cent of the overall southern African population, consumed 78 per cent of installed power-generating capacity, 84 per cent of the regional peak load, and 85 per cent of the electricity distributed and sold.[14] In the same year, about 50 per cent of South Africa's population had access to electricity. Other initiatives, such as the government's electrification policies, were spearheaded under former South African president Thabo Mbeki, who in 2004 pledged that by 2012 all of South Africa's households would have access to electricity.[15] By 2009, just under 85 per cent of South African households had access to electricity.[16] South Africa has taken the leading role in providing power to the region; it is by far the largest consumer of power in southern Africa, and has an economy that is twenty times the size of that of the next-largest SADC country.[17]

SAPP's overall objective is to provide reliable and economical electricity supply to the consumers in its member states, consistent with reasonable utilization of natural resources and environmental impact.[18] Ideally, the intention of SAPP is to create an increase in regional trade in electricity and to further foster economic integration in SADC. By 2027, it is envisaged that

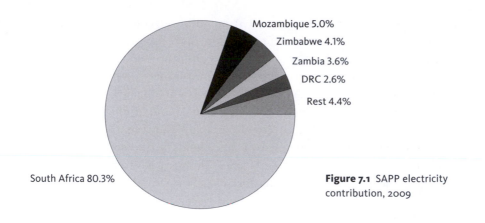

Mozambique 5.0%

Zimbabwe 4.1%

Zambia 3.6%

DRC 2.6%

Rest 4.4%

South Africa 80.3%

Figure 7.1 SAPP electricity contribution, 2009

Source: Alison Chikova, 'Energy trading in the Southern African Power Pool', 2009, www.sapp.co.zw.

SAPP will increase SADC's total electricity generation by 42,000 megawatts (MW) compared to its electricity capacity in 2007, which stood at 52,742 MW and of which 41,000 MW was supplied to meet consumer demand.[19] In April 2009, 48,649 MW of SADC's overall installed capacity of 55,927 MW was available for the region. SAPP's grid interconnectors had solid margins as well, with installed capacity at 53,445 MW against available capacity of 46,772 MW, while the demand during this time peaked at 43,267 MW.[20]

Through its SDIs, the southern African region is seeking to develop other energy resources such as biomass energy and biofuels, thus enhancing the overall power sector capacity.[21] By 2020, a decrease of 15 per cent in non-commercial final energy is envisaged, giving priority to alternative approaches to generating electricity.[22] The region has been making use of mainly non-renewable energy resources such as coal, gas and liquid fuels such as paraffin to produce electricity. Southern Africa also has an abundance of renewable energy resources such as wind, water, biofuels (corn, sugar cane and soya) and geothermal heat that can be harnessed as alternative approaches to generating electricity. South Africa is also considering other alternative energy resources, such as gas/diesel and nuclear power in order to reduce its greenhouse gas emissions.[23] (See Simon in this volume.) However, use of nuclear power, though the most cost-effective means of generating of electricity, may prove unpopular in the wake of the 2011 earthquake and tsunami in Japan, whose Fukushima nuclear plant suffered serious complications as a result of the natural disaster.[24]

In 1998, Eskom, South Africa's power utility, was ranked the fifth largest power utility globally, with annual sales of US$4.8 billion, 40,000 employees, a net income of US$800 million, and total assets of US$14.4 billion. Its research and development department was equivalent in size and annual budget to the departments of the other power utilities in the southern African region.

However, in the early 2000s Eskom began to experience difficulties and had to look outward, to its regional neighbours, to meet South Africa's electricity needs.[25]

In 2003, Eskom had a net loss of R719 million on revenues of R3.3 billion, in comparison to a R9 million profit on R2.9 billion revenues in 2002; and its cash flows from operations declined to R285 million, from R324 million in 2001.[26] In October 2010, South Africa's National Treasury injected loan guarantees of R350 billion for Eskom to build new Medupi and Kusile coal-fired power stations.[27] This investment was presumably due to South Africa's massive coal reserves in relation to the rest of the region. However, Eskom has faced challenges in securing coal from South African mining companies, who are increasingly looking beyond the region and focusing on exporting to investors such as Asia for much higher returns.[28]

The World Bank is also thinking of making available US$300–400 million (2013–16) to rehabilitate and strengthen existing energy plants in the region, such as to refurbish the DRC's Inga I and II hydroelectric projects.[29] SAPP has, on the whole, had positive spin-offs for the region's economy, and South Africa's viable market creates a pull factor for outside investment interests to the region. South Africa is now in a much more advantageous position in the region, with Eskom comprising thirty-four networks in 2006; the country also is the leading driver of SAPP, having technical and development expertise as well as regional transmission systems and investments.[30] South Africa constituted 85 per cent of electricity consumption (compared to an 80.4 per cent contribution – see Figure 7.1)[31] in the region in 2009, and it seems that South Africa consumes more than it contributes. This dominance is unlikely to change significantly in the future. Given the high demand for electricity in South Africa, Eskom's role (in comparison to the other members' contributions of resources to the electricity grid) may not necessarily equate to 'full recovery of costs and equal sharing of profits', as defined in the SAPP agreement for its users.

The 1995 SAPP agreement in its current form may not be that equitably designed, since South Africa is the largest consumer of overall electricity supplied among its members, as evidenced by Table 7.1. Some measures have been put in place to address the varying tariff-setting principles for electricity among SADC's fifteen member states. These wide variations are seen as a major factor in trade diversion and overall investment in the power sector in the region. SADC estimates that the regional power deficit among member states could be addressed should funding be secured to allow the planned power projects such as Zizabona and the West Power Corridor (Westcor) to be completed.

For SDIs to work effectively in achieving their goals, governments need to relinquish some of their power to SADC. Southern Africa was in a strong position to attract the DRC's abundance of hydroelectric resources through its 2003 Westcor project as well as through the lure of permanent membership in SAPP.

Table 7.1 SAPP electricity demand and supply (MW), 2009

no.	Country	Utility	Installed capacity	Available capacity as at Feb. 2009	Installed minus available	Peak demand 2008	Capacity required	Shortfall
1	Angola	ENE	1,128	870	258	668		
2	Botswana	BPC	132	90	42	503		
3	DRC	SNEL	2,442	1,170	1,272	1,028		
4	Lesotho	LEC	72	70	2	108		
5	Malawi	ESCOM	302	246	56	259.6		
6	Mozambique	EDM	233	174	59	415,64		
		HCB	2,250	2,075	175			
7	Namibia	NamPower	393	360	33	444		
8	South Africa	Eskom	43,061	38,384	4,677	35,959		
9	Swaziland	SEB	51	50	1	200		
10	Tanzania	TANESCO	1,186	680	506	694		
11	Zambia	ZESCO	1,737	1,200	537	1,495		
12	Zimbabwe	ZESA	2,045	1,080	965	1,397		
	TOTAL SAPP		55,032	46,449	8,583	43,171	47,575	(1,126)
	TOTAL interconnected SAPP		52,426	44,653	7,763	41,550	45,788	(1,135)

Source: Alison Chikova, 'Energy trading in the Southern African Power Pool', 2009, www.sapp.co.zw

Westcor aimed to generate 5,000 MW of electricity among the national utilities of five SADC states: Angola, Botswana, the DRC, Namibia and South Africa. Inga III, the site that was earmarked for a hydroelectric plant along the Congo river and Inga Falls and targeted to explore renewable energy options in the region, was abandoned by the Congolese government in the last quarter of 2010. Kinshasa also abandoned the Westcor project, since it argued that the project would have benefited the region more than itself.[32] It appears that southern Africa must still grapple with national projects taking priority over regional projects that have the potential to promote regional economic development. Member states pushing national agendas also opposed to regional ones will inevitably negatively affect and hamper the regional economic development envisaged through SADC trade policies.

If southern Africa is serious about pooling its resources through a resource-led development strategy, using SDIs as a mechanism, SADC should take seriously the hegemonic position of South Africa, given the dominance of its parastatal power utility, Eskom, whose failure to secure a partnership with the DRC in the Westcor project played a large role in the Congo's abandonment of that initiative. The DRC has agreed to an entirely new memorandum of understanding and project to oversee the resources of its Grand Inga Dam, a project that is envisaged to require significantly more funding in order to generate the dam's hydroelectric potential of 100,000 MW. The lesson is clear: SADC member states do not want to be disadvantaged as a result of South Africa's regional hegemony. SAPP is generally seen as a vehicle to enhance power in the region and reduce or eradicate supply deficits that negatively affect trade, as well as to increase economic development regionally.[33] SADC member states need to show deeper allegiance to the principles of the 1996 SADC Protocol, which commits them to develop and use energy to support economic growth, eradicate poverty and improve the quality of life for the region's 257 million citizens.

Southern Africa's regional body should use every opportunity to balance economic discrepancies among its members through more robust policies, even though this would mean fewer benefits for the dominant power, South Africa. The most noticeable effect of the abandoned Westcor Inga III power project has been the dashed hopes of many energy-starved southern African citizens. The DRC government has instead brokered a deal with Australian aluminium-mining giant BHP Billiton (the biggest mining company globally) to generate power for the country's new aluminium smelter. A lucrative partnership was signed in 2010 between BHP Billiton and the DRC government to build a US$3.5 billion, 2,500-megawatt hydroelectric plant at the same location as the Westcor Inga III project, previously earmarked for the SADC initiative. The remaining hydroelectric power generated by BHP Billiton will be for the use of the DRC.[34] Significantly, the DRC should capitalize on SADC's support, and align its national economic policies to benefit the region, lest it appear to have joined SADC in 1997 only because it foresaw a need to use SADC's military muscle against Rwanda and Uganda and prevent Laurent Kabila's ouster from government.

SADC free trade area

The central idea behind the creation of a SADC free trade area (FTA) in August 2008 was to attempt to ensure maximum regional industrial development and integration in southern Africa, and to derive economic benefits from these initiatives.[35] However, the FTA is not a means to an end and cannot benefit SADC's overall market economy without creation of the SADC Customs Union by 2010, the common market by 2015, and the monetary union by 2016.

That SADC members belong to more than one regional grouping (with the exception of Mozambique) poses many challenges. Member states belonging to different economic blocs are confronted with protocols when they try to negotiate agreements – implementation of these protocols is complicated and can delay trade-enhancing efforts.[36] Most SADC member states currently belong to more than two of several regional groupings: the Southern African Customs Union (SACU) – Botswana, Lesotho, Namibia, South Africa and Swaziland (see Gibb in this volume); the Economic Community of Central African States (ECCAS) – Angola and the DRC; the Indian Ocean Commission (IOC) – Mauritius; the East African Community (EAC) – Tanzania; the Common Market for Eastern and Southern Africa (COMESA) – Angola, the DRC, Madagascar, Malawi, Mauritius, Seychelles, Swaziland, Zambia and Zimbabwe.

Economic opportunity and development are important factors in why states join regional economic communities. Although SADC did not manage to attract to its FTA the membership of Angola, Seychelles and the DRC, which could increase its current intra-market trade population by 170 million, other areas of cooperation have been pursued.

In October 2008, SADC, COMESA and the EAC held a meeting in Kampala, Uganda, to discuss the possibility of forming a tripartite FTA. Such efforts by these three regional economic communities could ultimately alleviate many problems, such as unequally derived benefits due to competition between economically powerful SADC states like South Africa and economically vulnerable states like Lesotho. In August 2010 the SADC Summit, held in Windhoek, Namibia, spent two days discussing timelines for a free trade area and how to fast-track preparations for the creation of a SADC Customs Union, originally scheduled for completion by 2010.[37] Southern Africa's regional integration efforts have produced little real trade liberalization within SADC. Where strong trade links exist, they have generally been created by strong bilateral deals with South Africa, such as those agreed with Mozambique, Zambia and Zimbabwe in 2000.[38]

Also, South Africa's unilateral trade agreement with the EU – the Trade, Development and Cooperation Agreement (TDCA) of 1999 (see Qobo in this volume) – is still viewed negatively in the region.[39] The TDCA envisages a reduction in trade and tariff preferences for EU goods into South Africa's market, and is seen as a major threat to the region's development and the success envisaged for the FTA. Concerns have also been raised about the impact of the EU–South Africa free trade agreement by SACU's other members – Botswana, Lesotho, Namibia and Swaziland (BLNS) – as well as by non-SACU SADC members. For example, Europe still pays its wheat farmers a production subsidy of US$103 per tonne, while SADC wheat farmers have no access to this kind of luxury; and Europe's beef-dumping in South Africa accounts for 70–80 per cent of highly subsidized canned meat, sold at 'a fourth of its market value' in Europe, making it cumbersome for southern Africa's beef producers to compete.[40]

From a global perspective, in 2001 rich countries' agricultural subsidies alone amounted to US$311 billion, exceeding sub-Saharan Africa's total national income of US$301 billion.[41] SADC's regional integration attempts will be hampered by heavily subsidized European farmers, who have an unfair competitive advantage over SADC farmers. The EU's US$50 billion yearly Common Agricultural Policy also negatively hampers Africa's development prospects overall, given that around 70 per cent of Africa's population work in the agricultural sector.[42]

For the FTA to prosper in the SADC region, efforts by all its members are critical. South Africa's lopsided trading patterns can only move the posts farther from the goal. In 2004, South Africa's total exports and imports, respectively, stood as follows: with the EU, R20.5 billion and R26.8 billion; with East Asia, R10.9 billion and R12.1 billion; with North America, R7.0 billion and R6.2 billion; with the Middle East, R1.9 billion and R2.4 billion; and finally, with all of Africa, R7.0 billion and R2.4 billion.[43]

Intra-regional trade has also increased, with southern Africa increasingly becoming a major export partner for South Africa. In 2010, South Africa's export trade with its key partners stood as follows: EU, R13 billion; Asia, R19.5 billion; China, R7.3 billion; and all of SADC, just under R6 billion.[44]

These glaring discrepancies seen in the import and export trade patterns of the region's hegemon, South Africa, should be a major concern. With a gross domestic product (GDP) of US$213 billion in 2010, South Africa accounts for 85 per cent of foreign direct investment and 70 per cent of all multinational corporations (MNCs) within SADC. South Africa's high level of trade interaction in the region does not benefit other SADC member states. Therefore, the organization must address strengthening its current FTA first. The 'imperialist' mercantilist behaviour and influx of some of South Africa's oligopolistic MNCs into the region, such as MTN, Vodacom and Shoprite Checkers, has caused resentment among other SADC member states.[45]

SADC's approach in the formulation of the FTA is geared towards ultimately attracting foreign investment and further interest in the region, but efforts must first focus on strengthening the region. Though there has been an increase in exports from South Africa to the southern Africa region, more needs to be done for significant impact to be felt in the region. Exports from South Africa to Mozambique, which is South Africa's largest trading partner in the region after Angola, increased from R899.5 million in 1992 to R6.419 billion in 2002, resulting in an exceptional regional spillover that increased Mozambique's investment growth from R47 million to R403 million over the same period.[46] In 2007, Angola was South Africa's second-largest trading partner with bilateral trade at $14.3 billion.[47] South Africa's regional exports and imports will have a profound impact on southern Africa's integration efforts. Given the lopsidedness of South Africa's economy and the rest of southern Africa, it is doubtful whether initiatives such as the FTA will make a significant difference in the region's overall economic stability unless properly designed to reduce these inequalities.

Southern Africa's FTA aims to eliminate barriers to trade in goods and services for its twelve members, establish a common external tariff, and to then redistribute tariff revenue among its members. It is hoped that these principles of engagement will ultimately promote spillover effects for the region. The comparative advantage that trade in agricultural goods has among such SADC members as Madagascar, Malawi, Mozambique and Tanzania is positive and should be built upon through rigorous policy reform for the region.[48] As earlier outlined, the current TDCA will result in a negative impact on trade in the region, and will weigh heavily on already weak economies.

It is unlikely that the FTA will reduce the economic imbalance between SADC's members and South Africa, and these efforts will thus not strengthen the region substantively.[49] The current and disproportionate share of tariff revenues in place for smaller states that are dependent on South Africa, Lesotho, Botswana, Swaziland and Namibia within SACU may also not be enough. Since the inception of SADC in 1992, regional integration has not accelerated significantly. With South Africa accounting for more than 70 per cent of SADC's GDP of $471 billion[50] and with the tight noose around the necks of SADC's BLNS states requiring them to establish a common negotiating mechanism according to Article 31 of the 2002 SACU Agreement, BLNS economies are finding it difficult to prioritize SACU over perceived national interests.[51] It is no wonder, then, that the BLNS states ignored their Article 31 obligations and signed interim economic partnership agreements (IEPAs) with Brussels in order to protect their access to the vital European market. (For contrasting arguments, see Gibb as well as Qobo in this volume.)

A two-pronged approach has been advocated by Harry Stephan: 'to first minimize South Africa's trade within SADC, and to maximize trade of SADC's members with the region's hegemon; and second, for the desired increase in trade envisaged, to put in place support of government industries, increased flow of FDI [foreign direct investment] and inter-governmental cooperation on major developmental projects seen in SDI projects'.[52] It is critical that South Africa revisit its foreign policy, and align itself with more progressive strategies and approaches in order to direct its skewed trade in favour of the southern African region. South Africa can assist in redefining a more nuanced model that is disproportionately in favour of weaker SADC member economies in order to leverage the economic gap between itself and its neighbours.

Also hampering regional trade efforts is the excessive overlapping membership that could undermine the FTA process. Removal of trade barriers envisaged in the FTA, viewed as essential to creating an enabling environment for economic integration, may not be effective. More refined trade agreements that incorporate non-reciprocity could possibly be adopted, to allow weak economies such as Lesotho and Swaziland preferential access to the South African market for sensitive goods. As SADC forms its tripartite alliances with COMESA and the EAC, more emphasis should be placed on strengthening SADC's FTA.[53] The SADC–EAC–COMESA tripartite agreement, whose membership comprises more than half of Africa's states, aims to establish a single FTA by 2012. Already in place is the 2009 Zambia and Zimbabwe 'one-stop border post', with a second one between Tanzania and Kenya under way.[54]

The 2000 SADC Trade Protocol provides a framework for free trade negotiations and tariff reduction obligations. In 2008, 85 per cent of goods were traded duty free, with 99 per cent duty-free trade envisaged within southern Africa by 2012.[55] Despite SADC's liberal trade policy framework which attempts to open its markets and promote trade creation rather than trade diversion, intra-SADC trade is still limited. Adopting more liberal trade policies nationally does not automatically mean easy access to markets regionally, nor would liberal policies lean more in favour of regional trade. Viable economic regional integration efforts can succeed only if SADC capitalizes more robustly on its comparative advantage and conducts trade in commodities such as textiles, clothing and sugar.

In April 2011 South Africa was also admitted into the BRIC (Brazil, Russia, India and China) forum – the fastest-growing economies globally. Together, the BRIC countries account for 40 per cent of the global population, 16 per cent of global economic output, and 50 per cent of global growth.[56] This is not necessarily a bad thing for southern Africa, since it can strengthen the SADC region and assist South Africa in addressing its R25 billion trade deficit with China.[57] It is highly unlikely that South Africa's Jacob Zuma administration will forgo its 'golden handshake' deal undertaken with the BRIC countries and sign up to a most-favoured-nation clause with Brussels. Whether South Africa would enter into such an agreement with Europe for the sake of its neighbours remains to be seen.

SADC's Regional Indicative Strategic Development Plan

Is the Regional Indicative Strategic Development Plan a viable instrument to promote southern Africa's political and economic sustainability?[58] In March 2001 at an Extraordinary Summit meeting in Windhoek, Namibia, SADC's institutions were restructured, and the RISDP was approved in 2003 in order to complement the restructuring and to provide direction for SADC policies and programmes. The RISDP is the blueprint for SADC's regional development strategy and outlines key interventions necessary to deepen integration and to reduce poverty. The formulation and preparatory stages of the RISDP took into account the protocols and plans of the New Partnership for Africa's Development (NEPAD), the African Union (AU) established in 2002, the World Trade Organization (WTO) created in 1995, the EU/African, Caribbean and Pacific (ACP) Cotonou Agreement of 2000, and the Millennium Summit Declaration of 2000. The RISDP emphasizes the critical importance of good political, economic and corporate governance as a prerequisite for socio-economic development and sustainability in southern Africa.

The RISDP, as revised in 2006, sets out a fifteen-year framework for implementing social and economic policies, and embodies SADC's overall implementation and developmental agenda. The Plan's implementation framework in its current form relies heavily on the ideals of NEPAD,[59] which has put forward a five-sector plan, with economic and corporate governance initiatives constituting one of these sectors. The economic dimensions of NEPAD have been controversial, akin to South Africa's macroeconomic Growth, Employment and Redistribution Policy (GEAR), which replaced the RDP in 1996.[60] It has been strongly argued that NEPAD's neoliberal policies are not benefiting ordinary people and should be reshaped into a developmental model that benefits the region.[61] With NEPAD still trying to find its feet, the RISDP should be careful not to place all its eggs in one basket. It is also perceived that the regional plan is not aligning its operational framework to NEPAD's principles, values, objectives and priorities.[62] Because the RISDP is southern Africa's economic and political guiding framework, it will have to revisit its current economic and political strategies, as well as correct any anomalies that still exist, for the benefit of regional integration.

The RISDP has prioritized a long-term development strategy to target political stability, which will inevitably lead to economic growth and development within the region. High on SADC's agenda should be the stability in the DRC, a member of SADC since 1997, and the impact that this could have on the region. Continued growth is believed to be dependent largely on a stable political environment. Should the DRC become more politically stable, the SADC region could envisage a much higher growth rate benefiting from the rich mineral wealth of the country, such as diamonds, gold, coltan, copper, coal and the Grand Inga Dam. SADC is encouraged to play a more active role in the DRC and remain closely tied to its developments, work more closely with the AU's policy on Post-Conflict Reconstruction and Development (PCRD), build good governance institutions, and encourage effective management and utilization of the Congo's resources.

External actors are still often seen as 'scrambling' for southern Africa's resources: Congo's wealth, Angola's oil and diamonds, Zambia's copper and Botswana's diamonds.[63] SADC must devise clear plans about how to benefit from such external interest. China's multibillion-dollar agreement with DRC president Joseph Kabila involves US$9 billion for direct access to the DRC's mineral wealth in exchange for infrastructure projects – building of railways, roads, hospitals and healthcare centres, and two hydroelectric projects.[64]

SADC has an overall intra-community trade of 24 per cent, with the remaining trade percentage being outside the region. Of the organization's fifteen member states, six have a comparative advantage in oil and mineral resources. Only two – South Africa and Mauritius – play a significant role in industry and could use this advantage positively from the core to the periphery for the benefit of regional integration. The RISDP's framework – as described in its 'main economic characteristics and current economic developments' section[65] – identifies member states' strengths and weaknesses, but does not provide them with a viable implementation tool to address, for instance, how members with large manufacturing sectors, such as South Africa and Mauritius, can use their comparative advantage; nor does it define how smaller economies manufacturing the same goods can diversify their interests to further economic integration in southern Africa.

Conclusion

SADC should use its comparative advantage to bolster the economic development of southern Africa through a more robust RISDP framework. Southern Africa should take into account the hegemonic position of South Africa, which accounts for over 70 per cent of the regional economy. SADC's regional economic development policy instruments – with their main focus being to reverse the economic discrepancies evident in the varying stages of development of SADC members – have the potential to substantially improve economic integration in the SADC region. The regional body must use its power pool and free trade area more effectively to deepen regional integration in southern Africa.

It is important to redefine how regional integration is able to address southern Africa's 'economic curse', given the huge economic disparities evident between SADC members and the region's hegemon, South Africa. Hence, strides towards a more robust policy for southern Africa's economic growth must be further explored. South Africa's role in SADC versus its domestic situation, evident in its current struggles to narrow the gap between rich and poor South Africans, with 5 per cent of its population still owning 88 per cent of its entire wealth while four large corporations control 81 per cent of share capital,[66] should not give rise to the overbearing role played by its MNCs in the region and elsewhere in Africa.

More emphasis must also be placed on SADC members' different stages of economic development in order to boost poor economies. Furthermore, coherent policies need to be adopted that allow vulnerable economies to benefit more from South Africa-led institutions such as the Development Bank of Southern Africa (DBSA) and the Industrial Development Corporation (IDC). (See Monyae in this volume.) Initiatives like the South Africa/Maputo trade corridor and others such as Beira and Zambezi, Limpopo, Mtwara, Nacala, Tazara and Lobito development corridors, as well as the Lubombo and the Okavango Zambezi international tourism SDIs, must be actively pursued. SADC can become more effective in pooling the region's resources through increasing regional electricity supply and accessing the DRC's wealth, as well as by exploiting the mineral wealth of Angola, Botswana, Zambia and other member states to ensure more effective regional integration in southern Africa.

Notes

1 See Immanuel Wallerstein, 'Regional unity and African unity', in Wallerstein, *Africa: The Politics of Independence and Unity* (Lincoln: University of Nebraska Press, 2005). See also Guy Martin, 'African regional cooperation and integration', in Martin, *African World Politics: A Pan-African Perspective* (Trenton, NJ: Africa World, 2002).

2 John Pinder and Simon Usherwood, *The European Union: A Very Short Introduction* (Oxford: Oxford University Press, 2007). See also Anne Deighton, 'The remaking of Europe', in Michael Howard and William Roger Louis (eds), *The Oxford History of the Twentieth Century* (Oxford: Oxford University Press, 1998); Chris Hill and Michael Smith, *International Relations and the European Union* (Oxford: Oxford University Press, 2005); Anand Menon, *Europe: The State of the Union* (London: Atlantic, 2008).

3 Pinder and Usherwood, *The European Union.* See also Michael Efler, Gerald Häfner, Roman Huber and Percy Vogel, *Europe: 'Not without the People!'* (Hamburg: VSA, 2009).

4 Adebayo Adedeji, 'Comparative

strategies of economic decolonization in Africa', in Ali A. Mazrui and C. Wondji (eds), *General History of Africa*, vol. VIII: *Africa Since 1935* (Oxford: James Currey, 1999).

5 Harry Stephan, Michael Power, Angus Fane Hervey and Raymond Steenkamp Fonseca, 'Regional theory and southern African regional solutions', in Stephan et al., *The Scramble for Africa in the 21st Century: A View from the South* (Cape Town: Renaissance, 2006). See also Adebayo Adedeji, 'Within or Apart?', in Adedeji (ed.), *South Africa and Africa: Within or Apart?* (London: Zed Books, 1996); John Ravenhill, 'The future of regionalism in Africa', in Ralph I. Onwuka and Amadu Sesay, *The Future of Regionalism in Africa* (London: Macmillan, 1985).

6 David Simon, 'Shedding the past, shaping the future', in Simon (ed.), *South Africa in Southern Africa: Reconfiguring the Region* (Oxford: James Currey, 1998). See also Abillah H. Omari and Paulino Macaringue, 'Southern African security in historical perspective', in Gavin Cawthra, Andre du Pisani and Abillah Omari, *Security and Democracy in Southern Africa*

(Johannesburg: Wits University Press, 2007).

7 See Stephan et al., 'Regional theory', p. 290.

8 Stephan et al., *The Scramble for Africa*, pp. 308–12.

9 *Southern African Development Community (SADC) Today*, 10(2), August 2007.

10 See Southern African Power Pool website, www.dme.gov.za/energy/electricity.stm#5.

11 Tore Horvei, 'Powering the region: South Africa in the Southern Africa Power Pool', in Simon, *South Africa in Southern Africa*.

12 Ibid.

13 Ibid. See also 'SADC Infrastructure Development Status Report for Council and Summit', September 2009, www.sadc.int/cms/uploads/K-7543%20RTFP%20SADC%20Infrastructure%20brochure_English_V11_LR.pdf.

14 Horvei, 'Powering the region'.

15 Ibid., p. 149.

16 South African Institute of Race Relations 2009/10, 'South Africa survey report', Johannesburg, p. 64. See also Thabo Mbeki, Speech at the Second Joint Sitting of the Third Democratic Parliament, Cape Town, 11 February 2005, www.info.gov.za/speeches/2005/05021110501001.htm.

17 Horvei, 'Powering the region', p. 159.

18 See Southern African Power Pool website, www.dme.gov.za/energy/electricity.stm#5.

19 *SADC Today*, 10(2).

20 'SADC Infrastructure Development Status Report', pp. 24–5.

21 Ibid., pp. 24–5.

22 Horvei, 'Powering the region', p. 148.

23 South African Institute of Race Relations, 'South Africa survey report', p. 9.

24 See, for example, 'Fukushima radiation from Japan's stricken plant detected across UK', *Guardian*, 29 March 2011, www.guardian.co.uk/uk/2011/mar/29/fukushima-raditation-found-across-uk.

25 See Eskom, 'Reuel Khoza on Eskom's new focus and outward looking policies', Chairperson's report, in Stephan et al., *The Scramble for Africa*, p. 315.

26 Alison Chikova, 'Energy trading in the Southern African Power Pool', 2009, www.sapp.co.zw.

27 Lynley Donnelly, 'Eskom's early xmas gift', *Mail and Guardian*, 29 October 2010, p. 11.

28 Agnieszka Flak, 'South Africa says coal for power a priority', Reuters, 2 February 2011, www.reuters.com/article/2011/02/02/mining-safrica-idUSLDE7110IC20110202.

29 'BHP seeks Congo power project to replace Westcor', Reuters, 26 February 2010, www.reuters.com/article/2010/02/26/congo-democratic-ingax-idUSLDE61O2QK20100226.

30 Ibid.

31 See also Lawrence Musaba's report on the SAPP, 'South Africa country seminar on cross border trading and SAPP day ahead market', 2010, www.sapp.co.zw.

32 'SADC Infrastructure Development Status Report', p. 30.

33 Ibid., pp. 20–4.

34 See International Rivers, People, Water, Life, 'African dams briefing', Report (Berkeley, CA: International Rivers Africa Program, 2010), p. 19.

35 See SADC website, www.sadc.int/fta. See also Jacob Nyambe and Klaus Schade, 'Progress towards the SADC free trade area: the challenges', in Jonathan Mayuyuka Kaunda and Farai Zizhou, *Furthering Southern African Integration: Proceedings of the 2008 FOPRISA Annual Conference* (Gaborone: Botswana Institute for Development Policy Analysis and Lightbooks, 2009), pp. 33–51.

36 Kaunda and Zizhou, *Furthering Southern African Integration*, pp. 33–4.

37 'SADC pushes free trade, Customs Union', 18 August 2010, www.southafrica.info/africa/sadc-180810.htm.

38 See Margaret Lee, *The Political Economy of Regionalism in Southern Africa* (Lansdowne, South Africa: University of Cape Town Press, 2003), pp. 114–35.

39 See ibid., p. 212.

40 See ibid., p. 218.

41 Joseph Stiglitz, *Globalisation and Its Discontents* (London: Penguin, 2006), p. 76. See also Adekeye Adebajo, 'Chronicle of a death foretold: the rise and fall of UN reform: ending global apartheid: sustainable development, aid, and trade', in Adekeye Adebajo and Helen Scanlon (eds), *A Dialogue of the Deaf: Essays on Africa and the United Nations* (Auckland Park, Johannesburg: Jacana, 2006).

42 Centre for Conflict Resolution (CCR), 'Eurafrique? Africa and Europe in a new century', Seminar report, 31 October/1 November 2007.

43 South African Department of Trade and Industry (DTI), 'A South African trade policy and strategy framework', May 2010, pp. 69–71, www.dti.gov.za/TPSF.pdf.

44 See ibid., pp. 64–82. See also www.saexpo2010.com/english/iframe/trade.htm; http://www.thedti.gov.za/econdb/raportt/rapcont.html; and www.thedti.gov.za/econdb/raportt/rapregi.html.

45 Judi Hudson, 'Economic expansion into Africa', in Adekeye Adebajo, Adebayo Adedeji and Chris Landsberg (eds), *South Africa in Africa: The Post-Apartheid Era* (Scottsville: University of KwaZulu-Natal Press, 2007).

46 Ibid.

47 Adekeye Adebajo, *The Curse of Berlin: Africa After the Cold War* (Scottsville: University of KwaZulu-Natal Press, 2010), p. 197.

48 Arne Wiig and Tebogo B. Seleka, 'Will intra-regional trade liberalisation within SADC reduce poverty? The case of Malawi', in Gavin Cawthra and Jonathan Mayuyuka Kaunda, *Towards Political and Economic Integration in Southern Africa: Prospects of the 2007 FOPRISA (the Formative Process Research on Integration in Southern Africa) Annual Conference* (Gaborone: Lightbooks, 2008).

49 Elias Links, 'The European Union and southern Africa: between Lomé and a free trade agreement', in Greg Mills, *Southern Africa into the Next Millennium* (Johannesburg: South African Institute of International Affairs, SAIIA, 1998).

50 SADC, 'Investment Promotion Strat-egy to Promote Sustainable Investment into the SADC Region During the 2010 CAF Africa Cup of nations [10–31 January 2010] and the 2010 FIFA World Cup [11 June–11 July 2010]', Strategy document, pp. 1–33, www.sadc.int/cms/SADC%20 2010%20strategy(2).pdf.

51 Brendan Vickers, 'SADC's international trade relations', in Charles Harvey (ed.), *Proceedings of the 2009 FOPRISA Annual Conference* (Gaborone: Botswana Institute for Development Policy Analysis, 2010), p. 146.

52 See Harry Stephan , 'Open regionalism in southern Africa', in Stephan et al., *The Scramble for Africa.*

53 Xavier Carim, 'Keynote address from the Sixth Southern African Forum on Trade', *From Cape to Cairo: Exploring the COMESA-EAC-SADC Tripartite FTA*, 3/4 August 2009.

54 James Mwapachu (secretary-general of COMESA–SADC–EAC Tripartite), 'Southern Africa: region moves to set up free trade area', *All Africa*, 25 January 2011.

55 Ibid.

56 'Why China invited SA to join BRIC', *Independent Online*, January 2011, www.iol.co.za/business/business-news.

57 See ibid.

58 See SADC, 'Regional Indicative Strategic Development Plan (RISDP)', 2003, www.sadc.int/index.php.

59 See ibid.

60 See the discussion on NEPAD in Christopher Landsberg, *The Quiet Diplomacy of Liberation: International Politics and South Africa's Transition* (Johannesburg: Jacana, 2004), pp. 196–8. See also Christopher Landsberg, 'The making of the AU and NEPAD', in Adebajo et al., *South Africa in Africa.* See also Sheila Bunwaree, 'NEPAD and its discontents', in John Akokpari, Angela Ndinga-Muvumba and Tim Murithi (eds), *The African Union and Its Institutions* (Johannesburg: Jacana, 2008).

61 See the discussion on NEPAD in Landsberg, *The Quiet Diplomacy of Liberation*, pp. 196–8.

62 See John Rocha, 'The implementation of NEPAD in the SADC region', *Pax-*

Africa: African Peace and Security Agenda, 5(1), March 2009.

63 David Mwaniki, 'Supporting the peace in the DRC', *Pax-Africa: African Peace and Security Agenda*, 5(1), March 2009.

64 Ibid.

65 See SADC, 'Regional Indicative Strategic Development Plan', chs 1–2, 'Political and socio-economic situation in SADC' and 'Political situation'.

66 Adedeji (ed.), *South Africa and Africa: Within or Apart?*

8 | The Southern African Customs Union: promoting stability through dependence?

Richard Gibb

The Southern African Customs Union (SACU), established in 1910, is a remarkable regional institution. It is the most effectively functioning example of customs-led integration in Africa and the oldest customs union in the world, pre-dating the European Union (EU) by almost fifty years.[1] SACU has five member states: Botswana, Lesotho, Namibia, South Africa and Swaziland (see Map 8.1). The SACU Agreement has twice been renegotiated, in 1969 and 2002, following the end of colonialism and apartheid respectively. However, the 2002 SACU Agreement is under considerable pressure from South Africa, which wants to restructure several strategic elements underpinning the arrangement,[2] including the institutional infrastructure, associated decision-making mechanisms, and the all-important revenue distribution formula.[3]

Somewhat paradoxically, given that SACU has its origins in the fundamentally unstable colonial and apartheid regimes that governed and dominated southern Africa until 1994, it has nevertheless been instrumental in the promotion of economic development and stability among its member states. For most of its existence, SACU has been a profoundly undemocratic institution, structurally challenged by the existence of significant absolute and relative inequalities in levels of development among its member states. One hundred years old in 2010, SACU is an institution that has survived against the odds. This chapter examines the contemporary nature of SACU and its role in promoting economic and political stability, development and integration in southern Africa.

The geopolitical imperative

Regional integration in southern Africa is a critical component in securing sustained and sustainable geo-economic and political stability throughout the region. Geographically, the economic and political appeal of regionalism in sub-Saharan Africa is almost intuitive. Southern Africa's key regional economic community (REC), the Southern African Development Community (SADC), which was established in 1992, comprises fifteen countries and represents a small and peripheral component of the world economy, with a combined estimated gross domestic product (GDP) of $471 billion (about the size of Belgium's GDP of $444 billion) and a population of 257 million people in 2010. The individual countries of southern Africa, including South Africa, are

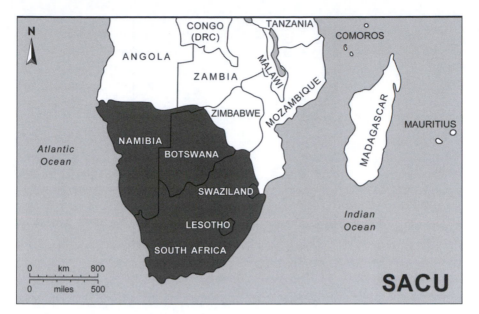

Map 8.1 SACU member states

marginal players in global trade and the world economy. The whole of Africa accounts for approximately 2 per cent of global merchandise exports and 3 per cent of global imports, roughly equivalent to exports and imports of the Spanish economy, valued at $1.3 trillion in 2010.[4] The individual countries of southern Africa are mainly small and vulnerable. In the case of SACU, four of its five member states can justifiably be categorized as 'micro-states', with South Africa, of course, being the exception. Notwithstanding the large surface area of Botswana and Namibia, as Map 8.1 illustrates, these countries have small populations, small markets and vulnerable economies (often mono-economies). Regional integration is widely perceived to be a powerful instrument to combat the feeding of core economies on peripheral ones, through the promotion of economic development and stability.

Throughout Africa, and southern Africa in particular, extreme geographical fragmentation, combined with the problems of economic and political survival, has encouraged the formation of a large number of interstate organizations and regional economic communities. There are a bewildering number of overlapping regional institutions in southern Africa (see Figure 8.1). These institutions overlap spatially, with many countries belonging to several institutions simultaneously, and overlap structurally, with shared objectives that are incompatible and insufficient for the creation of customs unions and, ultimately, economic and political unions.

Theoretically, states that are joined together are better placed to exploit larger-scale economies while simultaneously being able to restructure regional

TABLE 8.1 SACU economic indicators, 2007/08

	Population (million)/ SACU %	GDP at market price/ SACU (%)	Real GDP growth rate (%)	GDP per capita (US$)	Public expenditure and net lending	Budget balance to GDP ratio (%)	Debt to GDP ratio (%)	Annual inflation rate (%)	Prime interest rate (%)	Current account to GDP ratio (%)
Botswana	1.7 (3.0)	92.3 (4.2)	3.3	6,000.0	28.6	3.1	5.6	12.6	16.5	11.0
Lesotho	1.9 (3.4)	11.8 (0.5)	5.1	663.5	5.3	10.7	45.6	10.7	16.6	15.6
Namibia	2.0 (3.6)	62.7 (2.9)	4.1	4,130.0	17.7	4.7	18.7	10.3	14.8	9.2
South Africa	48.5 (88.0)	1,999.1 (91.5)	5.1	5,701.0	606.7	1.7	34.4	11.5	15.0	−7.3
Swaziland	1.1 (2.0)	19.4 (0.9)	3.5	2,777.6	6.2	3.2	18.8	12.9	14.5	−1.4

Source: SACU, 2010

Country	COMESA	COMESA FTA	ESA-EPA Config.	SADC	SADC's EPA Config.	SACU	Common Monetary Area	EAC	WTO
Angola	■			■	■				■
Botswana				■		■	■		■
Burundi	■	■	■					■	■
DR Congo	■		■	■					■
Comoros	■		■						
Djibouti	■	■	■						■
Egypt	■	■							■
Eritrea	■	■	■						
Ethiopia	■		■						
Kenya	■	■	■					■	■
Libya	■								
Lesotho				■	■	■	■		■
Madagascar	■	■	■	■					■
Malawi	■	■	■	■					■
Mauritius	■	■	■	■					■
Mozambique				■	■				■
Namibia				■	■	■	■		■
Réunion									
Rwanda	■	■	■					■	■
Seychelles	■		■						
Somalia									
South Africa				■	Observer Status	■			■
Sudan	■	■	■						
Swaziland	■	■	■	■	■	■			■
Tanzania				■				■	■
Uganda	■	■	■					■	■
Zambia	■		■	■					■
Zimbabwe	■	■	■	■	■				■

Figure 8.1 Regional institutions in southern Africa

economies in ways that benefit regional production bases. Regional integration can also be seen as a way to promote stability by reducing the exploitative dependency relationships arising from limited and unspecialized internal markets. This economic rationale explains why the creation of trading blocs has been, and continues to be, at the very centre of intra-African cooperation. Hence, regionalism is seen as a mechanism to integrate smaller markets by creating larger ones that are more successful within the global economy. In 2000, Prega Ramsamy of Mauritius, then SADC Executive Secretary, argued for greater regional integration on the grounds that the 'individual economies of most member states are not internationally viable and competitive, as they are not in a position to enjoy the required economies of scale and to effectively deal with constraints to international competitiveness'.[5]

Furthermore, regional integration has an important role to play in facilitating peace, security and stability. The classical liberal argument is that greater economic interdependence reduces conflict and enhances security. The mutually reinforcing relationship between regional economic integration and peace and security is, as observed by Phillipe De Lombaerde, 'an assumption behind many contemporary discourses in favour of more cooperation and integration'.[6] Much of the literature focuses on the potential to create a positive feedback mechanism fuelled by regional integration promoting trade, which in turn promotes the economic development necessary for greater human security, which in turn promotes greater integration. In peace and security terms, this argument focuses on the critical importance of human security, including economic and food security, underpinning 'traditional realist' security. Furthermore, in a regional context, by providing an institutional rules-based framework for trade, integration and interstate regional governance, regional integration has the potential to promote a more robust interstate security framework. While this is not the place for a Eurocentric analysis of regional integration, it is worth noting that regional stability, peace and the regulation of interstate economic and political governance were the foundations upon which the EU was built. While the relevance of the European experience has been widely questioned in Africa, as it depends on regional integration stimulating intra-regional trade and economic interdependence, SACU has indeed been successful in promoting high levels of intra-regional trade and interdependence.[7]

Regionalism is all-encompassing and should be viewed in terms of both security and politics, as much as economics and trade. In reality, regionalism has always been as much political as economic, in Africa as much as elsewhere. In other words, economics and trade should not be viewed as the sole and primary driver of regional integration. Instead of promoting trade that creates security, perhaps regional integration in southern Africa could be better focused on promoting peace and security and, in so doing, help create conditions suitable for trade. In a review of African integration, Christopher Clapham argues that 'where regional economic organisations did have any significant impact on regional relationships, this was much more likely to be in the field of security than that of economic development'.[8]

SACU trade and inequality

From a regional perspective, the principal hurdles facing regional integration in southern Africa, and SACU in particular, arise from the considerable and absolute inequalities between South Africa and its SACU partners in terms of development levels, populations and economies. Issues of inequality and imbalance transcend the colonial era of the 1960s and remain alive today in the post-apartheid period since the mid-1990s. Inequality among SACU member states is deep rooted, consistent and persistent.[9] It could be argued that, with South Africa's reintegration into southern Africa following the demise of apartheid in 1994, the issue of inequality has become even more pronounced and South Africa's economic dominance of the region has become more entrenched.

The patterns and extent of inequality in SACU member states have been well documented elsewhere.[10] A few key figures serve to illustrate the severity of this imbalance. Intra-SACU trade is characterized by the dominant position of South Africa within the BLNS grouping (Botswana, Lesotho, Namibia and Swaziland) in trade, especially imports. South Africa dominates completely the import markets of the BLNS states, enjoying more than 75 per cent of the market in each country and over 90 per cent in Swaziland and Lesotho.[11] However, given its size and diversification in terms of export destinations and import sources, South Africa's trade with its SACU partners is a relatively minor component of the South African economy. SACU imports stand at approximately 2 per cent of South Africa's total imports. There is a marked asymmetrical imbalance of trade, leaving South Africa with a multibillion-dollar regional trading surplus. Furthermore, these quantitative descriptors reveal only part of a much more complicated dynamic of dominance. South Africa is more developed in financial services, transport infrastructure, manufacturing, agriculture, and technological research. These dynamics place South Africa in a much more dominant position in the SACU political economy, and this dominance will continue for the foreseeable future.

Therefore, an important question in determining the nature, evolution and success of SACU is how best to manage South Africa's economic and political dominance. Two sets of data serve to illustrate the extent of this dominance: GDP and population size. In 2007/08, over 91 per cent of SACU's GDP was produced in South Africa (see Table 8.1), with the other four member states collectively representing less than 9 per cent. Lesotho's economy, the smallest among SACU states, represented only 0.5 per cent of SACU's GDP. Approximately 88 per cent of SACU's combined population was South African. The next most populous country was Namibia, with 3.6 per cent of SACU's total population.

Such large strategic and structural inequalities create a number of serious obstacles that regional institutions need to address. Most important, they raise the question of how best to integrate a semi-developed country like South Africa with small vulnerable economies (SVEs) like Botswana, Lesotho, Namibia and Swaziland.[12] Traditional customs union theory supports the idea that states have to be at broadly comparable levels of development for integration to succeed.[13] Otherwise, polarized economic development is likely to occur that will favour the developed state at the direct expense of the underdeveloped state. SACU's future success in promoting regional integration and stability is, in large part, dependent on how it manages this inequality.

Redistribution?

In a regional institution like SACU, characterized by such intense inequalities, economic integration based on the principles of a free market will promote a tendency towards agglomeration. In other words, growth and development will focus on South Africa's economic core at the expense of the periphery of the BLNS. This raises the controversial question of how best to reduce, or to compensate for, the trend towards industrial and economic polarization. In order for a regional institution like SACU to secure the allegiance of all member states, there must be an explicit and tangible gain achieved from membership. Part of the political and economic success associated with SACU is a product of its longevity, which has been dependent on the smaller SACU economies gaining financially from membership.[14]

From 1969 to 2004 the SACU Agreement contained a powerful and positive redistributive mechanism aimed at compensating the BLNS states for being in a customs union dominated, economically and politically, by South Africa. The 1969 SACU Agreement contained a revenue-sharing formula (RSF) designed to apportion the monies collected through the common revenue pool (CRP). Revenue from the pool was distributed according to a complex formula.[15]

The revenue-sharing formula resulted in the following:

1 The share of total CRP monies paid to the BLNS states was calculated based on the level of their own imports, customs duties, excise, import surcharges and sales duties as a percentage of the customs union as a whole.
2 This sum was then augmented by a 'compensation rate' of 42 per cent in order to offset the disadvantages of smaller countries belonging to a customs union dominated by a more developed industrial economy.
3 In 1976, probably as a result of the Soweto uprising and associated political crisis, the formula was amended to provide a 'stabilization factor' that ensured that the BLNS states received at least 17 per cent of the total value of all imports and other duties paid.[16]

After 1976 the stabilization factor was the binding element within the formula and increased the effective rate of compensation paid to the BLNS to 77 per cent.[17] The BLNS states therefore derived substantial and significant benefits from the 1969 SACU Agreement. The most important benefit for the BLNS states was the very significant contribution to state revenue provided by the CRP, which in 2004 stood at between 35 and 55 per cent.

The 2002 SACU Agreement introduced a new, and significantly modified, revenue distribution formula (RDF) designed to limit payments to the actual size of the CRP (as opposed to the total value of all imports and other duties paid). However, the RDF has consistently been the most contentious and divisive policy among SACU member states. More precisely, it divides sharply the interests of South Africa, which focuses on tariff and trade policy in terms of economic growth and development, from the interests of BLNS states, which focus (although far from homogeneously) more on the fiscal implications of revenue generated through the CRP.

Under the 2002 SACU Agreement, the total CRP is disaggregated and distributed into three basic components, each with a different set of distribution criteria:

1 *Customs* (based on intra-SACU trade). The customs component consists of all duties and surcharges collected by SACU's common external tariff (CET). However, although this income is derived from imports into SACU, the determining criterion for distribution is intra-SACU imports. As a result, the distribution of the customs component has no relation to contributions made to the CRP. This component therefore represents the most distortionary element of the RDF. In short, this formula discriminates positively in favour of the BLNS states, whose trade profiles, especially imports, are heavily distorted in favour of intra-SACU trade.

2 *Excise.* The excise component consists of all excise duties outside the 15 per cent that are directed towards a development fund. Thus, 85 per cent of excise is distributed in relation to each member state's share of SACU's GDP. South Africa therefore attracts the largest share of the excise component.

3 *Development.* The development component consists of the 15 per cent share of the excise component (described above), which is allocated to member states according to the inverse of each country's GDP per capita. The poorest states therefore receive a disproportionately larger share of the development fund.

Overall, BLNS states have received a significant proportion of total government revenue from the development component and there has been a considerable amount of fiscal redistribution from South Africa to BLNS states. Importantly, the RDF has resulted in South Africa receiving approximately 90 per cent of the SACU revenue from the excise component, whereas the BLNS states have received almost 80 per cent of their income from the customs component.[18] Hence, BLNS states have a dependence, indeed overdependence, on the revenue generated through tariffs. South Africa, on the other hand, regards the income generated via tariffs to be a secondary consideration to industrial and economic policy.

South Africa, which essentially drove the negotiations that led to the 2002 RDF formula, had a flawed assumption underpinning its negotiating strategy. Tshwane (Pretoria) felt that the income generated through the CET would reduce sharply as a result of multilateral trade liberalization and bilateral free trade agreements, such as the Trade, Development and Cooperation Agreement (TDCA) with the EU.[19] The absolute size of the CRP has experienced considerable and sustained growth, driven by strong consumer-led consumption of imported goods from outside SACU. Table 8.2 lists the absolute and relative distributions of the CRP for the years 2005/06 to 2009/10, during which time the CRP more than doubled. This has resulted in a significant increase in the CRP payments to the BLNS states.

TABLE 8.2 SACU common revenue pool, 2005/06–2009/10: absolute revenue (R billions)/SACU %

	2005/06	2006/07	2007/08	2008/09	2009/10	Annual growth (%)
Botswana	4,007.55 (16.00)	5,549.24 (16.39)	8,329.58 (19.13)	9,472.80 (17.82)	9,166.67 (17.63)	−3.2 (−1.0)
Lesotho	1,983.98 (7.92)	2,784.02 (8.22)	3,822.29 (8.78)	4,901.10 (9.22)	4,918.21 (9.46)	0.3 (2.6)
Namibia	3,228.19 (12.89)	5,393.87 (15.93)	6,014.53 (13.81)	8,502.20 (16.00)	8,585.46 (16.52)	1.0 (3.2)
South Africa	13,027.10 (52.02)	16,477.91 (48.67)	20,795.90 (47.75)	24,264.40 (45.65)	24,124.59 (46.41)	−0.6 (1.7)
Swaziland	2,794.96 (11.16)	3,653.63 (10.79)	4,591.06 (10.54)	6,009.00 (11.31)	5,188.95 (9.98)	−13.6 (−11.7)
Total payment out of CRP	25,041.78	33,858.67	43,553.35	53,149.50	51,983.89	−2.2

Source: SACU, 2010

For example, although Lesotho's relative percentage share of the CRP has risen marginally from 7.9 to 9.4 per cent in the period 2005/06 to 2009/10, its absolute revenue has increased dramatically, from R1,983 to R4,918 billion, representing a 250 per cent increase over four years. For many BLNS states, SACU payments are seen as a critical source of income, underpinning and dominating government revenue and finance. In Lesotho, SACU payments accounted for over 60 per cent of government revenue in 2008.[20]

South Africa is now determined to renegotiate the distribution formula, and in June 2010 the Namibia-based SACU Secretariat issued a tender to conduct a study on an alternative formula to manage the CRP. This would represent a significant threat to SACU and in particular to the needs and interests of the BLNS states. The longevity of SACU has depended on an RDF formula that effectively guarantees BLNS support of the organization. Without an effective redistributive mechanism, the future of SACU could be challenged.

Democratization and decision-making

The end of apartheid in South Africa inevitably changed Pretoria's geopolitical priorities and provided an opportunity to renegotiate and restructure SACU. Post-apartheid South Africa prioritized 'democratization', both domestically and throughout southern Africa, and the 2002 SACU Agreement reflects this fundamental reorientation of foreign policy. Between 1910 and 1969, SACU agreements were profoundly undemocratic, enabling Pretoria to determine tariffs and excise rates unilaterally for the whole SACU region. For example, Article 4 of the 1969 SACU Agreement stipulates that 'the Government of South Africa shall give the other contracting parties adequate opportunities for consultation *before imposing, amending or abrogating* any customs duty with respect to goods imported into the common customs area from outside' (emphasis added).[21]

SACU tariff policy was therefore formulated and determined by South African institutions. In practice, the South African Board of Tariffs and Trade (BTT), which had no BLNS representation, made recommendations (over tariffs, not excise) to the South African minister of trade and industry. Although the 1969 SACU Agreement required South Africa to consult with the BLNS states, this rarely took place.[22] The BTT was an influential quasi-non-governmental organization, funded by the South African Department of Trade and Industry, whose recommendations had authority and were generally accepted. The minister had the power to accept or reject but not amend BTT proposals. In addition, SACU excise policy (as opposed to tariffs) was determined exclusively by South Africa. The South African minister of finance was obliged 'to consult the Governments of Botswana, Lesotho and Swaziland prior to the introduction of changes in the fiscal structure of South Africa'[23] (as with tariffs, the BLNS states had no statutory powers and very little influence over excise policy). SACU tariff and excise policy was thus unilaterally formulated and determined by South African institutions. This represented a major loss of sovereignty for the BLNS states, affecting several key policy areas, including industrial, fiscal and development.

On 21 October 2002, after eight years of negotiations, a new SACU agreement was signed and ratified by the five member states. It entered into force on 16 July 2004. Article 2 of the new agreement set out eight objectives for the new SACU, including a desire 'to create effective, transparent and democratic institutions that will ensure equitable trade benefits to Member States'.[24] Articles 7 to 17 of the new agreement provided for the establishment of six new SACU institutions: Council of Ministers, Customs Union Commission, Secretariat, Tariff Board, Technical Liaison Committees, and Tribunal (see Box 8.1). In addition, each member state could establish its own investigating 'National Body' to conduct tariff and trade remedy investigations (Article 14.1). For the first time in ninety-four years, SACU had a dedicated set of permanent institutions that were intergovernmental in nature and 'independent' of South African national institutions and ministries.

Several new institutions were established that operate through consensus decision-making.[25] The new SACU Agreement established a democratic rules-based structure to govern the regional trading bloc that is in sharp contrast to the structures of the colonial and apartheid periods.[26] Decisions have to be taken at meetings with all five member states present and on the basis of

Council of Ministers The Council of Ministers is the supreme decision-making and -taking authority on SACU matters. It consists of at least one minister from each member state and is responsible for overall policy direction and the proper functioning of SACU institutions. The Council is also responsible for appointing the Executive Secretary of the Secretariat and members of the SACU Tariff Board. According to Article 8.7, 'the Council shall approve customs tariffs, rebates, refunds or drawbacks and trade related remedies'. The Council is chaired by each member state, in rotation, for twelve months.

Customs Union Commission The Customs Union Commission (Article 9.3) is responsible for the implementation of the 2002 SACU Agreement. The Commission, comprising senior civil servants from each member state, therefore oversees the management of the CRP and supervises the Secretariat. According to Article 9.2, 'the Commission shall be responsible to and report to the Council'.

Secretariat The Secretariat is headed by an executive secretary, appointed by the Council, who must be a citizen of a member state. Other Secretariat staff are determined by the Commission. The Secretariat is responsible for the day-to-day administration of SACU (Article 10.1), arranging meetings, disseminating information, and keeping minutes. After prolonged discussion, member states decided to locate the Secretariat in Windhoek, Namibia.

Tariff Board Importantly, the SACU Agreement states that 'the Tariff Board

consensus. The important issue, for both South Africa and the BLNS states, of the consensus decision-making process is that it requires a 'collective unanimous opinion'. This means that decisions in the Council and Tariff Board require unanimous support from all member states, giving each state an effective right of veto. The BLNS states, under the 2002 SACU Agreement, thus have a *de jure* right of veto over all SACU legislation that includes the setting of tariffs and rebates. In sharp contrast to the 1910 and 1969 SACU Agreements, each BLNS state now participates on an equal footing with South Africa. Individual SACU member states have equal power to determine, and at the very least veto, policy proposals at the Council and Tariff Board levels. Under the 2002 SACU structure, member states are able to share sovereignty over tariff matters.

As a consequence, SACU will be involved in all future trade negotiations with third parties. Article 31 of the 2002 SACU Agreement stipulates that: 'No shall be an *independent institution* made up of full-time or part-time members' (Article 11.1, emphasis added). The Board makes recommendations to the Council on the level and changes of customs, anti-dumping, countervailing and safeguard duties on goods imported into SACU. However, the terms of reference, policy mandates, procedures and regulations of the Tariff Board are determined by the Council.

Technical Liaison Committees Four Technical Liaison Committees on matters related to agriculture, customs, trade and industry, and transport advise and assist the Commission in its work. The Council has the authority to determine and alter the terms of reference of these committees.

Tribunal The Tribunal, at the request of the Council, adjudicates (and settles, Article 13.1) any issue concerning the application or interpretation of the SACU Agreement. The Tribunal also plays an advisory role on any issue referred to it by the Council. According to Article 13.2, 'the Tribunal shall be composed of three members', and according to Article 13.5, 'the parties to the dispute shall choose the members of the Tribunal from amongst a pool of names, approved by the Council, and kept by the Secretariat'. Importantly, the Tribunal determines its own rules of procedure (Article 13.8).

National Bodies The SACU member states may establish specialized, dedicated and independent National Bodies entrusted with receiving requests for tariff changes and other SACU-related issues. National Bodies study, investigate and determine the impacts of tariff changes and make recommendations to the Tariff Board and/or the Commission.

Member State shall negotiate and enter into new preferential trade agreements with third parties or amend existing agreements without the consent of other Member States' (31.3) and that 'Member States shall establish a common negotiating mechanism in accordance with the terms of reference to be determined by the Council' (31.2). This is a clear and decisive break from past practices in which South Africa negotiated and concluded trade agreements unilaterally.

As with the RDF, South Africa is now keen to renegotiate the 2002 institutional arrangements that it considers as acting, or having the potential to act, against its vital national interests. It is also concerned about the democratic credibility of this arrangement. These concerns are best illustrated by the acrimonious, ill-coordinated and contentious way that SACU has managed negotiations with the European Union over the creation of economic partnership agreements (EPAs). (See Qobo in this volume.)

The BLNS states have been negotiating an EPA with the EU through a SADC grouping that excludes both South Africa and several SADC member states. South Africa entered the SADC EPA negotiations in February 2006 to consolidate and protect the SACU configuration and to avoid further fragmentation of SADC, as earlier noted. South Africa had already negotiated its own trade agreement with the EU in 2000. The Trade Development and Cooperation Agreement, which is legally separate from the EPA process (and the Lomé and Cotonou trade regimes of 1975 and 2000 respectively), is based on reciprocity and a free trade area (FTA).

Within the seventy-nine member states of the African, Caribbean and Pacific (ACP) bloc, the Caribbean is the only regional grouping to have negotiated a full EPA with the EU by the 31 December 2007 deadline. The mounting pressure of the World Trade Organization (WTO) to have a compatible trade regime from 1 January 2008, and to preserve preferential access to the EU market, has led almost all ACP developing countries to negotiate interim EPAs (IEPAs) with the EU. In other regions, progress in the negotiations to establish EPAs has been more acrimonious and time-consuming than expected.

On 23 November 2007, the EU and a few SADC member states initialled an IEPA, including a WTO-compatible market access schedule, provisions on development cooperation, and several other measures. The SADC IEPA included the BLS (Botswana, Lesotho and Swaziland) states. South Africa, and later Namibia, opposed several issues contained in the IEPA, including the compulsion to negotiate new-generation trade issues (for example, public procurement, banking and insurance) and the negative impact the trade provisions will have on the integrity of SACU.

Article 19 of the SADC IEPA states: 'this Agreement establishes a free trade area (FTA) between Parties, in conformity with the General Agreement on Tariffs and Trade, in particular Article XXIV'; and 'for the purposes of this Annex, the term "SADC EPA States" shall not include South Africa'. Thus, the BLS states committed themselves, and by default SACU, to an IEPA that South Africa was opposed to. Under a reciprocity clause, Botswana, Lesotho and Swaziland have agreed to 86 per cent liberalization by value. For forty-four sensitive tariff lines, liberalization is envisaged in 2015, with liberalization of a remaining three tariff lines in 2018.[27]

Although not a signatory to the IEPA, South Africa is the key player in the region and remains hostile to the EU's agenda of extending the scope of the EPAs. Tshwane forwarded several key arguments to denounce the EU's agenda, the most important aspects of which are the following:

1 There is no compulsion to negotiate 'new-generation' trade issues in order to meet WTO requirements.

2 There is limited negotiating capacity in SACU and there is already evidence

to suggest that some states, in particular Swaziland, did not appreciate fully the implications of signing the IEPA.

3 'New-generation' issues have not been addressed at the regional level, by either SADC, the Common Market for Eastern and Southern Africa (COMESA) or SACU. By negotiating an EPA based, in part, on 'new-generation' issues, the EU–SADC trading regimes would be deeper and more comprehensive than those of these regional economic communities.

The EU–SACU economic partnership agreement is therefore a significant challenge to SACU, and to South Africa in particular. Above all else, it highlights South Africa's inability to determine unilaterally the tariff and trade regime for SACU. South Africa may therefore be subject to a tariff and trade regime, through the SADC EPA, that it fundamentally opposes. Equally, if the SACU 2002 Agreement were adhered to, South Africa would be in a better position to veto such an agreement. While this is clearly an emerging policy area, what it highlights is South Africa's discomfort at sharing trade and tariff sovereignty with the BLNS states on the basis of an equal partnership. (For a different perspective, see Qobo in this volume.)

Conclusion

Regional integration is essentially a state-led process. In reality, it can only be as strong as its constituent parts, placing SACU in a difficult transition as it explores how strong its member states want to be. Difficult issues concerning revenue, sovereignty and democracy are being negotiated, renegotiated and reconfigured through SACU. However, the temptation to examine SACU solely in terms of economic and technical issues must be avoided. Regionalism is as much a political and social process as it is an economic one.[28] Regional trade and regional security, development and peace, are heavily interlinked and related to the condition of the African state. Given the extreme geographical segmentation of sub-Saharan Africa and the economic vulnerability of many states, regional integration, both economic and political, will help determine the future of southern Africa. SACU already forms a core component of the architectural infrastructure of regionalism in southern Africa. Furthermore, because all five SACU member states belong to SADC, there is already a form of 'variable geometry regionalism' operating within southern Africa. Given SACU's longevity, stability and depth of integration, the organization has a continuing role to play in the development of peace and security in southern Africa.

Notes

1 World Trade Organization (WTO), Trade Policy Review: Southern African Customs Union, Report no. WT/TPR/S/114, Geneva, 2003.

2 Talitha Bertelsmann-Scott, 'SACU – one hundred not out: what future for the Customs Union?', SAIIA Occasional Paper no. 68, September 2010; J. B. Cronje,

'Possible changes to the SACU revenue sharing formula', Tralac, 2010, www.tralac.org.

3 South African Institute for International Affairs (SAIIA), 'One hundred years and not out: what future for SACU', Conference held by SAIIA, Pretoria, June 2010, www.saiia.org.za/component/registrationpro/event/198/One-Hundred-Not-Out--What-Future-For-SACU.

4 WTO, *Annual Reports*, vols. 1–2, Geneva, 2008.

5 Prega Ramsamy, *Poverty Reduction: A Top Priority in SADC's Integration Agenda* (Gaborone: SADC Review, 2000).

6 Phillipe De Lombaerde, 'Regional integration and peace', *Peace and Conflict Monitor*, May 2005, www.monitor.upeace.org/innerpg.cfm?id_article=268.

7 Richard Gibb, 'Regional integration in post-apartheid southern Africa: the case of renegotiating the Southern African Customs Union', *Journal of Southern African Studies*, 23(1), 1997, pp. 67–86.

8 Christopher Clapham, 'The changing world of regional integration in Africa', in Christopher Clapham, Greg Mills, Anna Morner and Elizabeth Sidiropoulos (eds), *Regional Integration in Southern Africa* (Johannesburg: South African Institute of International Affairs, 2001), p. 62.

9 James Sidaway and Richard Gibb, 'SADC, COMESA, SACU: contradictory formats for regional integration', in David Simon (ed.), *South Africa in Southern Africa: Reconfiguring the Region* (Oxford: James Currey, 1988), ch. 10, pp. 164–84.

10 Anton Bösl, Gerhard Erasmus, Trudi Hartzenberg and Colin McCarthy, 'Introduction: monitoring the process of regional integration in southern Africa in 2009', *Monitoring Regional Integration in Southern Africa Yearbook 2009* (Stellenbosch, South Africa: Trade Law Centre for Southern Africa, Konrad-Adenauer-Stiftung, 2010); Colin McCarthy, 'Perspectives on the Southern African Customs Union', *TRALAC: Trade Law Centre for Southern Africa*, 29 July 2009, www.tralac.org/cgi-bin/giga.cgi?cmd=cause_dir_news_item&news_id=70726&cause_id=1694.

11 Robert Kirk and Matthew Stern, 'The new Southern African Customs Union Agreement', Africa Working Paper no. AWPS57 (Washington, DC: World Bank, 2003).

12 Brendan Vickers, 'SADC's international trade relations', in Charles Harvey (ed.), *Proceedings of the 2009 FOPRISA Annual Conference* (Lentswe La Lesedi, Gaborone: Botswana Institute for Development Policy Analysis, 2010), p. 132.

13 Peter Robson, *The Economics of International Integration* (London: Allen and Unwin, 1980).

14 Bertelsmann-Scott, 'SACU – one hundred not out'.

15 Colin McCarthy, 'The challenge of reconciling revenue distribution and industrial development in SACU', in Brendan Vickers (ed.), *Industrial Policy in the Southern African Customs Union: Past Experiences, Future Plans* (Midrand, South Africa: Institute for Global Dialogue (IGD), 2008), p. 30. (The revenue-sharing formula is as follows: $R = (m + q)/(M + Q)$. H. 1.42, subject to the constraint $R \geq 0.17 \, (m + q)$ and $R \leq (m + q)$, where R equals the revenue share of a BLNS country, m the value of its dutiable imports, and q its excisable consumption and production; where M equals the dutiable imports into and Q the excisable production in the common customs area; and where H equals the revenue (customs and excise) in the customs union pool. The stabilization factor was constructed to produce a multiplier that would equal 1.42 only when the revenue rate prior to stabilization equalled precisely 20 per cent. When the revenue rate fell to below 20 per cent, as it mostly has since the introduction of the stabilization factor, the enhancement would exceed 42 per cent.)

16 Richard Gibb, 'Regional integration in post-apartheid southern Africa'.

17 Ibid.

18 McCarthy, 'Perspectives on the Southern African Customs Union'.

19 Richard Gibb, 'Globalisation and Africa's economic recovery: a case study of the European Union–South Africa

post-apartheid trading regime', *Journal of Southern African Studies*, 29(4), 2003, pp. 885–901.

20 Lesotho Ministry of Finance, Minister of Finance, 'Budget Speech to Parliament', 2010, www.lesotho.gov.ls/documents/speeches.php.

21 Republic of South Africa, 'Customs Union Agreement Between the Governments of the Republic of South Africa, the Republic of Botswana, the Kingdom of Lesotho, and the Kingdom of Swaziland', *Government Gazette*, 54(1212), 1969, pp. 1–16.

22 Kirk and Stern, 'The new Southern African Customs Union Agreement'.

23 Republic of South Africa, 'Customs Union Agreement', Article 14(7).

24 SACU Secretariat, *Southern African Customs Union Agreement 2002*, Windhoek, 2003.

25 Colin McCarthy, 'The Southern African Customs Union in transition', *African Affairs*, 102, 2003.

26 Gerhard Erasmus 2004, 'New SACU Institutions: Prospects for Regional Integration', working paper, Trade Law Centre for Southern Africa: Stellenbosch, South Africa.

27 European Commission, 'What will an economic partnership agreement do?', *Trade Policy in Practice: Global Europe* (Brussels: Commission of the European Communities, External Trade, 2008); Rob Davies, 'Bridging the divide: the SADC EPA', *Trade Negotiations Insights*, 7(4), 2008, p. 1. See also trade.ec.europa.eu/doclib/docs/2009/july/tradoc_143981.pdf, p. 20.

28 Wieslaw Michalak and Richard Gibb, 'Trading blocs and multilateralism in the world economy', *Annals of the Association of American Geographers*, 87(2), 1997, pp. 264–79.

9 | South Africa's development finance institutions

David Monyae[1]

The global financial turmoil of 2007–10 refocused the world's attention on the growing importance of development finance institutions (DFIs) in building sustainable peace and security through infrastructure development.[2] Lack of infrastructure remains a major source of insecurity and a barrier to economic growth and development, particularly in southern Africa. Although scholars prefer to study political actors such as elites, parties and nation-states as the main authors of conflicts, lack of infrastructure is a critical element in fuelling conflicts and tensions in underdeveloped countries. Within this context, this chapter examines the roles of two South African DFIs, the Development Bank of Southern Africa (DBSA) and the Industrial Development Corporation (IDC), in promoting infrastructure development in the rest of southern Africa. Although South African DFIs operate largely independently of direct government entities, their vision and mission are guided by the country's post-apartheid foreign policy and relations with other African countries. As this chapter will show, South African DFIs are increasingly becoming key vehicles in the implementation of the country's foreign policy objectives in the region.

At the African Union (AU) Summit of Heads of State and Government held in Kampala in 2010, South African president Jacob Zuma was appointed chair of the New Partnership for Africa's Development (NEPAD) High-Level Subcommittee on Infrastructure. The subcommittee, comprising eight African heads of state and government,[3] has been tasked with prioritizing and consolidating high-impact regional and continental infrastructure projects in order to promote regional integration and economic development in Africa. It has already begun giving the development of pan-African rail and road infrastructure much needed impetus, with a strong focus on the North–South Corridor, linking Durban in southern Africa to Mombasa in Eastern Africa.[4] The North–South Corridor has been prioritized because it is the busiest corridor in the region in terms of value and volume of freight. It is also of strategic importance for the proposed tripartite free trade area comprising the Common Market for Eastern and Southern Africa (COMESA), the East African Community (EAC) and the Southern African Development Community (SADC).

President Zuma's leadership role in infrastructural development in relation to Africa as a whole clearly demonstrates the continued recognition of South Africa as a 'voice' and 'anchor', as well as a partner, in development on the continent.[5] That South Africa relies heavily on its DFIs as vehicles to fulfil its long-held quest for infrastructure development on the continent is in line with its foreign policy objective of creating a 'Better Africa and a Better World'.[6] The 2010 New Growth Path for South Africa's economy explains the rationale underlying the country's leadership role in supporting economic development and regional integration elsewhere on the continent:

> Support for regional growth is both an act of solidarity and a way to enhance economic opportunities. ... South Africa should be the driving force behind the development of regional energy, transport and telecommunication. Government will work jointly with African partners to identify mutually beneficial opportunities for trade and development, mindful of regional differences in resources and development. On this basis, South Africa will undertake initiatives to strengthen SADC and connect it with the East African community and COMESA.[7]

To achieve this goal, the New Growth Path maintains that

> [g]overnment will work with South African development finance institutions (DFIs) and state-owned enterprises (SOEs) to address backlogs in regional logistics, water and electricity infrastructure. Government will launch an appropriately structured Africa Development Fund to assist in financing this kind of infrastructure, and at the same time play the role of a sovereign wealth fund in helping to achieve a more competitive rand. Priorities include: a) by 2012, developing and implementing proposals to improve the road/rail/ports system serving southern and central Africa; b) strengthening regional integration on energy, including the Southern Africa Power Pool, linked to urgent improvements in electricity interconnectors, and exploring other opportunities for enhancing clean energy across central and southern Africa, including gas; c) developing proposals to improve telecommunications and internet connectivity across the region and from the region to Europe, Asia and Americas.[8] (See Nagar in this volume.)

South Africa's post-apartheid Africa policy

Following South Africa's historic 1994 democratic elections and the end of its pariah status, the country began to transform its foreign policy agenda. The search for a new foreign policy identity was informed by three key factors. First, the demise of apartheid in South Africa in 1994, in conjunction with the end of the Cold War in 1991, meant that South Africa's foreign policy had to be formulated in a new global terrain mainly defined by the triumphant Western countries, with the United States at the helm. The Soviet Union – a former ally of some African liberation movements, including the African National Congress (ANC) in South Africa – had disintegrated and lost its sphere of influence in eastern Europe. Secondly, the African continent was engulfed in intrastate conflicts, massive civil strife and poverty. Thirdly, despite the demise of apartheid and the dawn of a democratically elected government in South Africa, the country's position on the continent remained questionable. From the late 1970s, apartheid South Africa had pursued a policy of regional destabilization that caused massive loss of human and infrastructural capital. The end of apartheid left lingering fears among southern African states of post-apartheid South Africa's military and economic hegemony.[9]

South Africa had five basic objectives in transforming its foreign policy:

1 Integrate South Africa into SADC and the continent as a whole in a manner that promotes Africa's development and security as well as South Africa's economic interests.
2 Prioritize an African peace and security agenda as preconditional to generating momentum for African developmental and economic growth.
3 Emphasize effective good governance by African governments as a corollary to peace and security.
4 Support South–South cooperation in order to ensure that Africa, as an integral part of the global South, benefits from the economic emergence of the South and is integrated into the global economy within an emerging market context.
5 Ensure that an African peace, security and development agenda is integral to North–South dialogue as reflected in the Group of Eight's (G8) Africa Action Plan in response to Africa's NEPAD initiative.[10]

The role of South African DFIs in region-building in the post-apartheid era is best understood in the context of Pretoria's transformed foreign policy in general, and towards Africa in particular. Beginning in 1994, South Africa's foreign policy under the ANC-led government assumed a more Third World, non-aligned, pan-Africanist posture, in contrast to the Eurocentric, pro-Western, Cold War orientation of the apartheid years. The foreign policy transformation occurred in an atmosphere of international goodwill towards democratic South Africa given the iconic status of the country's first post-apartheid president, Nelson Mandela, after a 'negotiated revolution' had given birth to the much-touted 'rainbow nation'.[11]

South Africa's post-apartheid foreign policy had a clear bias towards countries inside and outside Africa that had rendered unwavering support for the South African liberation struggle in general, and for the ANC in particular. South Africa's new ruling class effectively assumed the guilt of the erstwhile apartheid oppressors, who had ruthlessly destabilized the region in the interests of maintaining the apartheid system. Thus the liberators of South

Africa decided to absorb responsibility for the depredations of an enemy they had fought – an enemy that had done grievous harm to the rest of the region and for whom the post-apartheid elite felt they must atone.

A section of the Reconstruction and Development Programme (RDP), formulated by the ANC and its tripartite alliance partners – the Congress of South African Trade Unions (COSATU) and the South African Communist Party (SACP) – to serve as its election manifesto, was focused on South Africa's policy towards the rest of southern Africa. The RDP acknowledged that South Africa had an important role to play in the region and that development of the country's trade, investment, labour and financial sectors was required to benefit southern Africa as a whole. Proposals were thus put forward by experts and senior government officials in favour of deploying government institutions, including DFIs, to support regional integration and development efforts.[12]

Development finance institutions are important for southern Africa because they provide finance to projects, economic sectors or sections of the population that are not well served by the financial system as a whole. They complement both government resources and market funding. In addition, DFIs also help in building capacity through the provision of technical assistance, including project preparation and feasibility studies, and the promotion of entrepreneurship and business development. They contribute to national policy objectives such as supporting society through private sector development, employment creation, income redistribution, import substitution and development of poor groups, regions or sectors. DFIs also serve as the financial arm for government development policies, assist government in the formulation of such policies through lessons learned, bridge the gap between government and the private sector, and promote regional trade and cooperation.[13]

The Industrial Development Corporation

The IDC was established in 1940 by General Jan Smuts's government to promote economic growth and industrial development in South Africa specifically by assisting the diversification of the country's economy, which was over-reliant on the export of gold and agricultural production.[14] The IDC also had the objective of supporting the import substitution policy formulated by the South African government during the Second World War.[15] It provided financing for local industries to produce alternatives when imported goods were scarce, and to empower Afrikaners economically in order to ensure the country's independence from the former British colonial power.[16]

After South Africa's democratically elected government came to power in 1994, the IDC was reinstituted to pursue a developmental agenda in both South Africa and the rest of Africa. The IDC's mandate allows it to fund private sector projects that contribute to sustainable economic growth, employment creation and poverty reduction. This is achieved through the promotion of entrepreneurship by building competitive industries and enterprises based on sound business principles. The IDC aims to 'be the primary source of commercially sustainable industrial development and innovation to benefit South Africa and the rest of the African continent'.[17] It provides capital for equity, quasi-equity, commercial debt, export finance, guarantees and wholesale finance.

An amendment to South Africa's Industrial Development Act in 1997 opened the way for the IDC to extend its reach beyond South Africa to the rest of the SADC region in 1998 and to the rest of Africa in 2002. This allowed the IDC to provide financial assistance to industries and enterprises in South Africa, southern Africa and the rest of Africa in line with South Africa's policy of supporting NEPAD. The decision to expand the operations of the IDC into the rest of Africa was based on the following facts:

- South Africa's future prosperity is inextricably linked to the economic development of the rest of Africa. The IDC is committed to improving industrial capacity in Africa.
- The rest of Africa represents enormous market potential and untapped resources. The IDC leverages private sector investment for economic development. It also has an international network of partners that support its projects and initiatives.
- Existing South African products and services can contribute to the development of the continent's diverse economies.
- Africa is projected as one of the last bastions of economic growth and the IDC wants to make its mark in this significant era.[18]

The IDC works with locally based partners in order to overcome local and regional challenges to the implementation of its projects. It has established working relationships with DFIs and regional forums in thirty-four African countries. The IDC operates in the mining and beneficiation sector, as well as the agro-processing and forestry sector. It also supports projects in the manufacturing, infrastructure (such as telecoms, energy, water and sanitation, transport), information and communication technology (ICT), transport and construction sectors. In terms of social services, the IDC has been involved in the healthcare and education sector. The IDC also focuses on tourism, public–private partnerships and franchising. These areas in which the IDC is involved resonate with SADC's vision and existing programmes for regional integration.

The IDC's regional presence is legitimized by its accreditation to the SADC Development Funding Regional Council. It is mandated to enhance capacity-building initiatives and extend credit lines to all SADC DFIs. The IDC also works in partnership with South Africa's Department of Trade and Industry to identify and pursue investment and trade opportunities in Africa. The IDC's focus on economic growth and poverty reduction enables it to work with NEPAD. For example, the IDC played an advisory role to the NEPAD e-Africa commission on the East African Submarine Cable System (EASSY) project, aimed at linking eight African countries and islands on the continent's eastern coast, from South Africa to Sudan.[19] The IDC also provided consultative services during the development of the protocol for the NEPAD ICT Broadband Infrastructure for Eastern and Southern Africa. The African Development Bank (AfDB) has also provided the IDC with lines of credit in the past to help it effectively meet its infrastructure development objectives in Africa.

In 2010 the IDC had over eighty projects under implementation or consideration in twenty-five African countries.[20] It had approved over US$1 billion for these projects.[21] IDC-funded projects between 2005 and 2009 were expected to generate an estimated 147,000 jobs in South Africa and the rest of Africa. In the 2008/09 financial year alone, IDC funding was expected to create about five thousand new direct jobs in the rest of Africa (excluding South Africa).

The reputation of the IDC in Africa was enhanced in 2009 when the Association of African Development Finance Institutions (AADFI) voted it the best DFI in a peer review exercise. The IDC won the award mainly in recognition of the outstanding contribution of its infrastructure investments to promoting regional integration. It had also shown high standards in the three key areas of AADFI rating, namely good corporate governance, operational efficiency and financial performance.

The IDC is well placed to assist African countries emerging from various crises, including wars, since most private and international financiers are wary of committing funds to such environments. Generally, the IDC follows markets where South African foreign relations with the host country create an environment conducive to economic activities through, for example, the signing of bilateral investment agreements. However, these agreements are not a prerequisite for the IDC to enter a specific country. The biggest risk factors are normally political, as political uncertainties or violence can threaten the huge investments made in any specific country or region. Therefore, DFIs such as the DBSA carefully consider the political environment before committing to massive project investment.

The role of the IDC in Mozambique

In 1997 the IDC co-launched the Mozambique Aluminium Smelter (Mozal) 1 project along with BHP Billiton (Australia), Mitsubishi Corporation (Japan) and the government of Mozambique to build an estimated US$1.36 billion greenfield aluminium smelter near Maputo with annual production capacity of 253,000 tonnes of primary aluminium for export. The first aluminium was produced by the project in June 2000. Mozal was the first major foreign investment project in Mozambique and its implementation contributed significantly to putting Mozambique on the foreign investment map, encouraging others to invest in a poor country still recovering from a devastating civil war in 1992 after the signing of the Rome Treaty. Mozal is a key FDI project in the Maputo Development Corridor (MDC), one of the first Spatial Development Initiatives (SDIs) in SADC (discussed later in this chapter; see also Khadiagala, Nagar in this volume). Mozal also boosted the economies of Mozambique's major trading partners in the region, South Africa and Swaziland. The corridor has enabled the two countries to increase trade exchanges as well as reduce traffic congestion and fatalities.

The South African government viewed the IDC's involvement in the Mozal project as a practical illustration of its foreign policy objective to promote economic development in southern Africa, including through public–private partnerships. In 2001, Mozal generated 55 per cent of Mozambique's exports and accounted for approximately 8 per cent of the country's gross domestic product (GDP).[22] Other net direct benefits to the Mozambican government accrued through the 1 per cent sales tax on aluminium. Mozal 1 created full-time jobs for about 750 people, of whom 88 per cent were Mozambican. Mozal II, which was commissioned in August 2003, doubled the output of the smelter, and during construction created full-time jobs for about three thousand people, of whom approximately 70 per cent were Mozambican.[23] Mozal workers have also received substantial training, allowing for their development into a highly skilled labour force.

Mozal has contracted with several private local companies for services such as transport, catering, cleaning and security. For these services alone, at least four hundred non-Mozal staff are employed on-site. The project spends approximately US$35 million annually with the local companies. Mozal has also initiated a Graduate Development Programme, aimed at exposing graduate technicians to an actual heavy-industry environment with world-class process facilities. Furthermore, Mozal has developed two significant programmes, the Mozal Community Development Trust (MCDT) and the Small and Medium Enterprises Empowerment Linkage Programme (SMEELP), in order to more effectively channel its resources to the local small and medium enterprises and the local community.[24] Through all these initiatives and programmes, Mozal has completely changed Mozambique's infrastructural outlook.

In 2008 the IDC also approved R850 million in funding to facilitate the transfer of the majority stake in the Cahora Bassa hydroelectric project to the Mozambican government. Cahora Bassa is a strategic asset for the southern Africa region, with most of the power generated from the plant utilized by South African energy utility Eskom under long-term power purchase agreements. Cahora Bassa accounts for about 3 per cent of electricity consumed in South Africa and is a relatively cheap and clean source of power in the region.

The Development Bank of Southern Africa

The DBSA was established by South Africa's apartheid government in 1983 with a share capital of R2 billion.[25] It had a twofold objective. First, it was to support the government's policy of separate development by propping up Bantustans (Transkei, Bophuthatswana, Ciskei and Venda) and non-independent, self-governing territories such as KwaZulu. It financed the apartheid regime's development and maintenance of infrastructure in these areas essentially to enable the state to effectively monitor and control the South African public. This was envisaged as lightening the load borne by the government in developing the Bantustans.[26] Secondly, the government aimed at establishing a developmental bank that would provide, monitor and manage funds for the development of small enterprises in cooperation with the private sector.

Over the years, the mandate of the DBSA evolved in response to South Africa's transition to democracy and to promote the new government's developmental objectives. The DBSA assumed the functions of a post-conflict and reconstruction organization, providing funds to help rebuild infrastructure that had been destroyed or neglected during the apartheid era. Its reconstruction work was solely funded by the South African government and focused mainly on South Africa until the promulgation of the DBSA Act in 1997 allowed the bank to expand into other SADC states in line with the foreign policy objectives of the new government.

With its official reconstitution as a DFI in 1997, the DBSA assumed new roles such as assisting the South African government in achieving its strategic objectives at home and in the rest of southern Africa. These objectives included the promotion of broad-based economic growth, job creation, and integration, the building of human and institutional capacity, and the co-financing of infrastructure development in South Africa and the rest of SADC. Areas contributing to social transformation and economic stimulation have been singled out as potential investment destinations, to help alleviate the existing backlogs in the provision of water, sanitation, electricity, communication and healthcare. In South Africa, the DBSA focused mainly on the local government sector, which was in dire need of infrastructure development in order to improve access to services for the general public. The bulk of DBSA investments are in local municipalities. This is why matters of infrastructure development, capacity development and governance are handled through the development fund and Vulindlela Academy.

The DBSA in the SADC region

The DBSA has done extensive work outside South Africa in line with its mandate to provide infrastructure development support in the entire southern Africa region. Its first investment initiative outside South African borders was in 1987 in the form of a small-farmer development programme in Mozambique,

Swaziland, Lesotho and Namibia.[27] While some saw this programme as small and insignificant at the time, it has since proved to be the first of many steps that the DBSA would undertake in promoting southern Africa's development. By 2009 the DBSA had made loans to ten SADC countries: Zambia (the largest recipient, with R2 billion), Mozambique, Tanzania, Namibia, Mauritius, Lesotho, Angola, Malawi, Swaziland and Botswana (the smallest recipient, with R83 million).[28] The DBSA is involved in a range of development projects, including energy, telecommunications and mining, with energy composing just under a third of its investments. Let us examine the role of the DBSA in Zambia, Mozambique and Lesotho.

Zambia The Zambian economy is mostly centred on the mining of copper and cobalt, but the country also has an extensive freshwater supply that has not been effectively exploited for agricultural support, because of lack of expertise and resources. The DBSA has devoted much effort to the diversification of the Zambian economy. In accordance with the Zambian National Development Plan, it has focused on sectors such as electricity (Zambia Electricity Supply Corporation Limited [ZESCO], Copperbelt Energy Corporation, Lunsemfwa Hydro Power Company and Kariba North Hydropower), communications (Celtel and Zamcell), mining (the Konkola deep mine and smelter) and finance (Development Bank of Zambia).[29] The DBSA contributed US$100 million of the total project cost of US$1.1 billion for the Konkola mining projects. Konkola Copper Mines Plc (KCM) is a Zambian registered company and the largest mining and metal company in the country. KCM's principal activity is the mining, production and marketing of copper and cobalt, and production of acid. It has both underground and open-pit mining operations as well as concentrators, a leaching plant, a smelter and a refinery spread across locations in the Copperbelt province.

The US$100 million that KCM sought from the DBSA was for partly financing its deep-mining project and the smelting facilities in Chingola Zambia. The deep-mining project involves the sinking of one main shaft to 1,490 metres, along with other supporting shafts for ventilation, dewatering and equipment. The project seeks to access the rich body of ore that lies below the current levels of production. As the largest single investment in Zambian mining ever, the project will increase the production capacity of the Konkola mine from 2,000,000 to 7,500,000 tonnes of copper ore per annum.[30] The second component of the project, the Nchanga smelter project, is a new, state-of-the-art smelter and acid plant with a production capacity of 250,000 tonnes of copper per annum. It will handle not only the increased output from the deep-mining project but also the concentrates from other mines in Zambia. The 1,850-tonne-per-day sulphuric acid plant will capture the sulphur dioxide gases from the smelter and convert them into acid, making this smelter environmentally friendly.

Mozambique At the end of a devastating sixteen-year civil war in 1992, Mozambique faced extreme infrastructural problems. The country required toll roads to Maputo from Johannesburg, railway lines, power transmission lines from South Africa via Swaziland to Mozambique, and rehabilitation of power lines from Cahora Bassa to Secunda and Mozal (the aluminium smelter plant), to name just a few of its necessities. According to SADC Executive Secretary and former Mozambican planning minister Tomaz Salomão, Mozambique's lack of infrastructure and failure to attract domestic and foreign investment led SADC to encourage the South African government to financially assist Mozambique in addressing its infrastructure challenges in the post-conflict era from 1992 to 2005.[31] The Nelson Mandela-led South African government at the time responded by forming a team of South African and Mozambican officials, with DBSA support, to assist Mozambique in meeting its infrastructure needs.

The DBSA provided financial and project management advice for the US$8 billion Maputo Development Corridor – one of the major resultant development projects – which was launched in 1996.[32] The MDC project was undertaken to rehabilitate the core infrastructure in the corridor (the N4 toll road, rail, port and dredging facilities, and the Lebombo/Ressano Garcia border post between Mozambique and South Africa), through public–private partnerships (cognizant of state fiscal limitations) in order to re-establish key linkages and open up underutilized economic development opportunities. The project was important to Mozambique and South Africa's respective reconstruction and development programmes, which sought to increase GDP and employment growth as well as local and foreign investment and exports. The project also aimed at promoting regional economic integration, international competitiveness, and broadening of the ownership base in the economy of the corridor. The corridor runs through the most highly industrialized and productive countries of southern Africa, from Gauteng to the port of Maputo on Africa's eastern coast. As one of the region's success stories, the MDC since its inception has improved trade and foreign direct investment in Mozambique and South Africa. For example, cargo traffic through the Lebombo/Ressano Garcia border post grew from almost nothing in mid-2002 to 3.4 million tonnes per year in 2007. This traffic, composed largely of South African exports and transit imports/exports through the port of Maputo, totalled 7.6 million tonnes in 2002, an increase of more than 13 per cent over the previous year.

By the end of 2004, Port Maputo was working around the clock in full compliance with the highest international security standards. The port was the first on the African continent to achieve compliance with International Ship and Port Facility Security (ISPS). During 2008, seismic surveys were conducted to establish the cost and viability of increasing the depth of the entrance channel and approaches to the port. In 2007 the first phase of a car terminal was launched, and in 2008 a ferrochrome terminal was built, with a capacity in excess of one million tonnes, and the bulk sugar terminal was expanded. The Matola coal terminal is being modernized and doubled in capacity, while R144 million of infrastructure improvements to the container terminal have led to significant growth in throughput.[33] The Maputo Port Development Company, which manages the port, recently completed a fifty-year master plan indicating that regional demand for the port will exceed 40 million tonnes per annum by 2028. Port Maputo will provide employment for many thousands of people, and award contracts worth more than R120 million per annum to local companies.[34]

As a result of the MDC, among other economic policies and industrial and infrastructural development projects, Mozambique, which ranked as the world's poorest country at the end of its civil war in 1992, has been able to transform itself from a nationalized economy into a market-oriented one. Because of the abundance of natural resources such as coal and natural gas, the international community now views Mozambique as a destination for energy investment. Furthermore, the International Monetary Fund (IMF) and the World Bank have agreed to provide Mozambique with much-needed debt relief to give the country a chance to achieve a sustainable economy (in 2001, with a debt of US$2 billion, Mozambique officially became a Heavily Indebted Poor Country, HIPC).[35] Despite being prone to natural disasters such as recurrent floods, which have an immense impact on the economy in terms of infrastructure, human capital and production, the country's economy consistently grew by an average of 7 per cent per annum between 2000 and 2010.

The DBSA's involvement in Mozambique now amounts to a total current exposure of R1.36 billion. This portfolio spans sectors such as energy, telecommunications, water, industry and agriculture.[36]

Lesotho Lesotho, a landlocked country completely surrounded by South Africa, has a population of 2 million, 82 per cent of whom live in the poverty-stricken rural areas. Although the country is facing dire economic and health issues, it has experienced positive economic growth, from 4.6 per cent in the 1980s and 4.4 per cent in the 1990s to 7.2 per cent in 2006. The growth in 2006 was largely because of the activities associated with the Lesotho Highlands water project, the reopening of the Letseng diamond mine and the opening of the new mines of Kao and Liqhobong, along with the revival of the textile industry.[37] The DBSA has supported the government of Lesotho's initiatives to improve key sectors of the country's economy, such as mining, energy, financial services and manufacturing. The DBSA's approach to assisting Lesotho involves direct loan financing, capacity support and advice on specific projects. The DBSA has approved loans to Lesotho in the amount of R2 billion total, with an exposure of R602 million in 2010 alone. At the centre of Lesotho's development are two projects: the Highlands water project and a public–private partnership hospital.

The Highlands project transfers water from the Lesotho Highlands to South

Africa's Vaal river system and generates hydroelectric power for Lesotho. It is Africa's largest-ever water transfer project as well as the largest ongoing binational construction project on the continent. According to former South African president Thabo Mbeki, the project seeks to harness Lesotho's 'white gold' for the benefit of both countries. It aims to improve the security of water supply for South Africa's rapidly expanding Gauteng province, which generates almost 60 per cent of the country's industrial output and 80 per cent of its mining output, and where over 40 per cent of South Africa's population live.[38] The province needs more water than its main source, the Vaal river, can provide. For Lesotho, the project has provided new infrastructure, including roads, expanded communication and electricity systems, health facilities, job opportunities, improved water supply and sanitation to numerous communities, and many additional secondary benefits associated with the revenue streams from this huge capital investment.[39]

Construction on phase 1A of the project began in 1984, and the first dam, Katse, began delivering water in 1998. Construction on phase 1B of the project began in 1998, and comprises the 145-metre-high Mohale Dam on the Senqunyane river, the 32-kilometre Mohale Tunnel, linking Mohale Dam to Katse Dam, and the 6-kilometre Matsoku weir and tunnel, which diverts flood water from the Matsoku river into the Katse reservoir. Water transfer from Mohale Dam and the Matsoku river to Katse Dam has begun, and will gradually increase the volume of water delivered to South Africa from 20 to 26 cubic metres per second. While Katse Dam is the highest concrete arch dam in Africa, Mohale Dam is the highest rockfill dam on the continent, consisting of 7.8 million cubic metres of rock that was placed and compacted before the addition of concrete face. The dam features a flexible outlet structure that ensures high-quality water for downstream releases in order to ensure the sustainability of aquatic life.

Other infrastructure completed during phase 1B includes three mountain passes, 72 kilometres of tarred roads, 75 kilometres of power lines, and over one hundred construction houses. At the peak of construction, phase IB created more than eight thousand jobs for local and regional workers. The entire project is expected to cost US$8 billion by the time of its completion in 2020. In November 2003 the South African Institute of Civil Engineering named Lesotho Highlands the 'project of the century' for its 'immense impact on the betterment of the lives of South Africans and Basotho, the benefits it brought to the economies of both countries, the manner in which the environmental impacts were addressed, and the effective and efficient overall management of the project'.[40]

In a project unique to the health sector in the region, the government of Lesotho has also entered into a public–private partnership with Tsepong, a Lesotho–South Africa consortium anchored by Netcare, a leading South

African healthcare provider, to replace the collapsing and only national referral hospital in Lesotho with a new, 390-bed hospital in Maseru, while refurbishing four existing filter satellite clinics. This hospital was approved in December 2009.[41] In 2010 the DBSA was appointed lead arranger after committing R740 million to the project, including R60 million to facilitate the participation of a local empowerment group.

Conclusion

South Africa's DFIs have financed projects vital to regional integration and development in southern Africa. While these institutions are increasingly becoming important foreign policy tools for South Africa, what is required is clear coordination of the activities of DFIs under the auspices of the envisaged South African Development Partnership Agency (SADPA). South Africa's DFIs confront stiff competition from similar institutions from both developed countries and emerging markets, but they occupy a relatively privileged position because they understand African markets better and have been in the field much longer than their counterparts from elsewhere in the world. The IDC and DBSA will therefore play a key role in region-building through infrastructure development in SADC and beyond, as SADC plans to create a single trading bloc with COMESA and the EAC. As the most economically developed country on the continent, South Africa is critical to the promotion of infrastructure development in southern Africa.

Notes

1 David Monyae is a policy analyst at the Development Bank of Southern Africa (DBSA). He writes in his personal capacity. He thanks Mbongeni Myende, Zama Hlophe and his colleagues Mohammed Jahed, Zulaikha Brey, Francis Kornegay, Admassu Tadesse, Sam Muradzikwa, Melissa Govender and William Gumede.

2 There is no universally agreed definition of infrastructure. For the purposes of this chapter, I adopt the *American Heritage Dictionary*'s definition: 'basic facilities, services, and installations needed for the functioning of a community or society, such as transportation and communications systems, water, and power'.

3 South Africa (as chair), Algeria, Benin, Egypt, Nigeria, Republic of the Congo, Rwanda and Senegal.

4 Development Bank of Southern Africa (DBSA), 'DBSA and Zambian RDFA sign a historic road development loan', Press release, 26 January 2011.

5 Chris Landsberg and David Monyae, 'South Africa's foreign policy: carving a global niche', *South African Journal of International Affairs*, 13(2), Winter–Spring 2006, pp. 131–45.

6 South Africa's Foreign Policy Discussion Document, South African Department of Foreign Affairs, 2006.

7 South African Department of Economic Development, *The New Growth Path*, 2010.

8 Ibid.

9 Sam C. Nolutshungu, 'Sceptical notes on "constructive engagement"', *Issue: A Journal of Opinion*, 12(3/4), 1982, p. 8.

10 David Monyae, 'South Africa's foreign policy and the United Nations in Africa', Paper written for the United Nations Development Programme, 2010.

11 Ibid.

12 African National Congress, *The Reconstruction and Development Programme: A Policy Framework*, 1994, www.anc.org.za. See also Alan Hirch, *Season of Hope: Economic Reform Under Mandela and Mbeki* (Scottsville: University of KwaZulu-Natal Press, 2005).

13 Stephany Griffith-Jones, David Griffith-Jones and Dagmar Hertova, 'Enhancing the role of regional development banks', G-24 Discussion Paper no. 50, July 2008.

14 Mthokozisi S. H. Thabede, *The IDC in SADC*, 2008, ujdigispace.uj.ac.za:8080/dspace/bitstream/.../IDCinSADCreport.pdf.

15 Geoffrey Qhena, 'DFI positioning', IDC case study, 23 November 2006, www.idc.co.za/Conference%20Papers/2006/Africa%20Development%20Finance%20Week/GeoffreyQhena.pdf.

16 Ibid.

17 Industrial Development Corporation (IDC), *Annual Report: Towards a New Developmental Growth Path*, 2010, www.idc.co.za.

18 Ibid.

19 The eight countries are South Africa, Mozambique, Madagascar, Tanzania, Kenya, Somalia, Djibouti and Sudan.

20 DBSA, 'The evolution of the Development Bank of Southern Africa 2010: development activism through development finance', 2010, pp. 201–9.

21 IDC, *Annual Report*. http://www.idc.co.za/Conference%20Papers/2006/Africa%20Development%20Finance%20Week/LumkileMondi.pdf.

22 IDC website, www.idc.co.za.

23 Ibid.

24 'IDC pushes for more support for local SMMEs', *Business Report*, 17 June 2009.

25 DBSA, 'The Evolution of the Development Bank of Southern Africa', p. 44.

26 DBSA, *25th Anniversary Book*, 2008, pp. 44–6.

27 Ibid., p. 148.

28 DBSA, *Board of Directors project visits to the SADC region*, Briefing booklet, 2009.

29 Ibid.

30 DBSA, Presentation for the Chamber of Commerce and Industry of Japan, 1 February 2011.

31 SADC, 'Perspectives on DFIs and on the DBSA's role in regional economic development', Interview with Tomaz Salomão, SADC Executive Secretary and former Mozambican planning minister, 2009.

32 Ibid.

33 *Construction for Development Magazine*, October 2009, www.isiza.co.za/features/bric-nations/303573.htm.

34 Ibid.

35 DBSA, *Board of Directors project visits*.

36 DBSA, *International Division 'Portfolio Analysis'*, 31 October 2010, p. 4.

37 DBSA, *Board of Directors project visits*.

38 SouthAfrica.info, 'Africa's biggest water project', 17 March 2004, www.safrica.info/business/economy/infrastructure/sa-lesothowaterproject.htm.

39 Ibid.

40 Ibid.

41 DBSA, *Board of Directors project visits*.

PART FOUR

Human security

10 | Food insecurity

Scott Drimie and Sithabiso Gandure

There is now an extensive literature on the underlying causes of the food insecurity that has intermittently affected countries in southern Africa, particularly since 2001.[1] Many of these studies concur that there has been a long-term erosion of resilient livelihood strategies over a period of time, indicative of increased levels of hunger in the region. While harvest failures were evident in the drought years of 2001 and 2002, and harvest failure was again the main causal factor in 2005, these studies outline a much broader set of underlying causes, among them the growing levels of extreme poverty, the AIDS epidemic and weaknesses in regional governance.

Realization of the United Nations (UN) Millennium Development Goals (MDGs), particularly that of halving the number of hungry people before 2015, remains elusive in many countries in sub-Saharan Africa.[2] The Global Hunger Index, developed by the International Food Policy Research Institute (IFPRI), which monitors reduction of food insecurity, shows that sub-Saharan Africa made only marginal progress between 1990 and 2008.[3] Nine of the ten worst-performing countries in terms of percentage change in the index during this period were in Africa.[4] Indeed, the 2009 *State of Food Insecurity* report, jointly authored by the UN's Food and Agricultural Organization (FAO) and the World Food Programme (WFP), estimates that more than 40 per cent of the 257 million people in the Southern African Development Community (SADC) region are undernourished.[5]

Food security is the cornerstone of human security. Without it, attempts to build peace in southern Africa will remain elusive. A former executive director of the WFP told the UN Security Council in December 2002: 'Never before has WFP had to contend with potential starvation of this magnitude on the African continent, with the simultaneous outbreak of two enormous and complex crises in the Horn and Southern Africa exacerbated by HIV/AIDS and economic policy failures.'[6] The Security Council expressed its concern about Africa's food crisis, which it saw as presenting a major threat to peace and security on the continent.[7]

Theoretical constructs: freedom from hunger

Food security can be defined as the success of local livelihood strategies in guaranteeing access to sufficient food at the household or family level.[8] To use a more workable definition, one accepted by SADC states, 'food security is when all people, at all times, have physical, social and economic access to sufficient, safe and nutritious food that meets their dietary needs and food preferences for an active and healthy life'.[9] Nutrition security is achieved when secure access to appropriately nutritious food is coupled with a sanitary environment and adequate healthcare services to ensure a healthy and active life for all household members.

Food and nutrition security fundamentally determine life possibilities, and people's ability to convert opportunities into outcomes. Improved nutrition significantly reduces child and maternal mortality, improves educational outcomes, and increases economic productivity and growth. According to a 2010 report by the United Kingdom's Department for International Development (DfID), the strategy adopted for tackling malnutrition in developing states should take into account that the consequences of food and nutrition insecurity are long-term, intergenerational and irreversible, with the effects of poor foetal growth and stunting in the first two years of life sustained into adulthood.[10] SADC member states have recognized food and nutrition security as the foundation essential for attaining the MDGs and other interlinked policy objectives in the region.[11] This is articulated in the SADC Dar es Salaam Declaration on Agriculture and Food Security of May 2004.[12]

In his influential work *Development as Freedom*, Amartya Sen argues that development consists of the removal of various types of 'un-freedoms' that leave people with little choice and little opportunity of exercising their reasoned agency.[13] He posits that the persistence of extensive hunger in a world of unprecedented prosperity is an unparalleled tragedy, particularly as it is accepted and tolerated as an integral part of the modern world – as a tragedy that is essentially unpreventable. Echoing this, the United Nations has argued that no human right has been so frequently violated in recent times as the right to food, despite the fact that it is one of the most consistently enshrined rights in international human rights law, one constantly reaffirmed by governments.[14]

In order to eliminate hunger, it is crucial to understand the causal factors in sufficiently broad terms, and it is not enough to understand only the balance between food and population, as is often argued. Sen's work has consistently posited since the early 1980s that what is crucial in analysing hunger is the substantive freedom of the individual and the family to establish ownership over an adequate amount of food, which can be done either by growing the food oneself or by buying it in the market.[15] A more recent analysis of hunger, famine and food insecurity focuses attention on 'response failure', or the failure of governments and agencies to intervene to protect household food security following supply and demand failures.[16] In *Development as Freedom*, Sen writes that 'there has never been a famine in a functioning multi-party democracy'.[17] He argues that democracies confer a range of freedoms – not least the right to vote out an incompetent government, but also the right to protect citizens against violations of basic rights, including the right to food. However, Stephen Devereux has questioned this assertion, considering that famines have been experienced in countries such as Ethiopia, Malawi and Niger in the first decade of the twenty-first century, soon after these states became multiparty democracies.[18] A plausible explanation might be that during the infancy stages of states becoming democratic, 'anti-famine political contracts' may not yet be in place or consolidated as an effective policy instrument.[19] Devereux thus argues that fully functioning democracies are more able to provide effective protection against famine,[20] while, as Alex de Waal observes, weak or infantile democracies may not be.[21]

Thus, hunger relates not only to food production and agricultural expansion but also to the functioning of the entire economy, as well as to the operation of socio-political arrangements that can, directly or indirectly, influence people's ability to acquire food, achieve health, and maintain nourishment.[22] The danger of this definition is that it leads to an all-encompassing assertion of food and nutrition security that is morally unimpeachable and politically acceptable, but also unrealistically broad.

Regional food security and root causes

SADC's food and nutrition security is highly dependent on the performance of agriculture, which is the main form of livelihood for 70 per cent of the region's population.[23] Food availability is largely assessed through cereal production levels (see Figure 10.1). During the 1990s there were sharp yearly variations in SADC's cereal and maize production levels, which have steadily risen since 2001. Notable low production was recorded in the 2002/03 and 2005/06 seasons. More recent regional cereal production levels show marked upward

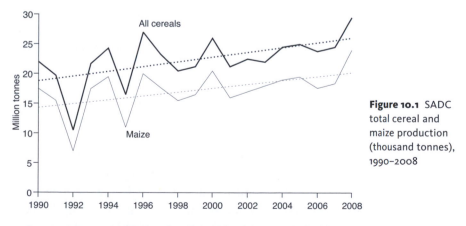

Figure 10.1 SADC total cereal and maize production (thousand tonnes), 1990–2008

Source: SADC, *Food Agriculture and Natural Resources Directorate Annual Report, April 2008–March 2009*, 2009 (shows twelve of the fifteen SADC countries)

improvements, owing to improved access to fertilizers and seed provisions through subsidy programmes as well as good rains and enabling economic policies in some countries.[24]

The improvement in overall cereal production at a regional level in southern Africa should not be taken as an indicator of overall improved food security in every country, as many countries continue to produce less than their national requirements. During the 2009 season, only South Africa, Malawi and Zambia produced more than their national requirements, while the remaining countries in the subregion faced food deficits.[25] Despite the recent increases in cereal production in southern Africa, the 2008 *State of the World's Children* report, authored by the United Nations Children's Fund (UNICEF), found that 28 per cent of children (children aged 0–59 months) in southern and eastern Africa were moderately and severely underweight, 7 per cent were moderately and severely wasted, and 40 per cent were moderately and severely stunted.[26] UNICEF argues that the trend of slow improvement in national nutrition across the subregion stopped in the late 1990s before declining sharply in the early part of 2000, particularly in drought-stricken areas with a high HIV prevalence.[27]

These nutrition figures are indicative of the chronic food insecurity that has unfolded across southern African since early 2000, with many more people living 'on the borderline'. Southern African countries are now less able to absorb shocks or stresses than during the 1990s, owing largely to the region being more vulnerable to external shocks than previously.[28] The negative outcomes and indicators not only point to malnutrition, but also indicate lower life expectancy, increased child mortality, higher levels of poverty, and the rapid spread of the HIV/AIDS epidemic.[29]

Underlying causes of regional food insecurity

The underlying causes of regional food security are poverty, climate change and periodic floods and droughts, weak state capacity for service delivery, inappropriate agricultural practices and disruptive government policies, as well as the global food price hikes due to the 2007/08 global financial crisis. Food insecurity has been compounded by the HIV/AIDS epidemic.[30]

Poverty, malnutrition and gender Although the region is well endowed with natural resources and rich biodiversity, poverty is one of the deep-rooted causes of food insecurity. Close to three-quarters (70 per cent) of the region's population of 257 million people live on less than two dollars a day, and 40 per cent live on less than one dollar a day.[31] Besides South Africa and Botswana, in all countries of the region over half, and in some instances over three-quarters, of the population live on less than two dollars a day. Recognizing the need to achieve greater food security, SADC Heads of State and Government signed a declaration on poverty eradication and sustainable development in April

2008. In addition, the SADC Task Force of Ministers of Trade, Agriculture and Finance was established to foster regional collaboration efforts to facilitate cross-border and internal food flows alongside improved infrastructure and distribution networks.[32] However, member states need to realize that poverty is as much a socio-economic issue as a political one; therefore, political will and appropriate and coherent policies, as well as accountable governments at the subregional level, are needed to realize these intended objectives and commitments.

While the regional strategy to combat malnutrition has tended to focus on the underlying economic and environmental causes, international research on malnutrition in the period 1970–95 indicates that extreme poverty accounts for only half the variability in malnutrition rates.[33] As shown in Table 10.1, many other factors, such as educating and empowering women, can help deal with malnutrition. Hardly any analysis has been conducted on the impact that declining quality of key social services such as health and education has on food insecurity.[34]

TABLE 10.1 Contributions to reduction in child malnutrition, 1970–95

Factor	Percentage contribution
Women's education	43
Per capita food availability	26
Health environment improvements	19
Women's status relative to men	12

Source: L. Haddad and L. C. Smith, *Explaining Child Malnutrition in Developing Countries: A Cross-Country Analysis* (Washington, DC: International Food Policy Research Institute, IFPRI, 2000)

Women's educational status has the strongest impact on child malnutrition, followed closely by per capita food availability.[35] In addition, child malnutrition results from major diseases such as malaria, acute respiratory infections (including pneumonia) and HIV/AIDS. Women's vulnerability is exacerbated by limited access to and control of land, despite the fact that women are the majority agricultural producers in the region.

In many SADC states, people have a diet high in carbohydrates relative to proteins and fats.[36] Clearly, having enough food available per person at a national level is a necessity but not a sufficient condition for a country to achieve food security. The correct food security ration per person at national levels does not guarantee food security, which can only be achieved when food is available to all households.

The HIV/AIDS epidemic and 'new variant famine' The pervasive HIV/AIDS epidemic is widely acknowledged to be a major driver of food insecurity in the region. One third of those who are affected by the global epidemic live in southern Africa; one third of global AIDS deaths in 2006 occurred in the region, and adult HIV prevalence exceeded 20 per cent in four countries: Swaziland, Lesotho, Botswana and Zimbabwe.[37] HIV/AIDS undermines livelihoods in four major ways: it reduces farm production and income and diminishes labour and capital owing to disease and death; it undermines the ability of households to cope with liquidation of assets and to take care of sick family members; it prevents household breadwinners from finding work and stunts migration; and it diminishes skilled staff in public service and private sectors.[38] HIV also contributes to the rise in inequality.[39] Alex de Waal and Alan Whiteside suggest that the coexistence of and interaction between acute food insecurity and high HIV prevalence could precipitate a downward spiral of households and communities into destitution, thus precipitating famine.[40] Not only does AIDS interact with and worsen other shocks to livelihood, but it also selectively undermines the very strategies that historically were employed to respond to such shocks. Such strategies vary, from reallocation of discretionary expenditures in sacrificing less essential goods, to allocations for essential assets such as livestock and farming equipment. The new variant famine (NVF) hypothesis posits that populations that are highly burdened by AIDS have difficulty recovering from transitory shocks and are forced to take more immediate measures, and for a longer period of time, compared to populations that are not affected by AIDS.[41]

One of SADC's member states, Swaziland, has experienced falling agricultural production among subsistence farmers and increased food insecurity resulting from loss of formal work by healthy breadwinners who must care for HIV-infected family members.[42] High adult morbidity and mortality deplete the asset bundles of households, leading to the liquidation of physical goods and livestock and an inability to pay for medical care and funerals. Increasingly, the burden of care is falling on those who are traditionally deemed as dependants. According to the theory's proponents, the full impact of NVF is yet to be felt.

Food price increases The global food price crisis of 2007/08 was superimposed on the broader and deeper livelihood crisis experienced in southern Africa. Rising energy prices, subsidized biofuel production, income and population growth, globalization and urbanization were among the major forces contributing to surging demand for global food. Productivity and growth were impaired by land and water constraints; underinvestment in rural infrastructure and agricultural innovation; lack of access to inputs; and unstable weather patterns due to climate change. Between 2005 and 2008, international prices of wheat and maize tripled, while rice prices increased fivefold.[43] High food prices meant that poor households were forced to allocate high proportions of their expenditures to staple foods, sometimes leading to a reduction in the frequency and consumption of diverse and nutritious diets. From 2005 to 2007, the number of undernourished people in the world increased from 848 million to 923 million, owing largely to the food price crisis.[44] Of this, the FAO estimates that rising food prices plunged an additional 24 million people in sub-Saharan Africa below the hunger threshold.[45]

As food prices declined in late 2008, the world became ensnared in a global financial crisis. The ensuing financial recession and food price hikes have seriously affected poor and vulnerable groups in southern Africa and other low-income countries, who will continue to suffer until the crisis abates.[46] It is the poorest of the poor, households headed by elderly members, and families living with HIV/AIDS, who have suffered the greatest food insecurity owing to the financial crisis.[47] Research in southern Africa indicates that the impact of increased food prices has differed from the impact of other price shocks such as increased electricity or transport prices in that the poorest people dedicate the largest share of their budget to food.[48] Thus, when food prices rise, the poor have the least ability to cut non-food expenditures to compensate for the increased costs. Higher food prices increase the burden for women, who must stretch the already limited food budget even farther. In this volatile context, food prices will remain unstable until the underlying conditions that led to the dramatic increases are corrected.

Climatic conditions In 2007 the Intergovernmental Panel on Climate Change (IPCC) concluded that global warming and climate change have direct implications for food security in southern Africa.[49] Changing weather patterns such as increased temperatures, erratic rainfall and recurrent droughts and floods threaten agricultural production and food security in the subregion. The consensus of scientific opinion is that countries in the temperate, high- to middle-latitude regions are most likely to enjoy increased agricultural production, whereas countries in tropical and subtropical regions are more likely to suffer agricultural losses as a result of climate change in future.[50] Some analysts have predicted that climate change will cause a 10 per cent reduction in maize productivity in Africa by 2055.[51] However, local agro-ecological and soil conditions, among other factors, will determine the magnitude and severity of the impacts on individual countries. Climate change is also linked directly to ecosystem services and impacts negatively on health and livelihoods under stress.[52] For example, soil degradation, already widespread, is rapidly eroding the capacity of the region's ecosystems to support food production, and water resources are coming under ever greater pressure owing to competing demands of urbanization, industry and agriculture.[53]

SADC's regional strategic framework for addressing food insecurity

SADC's strategic framework for addressing food insecurity is guided by initiatives operating at four levels. At the global level, the first MDG commits UN member states to halve the number of people who suffer from hunger by 2015. At the continental level, African leaders endorsed the Comprehensive Africa Agriculture Development Programme (CAADP) in 2003 as a plan of action for revitalizing the agriculture sector, after recognizing this sector's capacity to alleviate poverty and improve food security. One of the four pillars of the CAADP – the Framework for African Food Security (FAFS) – specifically aims at addressing inadequate food supply, widespread and persistent hunger and malnutrition, and inadequate management of food crises.[54] At the regional level, SADC's Regional Indicative Strategic Development Plan (RISDP) of 2003 provides a framework to guide member states on how to attain food security. Finally, at the national level, SADC countries have formulated various food security policies and poverty reduction strategies. However, despite this elaborate scaffolding, major implementation challenges exist.

Framework for African food security The FAFS is the first continent-wide attempt to address food insecurity. It provides an overall strategy, including recommended actions and tools from which Africa's subregional and country-specific policies can be developed. While recognizing the role of non-agricultural interventions in ensuring food security, the framework also ensures that the CAADP's agriculture growth agenda supports the chronically poor and food insecure.

Each African regional economic community (REC), including SADC, is required to prepare and adopt a long-term strategy and a medium-term operational plan for enhancing food security. However, the FAFS has not been adequately embraced at both SADC and individual country levels, as many activities are driven by the RISDP. There is little evidence that development budgets have been made available to tackle the structural causes of food insecurity, despite political commitments by donors and governments to align and coordinate their support for these national, subregional and regional interventions.[55] For example, Malawi and Zimbabwe are the only two SADC countries that have abided by the CAADP commitment to allocate 10 per cent of their national budgets to agriculture.[56]

Clearly, the FAFS is a well-designed model for addressing food insecurity. However, its implementation has been affected by significant challenges of coordination and overlap. The lack of policy frameworks and poor definition of mandates and responsibilities of line ministries in individual countries have hindered effective implementation. While the idea of creating national coordination platforms to drive the FAFS agenda at country levels is well intended, it can lead to a loose arrangement that does not guarantee success. Given that the responsibility for implementation of the FAFS lies with individual countries, it is highly likely that progress will be slow, or that the FAFS may fail to take off.

The Regional Indicative Strategic Development Plan

The SADC's RISDP identifies sustainable food security as a key priority across the region. As part of efforts to implement food security strategies under the RISDP, SADC Heads of State and Government adopted the Dar es Salaam Declaration on Agriculture and Food Security in May 2004. One of the agreed measures is increased availability of and access to key agricultural inputs for farmers, consisting of improved seed varieties, fertilizers, agrochemicals, tillage services and farm implements. For the medium to long term, SADC governments agreed to target 10 per cent of national budgets to agriculture and rural development, as mentioned earlier. SADC governments also identified the need to develop a regional food reserve facility, and improve infrastructure to promote trade and open the market, as well as construct dams for irrigation purposes. However, lack of capacity for implementation at the national level as well as within the SADC directorate charged with supporting this process, coupled with weak institutional policy frameworks, has hindered progress.[57]

In line with the RISDP goal of strengthening institutional frameworks for the implementation of the region's food security strategy, the SADC Regional Agriculture Policy (RAP) had reached an advanced stage of development by July 2010. The policy is expected to be a binding legal instrument for the implementation of the region's food, agriculture, natural resources and environmental strategies. However, there is concern that this policy may not be compatible with other regional strategies, not least the SADC biofuels strategy released in 2005, which calls for the region's self-reliance in energy through the production of biofuels.[58] (See Nagar in this volume.) Increasing farmland under production for fuel rather than food is an obviously contested issue in a context of high food insecurity.

FAFS and RISDP: the linkages

Although SADC's food security strategy purports to be guided by the FAFS, this is not clear on the ground. There are currently marked differences between the two frameworks. The implementation of the RISDP is largely tied up with addressing food availability through agricultural production. The FAFS addresses not only production concerns but also 'persistent hunger and malnutrition', highlighting issues of accessibility and utilization of food. Indeed, the emphasis transcends agricultural production, as the FAFS also emphasizes social protection, nutrition concerns and, importantly, the alignment of policies across sectors. Thus, a focus on food accessibility, availability and to some extent utilization is the core tenet of the FAFS. That access to food is a major problem in southern Africa makes it imperative not only to address food availability but also to develop a deeper and nuanced understanding of vulnerability. It is therefore critical that SADC lean towards a model that addresses the underlying causes of hunger.

Besides providing general guidelines for informing national and regional policies, the FAFS provides specific tools for assessing, measuring and implementing programmes. The RISDP was formalized in 2003 and is far more embedded within the region than the more recent FAFS, which came under discussion at the regional level only in 2008. However, integrating the RISDP within the broader and more comprehensive FAFS may strengthen the limited impact of the more production-focused regional initiative. That said, the jury is still out on the effectiveness of the CAADP process, particularly around the perennial challenge of ensuring coordination mechanisms at the country level that transcend agriculture, health, environmental services and other sectors necessary to underpin food security.

The Malawi 'success story'

One of the often-cited 'success stories' of the RISDP approach is the turnaround of Malawi from a situation of severe famine in 2001 to a position of exporting surplus food in 2009.[59] In 2004 the government of Malawi launched a nationwide agricultural inputs subsidy programme, targeting 1.3 million smallholder farmers initially and 1.75 million by 2007. The subsidies entailed coupons to buy fertilizer and seed at rates below the market price.[60] The government used discretionary budget funds and support from the UN to import fertilizer and procure improved maize seed for distribution to farmers. It invested in farmer training programmes consisting of new irrigation methods and management techniques in order to improve yields. The government created a fund to buy a percentage of the farmers' maize crops and stored the surplus for future emergencies. The result was a significant improvement in Malawi's food security strategy. After the series of food crises between 2001 and 2005, the country recorded a surplus cereal production of 1.2 million metric tonnes in the 2009/10 consumption year, and doubled the 2008 surplus of 0.5 million metric tonnes.[61]

It is on the basis of this 'success story' that the Earth Institute at Columbia University, New York, has argued that an African 'Green Revolution' is possible.[62] Nonetheless, the institute has acknowledged that Malawi's smallholder farmers would need more than subsidized farm inputs to escape the trap of dependency on the state. Land size is a major factor: the combination of a growing population and limited arable land has hampered Malawi's ability to produce food. In addition, investment in water harvesting and irrigation, diversified agriculture, village-based clinics, rural electrification, rural roads and other infrastructure is required for long-term growth. Another worrying factor is that Malawi devotes at least 60 per cent of the national agricultural budget to input and crop-marketing subsidies, leaving relatively little for the long-term investments necessary for sustainable reductions in hunger.[63]

Despite these concerns, after decades of food insecurity and recurring emergencies, Malawi has successfully implemented a national response that has led to major surpluses. The Earth Institute has argued that this could lay the foundation for achieving long-term food security: 'drawing on their core resources of land and labour [and] [d]etermined to be self-reliant and free of food aid, Malawian smallholders demonstrated that they have the ability to respond to strategic material support and incentives in order to contribute to their own well-being'.[64] More generally, and as articulated in the FAFS, Malawi and other southern African countries will require a firm ten- to fifteen-year multi-stakeholder commitment to support rural economic transformation from subsistence farming to diversified and small-scale entrepreneurial farming, including huge complementary investments in health, nutrition, education, infrastructure, water and sanitation.[65]

Land reform and 'land grabbing': threat or opportunity?

Land issues are at the centre of agricultural development and livelihoods in the region, albeit often masked by great complexities. The complications of land issues relate to colonial land alienation policies and discriminatory development and investment patterns that have limited people's access to land.[66] Some of the major issues hinge around inequalities in distribution, inefficient utilization of land, discriminatory land laws, and weak government and judiciary capacities for implementation of the reform processes.[67] SADC clearly recognizes that land reform poses significant development challenges to member states. In August 2001, the SADC Heads of State and Government directed regional land ministers to develop a regional reform strategy to guide the formulation and implementation of sustainable programmes that respond to national development priorities. This was partly based on the premise that land reform was necessary in order to achieve sustainable food security. Land reform continues to be a major source of debate in the SADC region, requiring resolution and action from member states.[68]

A powerful but contentious trend has recently begun to sweep across the developing world: countries that export capital but import food are outsourcing farm production to countries that need capital but have 'land to spare'.[69] Instead of buying food on world markets, governments and politically influential companies buy or lease farmland abroad for production of food or fuel. Beneficiaries view these projects as an attractive and viable strategy that provides for new seeds, techniques and money for agriculture, which has been neglected for decades. Opponents call the projects 'land grabs', claim that the farms will be insulated from host countries, and argue that people tilling the soil will be pushed off. These dynamics have begun to play themselves out in the region, with countries such as Zambia, Tanzania, the Democratic Republic of the Congo, Mozambique and others becoming a frontier of land transactions with uncertain implications for local producers.[70]

Recent research relating to the character and volumes of large-scale land deals or leases (over a thousand hectares) provides a new approximation of the dynamic changes taking place regarding control, ownership and use of these large tracts of land.[71] Concern about the implications of this process is provided in formulations made by several institutions in a number of proposals, recommendations and principles that serve as a framework and road map for guiding land acquisitions in order to safeguard the interests and rights of rural people. The recommendations vary in character but show a consensus on large-scale land acquisitions and lease process:

- Negotiations must be transparent.
- Rights of local communities, including customary land rights, must be protected.
- There must be a sharing of benefits between local communities and investors.
- Environmental sustainability must be ensured.
- Food security must not be compromised.[72]

As Kjell Havnevik has argued, an increased concentration of land and an increased scale of operations have critical implications for the balance between smallholder and large-scale farming and the future livelihoods of southern African rural people; for the relative importance of subsistence and domestic food supply versus export-led agriculture; and for the role of global agribusiness in the region, connected with vertical integration in agricultural production, processing and distribution.[73]

Conclusion

For more than a decade, efforts to ensure food security in southern Africa have proved to be stopgap measures in the face of societal and environmental change.[74] There is a mismatch between the problem and the responses currently being implemented at both regional and country levels. These responses have remained relatively static and isolated in terms of protocols and declarations, a situation exacerbated by the way SADC directorates operate in silos. It is crucial that good intentions and lofty declarations in response to food insecurity are translated into concrete action on the ground, even in politically charged policy areas like land reform and climate change. These agreements often fail to assign specific responsibilities for implementation to specific actors, an omission that needs to be corrected if governments and international institutions are to be held accountable for their actions. Regional governments must address the urgent and immediate need of those experiencing acute hunger largely as a result of short-term shocks. Should governments and institutions ignore long-term solutions to boosting agricultural production – strengthening of programmes to ensure access to food, and reconceptualization of health and agricultural policies to underpin nutrition – they run the risk of prolonging hunger, malnutrition and starvation in the region.

A range of complementary activities designed to ensure food security of marginalized groups at the local level – the community, household and individual – is required. These activities should largely focus on exploiting opportunities centred on increasing local food availability through production, stimulating food accessibility by, for example, supporting small enterprises through microcredit, and supporting food utilization through education. These activities can loosely be described as a form of agrarian reform and would contain options that vulnerable people could adopt in promoting livelihoods beyond survival.

For this to happen, people need to be able to diversify livelihood strategies, to access and use land, and to access credit and extension services. There is also a need for a package of interventions facilitated by development partners, including encouraging greater agricultural and dietary diversity, focusing on more nutritious crops, and supplementing the diets of the most vulnerable to improve the nutritional situation in the region. This is particularly relevant to areas where agriculture production is limited, and where there are high levels of poverty. Where there are high levels of food insecurity, people do not have ready access to agricultural produce and dietary diversity is low, resulting in high malnutrition levels. Food insecurity has a localized context, which needs to be taken into consideration when developing appropriate interventions. For such 'agrarian reform' to succeed, the necessary institutional framework needs to be in place to enable a broad range of services from government and non-governmental actors. The practical realization of such a 'joined-up government' requires concerted political commitment from governments at national levels, facilitated by SADC at the regional level in order to achieve maximum regional impact.

Notes

1 Alex de Waal and Alan Whiteside, 'New variant famine: AIDS and food crisis in southern Africa', *The Lancet*, 362(9391), 2003, pp. 1234–7; Scott Drimie, 'The underlying causes of the food crisis in the southern Africa region: Malawi, Mozambique, Zambia, and Zimbabwe', Policy research paper (Oxford: Oxfam Great Britain; Oxfam International, 2004); 'Causing hunger: an overview of the food crisis', Oxfam Briefing Paper no. 91, 2006;

Nick Maunder and Steve Wiggins, *Food Security in Southern Africa: Changing the Trend? Review of Lessons Learnt on Recent Responses to Chronic and Transitory Hunger and Vulnerability* (Oxford: Oxfam Great Britain, World Vision International, CARE, RHVP, and OCHA, 2006).

2 United Nations, *Mixed Record on Millennium Development Goals Underlines Need for Sustained Push* (New York: Department of Public Information, News and Media

Division, 1 April 2008), www.un.org/News/Press/docs/2008/sgsm11487.doc.htm.

3 Klaus Von Grebmer et al., *Global Hunger Index: The Challenge of Hunger – Focus on Financial Crisis and Gender Inequality* (Washington, DC: International Food Policy Research Institute, IFPRI, 2009), www.ifpri.org/sites/default/files/publications/ghi09.pdf.

4 In eleven countries (all in sub-Saharan Africa, except for North Korea), the Global Hunger Index increased between 1990 and 2008. Listed in order from worst-performing, the ten sub-Saharan African countries were the Democratic Republic of the Congo (DRC), Swaziland, Guinea-Bissau, Zimbabwe, Burundi, Liberia, Comoros, Botswana and Zambia. Conflict and political instability in Burundi, Comoros, the DRC, Guinea-Bissau and Liberia have widened hunger. In Botswana and Swaziland, the high prevalence of HIV/AIDS, coupled with high inequality, has severely undermined food security despite greater national wealth.

5 Food and Agriculture Organization (FAO) and World Food Programme (WFP), *The State of Food Insecurity in the World 2009: Economic Crises – Impacts and Lessons Learnt*, Rome, 2009, ftp.fao.org/docrep/fao/012/i0876e/i0876e.pdf.

6 WFP, 'WFP issues global alert at UN Security Council', Press release, 2002, one.wfp.org/english/?ModuleID=137&Key=581.

7 Jenny Clover, 'Food security in sub-Saharan Africa', *African Security Review*, 12(1), 2003, www.iss.co.za/pubs/ASR/12No1/Clover.pdf.

8 Stephen Devereux and Simon Maxwell, *Food Security in Sub-Saharan Africa* (London: Intermediate Technology Development Group, 2001).

9 Overseas Development Institute (ODI), '1997 global hunger and food security after the World Food Summit', Briefing paper, www.odi.org.uk/publications/briefing-papers/1997/1-global-hunger-food-security-world-food-summit.pdf.

10 United Kingdom Department for International Development (DfID), *The Neglected Crisis of Undernutrition: DFID's Strategy*, 2010, www.dfid.gov.uk/.../The-neglected-crisis-of-undernutrition-DFIDs-strategy.

11 Caroline Harper, Rachel Marcus and Karen Moore, 'Enduring poverty and the conditions of childhood: lifecourse and intergenerational poverty transmissions', *World Development*, 31(3), 2003, pp. 535–54.

12 Southern African Development Community, 'Dar es Salaam Declaration on Agriculture and Food Security in the SADC region', 15 May 2004, www.sadc.int/index/browse/page/173.

13 Amartya Sen, *Development as Freedom* (Oxford: Oxford University Press, 1999).

14 United Nations Economic and Social Council, 'Substantive issues arising in the implementation of the International Covenant on Economic, Social, and Cultural Rights: International Code of Conduct on the Human Right to Adequate Food', 20th session, Geneva, 26 April–14 May 1999, www.unhchr.ch/tbs/doc.nsf/0/3d 02758c707031 d58025677f003b73b9.

15 Amartya Sen, *Poverty and Famines: An Essay on Entitlement and Deprivation* (Oxford: Clarendon, 1981); Sen, *Development as Freedom*.

16 Stephen Devereux, 'From "old famines" to "new famines"', in Devereux (ed.), *The New Famines: Why Famines Persist in an Era of Globalisation* (London: Routledge, 2007).

17 Sen, *Development as Freedom*, p. 178.

18 Devereux, 'From "old famines" to "new famines"'.

19 Alex de Waal, 'AIDS, hunger, and destitution: theory and evidence for the "new variant famines" hypothesis in Africa', in Devereux, *The New Famines*.

20 Devereux, 'From "old famines" to "new famines"'.

21 Alex de Waal, 'Democratic political process and the fight against famine', Working Paper no. 107 (London: IDS, 2000).

22 Sen, *Development as Freedom*.

23 International Union for Conservation of Nature (IUCN), 'The World

Conservation Union: 2010 scoping paper', Pretoria, South Africa, 2010, www.countdown2010.net/2010/wp-content/uploads/Scoping-paper-Final.doc.

24 Southern African Development Community (SADC), *Food Agriculture and Natural Resources Directorate Annual Report, April 2008–March 2009*, Gaborone, 2009.

25 Ibid.

26 Underweight is a measure of the ratio of weight to age as compared to a reference sample. Stunting is measured as low height for age, and underweight as low weight for age, as compared to a standard population of children under five. See United Nations Children's Fund (UNICEF), *The State of the World's Children: Maternal and Newborn Health*, December 2008, New York.

27 UNICEF, 'Nutrition fact sheet', June 2003, New York.

28 Maunder and Wiggins, *Food Security in Southern Africa*.

29 SADC, *SADC HIV and AIDS Epidemic Report* (Gaborone: SADC HIV and AIDS Unit, 2008).

30 Scott Drimie and Marisa Casale, 'Multiple stressors in southern Africa: the link between HIV/AIDS, food insecurity, poverty, and children's vulnerability now and in the future', *AIDS Care*, 21(S1), August 2009, pp. 21–6.

31 Ibid.

32 Ibid.

33 Nick Maunder, cited in Ann Witteveen, 'Chronic food insecurity and vulnerable livelihoods in southern Africa: Exploring the issues and reflecting on a role for Oxfam GB', Unpublished paper, Pretoria, 2006.

34 Witteveen, 'Chronic food insecurity'.

35 Lawrence Haddad and Lisa C. Smith, *Explaining Child Malnutrition in Developing Countries: A Cross-Country Analysis* (Washington, DC: IFPRI, 2000).

36 M. De Wit, 'Hunger in SADC with specific reference to climate change: a longer-term, regional analysis', Unpublished paper (Cape Town: OneWorld Sustainable Investments, 2009).

37 Stuart Gillespie et al. (eds), 'Poverty, HIV, and AIDS: vulnerability and impact in southern Africa', *AIDS*, 21(7), 2007 (special issue).

38 Maunder and Wiggins, *Food Security in Southern Africa*.

39 Linda Richter, Geoff Foster and Lorraine Sherr, *Where the Heart is: Meeting the Psychosocial Needs of Young Children in the Context of HIV/AIDS* (The Hague: Bernard van Leer, 2006); I. M. Timaeus, 'Deaths in the family: AIDS, demography, and poverty in Africa', Inaugural lecture delivered to the London School of Hygiene and Tropical Medicine, London, 26 February 2008.

40 De Waal and Whiteside, 'New variant famine'.

41 Scott Naysmith, Alex de Waal and Alan Whiteside, 'Revisiting new variant famine: the case of Swaziland', *Food Security*, 1(3), 2010, pp. 251–60.

42 Ibid.

43 Joachim von Braun, 'The food crisis isn't over (commentary)', *Nature*, 456(701), 2008.

44 FAO and WFP, *The State of Food Insecurity in the World*.

45 Ibid.

46 See Gillespie et al., 'Poverty, HIV, and AIDS'.

47 Sithabiso Gandure, 'High food prices in eastern, central, and southern Africa: assessing impact and tracking progress towards meeting the CFA objectives', WFP, 2008, home.wfp.org/stellent/groups/public/documents/ena/wfp197247.pdf.

48 Stuart Gillespie et al., 'Food prices and the HIV response: findings from rapid regional assessments in eastern and southern Africa', *Food Security: The Science, Sociology, and Economics of Food Preparation and Access to Food*, 10 July 2009, www.springerlink.com/content/9557g3121t5x202r/.

49 Intergovernmental Panel on Climate Change (IPCC), *Climate Change 2006: Impacts, Adaptation, and Vulnerability* (Cambridge: Cambridge University Press, 2007).

50 Gina Ziervogel et al., 'Climate

variability and change: implications for household food security', Assessments of Impacts and Adaptations to Climate Change (AIACC) Working Paper no. 20, 2006.

51 Peter G. Jones and Philip K. Thornton, 'The potential impacts of climate change on maize production in Africa and Latin America in 2055', *Global Environment Change – Human and Policy Dimensions*, 13(1), 2003, pp. 51–9.

52 Millennium Ecosystem Assessment, *Ecosystems and Human Well-Being: Synthesis*, Report of the Millennium Ecosystem Assessment (Washington, DC: Island, 2005).

53 R. E. Schulze, 'Climate change and water assessments and analysis in SADC region, through the SADC Regional Vulnerability Assessment Committee: a five year programme (2005–09)', Gaborone, 2005.

54 New Partnership for Africa's Development (NEPAD), *CAADP Pillar III Framework for African Food Security (FAFS)* (n.p.: African Union and NEPAD, 2009).

55 Maunder and Wiggins, *Food Security in Southern Africa*.

56 Shengenn Fan, Babatunde Omilola and Melissa Lambert, 'Public spending for agriculture in Africa: trends and composition', Regional Strategic Analysis and Knowledge Support System (ReSAKKS) Working Paper no. 28, IFPRI, April 2009, www.ifpri.org.

57 SADC, *Food Agriculture and Natural Resources Directorate Annual Report*.

58 SADC, *Feasibility Study for the Production and Use of Biofuel in the SADC Region*, Gaborone, 2005.

59 Stephen Devereux, 'Innovations in the design and delivery of social transfers: lessons learned from Malawi' (Brighton: Institute of Development Studies, 2008).

60 John M. Kadzandira, *Regional Evidence Building Agenda (REBA) Case-Study on the Input Subsidy Program, Malawi*, Report prepared for REBA on the Regional Hunger and Vulnerability Programme (RHVP), June 2007.

61 Malawi Vulnerability Assessment Committee, 'Vulnerability forecast', *Bulletin*, 5(1), July 2009, Government of the Republic of Malawi.

62 The 'Green Revolution' refers to a series of research, development and technology transfer initiatives, occurring between 1943 and the late 1970s, that increased industrialized agriculture production in India. The initiatives involved the development of high-yielding varieties of cereal grains, expansion of irrigation infrastructure, and distribution of hybridized seeds, synthetic fertilizers and pesticides to farmers. See G. Denning et al., 'Input subsidies to improve smallholder maize productivity in Malawi: toward an African Green Revolution', *PLoS Biol*, 7(1), 2009.

63 Andrew Dorward et al., 'Towards "smart" subsidies in agriculture? Lessons from recent experience in Malawi', *Natural Resource Perspectives*, 116, September 2008.

64 Denning et al., 'Input subsidies to improve smallholder maize productivity in Malawi'.

65 Ibid.

66 SADC, *Establishing the SADC Land Reform Support Facility and Inception Activities*, Final report, September 2007.

67 Ibid.

68 Sam Moyo and Ruth Hall, 'Conflict and land reform in southern Africa: how exceptional is South Africa?', in Adekeye Adebajo, Adebayo Adedeji and Chris Landsberg (eds), *South Africa in Africa: The Post-Apartheid Era* (Scottsville: University of KwaZulu-Natal Press, 2007), pp. 150–76.

69 *The Economist*, 23 May 2009.

70 Robin Palmer, 'An annotated guide to the bibliographies on biofuels, land rights in Africa, and global land grabbing', September 2010, www.oxfam.org.uk/resources/learning/landrights/downloads/annotated_guide_to_bibliogs_biofuels_africanlandrights_global_land_grabbing_sept_2010.pdf.

71 UN Special Rapporteur on the Right to Food (UN/SRRF, Olivier De Schutter), 'Large-scale land acquisitions and leases: a set of core principles and measures to address the human rights challenges', 11 June 2009.

72 Lorenzo Cotula et al., *Land Grab or Development Opportunity? Agricultural Investment and International Land Deals in Africa*, International Institute for Environment and Development (IIED), Food and Agriculture Organization (FAO) and International Fund for Agricultural Development (IFAD), 2009.

73 Kjell Havnevik, 'Outsourcing of African lands for energy and food: challenges for smallholders', Paper presented to IPD's African Task Force, Pretoria, South Africa, July 2009.

74 Maunder and Wiggins, *Food Security in Southern Africa*; Drimie and Casale, 'Multiple stressors in southern Africa'.

11 | HIV/AIDS and human security

Gwinyayi A. Dzinesa

HIV/AIDS has adverse effects on all sectors of society. It is, in fact, the breadth and scope of these effects that make AIDS a threat to human security and a potentially destabilizing force worldwide. (Peter Piot, former UNAIDS executive director)[1]

HIV/AIDS is one of the most pervasive human security threats facing southern Africa. The pandemic has affected the Southern African Development Community (SADC) region more severely than any other subregion in the world. In 2007 the Joint United Nations Programme on HIV/AIDS (UNAIDS) estimated that southern Africa, home to 4 per cent of the global population, accounted for 35 per cent of all people living with HIV/AIDS worldwide and 32 per cent of the world's new HIV infections and AIDS-related deaths.[2] About 1.15 million southern Africans were infected during 2008, which translates into an average of 3,150 new infections each day.[3] While southern Africa's HIV/AIDS epidemics appear to have stabilized, in 2009 nine SADC countries (Botswana, Lesotho, Malawi, Mozambique, Namibia, South Africa, Swaziland, Zambia and Zimbabwe) continued to bear a disproportionate share of the global AIDS burden, with each having a national adult HIV prevalence higher than 10 per cent.[4] In 2009, Swaziland had an adult HIV prevalence of 25.9 per cent, making it the country with the highest level of infection in the world.[5] South Africa, the region's economic powerhouse, has the world's largest number of people living with HIV/AIDS, estimated at 5.5 million in 2010.[6] The pandemic has ceased to be primarily a health concern but is at the core of human security in southern Africa,[7] which has been grimly described by UNAIDS as the 'global epicentre of HIV/AIDS'.[8]

The susceptibility of southern Africans to HIV infections, including the social, cultural, economic and political dimensions, has been well documented.[9] In examining the impact of HIV/AIDS on human security in southern Africa, this chapter evaluates SADC's policy and institutional framework for HIV/AIDS; assesses the development of regional minimum standards for the harmonized control of HIV/AIDS among SADC militaries – a sector particularly vulnerable to the pandemic – as well as lessons that other SADC sectors can draw; and analyses the engagement of civil society in the region's human security agenda and fight against the pandemic.

Human security in southern Africa: a conceptual brief

With the end of armed conflicts in Mozambique and Angola in 1992 and 2002 respectively, the transition from apartheid to democracy in South Africa in 1994, and the holding of first elections in the Democratic Republic of the Congo (DRC) in 2006/07, an era of relative stability in southern Africa began. The main contemporary threats confronting the region are not military threats to the security of member states but socio-economic risks to human survival, dignity and livelihood such as HIV/AIDS, otherwise popularly known as non-military threats to human security.[10] The term 'human security' was introduced at the global level in the United Nations Development Programme's 1994 *Human Development Report*.[11] The term embraces far more than the absence of violent conflict, also encompassing economic, food, health, environmental, personal, community and political security. It views 'freedom from want' and 'freedom from fear' as two of the building blocks of human – and therefore national – security.[12] Basic human security elements that HIV/AIDS impacts negatively include survival, safety, opportunity, dignity, agency and autonomy.[13] The human security concept has garnered strong recognition at the continental and regional levels. It is important to note that human security and traditional state security are complementary and mutually dependent. The African Union's (AU) Constitutive Act of 2000 and the Common African Defence Pact of 2004 both define human security as a set of social, political, economic, military and cultural conditions that protect and promote human life and dignity.[14] According to the AU's Common African Defence and Security Policy of 2004, human security includes the right to participate fully in the process of governance; equal access to development as well as to resources and the basic necessities of life (food, shelter, safety and belonging); protection against poverty; equal access to education and healthcare; gender equality; and protection against natural disasters and ecological and environmental degradation.[15] At the regional level, SADC's key planning instruments, such as the 2003 Regional Indicative Strategic Development Plan (RISDP) and the 2004 Strategic Indicative Plan of the Organ (SIPO) (Organ on Politics, Defence and Security Cooperation, OPDSC), acknowledge the threat posed by HIV/AIDS to regional integration and economic development.[16]

Impact of HIV/AIDS on human security in southern Africa

The high incidence of the HIV/AIDS pandemic has undermined the potential of southern Africa to achieve the Millennium Development Goals (MDGs) by 2015. Halting the spread of HIV/AIDS is intricately linked with the eight other MDGs that impact human security: eradicating extreme poverty and hunger; achieving universal primary education; promoting gender equality and empowering women; reducing child mortality; improving maternal health; combating other diseases such as tuberculosis; ensuring environmental sustainability;

and developing a global partnership for development. As former UN secretary-general Kofi Annan stated: 'Halting the spread of HIV is not only an MDG in itself; it is a pre-requisite for reaching most of the others.'[17] As in the rest of sub-Saharan Africa, HIV/AIDS has wreaked havoc on all sectors of society in the region, affecting health and education; agriculture and food security; the life and dignity of individuals, households and communities; the traditional safety net; and poverty and inequality.[18]

In southern Africa, HIV/AIDS has deepened and prolonged household poverty. The pandemic has caused reduction or loss of household income as a result of prolonged illness, medical costs and funeral expenses. Many households have also collapsed following the succumbing of breadwinners to HIV/AIDS. According to the RISDP, acute poverty among child-headed or elderly-headed households in southern Africa is increasing owing to the HIV/AIDS pandemic.[19] The pandemic has increased morbidity, with negative effects on the health sector. In 2004, for example, HIV/AIDS-related bed occupancy rates in public hospitals surpassed the 50 per cent mark in most SADC states.[20] In 2010, about 90 per cent of hospital bed occupancy in Swaziland's public hospitals was HIV/AIDS-related.[21] The great demand for health services by people living with HIV/AIDS has aggravated the already deficient public health services in the region. HIV/AIDS has also been a major cause of attrition among the region's health workforce and has undermined capacity to scale up services. The impact of the HIV/AIDS pandemic on tuberculosis (TB) has been particularly devastating, and the combination of the two infections has been gloomily called the 'cursed duet'. In 2006, SADC countries had the highest incidences of HIV-related TB in the world.[22] As recently as 2010, Swaziland, South Africa and Zambia had 80 per cent,[23] 73 per cent[24] and 60–70 per cent[25] HIV–TB co-infection rates respectively. There has also been a lethal convergence between the 'cursed duet', as TB is the leading cause of death in the region among people infected with HIV. Tuberculosis was the leading cause of death among people living with HIV/AIDS in South Africa in 2010; the number of people dying from TB in the country annually increased by 334.8 per cent between 1997 and 2005.[26] Against this background, implementation of integrated TB and HIV service delivery programmes is essential for improving the diagnosis, treatment and outcomes for patients affected by both diseases.[27]

SADC's education sector has seen its capacity depleted owing to the death of teachers and educational administrators. There have also been decreased enrolment rates as a result of infected children and orphans failing to register, while dropout rates have increased owing to AIDS-related factors as well. In some SADC countries the enrolment gap between orphaned and unorphaned children is very wide. For example, in Mozambique in 2000 only 24 per cent of children whose parents were dead attended school, compared with 68 per cent of those whose parents were both still living. The impact on education has negative ripple effects on the future human capital necessary for sustainable social and economic development in southern Africa. The lack of education foments HIV vulnerability as a result of illiteracy, gender inequality and poverty.

HIV/AIDS has had a severe impact on food security and nutrition. (See Drimie and Gandure in this volume.) The Food and Agriculture Organization (FAO) has estimated that between 13 and 26 per cent of agricultural workers in SADC will die between 1985 and 2020 owing to the pandemic. High morbidity and mortality levels among the agricultural workforce have led to reduced output and contributed to famine in some SADC states. There is a link between food shortage and the probability of HIV infection and progression to AIDS.

The direct impact of HIV/AIDS on human security in southern Africa is clearly demonstrated by demographic indicators such as life expectancy and mortality. There has been a marked reduction in regional average adult life-span, with some SADC member states experiencing life expectancy levels similar to those of the 1950s.[28] In Botswana, for instance, life expectancy dropped from almost seventy years to forty-four within a decade, owing mainly to HIV/AIDS. As already stated, the region suffers a disproportionate share of HIV/AIDS-related deaths. The pandemic has caused massive orphanhood – about six million children had been orphaned owing to AIDS by the end of 2003.[29] The trend has continued. By 2010, about 1.2 million children had been orphaned as a result of HIV/AIDS-related deaths in Zambia alone.[30] In South Africa in 2010, 43 per cent of maternal mortality and 57 per cent of under-five mortality were HIV-related.[31]

Women and girls have been disproportionately affected by HIV/AIDS in sub-Saharan Africa, where women account for 60 per cent of all HIV infections, with young women between ages fifteen and nineteen particularly vulnerable.[32] Analysts note that the HIV/AIDS pandemic has flourished along the 'well-worn path of gender inequality', where gender inequity, violence against women and childhood sexual abuse contribute to increased HIV risk among women.[33] Meanwhile, gender roles and relations influence access to, and use of, care and support services for females and males living with HIV.[34] Women and girls are more likely than men and boys to assume the responsibility of caring for the sick and orphans. Since young adult women are disproportionately affected by HIV/AIDS, it is often elderly women and young girls who step into these onerous roles, worse still in a context of inadequate public and private support services.[35] Furthermore, girls are more likely than boys to be withdrawn from school to assist in the household and as a cost-cutting measure.

There is a complex nexus between southern Africa's migration patterns, HIV/AIDS and human security.[36] In order to promote deeper integration, SADC member states adopted the Protocol on the Facilitation of Movement of Persons in 2005. (See Nyamnjoh and Mususa in this volume.) Migrant workers and other mobile populations are more vulnerable to contracting and transmitting

HIV/AIDS owing to factors such as oscillatory migration patterns; mobility and living away from spouses; separation from sociocultural norms that regulate behaviour in stable communities; isolated work environments with limited recreational options; limited access to health facilities and HIV/AIDS support programmes; overcrowded living quarters or having to sleep in trucks; sexual freedoms that come with a sense of anonymity; and lack of rights and legal protection.[37] In 2006, UNAIDS noted that the rates of HIV infection were growing fastest in those areas linked by major transport routes to Malawi, South Africa and Zimbabwe: the areas with a high degree of migrancy.[38] SADC has also specifically identified corridor border areas as a focus for high-risk activities and factors for HIV infection: sex work; sex with non-regular partners; low knowledge of HIV/AIDS; low condom use; high HIV prevalence among truck drivers and sex workers; weak implementation of national HIV prevention programmes; and illicit drug use.[39]

In some host southern African countries, such as South Africa, foreign immigrants have been victims of discrimination, exploitation, xenophobia and harassment. (See Nyamnjoh and Mususa in this volume.) At the same time, their access to legal and social protection, as well as health services, has been limited. In South Africa, for example, '[m]igrant and refugee women in the townships have been disproportionately affected by the recent xenophobia, not only because the violence has played out on the site of their bodies (through beatings and rape), but also because the violence has been directed towards their homes (through burning and looting)'.[40]

SADC policy and institutional framework for HIV/AIDS

Efforts by individual SADC member states to address HIV/AIDS pre-date the official SADC regional response to the pandemic. During the 1980s, individual SADC countries variously focused on HIV prevention, care and support, as well as mitigating the pandemic's socio-economic impact under the rubric of the Global Programme on AIDS, managed by the World Health Organization (WHO).[41] Since the 1990s, SADC countries have recognized that the pandemic affects all sectors of their economies, making it imperative to craft multi-sectoral strategies to address HIV/AIDS. To coordinate their plans, the region's governments have established national AIDS councils and commissions, which remain major actors in the regional fight to reduce the socio-economic impact of the pandemic. SADC's drive to develop harmonized HIV/AIDS policy and institutional mechanisms has built upon existing and proven country-level best practices.

SADC identified HIV/AIDS as one of its four key priority areas alongside military security, food security and governance. The pandemic was given prominence as a standing item on the agenda of the SADC Summit of Heads of State and Government, which committed itself to the formulation of a conducive regional policy environment and institutional framework to tackle the effects of HIV/AIDS.[42] SADC has also endorsed continental and global instruments and mechanisms to combat the impact of HIV/AIDS, such as the April 2001 Abuja Declaration, through which member states allocate at least 15 per cent of their national budgets to the health sector; the 2001 New Partnership for Africa's Development (NEPAD); the 2006 Brazzaville Commitment on Scaling up towards Universal Access to HIV/AIDS Prevention, Treatment, Care and Support in Africa; the MDGs, adopted at the United Nations Millennium Summit of 2000; and the UN General Assembly's 2001 Declaration of Commitment on HIV/AIDS.

SADC's overarching strategic framework comprises two major sections: the first provides an overview of the regional HIV/AIDS situation and analyses of responses; and the second lays out the operational planning, such as goals and objectives and the activities that need to be undertaken.[43] The subregional body recognizes that the war against HIV/AIDS needs a coordinated, sufficiently funded, innovative, interdisciplinary and multi-sectoral strategy.

SADC has established an HIV and AIDS Unit, comprising a core team of four experts complemented by project staff, within the SADC Secretariat's Department of Strategic Planning, Gender and Policy Harmonization, in order to coordinate the subregional body's response to the pandemic. The HIV and AIDS Unit is tasked with ensuring the successful operationalization of SADC's HIV/AIDS strategic framework. The common regional HIV/AIDS strategy focuses on six major areas: policy development and harmonization in key areas of prevention, care, treatment and support; mainstreaming HIV/AIDS strategy within all SADC policies and programmes; capacity-building to mainstream HIV/AIDS strategy; development of requisite technical resources; resource mobilization; and monitoring and evaluation of regional and global commitments.[44] Given the multidimensional and multi-sectoral nature of the HIV/AIDS pandemic, SADC's HIV and AIDS Unit is expected to work closely with the SADC Secretariat's directorates (those that have a focal point dedicated to HIV/AIDS) and other units.

SADC recognizes the roles of and importance of cooperating with other national, regional and international actors in a concerted and comprehensive fight against the HIV/AIDS pandemic. In 2009, SADC Executive Secretary Tomaz Salomão noted:

> For the SADC region to achieve success in preventing new HIV infections in the coming years, robust strategic partnerships must be consolidated between government, civil society groups, community-based and faith-based organisations, traditional authorities, regional bodies, international development partners and the private sector.[45]

The HIV and AIDS Unit works with member states (through national AIDS councils and commissions) and other regional and international stakeholders such as civil society organizations and international donors. It has played an instrumental role in the development of the policy documents mentioned earlier.

All Southern African countries have shown national commitment to combating HIV/AIDS and have formulated relevant policies and put in place structures to coordinate national multi-sectoral responses to the pandemic.[46] This is in accordance with the '3 Ones Principle': establishing one agreed HIV/AIDS framework, one national HIV/AIDS coordinating committee, and one agreed monitoring and evaluation framework. The national structures are the direct operational link with SADC's HIV and AIDS Unit and are critical to the implementation of the regional HIV/AIDS framework.

SADC's prevention strategy and action plan have underpinned efforts to harmonize and strengthen HIV prevention policies in the region. Twelve SADC member states reviewed their national policy frameworks and programmes in order to harmonize them with the regional strategy.[47] Six of these states were fully aligned to the regional framework, five were partially synchronized, while one was not aligned at all.[48] SADC member states have implemented several HIV prevention strategies, including information, education and communication programmes for the general public and relatively higher-risk groups (such as truck drivers, sex workers and men who have sex with men); condom promotion and distribution; voluntary counselling and testing; treatment of sexually transmitted infections; and promotion of abstinence.[49] Male circumcision and addressing multiple concurrent sexual partnerships (defined as having two or more partnerships that overlap in time) have recently emerged as popular preventive measures across the region. Coverage of prevention of mother-to-child transmission of HIV has also increased throughout southern Africa owing to a higher number of HIV-positive pregnant women accessing antiretroviral drugs to reduce transmission of the virus to their children.[50] At a June 2009 SADC meeting, member states undertook to halve new adult infections by 2015 and to eliminate mother-to-child HIV transmission.[51]

According to UNAIDS, the preventive measures are paying dividends, as there have been reductions in HIV incidence in some SADC countries.[52] For example, a drop in HIV incidence was reported among women in Zambia between 2002 and 2007. In Tanzania, national HIV incidence fell between 2004 and 2008. Zimbabwe has experienced a steady fall in HIV prevalence since the late 1990s, owing to changes in sexual behaviour.

In terms of treatment, southern Africa has made tremendous strides in recent years. According to UNAIDS, Africa's antiretroviral therapy coverage increased from 7 per cent in 2003 to 42 per cent in 2008, with particularly high coverage (48 per cent) in southern and eastern Africa.[53] This has lowered AIDS-related deaths but contributed to increased HIV prevalence owing to the longer life expectancy of those under treatment.

To facilitate regular and consistent tracking of the impact of the regional framework and programmes, the SADC Secretariat has since 2006 made efforts to produce annual HIV/AIDS epidemic reports based on data from member states. In order to address concerns about the difficulties of analysing regional HIV/AIDS trends owing to individual countries using different indicators, the SADC Secretariat, with financial support from the European Union (EU) and technical support from UNAIDS's Regional Support Team, developed an HIV/AIDS monitoring and evaluation framework for SADC in 2006.[54] This regional framework sensibly defines indicators in the priority areas identified in the Maseru Declaration, namely prevention and social mobilization; improving care and access to counselling, as well as testing services and support; resource mobilization; and strengthening of monitoring and evaluation. The framework uses two sets of indicators: the UN General Assembly's Special Session on HIV/AIDS indicators, and pointers to progress in the implementation of the Maseru Declaration. In 2007, SADC member states agreed on a set of twenty-six common HIV/AIDS indicators that would form the basis of standardized HIV/AIDS epidemic reports.[55] All SADC states have since put in place some monitoring and evaluation systems that are essential for the production of annual epidemic reports. Some SADC states have also conducted training on the design, planning and management of monitoring and evaluation systems. However, the production of comprehensive annual SADC HIV/AIDS epidemic reports has been undermined by the failure of member states to provide the SADC Secretariat with timely, complete, disaggregated data in line with the agreed SADC reporting format. The onus is on member states to submit complete reports in a sufficiently timely manner to allow the SADC Secretariat to objectively document HIV/AIDS trends in the region and craft concrete policy recommendations to enhance the regional response to the pandemic.

A major event in the development of technical resources was the completion of a regional HIV/AIDS database and online portal by 2006. SADC teamed up with the Faculty of Health Science at the University of the Witwatersrand in Johannesburg, South Africa, to develop the database. The project was part of an expanded multi-sectoral response to HIV/AIDS in the region funded by the EU in the amount of 7.6 million euros.[56] The database presented a valuable centralized depository of major regional HIV/AIDS documents and research. An evaluation of the project showed that SADC has significant home-grown research and expertise on the pandemic; the database enhanced well-informed regional collaboration in combating HIV/AIDS through the coordination and sharing of technical information and resources, as well as assisting in the monitoring and evaluation process.[57]

Through the Maseru Declaration, SADC member states reaffirmed their commitment to allocate at least 15 per cent of their annual budgets to the improvement of the health sector. However, in 2008, out of nine member states that reported on this commitment in their annual epidemic reports, only one exceeded the set target, while the range of allocations to the health sector was 5 to 19 per cent.[58] Meanwhile, the severe skills shortage in the health sectors in the region continued to present significant obstacles to effective implementation of HIV/AIDS programmes.

Funding for prevention, treatment, care and support activities in SADC has increased considerably in the past decade from sources like the World Bank's Multi-Country HIV/AIDS Programme for Africa (MAP) and the EU. From the United States, the President's Emergency Plan for AIDS Relief (PEPFAR) and the Global Fund to Fight AIDS, Tuberculosis and Malaria have been major sources of investment. (See Ngwenya in this volume.) PEPFAR, an initiative to combat the global HIV/AIDS pandemic, was launched in 2003 by former US president George W. Bush, who committed to providing US$15 billion to fund the plan's first five-year cycle (2003–08).[59] After assuming office in 2009, President Barack Obama announced a US$51 billion budget for PEPFAR, but over a period of six years – this was not in line with the US$48 billion that Obama promised would be rolled out by 2013, nor with the additional US$1 billion annual increase he had promised during his election campaign. The Global Aids Alliance estimated that the consequent shortfall would lead to 1 million people worldwide not receiving antiretroviral treatment and 2.9 million pregnant women transmitting HIV to their children, with Africa, especially southern Africa, the hardest hit. About 27 million people would also not have access to sexually transmitted infection prevention programmes, while 1.9 million orphans and vulnerable children would not receive care and support services. The Global Fund to Fight AIDS, Tuberculosis and Malaria was established in 2002 to prevent and treat these three profound health concerns. By 2009 the fund had approved US$15.6 billion for 572 programmes in 140 countries, with 57 per cent of the monies channelled to sub-Saharan Africa.

UNAIDS estimated that at the end of 2008, US$13.7 billion had been made available for the global AIDS response, representing a 21 per cent increase above the US$11.3 billion in 2007.[60] However, fears that the global financial crisis of 2007–09 would reduce political interest and financial support for HIV/AIDS programmes in the region at a time when treatment costs were increasing owing to longer life expectancy were realized when global AIDS funding flatlined between 2008 and 2009.[61] Critics of the notion that the uncertain global economic climate precluded increases in HIV/AIDS funding have pointed out that the trillions of dollars provided to bail out the banking sector show that the issue is one of political priorities rather than resource constraints.[62] Against this backdrop it is important that SADC states meet their commitment under the AU's Abuja Declaration to allocate at least 15 per cent of their national budgets towards health in order to alleviate the dire consequences of reduced HIV/AIDS funding.

HIV/AIDS, the military and human security

Human security and the traditional state-centred notion of security are complementary and mutually dependent. There is concern that HIV/AIDS can weaken SADC militaries and potentially compromise the territorial integrity of member states. An intense competition for national resources between HIV-ravaged military forces and civilian institutions might undermine other productive sectors of regional economies and intensify poverty. The military sector, along with other uniformed forces, is at the coalface of the pandemic as its demographics, deployment patterns, work environment and status and power make it particularly vulnerable to contraction and transmission of HIV/AIDS.[63] It is against this backdrop that the UN General Assembly's Special Session on HIV/AIDS identified national uniformed forces as a key area to be addressed in the global action against the spread of the HIV/AIDS pandemic.

While there are no accurate statistics for HIV infection rates within SADC militaries, some of the prevalence estimates range from 20 to 60 per cent.[64] HIV/AIDS potentially threatens military organizational effectiveness at the political, strategic, operational and tactical levels.[65] This makes it important to craft contextualized and comprehensive strategies to mitigate the implications of HIV/AIDS for SADC militaries. The 2003 Maseru Declaration specifically identified the region's uniformed services, including the military, as a vulnerable population requiring specially targeted interventions, but also as capable of acting as 'agents of change' to strengthen awareness and prevention among communities owing to its well-organized and disciplined structures.[66]

SADC is currently engaged in establishing a regional Stand-by Brigade (SADCBRIG) that will be part of an African Stand-by Force earmarked to be fully operational by the end of 2015. (See Saunders in this volume.) The high incidence of HIV/AIDS in the national militaries potentially threatens the military readiness of SADCBRIG.[67] UN Security Council Resolution 1308 of 2000 recognizes the possible damaging impact of HIV/AIDS on the health of international peacekeepers, including support personnel. UNAIDS therefore produced tools and information on HIV programming, activities and best practices in the uniformed services, including a programming guide, an awareness card, a peer education kit and a DVD.

SADC militaries have acknowledged the potential strategic, operational and tactical implications of HIV/AIDS. They have implemented independent HIV/AIDS prevention, treatment and care programmes at the national level but have struggled to fully operationalize harmonized policies and programmes at the regional level.[68] It is against this backdrop that SADC adopted the Regional Minimum Standards for Harmonized Control of HIV and AIDS, Malaria and Tuberculosis Among SADC Militaries in 2009. These standards were produced by the SADC Secretariat, working closely with the SADC Military Health Services and in collaboration with various stakeholders, including the Centre for

Conflict Resolution (CCR) in Cape Town, South Africa, the African Development Bank, the AU and the UN. The Regional Minimum Standards were based on a review of existing national, regional and global military HIV/AIDS policies to ensure relevance to, and implementability in, the SADC context, comprehensiveness and alignment with international standards. They provide regional contextualized guidelines for SADC militaries to synchronize prevention and control of AIDS, malaria and tuberculosis in line with the Maseru Declaration and Article 10 of the SADC Protocol on Health, which prioritize the control of communicable diseases through a harmonized regional policy.

A year after the adoption of the Regional Minimum Standards, an inaugural workshop of the SADC Military HIV Technical Committee, comprising the fifteen member states' military HIV coordinators, was convened in Victoria Falls, Zimbabwe, where the committee was officially launched. The committee used the workshop as a forum to begin developing a SADC military HIV strategic framework for implementing the Regional Minimum Standards as well as to share member states' experiences relating to HIV/AIDS. The progress in harmonizing control of HIV/AIDS policies among SADC militaries could present best practices and lessons for other regional sectors grappling with crafting common policies.

The Victoria Falls meeting postponed discussion of the critical training of SADCBRIG in HIV prevention. It is imperative that SADC's Military HIV Technical Committee complete the drawn-out process of producing a manual to provide pre-deployment training for militaries in preparation for peace support operations. Meanwhile, it is noteworthy that some southern African militaries have adopted CCR's manual, *HIV/AIDS in Integrated Peace Support Operations in Africa*, to educate their personnel on HIV/AIDS and other sexually transmitted infections.

Civil society, HIV/AIDS and human security in southern Africa

Civil society is, in principle, viewed as an important institution that can support, complement and enhance SADC's agenda. Article 23 of the SADC Treaty identifies civil society and non-governmental organizations (NGOs) as key stakeholders in regional processes. Article 5(2) stresses the need to 'encourage the people of the region and their institutions ... to participate fully in the implementation of the programmes and projects of SADC' as key to meeting the regional body's objectives. Notwithstanding these commitments, there has been concern that civil society participation in formal SADC processes has been 'marginal and ad hoc'.[69] During the past decade there have been efforts to enhance SADC–civil society cooperation in the area of human security and HIV/AIDS. For example, as previously discussed, CCR worked closely with the Namibian Ministry of Defence and SADC to support the development of the Regional Minimum Standards for Harmonized Control of HIV and AIDS, Malaria and Tuberculosis Among SADC Militaries, which were adopted in 2009.[70] CCR also produced a training manual in 2010, *HIV/ AIDS in Integrated Peace Support Operations in Africa*, in partnership with the Kofi Annan International Peacekeeping Training Centre (KAIPTC) in Ghana, which is being used by militaries in southern and western Africa.

In December 2008 the SADC Organ on Politics, Defence and Security and the SADC Council of NGOs (SADC-CNGO) co-hosted a meeting to discuss ways of collaborating and implementing programmes in specific areas. The SADC Organ and Pax Africa also hosted a conference in Johannesburg on 12 and 13 March 2009 on the theme 'Human security in SADC: accelerating achievement of the region's human security objectives through partnerships'. This meeting aimed to design an action plan for civil society support for regional human security priorities in collaboration with the SADC Secretariat and its Directorate for Politics, Defence and Security.[71] SADC's HIV and AIDS Unit has also organized meetings involving strong civil society participation to discuss regional frameworks and efforts to combat the pandemic.[72]

The engagement of civil society in a regional multi-sectoral response that also includes governments, business and the media is critical for designing effective programmes and ensuring their successful implementation. At the Johannesburg conference, the SADC Organ's director, Tanki Mothae, called upon civil society to provide complementary support to the directorate, such as institutional strengthening, training, capacity-building, technical assistance, policy advice and research and analysis.[73] An example of a prominent regional NGO with wide-ranging experience in HIV/AIDS interventions is the Southern African HIV and AIDS Information Dissemination Service (SAfAIDS), established in 1994. SAfAIDS is based in Tshwane (Pretoria), South Africa, and has two other country offices, in Lusaka, Zambia, and Harare, Zimbabwe. It works with local partners in Angola, Botswana, Lesotho, Malawi, Mozambique, Namibia, South Africa, Swaziland, Zambia and Zimbabwe to strengthen the capacity of HIV/AIDS organizations. SAfAIDS also focuses on advocacy; policy analysis; information production, collection and dissemination; as well as networking and building partnerships and leadership in promoting dialogue on cutting-edge issues related to HIV/AIDS in response to the needs of communities. Through its work, the NGO has promoted the understanding and analysis of HIV/AIDS in the region as a development issue rather than simply as a health issue.[74]

Civil society therefore plays important advocacy and education roles that raise HIV/AIDS awareness among citizens and policy-makers, making partnerships with NGOs imperative. NGOs may be more disposed to quickly and flexibly implement programmes, including reaching out to populations that governments may not be able to engage. Engaging religious and traditional leaders and organizations facilitates the harnessing of their potential for mobilizing broad societal support, rather than hampering effective prevention and education efforts. Civil society could also play a monitoring and evaluation role. Against this backdrop and the attendant potential for civil society to play strong roles in fighting the HIV/AIDS pandemic, the indications that SADC may be moving from rhetoric to action in terms of establishing partnerships with civil society are encouraging and need to be built upon.

Conclusion

Southern Africa remains the global epicentre of the HIV/AIDS pandemic. This exceptional 'hyper'-epidemic has had a tremendous impact on human security in the region. SADC states have formulated national-level responses, although these have been uneven. Though SADC has sought to develop a harmonized, innovative and comprehensive regional framework to combat HIV/AIDS, sound, self-implementing strategies are lacking and southern African countries face the challenge of executing them effectively on the ground.[75] The responses of SADC member states to HIV/AIDS can be criticized for not being evidence-based and thus not aligned with epidemiological realties, and compounded by limited capacity, resources and political will to implement the regional agenda.[76] In some cases, local and community responses have been weak. Overall, coordination challenges have hampered programme delivery. The development of strong, evidence-based strategies that are timely, coherent and relevant to the needs of countries is important. Partnerships and collaboration at the national, regional and global levels that include civil society and international agencies and institutions are vital to ensuring an effective response.

SADC should continue to prioritize the implementation of its prevention strategy; strengthen the community response to orphans and vulnerable children to ensure that those who are affected by HIV/AIDS remain in school; explore cross-border initiatives; and enhance member states' monitoring and evaluation mechanisms, such as through the promotion of a regional peer review system. The SADC Secretariat should ensure that its member states deliver on the continental and global commitments that it has endorsed, especially in terms of budgetary allocations to the health sector. The subregional body should share best experiences with Africa's other regional economic communities (RECs), such as the Economic Community of West African States (ECOWAS), the Economic Community of Central African States (ECCAS), the Intergovernmental Authority on Development (IGAD) and the Arab Maghreb Union (AMU). SADC, along with other RECs, should ensure the AU's operationalization of forums for the exchange of inter-regional experiences and identification of common issues among RECs.[77] This would ensure an integrated, synergistic and systemized continental approach, while promoting the comparative advantages of the RECs.

SADC's security structure, the SADC Organ on Politics, Defence and Security, remains preoccupied with more traditional threats. The SADC's peace and security blueprint, the Strategic Indicative Plan for the Organ, recognizes HIV/AIDS as a threat, but addressing the pandemic remains largely a responsibility of SADC's HIV and AIDS Unit and other SADC directorates that are separate from the SADC Organ.[78] The original SIPO expired in 2009; it remains to be seen whether the new SIPO will address these weaknesses. In particular, cooperation between the SADC Organ and other directorates should be institutionalized in order to more effectively address multifaceted human security challenges, including HIV/AIDS.[79]

Notes

1 Elhadj Sy, 'Gender, HIV/AIDS, and human security', 2001, www.un.org/womenwatch/daw/csw/Sy2001.htm.

2 See Southern African Development Community (SADC), 'SADC HIV prevention meeting: achieving prevention targets', Meeting report, Johannesburg, 7–9 June 2009; US Agency for International Development (USAID), 'HIV/AIDS health profile: southern Africa region', 2011, www.usaid.gov/our_work/global_health/aids/Countries/africa/southernafrica_profile.pdf.

3 SADC, 'SADC HIV prevention meeting', p. 1.

4 Joint United Nations Programme on HIV/AIDS (UNAIDS), 'Sub-Saharan Africa: latest epidemiological trends', 2010, www.unaids.org/en/media/unaids/contentassets/dataimport/pub/factsheet/2009/20091124_fs_ssa_en.pdf.

5 UNAIDS, 'Swaziland: HIV and AIDS estimates', 2010, www.unaids.org/en/regionscountries/countries/swaziland.

6 South Africa Department of Health, 'Universal access: treatment and prevention scale-up – the South African experience', Speech by Aaron Motsoaledi, South African minister of health, at the XVIII International AIDS Conference, 20 July 2010, www.doh.gov.za/search/index.html.

7 See Jacqui Ala, 'AIDS as a new security threat', in Mwesiga Baregu and Christopher Landsberg (eds), *From Cape to Congo: Southern Africa's Evolving Security Challenges* (Boulder, CO: Lynne Rienner, 2003), pp. 131–58.

8 UNAIDS, 'AIDS epidemic update: December 1998', 1998, data.unaids.org/publications/irc-pub06/epiupdate98_en.pdf.

9 See, for example, Angela Ndinga-Muvumba and Robyn Pharoah (eds), *HIV/AIDS and Society in South Africa* (Scottsville, South Africa: University of KwaZulu-Natal Press, 2008); Peter Fourie and Martin Schönteich, 'Africa's new security threat: HIV/AIDS and human security in southern Africa', *African Security Review*, 10(4), 2001, pp. 29–42; Robert Shell, 'Halfway to the holocaust: the economic, demographic and social implications of the AIDS pandemic to the year 2010 in the southern African region', in *HIV/AIDS: A Threat to the African Renaissance*, Occasional Paper Series (Johannesburg: Konrad Adenauer Foundation, 2000); Martin Schönteich, 'HIV/AIDS and security', Regional Governance and AIDS Forum, Institute for Democracy in Africa (IDASA)/United Nations Development Programme (UNDP), HIV Development Project for Southern Africa, 2–4 April 2003; Ala, 'AIDS as a new security threat'; SADC, 'Expert think tank meeting on HIV prevention in high-prevalence countries in southern Africa', Meeting report, Maseru, Lesotho, 10–12 May 2006.

10 Brittany Kesselman, 'Human security in the SADC region', *African Peace and Security Agenda*, 5(1), March 2009, p. 5.

11 See UNDP, *Human Development Report 1994* (New York: Oxford University Press, 1994).

12 Kofi Annan, 'Secretary-General salutes International Workshop on Human Security in Mongolia', Press Release SG/SM/7382, Ulan Bator, 8–10 May 2000, www.un.org/News/Press/docs/2000/20000508.sgsm7382.doc.html.

13 Sy, 'Gender, HIV/AIDS, and human security'.

14 Centre for Conflict Resolution (CCR), 'HIV/AIDS and militaries in southern Africa', Seminar report, Windhoek, Namibia, 9–10 July 2006, p. 6.

15 African Union (AU), 'Common African Defence and Security Policy', 2004, para. 6, www.africa-union.org/News_Events/2ND%20EX%20ASSEMBLY/Declaration%20on%20a%20Comm.Af%20Def%20Sec.pdf.

16 SADC, *The Regional Indicative Strategic Development Plan*, 2003, and SADC, *Strategic Indicative Plan for the Organ on Politics, Defence, and Security Cooperation*, 2004, www.sadc.int.

17 UNAIDS, 'Achieving the MDGs: why the AIDS response counts', 2008, www.unaids.org/en/KnowledgeCentre/Resources/FeatureStories/archive/2008/20080925_Achieving_MDG.asp.

18 See CCR, 'HIV/AIDS and militaries in southern Africa'.

19 SADC, *The Regional Indicative Strategic Development Plan* and *Strategic Indicative Plan for the Organ on Politics, Defence, and Security Cooperation*.

20 SADC, *Institutional Framework for the SADC HIV and AIDS Programme* (Gaborone: SADC HIV and AIDS Unit, 2004), p. 7.

21 Tsembeni Magongo, 'Umbutfo Swaziland Defence Force (USDF) HIV/AIDS programme', Presentation at the SADC Military HIV and AIDS Technical Committee Workshop, Victoria Falls, Zimbabwe, 2–4 August 2010.

22 World Health Organization (WHO), 'Report from the Expert Consultation on Drug-Resistant Tuberculosis', 2006, www.sahealthinfo.org/tb/expert.htm.

23 Magongo, 'Umbutfo Swaziland Defence Force (USDSF) HIV/AIDS Programme'.

24 South Africa Department of Health, 'Universal access'.

25 Lawson F. Simapuka, 'Challenges of management of HIV infection in the Zambia Defence Force (ZDF)', Presentation at the SADC Military HIV and AIDS Technical Committee Workshop, Victoria Falls, Zimbabwe, 2–4 August 2010.

26 South Africa Department of Health, 'Universal access'.

27 Andrea A. Howard and Wafaa M. El-Sadr, 'Integration of tuberculosis and HIV services in sub-Saharan Africa: lessons learned', *Clinical Infectious Diseases*, 50(supp. 3), 2010, pp. S238–S244.

28 SADC, *Institutional Framework for the SADC HIV and AIDS Programme*, p. 19.

29 SADC Parliamentary Forum, *Strategic Plan for SADC-PF on HIV and AIDS, 2007–2011*, 2007, p. 6, www.sadcpf.org.

30 Simapuka, 'Challenges of management of HIV infection in the Zambia Defence Force (ZDF)'.

31 South Africa Department of Health, 'Universal access'.

32 UNAIDS, 'Sub-Saharan Africa'.

33 See International AIDS Society, 'Advancing evidence and equity: report on the XVIII International AIDS Conference (AIDS 2010)', Vienna, Austria, 18–23 July 2010, p. 4.

34 UNAIDS, *Operational Guide on Gender and HIV/AIDS: A Rights-based Approach* (Amsterdam: UNAIDS Inter-Agency Task Team on Gender and HIV/AIDS and KIT Publishers, 2005), www.genderandaids.org/downloads/events/Operational%20Guide.pdf.

35 Ibid.

36 See Jonathan Crush, Bruce Frayne and Miriam Grant, 'Linking migration, HIV/AIDS, and urban food security in southern and eastern Africa', 2006, programs.ifpri.org/renewal/pdf/urbanrural.pdf.

37 International Organization for Migration, 'Partnership on HIV/AIDS and mobile populations in southern Africa', Pamphlet, April 2004. See also SADC, 'SADC HIV prevention meeting'.

38 UNAIDS, 'Report on the global AIDS epidemic', May 2006.

39 João Samuel Caholo (SADC deputy executive secretary for regional integration), 'Status of regional integration in the SADC region', 18 October 2010, www.un.org/africa/osaa/speeches/SADC_Presentation_18Oct2010.pdf.

40 Nadia Sanger, 'Foreigners know how to treat a woman: our South African brothers are players, abuse physically and emotionally; you can't depend on them – interrogating the links between xenophobic attitudes, gender, and male violence in Du Noon', Cape Town, 2008, www.boell.org.za/downloads/Report_on_Xenophobia_and_Gender.pdf.

41 SADC, *SADC HIV and AIDS Strategic Framework and Programme of Action: 2003–2007*, 2003, p. 7.

42 These initiatives have included the Maseru Declaration on HIV/AIDS of 2003; SADC HIV/AIDS Strategic Framework for 2000–2004; SADC HIV/AIDS Strategic Framework for 2003–2007, which replaced the 2000–2004 policy; SADC Code of Conduct on HIV and Employment; Regional Business Plan for HIV/AIDS for 2004–2008; SADC HIV/AIDS Monitoring and Evaluation Framework of 2006; SADC HIV/AIDS Strategic Framework for 2010–2015; SADC HIV/AIDS Business Plan for 2010–2015; SADC Framework on Best Practices; SADC Framework on Coordination; SADC Sexually Transmitted Infections (STI) Framework; People Living with HIV and AIDS (PLWHA) Advocacy Framework; and SADC Prevention Strategy and Plan of Action for 2008–2010.

43 See SADC, *SADC HIV and AIDS Strategic Framework and Programme of Action: 2003–2007*.

44 SADC, *Institutional Framework for the SADC HIV and AIDS Programme*, p. 7.

45 SADC, 'SADC HIV prevention meeting', p. v.

46 SADC, *Institutional Framework for the SADC HIV and AIDS Programme*, p. 19.

47 SADC, 'SADC HIV prevention meeting', p. 2.

48 Ibid., p. 2.

49 Kaka Mudambo, SADC Secretariat, personal communication, 5 August 2010.

50 Ibid.

51 SADC, 'SADC HIV prevention meeting'.

52 UNAIDS, 'Sub-Saharan Africa'.

53 UNAIDS, 'AIDS epidemic update: 2009', p. 9.

54 SADC, 'SADC member states HIV and AIDS epidemic update: proposed report format', July 2007, www.sadc.int.

55 Ibid.

56 SADC, SADC HIV Database *and Online Portal Project*, www.sadc.int.

57 Ibid.

58 Mudambo, personal communication, 5 August 2010.

59 Hilda Hecker, 'Effects of the global economic crisis: examining the impact on HIV and AIDS funding', 2009, www.sangonet.org.za/category/defined-tags/health/hiv-and-aids?page=. See also UNAIDS and World Bank, 'The global economic crisis and HIV prevention and treatment programmes: vulnerabilities and impact', June 2009, data.unaids.org/pub/Report/2009/jc1734_econ_crisis_hiv_response_en.pdf.

60 UNAIDS, 'Fact sheet: AIDS funding 2008', data.unaids.org/pub/FactSheet/2009/20090209_fs_available-funding_en.pdf.

61 International AIDS Society, 'Advancing evidence and equity', p. 5. See also SADC, 'SADC HIV prevention meeting', p. 6.

62 International AIDS Society, 'Advancing evidence and equity', p. 5.

63 See, for example, Martin Rupiya (ed.), *The Enemy Within: Southern African Militaries' Quarter-Century Battle with HIV and AIDS* (Pretoria: Institute for Security Studies, 2006).

64 See ibid.

65 John K. Sagala, 'HIV/AIDS and the military in sub-Saharan Africa: impact on military organizational effectiveness', *Africa Today*, 53(1), Autumn 2006, pp. 53–77.

66 SADC, Maseru Declaration.

67 Dawn Nagar, 'Africa's peace efforts

at risk from HIV/AIDS', *Business Day* (South Africa), 26 November 2010.

68 CCR, *HIV/AIDS in Integrated Peace Support Operations in Africa: A Training Manual*, Cape Town, 2010, p. 6.

69 Pax Africa, 'SADC and Pax Africa host conference on human security', *Africa Peace and Security Agenda*, 5(1), March 2009, p. 32.

70 See, for example, CCR, 'Whither SADC? An agenda for southern Africa's post-apartheid security', Seminar report, Cape Town, 18–19 June 2005; CCR, 'The peacebuilding role of civil society in southern Africa', Seminar report, Maseru, Lesotho, 14–15 October 2005; CCR, 'HIV/AIDS and militaries in Southern Africa'; CCR, 'SADC: building an effective security and governance architecture for the 21st century', Seminar report, Dar es Salaam, Tanzania, 29–30 May 2007; and CCR, 'Security and development in southern Africa', Seminar report, Johannesburg, 8–10 June 2008. CCR reports available at www.ccr.uct.ac.za.

71 Pax Africa, 'SADC and Pax Africa host conference on human security', p. 32.

72 See SADC, 'SADC HIV prevention meeting'.

73 Pax Africa, 'SADC and Pax Africa host conference on human security', p. 33.

74 Southern Africa HIV and AIDS Information Dissemination Service, 'About us', 2011, www.safaids.net/content/about-us.

75 SADC, *SADC HIV and AIDS Strategic Framework and Programme of Action: 2003–2007*, p. 7.

76 Innocent Modisaotsile (n.d.), 'HIV & AIDS in the SADC region: responses and challenges', www.uneca.org/tap/Inter Agency/HIV-AIDS-SADC-Region.ppt.

77 Ibid.

78 Kesselman, 'Human security in the SADC region', p. 5.

79 Ibid., p. 5.

12 | Migration and xenophobia

Francis Nyamnjoh and Patience Mususa

The major political and economic transitions that southern Africa has experienced in the past are likely to recur and create similar conflicts in contemporary patterns and trends of migration. While tensions often cannot be entirely resolved, owing largely to the stark inequalities in southern African societies, the timely recognition of potential problem areas of migration allows the development of plans to address issues before they escalate into crisis situations. This chapter explores views about the causes of the xenophobic attacks in South Africa in May 2008 and the discourse of the 'foreigner' in relation to the experiences of migrants in southern Africa. It assesses the different responses to xenophobia in the region, particularly in South Africa, and recommends that scholars, policy-makers, the media and other public figures adopt a critical but sensitive scrutiny of the violence that underlies migration in times of great social change such as southern Africa has been experiencing. We argue that a critical engagement with the region's experience of citizenship, ethnicity and the ideology of free markets is important in order to address effectively the link between migration and xenophobia.

The 2005 Southern African Development Community (SADC) Protocol on the Facilitation of Movements of People aimed at easing migration within the southern African region in order to promote regional integration and development. The protocol provided for the harmonization of the national migration laws of member states to facilitate hassle-free immigration, the entrance by people without a visa into the territory of another member state for a maximum period of ninety days per year, and the establishment of a SADC desk at ports of entry. Overall, the protocol aimed at standardizing migration as part of efforts to facilitate the free movement of people within the region. But despite the narrative of a better-integrated regional bloc and the neoliberal idea of the free movement of capital and labour, countries in the southern African region are moving towards tighter controls on the movement of people.[1] Indeed, in the more economically advanced economies within the region – South Africa, Botswana and Namibia – the discourse against free movement into these countries is growing stronger.[2] The number of repatriations or removals from South Africa of foreign nationals from other southern African countries has been increasing, with deportations almost doubling between 1994 and 2004.[3]

Furthermore, the idea of the free movement of people is generally not positively received in the region. A 2004 survey revealed overall negative attitudes towards immigrants and refugees in southern Africa, with respondents perceiving that their countries were being 'swamped'.[4] This attitude reflects not only the views of the wider public, but also the views of state migration policy. According to some research on South Africa, immigrant numbers have been conflated,[5] and this has been used to justify the push for better management – in other words, greater control of immigration into the country. This trend is sharply underlined in the 2008 Human Sciences Research Council's (HSRC) recommendations to close the South Africa border to new immigrants.[6] Scholars like John Sharp find this notion of inflexible citizenship worrying, especially because it disadvantages the poor, who rely on cross-border and other trade and remittances with or from 'outsiders'.[7] Tighter migration control is unlikely to stop the movement of people, but is more likely to increase the numbers of illegal or undocumented migrants, while simultaneously decreasing the legitimacy of spaces for belonging. For example, the African Peer Review Mechanism's (APRM) country report on South Africa, under the chairmanship of Adebayo Adedeji between 2005 and 2007, warned of a scourge of xenophobia, and twelve months after the release of the report, South Africa saw brutal attacks on fellow Africans in which sixty-two people were killed and about 100,000 displaced.[8]

While much has been written on migration and xenophobia in southern Africa in recent times,[9] there has been a failure to problematize assumptions of similarities (belonging together) and difference (not belonging together). There is a need to explain the underlying causes of migration and xenophobia as well as explore the manifestations of xenophobic violence.[10] We argue that while there is an urgency to resolve regional tensions of ever-diminishing circles of belonging in southern Africa, great care should be exercised in understanding the underlying dynamics.[11] This means addressing the hard questions about the politics of citizenship in the region, the impact of neoliberal economic policies on livelihoods, and also migration experiences, as well as engaging sensitively with questions of ethnicity.

Migration and the making of difference in southern Africa

Globalization has been coupled with the rise of identity politics and the drive to create ever more exclusionary circles of identification in southern Africa. Francis Nyamnjoh draws upon ethnographic and media sources across the region to show ways in which citizenship has largely been a fluid phenomenon and how attempts to bind it – for example, through a discourse of indigeneity – may be exclusionary.[12] He sees the role of capital accumulated in multinational investments as playing a role in aggravating tensions created by the inequalities and exploitation of labour. Other scholars, such as Michael

216

Neocosmos, make similar claims, but argue that the xenophobic violence witnessed in South Africa cannot be attributed to poverty and inequality alone, but also to a nationalist 'fear-mongering' discourse to obtain state control over immigration.[13] This 'fear-mongering' discourse is viewed as both a cause and a consequence of repressive state control mechanisms, including the deportation and harassment of 'illegal' immigrants by South African law enforcement agencies, which fuel the spread of a political discourse of violence.

While the violence in South Africa in 2008 particularly targeted 'foreigners' and was appropriately labelled 'xenophobic', it was similar to the forms of segregation practised in the past in South Africa by its apartheid government. These past practices involved various forms of violence such as restricting free movement of migrants and non-white South Africans, compulsory carrying of passes by all non-white South Africans as well as migrants, limited access to job markets, and limitations on the family life of migrant workers, in particular by restricting wives and children from visiting family members in mine camps. While migration does not always lead to violence, violence in some cases has tended to obscure the powerful ways in which migration has fostered close and cooperative relations across the region.[14]

Xenophobia can be defined as an extreme hatred of the 'other'.[15] Violence entails inflicting emotional, psychological, sexual and physical damage. According to Jamil Salmi's conceptual framework for violence, the phenomenon has diverse manifestations, including direct violence (deliberate injury to the integrity of human life), indirect violence (omission or lack of protection against poverty, hunger, disease and accidents), repressive violence (deprivation of fundamental human rights) and alienating violence (alienating working conditions, racism (and presumably sexism), social ostracism, cultural repression, and living in fear).[16] In explaining the tensions witnessed in xenophobic attacks, Salmi's broad conceptualization shows the dynamics of violence seen in migration, and the function it serves. For example, the xenophobic violence witnessed in townships and informal settlements in South Africa is seen by some as essentially a form of protest to compel the South African state to deliver much-needed public services. Treating violence as part of the tensions and contradictions in wider social, economic and political contexts allows for the examination of 'xenophobic events' beyond their temporality, and through the lens of history.

Migration histories of southern Africa show ways in which space and place have been configured and imagined through major social and political transformations. For example, colonialism has shaped the present spatial configuration of the nation-state and the formation of norms of state sovereignty. The acquisition and control of territorial space under colonialism were inseparable from capitalist expansion and were both inclusionary and exclusionary in nature. The control of spatial mobility in the modern nation-state, through migration control and restrictions on entitlement, is descended from these policies. Dispossessions of land associated with settler colonialism conflicted with the region's existing patterns of migration. In the pre-colonial era, people moved around to seek a livelihood, pasture, water and food sources, as well as shelter.[17] These movements entailed a flexible use of land, often held in trust by the community. Though colonialism predominates, prior spatial upheavals in southern Africa, such as the Mfecane,[18] also need to be examined in relation to colonial expansion and present-day constructions of ethnic belonging. It is especially relevant that the colonial enterprise used ethnicity in its rankings of entitlement, an architecture that the South African apartheid state adopted with great fervour. The legacy of these histories is imprinted in the present nation-state, which struggles to dismantle the structures that created second-rate citizens within the colonized body. However, the attempts to do so are undermined by the uncritical adoption of the same systems that structured exclusion during the colonial period.

Negative views of the 'foreigner' in southern Africa have not developed in a vacuum. There are varied and complex underlying causes of xenophobia apart from the impact of colonialism's 'othering' – which a number of African countries that achieved independence earlier than South Africa tried to counter through communitarian national ideologies such as Kenneth Kaunda's humanism in Zambia and Julius Nyerere's socialism in Tanzania. The diminished presence of the state in providing welfare and the widening spheres of illegality as a primary locus of livelihood for the majority in southern Africa are likely to contribute to the negative connotation of 'illegal' immigrant workers who compete against local citizens for jobs and public services as criminals. The construction of illegality needs to be explored in relation to the regulatory structures of the nation-state which grew out of colonialism.

The patterns of migration control in southern Africa partly explain present-day citizenship exclusion in the region. For example, rural–urban restrictions on movement during the colonial period regulated who was entitled to enter and stay in urban areas. Southern African men from rural areas were drawn, and coerced through having to pay hut taxes, to work in the mining hubs of Johannesburg, South Africa, and in the Copperbelt in Zambia, but they were prohibited from settling there permanently. To reinforce this lack of permanence for African mineworkers, black African women were not allowed to enter towns. This restriction did not fully deter women's presence in the mining areas, but theirs was an illegal existence. Caroline Moser argues that the restrictions on the movement of people contributed to the problem of fractured families in South Africa, the country that exercised the most stringent form of exclusion in the region.[19] Migration control also extended to where one could settle in urban areas. Colonial town planning created a spatial regulatory framework based on class and, in its extremes, race and ethnicity. Entitlements were thus structured spatially, and to reside outside these parameters was illegal and equated to fewer or no services and the possibility of eviction.

Despite migration restrictions, there was significant spatial mobility of the labour force in southern Africa. For example, cross-border labour migration occurred particularly between South Africa and its neighbours – Botswana, Lesotho, Namibia, Swaziland and Zimbabwe – with workers migrating from as far north as Malawi to work on two-year contracts in apartheid South Africa's mines.[20] However, the social mobility of the migrant workers inside South Africa was limited. The hierarchy of labour exploitation was based on race and ethnicity. Spatial partitioning in apartheid South Africa segregated mineworkers according to ethnicity. The struggles for independence in European-ruled southern African territories struck at the core of these spatial and social mobility restrictions. Countries like Tanzania and Zambia stopped supplying labour to the mines in apartheid South Africa after attaining their independence from colonial rule in the 1960s. However, other countries, such as Mozambique, Lesotho and Swaziland, whose economies were closely tied to that of South Africa, continued to supply labour to South Africa and still do so today,[21] despite tight migration controls.

In the contemporary period there is a problem of empirical substantiation of the definition of the nation as being culturally homogeneous and integrated, and using this as a form of legitimation of belonging or citizenship. Verena Stolcke notes that even though 'racist doctrines have become politically discredited in the post-second world war period and as African states moved towards independence from colonial rule, cultural fundamentalism as the contemporary rhetoric of exclusion' has instead replaced 'traditional racism' by 'reifying cultural boundaries and difference'.[22] According to Stolcke, the escape into cultural fundamentalism as an ideological position by nation-states, whereby the exclusion of groups is based on the idea that the 'foreigner, a stranger to the body politic' should attempt to assimilate and become culturally the same as the citizen (where the erroneous assumption is that citizens share a similar culture) is an 'essential prerequisite for access to citizenship rights', and thus 'the socio-economic exclusion of immigrants is a consequence of their political exclusion'.[23] This notion of cultural fundamentalism further spatially segregates groups based on culture.

Migration, xenophobia and ethnicity

According to a 2008 Southern African Migration Project (SAMP) study, South Africa has the highest ratings for anti-foreigner views in southern Africa. Earlier SAMP studies indicate that Botswana and Namibia also have a generally higher intolerance of 'outsiders'. For example, a 2003 SAMP study indicated that 94 per cent of Batswana, 90 per cent of South Africans and 97 per cent of Namibians would support the deportation of 'illegal' immigrants.[24]

The wave of xenophobic violence against foreign migrants in South Africa prior to, during and after May 2008 demonstrates the trauma of capitalist exploitation that had been masked by the country's racialized hierarchies. Some analysts see xenophobia, coupled with South Africa's struggles to manage rising income inequalities, unemployment and low economic growth, as a likely threat to the country's post-apartheid transformative foreign policy. During Nelson Mandela's presidency, Pretoria's foreign policy was based on the promotion of equality, democracy and human rights, drawing from the country's experience of the anti-apartheid struggle.[25] Former South African president Thabo Mbeki's subsequent leadership promoted the idea of an 'African Renaissance' that called for Africa's political and socio-economic renewal.[26]

A 2006 SAMP survey, reported by Jonathan Crush in 2008, indicated that a sizeable minority of the sampled population, 9 per cent,[27] were willing to use force to get rid of foreigners, underlining the failure by South Africa to address effectively the rising xenophobic attitudes, despite warnings in previous studies.[28] The perceived failure of the South African government to adequately tackle rising xenophobic views led commentators and the media to repeatedly warn that the country would likely witness a repeat of the 2008 xenophobic violence.[29] For example, M. B. Skosana, a member of parliament, in the newspaper *Sowetan* on 20 August 2009, called for a national debate on racism and for political education to 'confront racism, racial discrimination, xenophobia and Afrophobia'. Skosana further argued that it was impossible for the country to 'uphold and sustain the principle of non-racialism and at the same time sweep racism under the carpet ... without stirring a recipe for protracted social conflict'.[30]

An editorial in the newspaper *Mercury* on 2 June 2008 called on the South African leadership to address xenophobia and ethnicity, arguing that these were connected to the trauma resulting from apartheid, in order to curb possible repeats of violence. In an earlier warning in the newspaper *Star* on 17 May 2008, a Johannesburg-based Refugee Ministries Centre official commented that the xenophobic violence was 'misdirected frustration' and that 'ethnic or tribal attacks could follow on the violence on foreigners'. This warning was based on 30 September 2009 *Daily News* reports on violence at the Kennedy Road informal settlement in KwaZulu-Natal, during which a group of armed protesters lamented the alleged takeover of the settlement by the 'Ama-Pondo' when the settlement was for the 'Ama-Zulu'. This showed that violence was directed not just at those perceived to be foreigners, but also at those whose national citizenship should not be under dispute. The denial by a community safety and liaison officer, cited in the same newspaper article, that the violence was not ethnically motivated or xenophobic but simply crime, highlights the danger of disregarding the roots of the violence.

While South Africa is a prominent case study of xenophobia, other southern African countries cannot afford to be complacent. The increasing protectionist and defensive anti-foreigner discourse in other SADC countries can easily consolidate into strong xenophobic views and attitudes towards foreigners. The alleged abuse of Zimbabwean immigrants at the hands of state officials in Botswana is illustrative thereof.[31] So too is the 2009 beating of a Zambian national mistaken as a foreigner by Zambian immigration authorities because of appearing to be Tanzanian or West African.[32] For their part, Swazis, while more receptive to South African immigrants, have been less receptive to immigrants from other southern African countries, particularly Mozambicans.[33]

As Stolcke observes, the 'anti-immigrant rhetoric predicated on cultural diversity and incommensurability' and

> informed by certain assumptions implicit in the modern notions of citizenship, national identity, and the nation-state ... reifies culture conceived as a compact, bounded, localized, and historically rooted set of traditions and values transmitted through the generations by drawing on an ideological repertoire that dates back to the contradictory 19th century conception of the nation-state. ... Contemporary cultural fundamentalism is based, then, on two conflated assumptions: that different cultures are incommensurable and relations between cultures are hostile by nature because humans are inherently ethnocentric. Xenophobia is to cultural fundamentalism what the bio-moral concept of race is to racism, namely, the naturalist constant that endows with truth value and legitimates the respective ideologies.[34]

The quest to reconcile an idea of shared humanity with existing forms of domination has resulted in ideologies such as racism and xenophobia, with the thinking that:

> If the self-determining individual, through persistent inferiority, seemed unable to make the most of the opportunities society purported to offer, it had to be because of some essential, inherent defect. The person or, better, his or her natural endowment – be it called racial, sexual, innate talent, or intelligence – rather than the prevailing socioeconomic or political order was to be blamed for this. This rationale functioned both as a powerful incentive for individual effort and to disarm social discontent. Physical anthropology at the same time lent support both to claims of national supremacy among European nations and to the colonial enterprise by establishing a hierarchy of bio-moral races.[35]

Southern African countries grapple with this legacy, which is seen in the ambiguities of their construction of the nation-state. The colonial divide-and-rule systems that imposed identities 'circumscribed by arbitrary physical and cultural geographies' and the distinctions of a civilizing scale, which have left these post-independence states 'to capitalize on the contradictory and complementary dimensions of civic, ethnic and cultural citizenships',[36] are nowhere more apparent than in South Africa.

Free market policies and xenophobia

In the contemporary period, the rise of xenophobia in southern Africa and the rest of the world can be linked to the expansion of neoliberal global capitalism. Like colonialism, neoliberalism operates through the notion of comparative advantage, suggesting, for example, that a surplus in labour (offering cheaper prices) would somehow compensate for a surplus of capital. However, the global inequalities and restrictions on the movement of people from so-called cheap labour-supplying countries to rich countries have been ignored. So while people constantly try to migrate to rich countries, immigration restrictions, notions of sovereignty and regulations that structure territoriality all maintain the low value assigned to their physical labour. Those foreigners who enter the rich countries unlawfully become illegal immigrants, and are excluded from various entitlements, including full citizenship in the places where they offer labour.

To solve the contradictions in market ideologies of supporting free movement of capital and labour, a rhetoric of cultural difference is increasingly being used to structure and obscure these inequalities. Tayyab Mahmud locates the source of this rhetoric squarely within the contradictions inherent in the global system.[37] The drive to expand and increase the spheres of exchange requires easy movement of capital, commodities and labour to facilitate this expansion. However, this leads to strenuous attempts by the nation-state to maintain sovereignty in the face of this expansion of global capitalism. Mahmud argues that the latter works on the notion of exclusion, sifting and separating those deemed ineligible to the entitlements of citizenship, in what Nyamnjoh has described as ever-diminishing circles of citizenship.[38]

The process of inscribing the sovereign state increasingly draws on the exclusive notions of ethnicity and race. The mention of race and ethnicity in media reports of xenophobia in South Africa is particularly revealing. This also explains why a report found that xenophobic views in South Africa are widespread, cutting across income groups and race, and exposing xenophobia as a phenomenon in which not just the poor are turning against 'outsiders' in a competition for scarce resources, opportunities and services.[39]

Meanwhile, informal settlements in the urban areas of southern African cities continue to grow, showing that attempts to regulate them have largely been unsuccessful, arguably because social mobility is harder to achieve than physical spatial mobility. This causes a deadly overlap between race and class, in which ethnicity is associated with poverty and marginalization. Carol Paton argues that the xenophobic violence in South Africa in May 2008 was just another manifestation of the discontent or anger that underlies the violence in many of the country's townships.[40] Previous violence in townships was over service delivery, and took place in areas where little development had occurred.[41] That the most extreme forms of violence against foreigners in

South Africa were enacted upon those living in informal settlements highlights the multiple constructions of exclusion – as an ethnic other, as an illegal occupier, and as a poacher of resources. In this last sentiment, the impact of structural adjustment policies in southern Africa in structuring both inclusion and exclusion should not be underestimated.

The implementation of structural adjustment programmes in southern Africa was characterized by the diminished presence of the state in the provision of welfare,[42] the push towards an unregulated market, and a shift in focus from labour supply to entrepreneurship. The withdrawal of the state from welfare provision and the job losses that occurred as a result of the privatization of state-run industries contributed to the high rates of poverty in the region, notably in Zambia, Malawi, Mozambique and the Democratic Republic of the Congo (DRC), which have some of the highest poverty rates in the world.[43]

On the other hand, the widening of trade relations and the promotion of free enterprise have garnered the increased mobility of people seeking business opportunities and employment over a wider geographical area. Underlying the notion of free enterprise is also the dream of great social mobility, characterized by the few cases of people who have succeeded in this capitalist system. This mobility has come at a cost for some, as threats of xenophobic violence have reportedly been fuelled by resentment towards foreign business owners, who are seen as having out-competed local business owners.[44] The willingness of migrants to work for what are perceived by locals as low wages also led in November 2009 to the obstruction of work and eviction of Zimbabwean migrants from South Africa.[45] The links between poverty and migration, plus the contestation of resources based on an idea of exclusion, reveal the tensions that underlie these relations. However, these tensions should not obscure the ways in which cross-border relations are sometimes fostered across the region.

The attempts by some African nation-states to control cross-border migration are undermined by the porosity of their borders through the large absence of policed and physical barriers.[46] For example, cattle raiding has previously been a source of conflict for rural communities in areas along the Lesotho–South Africa border.[47] In addition, in most parts of Africa the similarities between ostensibly culturally distinct groups, most of whom were separated in the arbitrary carving up of Africa and the splitting of ethnicities by colonial powers at the Berlin Conference in 1884, mean that identification of foreigners as 'strangers' is more likely to be highly flawed. For instance, the use of language ability and physical features to identify foreigners during the xenophobic attacks in South Africa resulted in several locals being mistakenly identified as foreigners and victimized.[48] These similarities and the porosity of borders essentially present the possibilities of wider inclusion, rather than exclusion.

Labour and capital mobility in informal cross-border trade indicate the possibilities of inclusionary relations within southern Africa. A large volume of the region's cross-border trade, mainly between South Africa and its neighbours, is informal and dominated by women, who tend to trade in small volumes individually but overall contribute to a large volume of trade.[49] Most of the trips made by these small-scale cross-border traders are for short periods of time, depending on the turnover of their goods. The frequent movement involved in cross-border trade necessitates the establishment of cross-border relations. These relations can, however, be undermined by petty immigration and customs officials who occasionally employ exclusionary mechanisms of immigration control and customs levies that encourage underground cross-border trade.[50] This contributes to the narrative of illegality in southern Africa's immigration discourse. Cross-border trade within the region can be increased by easing migration restrictions that push up transaction costs and hinder economic investment. Several countries, notably Namibia, are reluctant to adopt an open border policy and have cited security concerns as the main reason.[51]

Meanwhile, the southern African mining sector is characterized by the casualization of labour, especially in countries like Tanzania, Zambia and Zimbabwe. The failure of the formal sector to provide sustainable livelihoods, given limited and unreliable employment opportunities, has led men and women to become informal miners. Reports from the DRC and Angola reveal a trend towards informal mining and the frequent deportation of foreign illicit miners and mineral traders.[52] The desperate position of migrant workers makes them vulnerable to the potential exploitation of multinational capital, which increasingly relies on casual labour, usually contracted from labour providers known as 'gang masters'. This mode of labour contraction allows the circumvention of national labour laws, especially because undocumented immigrant workers cannot lodge complaints about underpayment and mistreatment to authorities for fear of being deported.

Multinational companies, for their part, hire foreign labour as part of calculated attempts to avoid paying the market rates and benefits as well as possible labour-management disputes.[53] National governments can conveniently blame foreign nationals for the failure of the state to deliver public services. In addition, states can also use the perceived state failure to position themselves to attract foreign investment. Reports from Botswana[54] and Zambia,[55] where local artisans have queried the employment of foreign nationals in these two countries' mining industries in the context of existing massive unemployment of qualified local artisans, can be seen in this light. A news item on the deportation of four tobacco buyers from Malawi for allegedly buying tobacco on the local market at lower prices and thus undermining the country's development agenda[56] shows the difficulties that countries in the region face given their marginal position in global trade.

Conclusion

Some have posited the hypothesis that the xenophobic violence in South Africa's townships and informal settlements began as a form of protest to compel the state to deliver basic services to these poor communities. But there is uncertainty about whether the violence was motivated largely by competition for livelihood with foreign nationals, or whether ethnic-based hostilities were also at play. It would be misleading to seek to understand xenophobia in southern Africa in isolation.[57] There is a need for ethnographic enquiry into how the former colonial powers, which constructed and imposed or deformed cultural identities informed by pre-colonial local interconnected hierarchies, are, in the post-colonial and postmodern world of the late twentieth and early twenty-first centuries, using the very same constructed differences to discipline and punish immigrants from the former colonies, police ethnic minorities in Europe and North America, and contest claims to multiculturalism and flexible citizenship.[58] Such enquiry should be extended to former settler colonies like South Africa, where independence has not meant a departure of the settler minorities of European descent, nor led to citizenship, rights and entitlements for the majority indigenous populations beyond constitutional provisions and political rhetoric. In either case, citizenship and belonging have meant progressively encouraging a sort of cultural diversity that reflects a certain unity in diversity – a 'Rainbow Nation', however tenuous – among the settler and indigenous internal communities – as citizens, however unequal – while simultaneously tightly controlling the external borders. This approach would account for the active investment in political rhetoric and legislative measures that present immigrants, foreigners or strangers (outsiders) as undesirable, as a threat, and as morally and culturally inferior. Against the reality of citizenship as an unfinished business (especially economically and socially) for the majority of nationals (insiders), this rhetoric and practice only fuel the fears and insecurities of nationals, who tend to blame immigrants for all their socio-economic ills.[59]

Therefore, although the failures by the post-apartheid South African government to deliver on equality of citizenship beyond the constitutional provisions, and to curb rising unemployment, violent crime, housing shortage and deficient social services, are obviously not the fault of immigrants from Africa north of the Limpopo, these immigrants are effectively made into scapegoats for the socio-economic and political problems South Africans face.[60] Implicit in such hostility and reification of cultural difference is the assumption that immigrants or outsiders are not entitled to share in 'national' resources and wealth, especially in periods of growing scarcity of resources and economic uncertainties. Often forgotten or swept under the carpet is the fact that foreigners often do the jobs that locals will not or cannot do. Also, it seems to be taken for granted that fellow citizens cannot be as responsible for the insecurities and uncertainties that beget intolerance and aggression towards foreigners. Such arguments and perceptions have the universal effect of masking the political and economic roots of modern-day poverty, often misleadingly and aggressively directing attention to population control programmes that target particularly women in the poor South.[61] This myth of population control hinges on the argument that people are poor because they have large families, when in reality, in most cases, people have large families because they are poor.[62]

SADC's official discourse of greater social and economic integration in the southern African region is undermined on several levels by calls for the increased 'management' of migration at the national level, the absence of a clear agenda to address humanitarian situations that trigger migration within the region, the localized fight for resources within the region's large informal sector, and the inadequate interrogation of trends towards an identification of citizenship with ethnicity. In addition, the variations in the socio-economic and political history of the countries in the region make the weaving of any common migration policy difficult.[63] Xenophobia, and the xenophobic violence witnessed in South Africa, indicates just how high the stakes are in addressing migration in the region.

Notes

1 Francis Nyamnjoh, *Insiders and Outsiders: Citizenship and Xenophobia in Contemporary Southern Africa* (London: Zed Books, 2006). See also John Sharp, 'Fortress SA: xenophobic violence in South Africa', *Anthropology Today*, 24(4), 2008, pp. 1–3.

2 Jonathan Crush and Wade Pendleton, 'Regionalizing xenophobia? Citizen attitudes to immigration and refugee policy in southern Africa', Migration Policy Series no. 30 (Cape Town: South African Migration Project, SAMP, 2004), p. 2.

3 Darshan Vigneswaran, 'Free movement and the movement's forgotten freedoms: South African representation of undocumented migrants', Working Paper no. 41 (Oxford: Refugee Studies Centre, July 2007), p. 4. Reports from the South African Department of Home Affairs indicate that repatriations in South Africa rose from 90,692 in 1994 to 209,988 in 2004.

4 Crush and Pendleton, 'Regionalizing xenophobia?'

5 John Oucho and Jonathan Crush, 'Contra free movement: South Africa and the SADC migration protocols', *Africa Today*, 48(3), 2001, p. 146.

6 Suren Pillay, *Citizenship, Violence, and Xenophobia: Perceptions from South African Communities* (Pretoria: Human Sciences Research Council, Democracy and Governance Programme, 2008).

7 Sharp, 'Fortress SA'.

8 African Peer Review Mechanism (APRM), 'Country review report of South Africa', 19 October 2007.

9 See Oucho and Crush, 'Contra free movement'; Crush and Pendleton, 'Regionalizing xenophobia?'; Jack Fine and William Bird, *Shades of Prejudice: An Investigation into South Africa's Media's Coverage of Racial Violence and Xenophobia* (Johannesburg: Centre for the Study of Violence and Reconciliation, 2006); Vigneswaran, 'Free movement'.

10 See Nyamnjoh, *Insiders and Outsiders*; Michael Neocosmos, 'From "foreign natives" to "native foreigners": explaining xenophobia in post-apartheid South

Africa', in Council for the Development of Social Science Research in Africa, *Citizenship and Nationalism, Identity and Politics* (Dakar, 2006).

11 See Nyamnjoh, *Insiders and Outsiders*.

12 Ibid.

13 Neocosmos, 'From "foreign natives" to "native foreigners"'.

14 Owen Sichone, 'Xenophobia and xenophilia in South Africa: African migrants in Cape Town', in Pnina Werbner (ed.), *Anthropology and the New Cosmopolitanism: Rooted, Feminist, and Vernacular Perspectives* (Oxford: Berg, 2008), pp. 309–32.

15 Nyamnjoh, *Insiders and Outsiders*.

16 Jamil Salmi, 'Violence, democracy, and education: an analytical framework', LCSHD Paper Series no. 56 (Washington, DC: World Bank, 2000).

17 Aderanti Adepoju, 'Migration in Africa: an overview', in Jonathan Baker and Tade A. Aina (eds), *The Migration Experience in Africa* (Uppsala: Nordiska Afrikaninstitutet, 1995), p. 89.

18 This took place from about 1815 to 1840, involving large groups of people moving north to flee the expansion of the Zulu empire under Shaka Zulu.

19 Caroline Moser, 'Violence and poverty in South Africa: their impact on household relations and social capital', Poverty and Inequality Informal Discussion Paper Series (Washington, DC: World Bank, 1999).

20 See Robert Lucas, 'Emigration to South Africa's mines', *American Economic Review*, 77(3), 1987, p. 317.

21 Jonathan Crush, Vincent Williams and Sally Peberdy, 'Migration in Southern Africa', Paper prepared for the Policy and Research Programme of the Global Commission on International Migration, 2005, p. 3.

22 Verena Stolcke, 'Talking culture: new boundaries, new rhetorics of exclusion in Europe', *Current Anthropology*, 36(1), 1995, p. 12.

23 Ibid., p. 8.

24 Eugene K. Campbell and John

Oucho, 'Changing attitudes to immigration and refugee policy in Botswana', Migration Policy Series no. 28 (Cape Town: SAMP, 2003).

25 Chris Alden and Garth le Pere, 'South Africa's post-apartheid foreign policy: from reconciliation to ambiguity', *Review of African Political Economy*, 31(100), 2004, p. 284.

26 Ibid., p. 287.

27 Jonathan Crush, *The Perfect Storm: The Realities of Xenophobia in Contemporary South Africa* (Cape Town: SAMP, 2008), p. 38. According to Table 18, 'What sort of action would people take against foreigners?', 16 per cent said they would combine with others to force foreign nationals to leave the area, while most said they would 'snitch' – to the police, 44 per cent; to community associations, 36 per cent; and to employers, 32 per cent.

28 Ibid., p. 7.

29 Ibid.

30 This opinion followed a racial incident at South Africa's University of the Free State in which a group of white students gave dog food they had urinated on to five black university staff.

31 'Zimbabwe immigrants claim abuse', *Mmegi/The Reporter*, 16 February 2009.

32 'Businessman narrates beating ordeal', *Africa News/Times of Zambia*, 22 June 2009.

33 Hamilton Simelane and Jonathan Crush, 'Swaziland moves: perceptions and patterns of modern migration', Migration Policy Series no. 2 (Cape Town: SAMP, 2004).

34 Stolcke, 'Talking culture', pp. 4, 6–7.

35 Ibid., p. 7.

36 Francis Nyamnjoh, 'Ever diminishing circles: the paradoxes of belonging in Botswana', in Marisol de la Cadena and Orin Starn (eds), *Indigenous Today* (Oxford: Berg, 2007), p. 306.

37 Tayyab Mahmud, 'Migration, identity, and the colonial encounter', *Oregon Law Review*, 77, 1997, pp. 636–7.

38 Nyamnjoh, *Insiders and Outsiders*.

39 Crush, *The Perfect Storm*.

40 See 'Xenophobia: what lies beneath?', *Financial Mail* (South Africa), 30 May 2008.

41 Kate Lefko-Everett notes that 'we cannot afford a fresh outbreak of xenophobia' and that what are widely known as 'service delivery protests' in South Africa have xenophobic undertones. However, Lefko-Everett attributes the violence within these protests to the frustrations that informal settlement dwellers face in trying to draw attention from the South African state actors to the slowness of service delivery and its inadequacy when delivered. See 'We cannot afford a fresh outbreak of xenophobia', *Pretoria News*, 5 August 2009.

42 With the exception of South Africa, which has attempted to expand welfare through social grants to its citizens with great difficulty, because at the same time its free market ideology privileges the already affluent, thus widening socio-economic inequalities.

43 The United Nations (UN), in its 2009 *Human Development Report*, lists these SADC countries in the 'Low Development' index category.

44 The *Cape Times*, on 20 August 2009, reported on mediation by the Anti-Eviction Campaign and the UN High Commissioner for Refugees regarding the tensions between locals and Somali traders who had been threatened with eviction by their local counterparts. In the reported agreement, Somali traders were to raise the prices of their goods and operate at a certain distance away from local shops. The initiative also included plans by the local council to send local traders for business training.

45 The eviction of about three thousand Zimbabweans, reported in the *Sunday Independent*, 22 November 2009, in De Doorns in the Western Cape, highlights this perception. As a form of protest, the residents prevented Zimbabwean farm workers from being picked up as casual labour by gang masters. The workers were seen not only as 'stealing' local jobs, but also as undermining the resistance of South African residents to work for what were seen as low wages.

46 Adepoju, 'Migration in Africa', p. 93.

47 Gary Kynoch and Theresa Ulicki, 'Cross-border raiding and community conflict in the Lesotho–South African border zone', Migration Policy Series no. 21 (Cape Town: SAMP, 2001).

48 The *Pretoria News*, on 15 May 2008 in an article entitled 'Xenophobia the result of a broken African psyche', reported on the fact that Zulu- and Pedi-speaking South Africans were attacked during the xenophobic violence. The *Pretoria News* had also reported earlier, on 21 February 2008 in an article entitled 'Flames and mobs' fury', on a woman who had said foreigners could be identified by their 'dark and shiny faces'. Both reports indicated the arbitrary nature of these identifications in the xenophobic attacks, which have affected both foreign nationals and South Africans.

49 Sally Peberdy, 'Hurdles to trade? South Africa's immigration policy and informal sector cross-border traders in the SADC', Paper presented at a training course for the United Kingdom's Department for International Development, March 2002.

50 Ibid.

51 Bruce Frayne and Wade Pendleton, 'Mobile Namibia: migration trends and attitudes', Migration Policy Series no. 27 (Cape Town: SAMP, 2002).

52 The *Agence France Presse*, on 4 June 2008, reported that more than 400,000 migrants from the DRC had been deported from Angola in an attempt by the Angolan state to curb illegal mining and the trafficking of diamonds.

53 'Zambia protest by 360 workers should serve as a lesson', *Africa News/Times of Zambia*, 23 April 2008.

54 'Foreigners take our jobs – artisans', *Africa News/Mmegi*, 16 February 2009.

55 'Zambia protest by 360 workers'. The article reported on Indian workers who allegedly incited their Zambian counterparts to strike over work conditions in the mining industry. The strike

led to deportation of twenty-four of the Indian workers for misconduct. The strike apparently exposed the recruitment of foreign labour, as the article noted that locals had the same skills but were unemployed.

56 'Malawi expels foreign tobacco buyers', *Xinhua General News*, 8 September 2009.

57 Nyamnjoh, *Insiders and Outsiders*.

58 Stolcke, 'Talking culture'; S. Wright, 'The Politicization of Culture', *Anthropology Today*, 14(1), 1998, pp. 7–15.

59 Stolcke, 'Talking culture'; Nyamnjoh, *Insiders and Outsiders.*

60 Sichone, 'Xenophobia and xenophilia in South Africa'; Sharp, 'Fortress SA'; Pillay, *Citizenship, Violence, and Xenophobia.*

61 Stolcke, 'Talking culture', pp. 2–3.

62 Mahmud, 'Migration, identity, and the colonial encounter'.

63 John Oucho, 'Migration in southern Africa: migration management initiatives for SADC member states', Paper Series no. 157 (Pretoria: Institute for Security Studies, December 2007).

13 | Climate change challenges

David Simon

Addressing climate change has become one of the most profound challenges in southern Africa. It speaks directly to several of the themes of this volume: security and democratic governance; human security challenges; gender, migration and xenophobia; and regionalism and economic integration. This is because the impacts of climate change are being felt in various parts of the region, and as they increase in future they will have the potential to undermine anti-poverty programmes, development efforts, human security and ultimately peace. The objectives of this chapter are therefore to explain the relevance of the climate change challenge, to assess the extent to which the Southern African Development Community (SADC) and the Common Market for Eastern and Southern Africa (COMESA) are already engaging with the issue, and to identify broad priorities and directions for more substantive action. Clearly, numerous other climate change (and relevant disaster risk reduction) activities are occurring in the region through other forums at different scales, global, national and sub-national, but the focus here is on the two formal regional economic communities (RECs) that link southern African countries, SADC and COMESA.

The growing realities of climate change

Climate change – part of the broader and more inclusive concept of global environmental change (GEC), which embraces environmental dimensions beyond the climatic – has become one of the most pervasive global preoccupations. Although scientific research on climate change dates back over twenty-five years, the rise of climate change up the international political agenda is comparatively recent, driven by mounting evidence and reduced uncertainty about some of the principal parameters used to measure the phenomenon. The 2006 *Stern Review* on the economics of climate change argued convincingly that the cost of inaction greatly exceeded the cost of tackling climate change, as the latter would also provide vast new economic opportunities through the development and implementation of clean/green technologies such as wind turbines or solar forms of generating power.[1]

A rise in atmospheric temperatures of two degrees Celsius is generally regarded as the 'safe' limit needed to avoid highly damaging consequences such as catastrophic global water shortages and crop failure. Achieving this target is the focus of the hotly contested international negotiations over the successor to the Kyoto Protocol (1997–2012), because such a target will require cuts of 25 to 40 per cent in current emissions of greenhouse gases (GHGs) from 1990 levels by 2020. Current atmospheric GHG concentrations are about 435 parts per million (ppm) and are rising by 1.9 to 2 ppm annually. Pre-industrial levels were about 280 ppm, and around 480 ppm is thought to be the ceiling to avoid dramatic environmental changes.

These cuts will be difficult to implement and verify, and will impose differential burdens on different groups of countries and even people within countries. Who makes what cuts and bears which costs or receives what compensation are the core issues of contention. The December 2009 Copenhagen Climate Summit, formally known as the 15th Conference of the Parties (COP15) to the United Nations Framework Convention on Climate Change (UNFCCC), was intended to be the culmination of negotiations over a post-Kyoto regime.

The controversial and disappointing Copenhagen Accord that ultimately emerged is a non-binding document of intent, leaving much for future negotiating rounds.[2] This will prove difficult; moreover, the delay means that emission cuts will commence even later. Controversies over some of the Intergovernmental Panel on Climate Change (IPCC) data and sources used did not affect the overall picture significantly, but appeared to form part of a well-orchestrated campaign by powerful climate change deniers with their own agendas to avoid substantial GHG emissions reductions. This demonstrates what is at stake. This episode has set back the process, with public conviction about the importance of climate change declining in many wealthy countries and only modest progress achieved at COP16 in December 2010.

The geographies of GHG production and their impacts are diverse and unequal. Historically, the wealthy and industrialized countries have dominated GHG production as a result of energy-intensive industrialization and heavy reliance on motor vehicles, aircraft and the like. These countries – which also became wealthy and powerful as a result – therefore do bear a strong responsibility for tackling climate change and its impacts. Yet most have been reluctant either to accept major emissions cuts or to commit large sums of money to assisting poor countries in making cuts. Inevitably, this has become the principal stumbling block to a global deal, and has strengthened most poor countries' resolve to resist attempts to dilute the agreement. This is true for southern Africa.

However, rapidly changing international divisions of labour and production over the past three decades mean that every world region now contributes increasingly to GHG emissions, and at least one country in each region is represented in the top twelve and top twenty emitters. South Africa is Africa's leader in this respect. By 2008/09, China had overtaken the United States as

Box 13.1 Major likely GEC impacts in Africa

Rising temperatures, reduced rainfall

- rainfall decline and fluctuations continue in many areas;
- agricultural production declines, having likely food security implications;
- Sahara shifts farther southward;
- Kalahari expands;
- forest losses increase;
- intensified urban heat islands and health problems.

Rising sea levels and coastal inundation

- low-elevation coastal zones;
- much environmental damage to lagoons, estuaries, mangroves, etc.;
- effects on major coastal cities and ports;
- infrastructural and economic damage;
- urban poverty increases;
- many non-urban livelihoods depend on coastal areas;
- consequences for fishing, agriculture, tourism;
- salinization of water table;
- exacerbation of urban water supply shortages;
- undermining of (peri-)urban agriculture.

the world's largest emitter. However, its per capita emissions are still only 20 to 25 per cent of those in the USA. Although Africa contributes only about 5 per cent to global GHG emissions and is only a very small part of the problem, the continent will suffer more intensely from the consequences of GEC (see Box 13.1). With some exceptions, these consequences will likely consist of increased temperatures (accompanied by drought) and reduced and more variable rainfall.[3] This is why institutions like SADC and COMESA need to be proactive in their response to the challenges of climate change.

There is a significant mismatch between contributions to global emissions and their likely impacts in Africa, accentuated by poverty and lack of resources. Some detrimental impacts are already being felt, so that addressing the issue cannot be postponed. In the words of the IPCC: 'New studies confirm that Africa is one of the most vulnerable continents to climate variability and change because of multiple stresses and low adaptive capacity. Some adaptation to current climate variability is taking place; however, this may be insufficient for future changes in climate.'[4]

GEC, human security and human rights

Global environmental change is already beginning to generate a complex set of challenges at all levels, in all countries and agro-ecological zones in southern Africa and beyond. The principal priorities include ensuring sustainable urban and rural ecological footprints, guaranteeing food security, maintaining institutional and infrastructural integrity, and safeguarding shelter, utilities, economic activities and livelihoods. (See Drimie and Gandure in this volume.) GEC presents numerous potential threats to human security and development efforts if not addressed appropriately. Here are two examples. First, in relation to food security:

> Agricultural production, including access to food, in many African countries and regions is projected to be severely compromised by climate variability and change. The area suitable for agriculture, the length of growing seasons and yield potential, particularly along the margins of semi-arid and arid areas, are expected to decrease. This would further adversely affect food security and exacerbate malnutrition in the continent.
>
> Local food supplies are projected to be negatively affected by decreasing fisheries resources in large lakes due to rising water temperatures, which may be exacerbated by continued over-fishing.[5]

Secondly, water, the most basic human resource (already in deficit in many agro-ecological regions and urban areas), will clearly be affected by rising temperatures and variable rainfall. It will also be affected by increased abstraction from and pollution of surface and subterranean sources, and likely salinization of coastal aquifers as flooding becomes more frequent and sea levels rise. By 2008, the SADC region had sixteen cities of over one million inhabitants, located both in coastal zones and the interior, with high concentrations of industry, infrastructure and people, all of which require large volumes of water. Significant further erosion of vulnerable livelihoods of the poor and of the aspirations of the wealthy could easily lead to resource conflicts and instability, both within and between states, in the short, medium and long term (see Table 13.1).

The relationships between GEC and human security are extensive and complex, for they concern issues of equity and social and environmental justice, and the power relations that underlie them. These are some of the pressure points upon which policy should focus in addressing the sources of vulnerability to climate change impacts, rather than merely seeking to ameliorate or avoid the worst of the impacts themselves. The International Human Dimensions Programme on Global Environmental Change (IHDP), the umbrella scientific body focusing on social scientific research into climate change issues, devoted a decade-long core project to the subject (Global Environmental Change and Human Security).[6]

TABLE 13.1 Matrix of possible climate change/security interactions over time

	Direct impact	Indirect consequences						Slow onset
	Water	Food	Health	Mega-projects	Disasters	Biofuel		Sea level
Short term (2007–20)	Local conflict over water	Failure to meet MDGs	Failure to meet MDGs	Long history of development-induced displacement from 1950s	Nation-states begin to lose credibility owing to inability to prevent large disasters	Isolated competition over food and fuel, and price spikes		Small number of displacements
Medium term (2021–50)	Increased local and some international conflict over water	Significant displacement due to famine	Interaction with food production problems	Displacement of rural poor due to CDM and large-scale dams and other state-based mitigation and adaptation projects	Significant political unrest due to failure of DRR and inadequate recovery in many countries	Increased competition over food and fuel increases, and bio-diversity erosion		Increasing displacement and national/international tension
Long term (2051–100)	Major international conflict over water	Major displacement and political upheaval	Major displacement due to epidemics	Major urban upheaval and other political fallout from mega-project displacement	Major upheaval with international implications due to unattended weather catastrophes	Major discontent due to competition over food and fuel		Major international tensions due to population displacement
	All of these processes strongly interact with each other.							

Notes: CDM = Clean Development Mechanism (in terms of the Kyoto Protocol); DRR = disaster risk reduction; MDGs = Millennium Development Goals

Source: B. Wisner et al., 'Climate change and human security', 2007, www.radixonline.org/cchs.html and http://www.radixonline.org/cchs.doc

Flowing out of this perspective and the rights-based approach to development is a concern with the human rights dimensions of GEC.[7] Particularly in view of the tendency of political leaders to discount GEC as an uncertain and diffuse set of long-term impacts, and hence of far less immediate importance than their constituents' immediate needs, the rights-based approach has considerable value. It demonstrates that the human security effects of, and greater vulnerabilities to, GEC do affect immediate as well as future basic needs, many of which are enshrined as human rights in terms of international treaties and conventions. Moreover:

> Principle 1 of the 1972 Declaration of the United Nations Conference on the Human Environment (the Stockholm Declaration) states that there is 'a fundamental right to freedom, equality and adequate conditions of life, in an environment of a quality that permits a life of dignity and well-being'. The Stockholm Declaration reflects a general recognition of the interdependence and interrelatedness of human rights and the environment. While the universal human rights treaties do not refer to a specific right to a safe and healthy environment, the United Nations human rights treaty bodies all recognize the intrinsic link between the environment and the realization of a range of human rights, such as the right to life, to health, to food, to water, and to housing.[8]

The 2009 United Nations Human Rights Council report[9] explores these rights in greater detail in the context of climate change, and also the impact on particularly vulnerable groups, namely women, children and indigenous peoples.[10]

In view of these international instruments, governments and supranational organizations and agencies are under obligations to safeguard these human rights and need to prioritize them – and southern African regional progress should be assessed in this light too. An effective way of safeguarding these rights is through the approach advocated here, of 'mainstreaming' GEC policies and actions across the board. This means embedding them within all ongoing sectoral programmes and procedures so that addressing them becomes integrated into routine activities, rather than being regarded as something separate and an additional duty or burden to be tackled over and above normal business. A combination of mitigation and more complex adaptation policies and actions must be 'mainstreamed' into all routine as well as strategic planning and implementation activities of regional organizations and institutions in order to maximize the prospects of addressing GEC effectively. In this way, appropriate construction or maintenance standards can be applied, and conventional regulations, standards and budgeting practices can be altered accordingly. However, even such mainstreaming does not guarantee success or make these rights justiciable.

Global warming is now *everybody's* business and all countries and people have to take responsibility and act accordingly if the most serious impacts are to be averted. In seeking to establish a viable post-Kyoto global climate change regime, we need to recognize that the Kyoto Protocol formula is inadequate and outdated because of the deliberately asymmetrical burdens imposed upon wealthy and industrialized countries and 'developing countries'.

Southern African dimensions

In southern Africa, as elsewhere, awareness of climate change has risen substantially, and political leaders and civil society are devoting increasing attention to it. The increasing availability of empirical evidence and consensus about the severity and likely impact of future climate changes have undermined the often self-serving arguments of climate change sceptics.

However, there are profound challenges in addressing climate change in the contexts of widespread poverty and deprivation amid population growth (the ravages of HIV/AIDS notwithstanding) and increasing urbanization that prevail in southern Africa and other regions of the continent.[11] Perhaps most significant, immediate day-to-day survival challenges of meeting basic needs are often, and understandably, seen by politicians as being far more important than relatively vague future 'global' impacts that cross political boundaries and are thus far harder and more costly to tackle. There is also sometimes an element of political expediency, with 'greenwash' and rhetorical commitments to tackling climate change rapidly becoming an effective or even essential way to access targeted bilateral or multilateral aid funds or development facilities, just as has become the case with some private companies world-wide seeking to gain carbon credibility while continuing energy-inefficient business as usual.[12]

Awareness-raising and efforts designed to tackle GEC in southern Africa are predominantly taking place at the national and increasingly also at the local levels. However, climate change poses at least as important a challenge to the future of SADC as any of the more traditional military, security and trans-boundary economic issues. SADC, as the major regional institution in southern Africa, cannot afford to ignore this. The same applies to COMESA, which links southern Africa with East Africa and the Horn.

This also brings us back to the discussion about human rights in the context of climate change. South Africa's constitution is distinctive in providing that rights to a safe and clean environment are justiciable, and test cases are gradually being lodged. On paper, Zimbabwe's constitution also provides some such rights, but they have counted for little or nothing in practice in recent years. One pertinent issue in this context – which falls outside the scope of this chapter – is how citizens of southern African countries with very different enshrined rights might take legal recourse in defence of those rights in the context of these regional bodies' programmes and commitments.

Southern African regional institutions' engagement with GEC

Although by far the oldest regional institution, the Southern African Customs Union (SACU), which marked its centenary in 2010, has no direct role related to GEC, and so is not considered here. Since SADC is both the pre-eminent wholly southern African regional economic institution and the principal focus of this book, most attention is devoted to its GEC-related efforts. Thereafter, COMESA – which has an increasingly similar developmental role to that of, and shares seven southern African member countries with, SADC,[13] but stretches right up Africa to the Red Sea – inevitably therefore makes an interesting comparison.

The volumes on regional integration in Africa published from the late 1990s underscore this point: with the exception of a book by Ian Rowlands that is explicitly on the subject,[14] climate change is not mentioned.[15] In more general books on development trends and challenges in the southern African region, possibly the first mention of climate change in the context of desertification and water resource pressures came in 2004.[16] For other regions of the world, climate change challenges have been topical for longer.[17] Rowlands concentrated on regional integration experiences in southern Africa, the nature of climate change concerns in the middle to late 1990s, and possible regional initiatives on mitigation and adaptation via scaling up national studies in the UNFCCC context.[18] However, his focus was on energy, such as electricity demand and supply, natural gas utilization and transport sector coordination. Institutional climate change policies and programmes, which constitute the subject of this chapter, were not mentioned in the study. This reflects their absence, since uptake by southern African regional institutions has been very recent. Possible reasons for this include the particular institutional histories of the regional intergovernmental bodies, which represent a very diverse set of states and regimes and have differing priorities. There are also capacity constraints in terms of small secretariats; prioritization of existing sectoral and infrastructural programmes with perceived more immediate development dividends; and, related to the latter, some scepticism as to the relevance of climate change to the region.

SADC

Given that SADC is the region's premier development community, it would be logical to expect it to be a leading advocate of appropriate policies to respond to climate change. However, SADC's explicit engagement with climate change issues is only recent and its website contains little documentation on this issue. SADC's Programme of Action (SPA), described as 'a totality of Sectoral Programmes, with their policy objectives, strategies and projects designed to realize the overall goals and objective of SADC', still contains no mention of climate change.[19]

Nevertheless, the SADC Drought Monitoring Centre – perhaps the most logical focal point for GEC efforts – is devoted to 'climate monitoring and prediction for early warning and the mitigation of adverse impacts of extreme events' and undertakes several directly relevant monitoring and research activities, including 'climate change monitoring, detection and attribution'.[20] The centre exemplifies often long-standing regional initiatives in the disaster risk reduction (DRR) field, linked to environmental change and the vulnerability of poor populations, in particular, to fluctuating conditions. This work retains much relevance and represents a good starting point for GEC mitigation and adaptation, although some modification and scaling up of mechanisms is needed to cope with the distinct elements and magnitudes of likely impacts.

Through accreditation with and membership of the UN, SADC and its member states are party to the UNFCCC, the Montreal and Kyoto Protocols, and several other treaties, conventions and protocols of the 'Rio Process', which originated at the World Conference on Environment and Development in 1992, and these mechanisms have some relevance to climate change. Yet they often remain poorly connected with domestic or regional policies.

The first substantive and clear attempt by SADC to integrate climate change into its programmes and activities was not made until 2008, when the SADC Secretariat produced a sixty-page background document on the impact of climate change on the poverty situation for the SADC International Conference on Poverty and Development, held in Mauritius in April 2008.[21] This report is clear and forthright:

> The bottom line is that climate change affects the whole realm of humanity and should be tackled strategically and collectively. However, the region's capacity to address climate change challenges is very low. This study aims at addressing some of the outlined challenges.[22]

While noting that most development initiatives in the region have had poor social returns, often adversely affecting the environment, despite SADC and its member states having policies and strategies to promote environment and natural resource management for equitable and sustainable development, the report pulls no punches:

> Climate change and its impact on poverty, food security and sustainable development is reflected in most of regional and national policy and strategy frameworks. Unfortunately, the topic is not addressed with clarity. Much as Member Countries have adopted international initiatives on climate change, these are yet to be effectively and efficiently implemented at both regional and national levels.[23]

Indeed, the report is clear that climate change was not yet covered in any SADC policies, although it would be addressed in the environmental protocol that was then being formulated. There were – and still are – no collaborative mechanisms relevant to climate change. The draft protocol, in which climate change reportedly features 'very highly', was completed in early 2010 and is currently being finalized and ratified by member states.[24]

Following a survey of examples of climate change impacts and their costs within individual and groups of countries, the report outlines sectoral strategies to mitigate and adapt to climate change relating to agriculture, flood protection and drought mitigation, health, economics and policy, energy, ecosystems and weather. A prioritization matrix for action on constraints at the national and regional levels (see Table 13.2) reveals that the vast majority are of high priority, requiring urgent attention. It identifies institutional limitations of human, financial, and infrastructural resources as the single most binding constraint.[25]

The report concludes with a detailed action plan matrix for each of seven sectors or so-called programme areas corresponding closely to those listed above: food security and increased income from agriculture; water management; health; economics and policy; energy; institutional strengthening; and natural resource management and biodiversity. For each, the matrix identifies the policy issues, objectives, activities and implementing institution. Essentially,

the whole concept of natural resource and environmental management has been re-examined to mainstream climate change and its consequent impact. ... The major implementer of this Action Plan is the SADC Secretariat and the onus is upon this institution to come up with a time frame for the implementation or the proposed activities depending on availability of resources.[26]

The identification of institutional constraints as the principal limitation affirms my a priori hypothesis about the likely reasons for southern African RECs coming to the issue of climate change so late. Moreover, the importance of this document is not only its comprehensive survey of problems and issues but, crucially, also its advocacy of mainstreaming climate change across the whole programme portfolio rather than pigeonholing it into one arena. This is unusual for regional institutions and a progressive approach. The document provides no information on whether it was compiled by SADC Secretariat staff or external consultants.

SADC staff have also produced a short position paper outlining climate change impacts on health and SADC responses. Although brief and descriptive, its approach is similar to that of the SADC background document, revealing that most of the initiatives relevant to climate change have actually been targeted at health-related aspects of environmental sustainability. It affirms the importance of addressing the health challenges of climate change and that adaptive strategies to protect public health will be required regardless of any specific actions for climate change mitigation.[27]

The 2008 background document was followed by a call in August 2009 for

TABLE 13.2 Prioritization matrix for climate change constraints at SADC and member state levels

	Issue	Scale of the problem	Level of concern	Ability to adequately address issues	Priority ranking[a]
1	Inadequate institutional capacity at regional and national levels to deal with climate change.	National, regional	High	High at SADC; low at national level	1
2	Inadequate and/or inappropriate conservation measures.	National, regional	High	Low at national level	1
3	Weak enforcement of relevant laws and regulations.	National, regional	High	Low at national level	1
4	Weak/conflicting policies and legal framework.	National, regional	High	Medium at both levels	1
5	Ineffective and inefficient institutional linkages.	National, regional, global	Medium	Medium at all levels	1
6	Inadequate or lack of infrastructure and equipment.	National, regional, global	Low	Low at both levels	1
7	Inadequate and/or unsustainable funding mechanisms.	National, regional, global	High	Low at both levels	1
8	Inadequate awareness and understanding of indigenous and traditional knowledge systems.	Local, national, regional	Medium	Low at both levels	1
9	Limited participation of key stakeholders.	National, regional, global	Medium	Medium	1
10	Inadequate public awareness of the climate change issue.	National, negional, global	Medium	Medium	3
11	Unavailability and/or poor access to data and information systems.	National, regional, global	High	Low	1
12	Lack of mechanisms for development or access to relevant technologies.	National, regional, global	Medium	Low	3
13	Unsustainable utilization of natural resources and lack of mechanisms for equitable sharing of benefits.	National, regional	High at national level	Low	1
14	Limited staff incentives especially in the public services.	National, regional, global	High	Low at national level	3
15	Manpower inadequately skilled or trained in climate change and its impact.	National, regional	High	Low	1
16	Lack of or uncoordinated research on climate change and its impact.	National, regional, global	High	Low	1
17	Weak community participation in resource conservation and sustainable management.	National, regional	High	Low	1

Note: [a] Relative ranking from 1 to 5 of problems being faced by country, where 1 = most severe problem, 2 = second-most severe problem, and so forth

Source: Southern African Development Community, *The Impact of Climate Change on the Poverty Situation in the SADC Region*, Background document (Gaborone: SADC Secretariat, 2008)

a tender to develop an SADC regional environmental mainstreaming instrument to 'enforce compliance to environmental principles' and to 'ensure that environmental considerations are integrated into development decision-making with and across Member States'. The instrument's roles include facilitation of policy and legal frameworks, and 'integration of other cross-cutting issues such as climate change, water, HIV/AIDS, gender, education and energy into the trade and environmental management agenda'.[28] This work was still in progress at the time of writing.

The SADC Secretariat is also represented on the governing advisory board of the Southern African Regional Climate Change Programme (RCCP), launched in early 2009 with British and Swedish overseas development assistance funding for five years. The RCCP's objective is specifically 'to enable transboundary adaptation to climate change, with equitable access to climate funding, in Southern Africa', as part of broader socio-economic development. It aims to utilize local, indigenous and international knowledge and expertise in promoting dialogues about science, governance, policy and finance and forming appropriate regional partnerships.[29] Surprisingly, therefore, there appeared to be no mention of the RCCP on the SADC website even in early 2011 and it was not mentioned by the SADC Secretariat during my research for this chapter.

At the political level, both the Summit of Heads of State and Government in September 2009 and the meeting of Ministers of Environment and Sustainable Development in November 2009 reiterated their support for the common African negotiating position to be pursued at COP15 in December 2009. This position regards effective mitigation measures as binding on 'developed countries' (i.e. the Annex 1 countries to the Kyoto Protocol) but voluntary for 'developing countries', including the SADC region, where adaptation is seen as vital.[30] This position was duly upheld in Copenhagen as part of the Group of 77 developing countries' demands and carried forward to COP16 in Cancún in December 2010, but was somewhat undermined in practice by the jostling of individual African leaders for prominence. The reasoning behind this position on mitigation and adaptation was apparently that, since developing countries are not significant contributors to global GHG emissions,

> [a]ny mitigation efforts will not add much to global effort to reduce GHG emissions. On the other hand, while developing countries contribute less, they suffer most from the impacts of climate change since they don't have the capacity to adapt. Therefore developed countries should help developing countries in adapt[ing] to these impacts, while mitigation for them should be voluntary.[31]

Two other important elements of the African negotiating position relate to the need for accelerated transfer of 'green' technologies from industrialized to developing countries and for a substantial financing mechanism to facilitate this transfer and to promote mitigation and adaptation to climate change.[32]

COMESA

Like that of SADC, COMESA's political leadership has expressed appropriate formal commitments to the common African position on climate change – at the Thirteenth COMESA Authority meeting and also the Second Joint Meeting of the Ministers of Agriculture, Environment and Natural Resources, both of which were held at Victoria Falls in Zimbabwe during 2009. The declaration issued after the latter[33] urged the international community's support to Africa under the new climate regime to reflect African priorities, specifically: 'adaptation, capacity-building, research, financing and technology development and transfer, including support for South–South transfer of knowledge, in particular indigenous knowledge ...'. Moreover, the required international funds should be '... new and additional, adequate, predictable, apolitical, sustainable and provided primarily in the form of grants and other innovative financing mechanisms and instruments'.[34]

The ministerial meeting also agreed that adaptation to climate change should be closely aligned at national and regional levels around the world to foster collaboration and appropriate financing. More specifically, it committed member states to scale up climate-resilient food production technologies, and directed the COMESA Secretariat to develop a programme on two current international GHG-emission inventory and mitigation initiatives, namely Reduced Emissions through Deforestation and Forest Degradation (REDD) and Agriculture, Forest and Other Land Use (AFOLU).[35]

Pursuant to the African Union summit in January 2007, which called for governments and regional economic communities to integrate climate change strategies into their policies, programmes and actions, COMESA launched its Climate Change Initiative (CCI) to achieve 'economic prosperity and climate change protection'. Six of its seven 'specific objectives' are actually very general: consolidation of a shared African vision for the UNFCCC process; fostering regional and national cooperation; promoting integration of climate change issues into regional and national policies; planning and development and budgetary processes; enhancing the COMESA Secretariat's and member states' capacities in respect of the challenges; and promoting collaboration and partnerships. The seventh objective is the only exception in terms of specificity: 'Provide a framework for the establishment of an African BioCarbon Facility that combines market-based offsets, public and private funds'.[36]

COMESA's website listed the African BioCarbon Facility as one of eight thematic priority areas within the CCI.[37] However, the CCI strategy document[38] situates the facility/fund in the context of enhancing financing mechanisms to promote mitigation. It argues that such enhancement is essential, along with important changes to the Clean Development Mechanism (CDM) of the Kyoto Protocol, because the CDM currently excludes soil-based carbon sequestration, while its project-based and offset-based approach does not provide an appropriately broad and scaled incentive structure for the extensive, diverse and mass-participation nature of African agriculture. The CCI strategy document refers to several reviews and studies being undertaken as preliminaries to the establishment of the facility/fund.

Integration of climate change mitigation and adaptation into 'policies, sectoral planning and implementation at the local, national and regional levels' is the first principle of the CCI,[39] which itself seems comprehensive, well considered and realistically ambitious. The first CCI annual report itemizes events and actions under the respective objectives of the regional programme on climate change, namely to:

1 increase advocacy and policy dialogue through the establishment of an African Political Platform to enhance Africa's position in climate change negotiations;
2 increase knowledge management and enhanced capacity on climate change;
3 enhance civil society engagement in climate change negotiation processes; and
4 establish an African Climate Change Finance Facility/Fund.[40]

The CCI itself forms part of a regional programme being implemented jointly by COMESA, SADC and the East African Community (EAC) with Norwegian government funding.[41] COMESA used its share of the Norwegian funding to establish a Climate Change Unit (CCU) in February 2009 with a full-time staff of four. In 2009 the COMESA Secretariat devoted 12 per cent of its budget to climate change, reflecting the available external funding and the importance attached to it.[42] Surprisingly, the SADC documentation did not refer to this collaborative programme.

Conclusion

Even poor regions like southern Africa need to be far more proactive in both mitigation and adaptation activities. However, the vulnerabilities to GEC impacts in the region are not matched by the resources required to address them, and hence international treaties for the post-Kyoto regime need to resolve the funding and technology transfer mechanisms to assist poor countries and regions to mitigate and adapt successfully and rapidly. Since most public sector climate change engagement to date has been at the global, national and increasingly also local levels, regional initiatives – especially in poorer world regions – have often lagged behind. This certainly appears true in southern Africa, as revealed in this chapter, and the key challenge is now to translate the recent commitments into appropriate actions.

Though SADC was very much a late starter in addressing GEC, it has made substantial strides since 2007/08. The SADC Secretariat's assessment of the poverty–climate change nexus in 2008 was comprehensive and robust, and served to engender the required political buy-in from the leadership. The complete draft Environmental Protocol was due for approval and ratification by the end of 2010. The SADC's Mainstreaming Instrument – a central plank of its efforts to translate policies into practice – is currently under development. Overall, the SADC Secretariat has understood well the importance of mainstreaming climate change awareness and actions across the full range of activities so that they form part of normal routine and strategic practice.

These SADC climate change agendas appear broadly grounded and comprehensive. The COMESA Climate Change Initiative is focused on just eight areas, inevitably leaving some gaps, but the five-year strategy is well organized and comprehensive in relation to these foci, which are certainly important to the region.[43] The strategies of both RECs recognize that climate change concerns need to be integrated across the board rather than being added as extra sectors or agendas. SADC and COMESA are still in the relatively early stages of adopting the GEC agenda and especially in translating the policies into practice. The strongest activities are to be found in well-established units with technical competence and longer track records – which in southern Africa tend to be focused on agriculture, livestock and drought mitigation.

The regional bodies have not yet engaged with the human security or human rights approaches to climate change and their implications, although human security is being addressed in terms of social development. (See Dzinesa in this volume.) However broadly or narrowly conceived the RECs' respective programmes and actions therefore are, they appear at this early stage to be relatively superficial in the sense of not addressing the underlying social, economic and political forces that entrench inequalities and militate against the potential success of many well-intentioned interventions.

Furthermore, no evidence has been found of geographical disaggregation, other than perhaps in terms of agro-ecological regions in rural areas with respect to agriculture and livestock. In particular, no distinction is drawn between rural, peri-urban and urban areas and their overlapping but distinct challenges and interventions.[44] This lacuna is particularly important because South Africa, Zambia and Zimbabwe are comparatively highly urbanized and urbanization is continuing. The likely impacts of climate change on inland areas will increasingly lead to human displacement as rural livelihoods are undermined, especially in semi-arid areas or those that acquire these characteristics. Much of that displacement will take place towards urban areas, as is already occurring in other parts of the continent.

The leaders of SADC and COMESA have recently included climate change issues in their summit agendas and communiqués. Some of these statements have been general or vague, and there must be questions about the extent to which the heads of state and government have internalized the seriousness of the challenge and the need to become proactive. The leaders have also endorsed and adhered to the language and sentiments of the Kyoto Protocol. While understandable and perhaps a sound geopolitical negotiating strategy, there is little sign yet that the new realities of rapidly changing geographies of emissions and progressive mitigation and adaptive actions are being reflected in their understandings and strategizing.

In many respects, the likely reasons for the trends and lags identified here lie in the nature of the two RECs and their constituent governments. These are relatively recent institutions, at least in their current forms, and bring together groups of countries that diverge on every variable, including the strength and vitality of their democratic credentials. The leaderships of most countries in southern Africa remain of the liberation struggle generation, in most cases with authoritarian tendencies and in power for long periods. Reflecting these legacies, the summits tend still to be formalistic, performative events that are strong on ritual but weak on detailed engagement with the pressing issues of the day.

More generally, the diverse countries of southern Africa, saddled with poverty and myriad development problems, struggle to find and adhere to shared priorities, especially in terms of making the necessary trade-offs between narrow self-interest and wider regional benefits. Alena Drieschova and colleagues demonstrate these challenges in the context of trans-boundary water management and climate change adaptation.[45] SADC has the major advantage over COMESA and the New Partnership for Africa's Development (NEPAD) of geographical contiguity and thus great prospects of coherent programmes, but even so, the organization has yet to recover from the setbacks of the divisive engagement by several members in the conflict in the Democratic Republic of the Congo.

The explicit collaboration between SADC, COMESA and the EAC on the Norwegian-funded regional climate change programme represents a significant step forward. However, the long-standing issue of the geographical overlap in southern African membership of SADC and COMESA remains unresolved, and this exacerbates financial and human capacity constraints on the part of those countries and the respective secretariats of the RECs. In addition, this raises questions about possible conflicting interests, agendas and commitments among member states, not least in relation to climate change. SADC has for some years sought a realignment whereby it becomes the southern African component of COMESA in order to resolve these dilemmas, but to date no agreement has been reached and other permutations may be under discussion.

These issues notwithstanding, human security and human rights in southern Africa will increasingly be threatened by climate change, and on an uneven but large scale, with potentially serious implications for poverty, insecurity and resource conflict. There can be little doubt, therefore, that this challenge warrants urgent and specific attention in the context of regional integration and region-building. However, it remains to be seen how far the region's leadership is willing to prioritize and integrate it into the full range of ongoing development activities. Such 'mainstreaming', rather than stand-alone projects, is the most likely way to make progress in practice, while also avoiding direct competition for donor funds with basic-needs-type development assistance in a very constrained funding context.

Acknowledgements

I am most grateful to the Centre for Conflict Resolution for the invitation and financial support to participate in the workshop from which this book originates, and also to Alex Banda (SADC Secretariat) and Mclay Kanyangarara (COMESA Secretariat) for providing updated materials produced by their respective organizations. Both bodies were provided with the opportunity to comment on a revised draft of this chapter. A version of the original workshop paper was also presented at the annual conference of the Association of American Geographers in Washington, DC, in April 2010.

Notes

1 Nicholas Stern, *The Economics of Climate Change: The Stern Review* (Cambridge: Cambridge University Press, 2007).

2 United Nations Framework Convention on Climate Change, *The Copenhagen Accord*, Advance unedited version, 18 December 2009, unfccc.int/files/meetings/cop_15/application/pdf/cop15_cph_auv.pdf.

3 Department for International Development (DfID), 'Reducing the risk of disasters: helping to achieve sustainable poverty reduction in a vulnerable world – a DfID policy paper', London, 2006; Intergovernmental Panel on Climate Change (IPCC), *Climate Change 2007: Impacts, Adaptation, and Vulnerability – Working Group II Contribution to the Fourth Assessment Report of the Climate Change Intergovernmental Panel on Climate Change* (Cambridge: Cambridge University Press, 2007).

4 IPCC, *Climate Change 2007*, p. 13; see also ch. 9.

5 Ibid., p. 13.

6 Global Environmental Change and Human Security project, www.gechs.org. For diverse approaches to this theme, see also Jon Barnett, 'Climate change, insecurity, and injustice', in W. Neil Adger et al. (eds), *Fairness in Adaptation to Climate Change* (Cambridge, MA, and London: Massachusetts Institute of Technology Press, 2006), pp. 115–29; Karen O'Brien, 'Are we missing the point? Global environmental change as an issue of human security', *Global Environmental Change*, 16(1), 2006, pp. 1–3; Karen O'Brien and Robin Leichenko, *Human Security, Vulnerability, and Sustainable Adaptation*, 2007; United Nations Development Programme (UNDP) Human Development Report 2007/2008, *Fighting Climate Change: Human Solidarity in a Divided World*, Human Development Report Office Occasional Paper 2007/9; Ben Wisner et al., 'Climate change and human security', 2007, www.radixonline.org/cchs.html and www.radixonline.org/cchs.doc; Jouni Paavola, 'Science and social justice in the governance of adaptation to climate change', *Environmental Politics*, 17(4), 2008, pp. 644–59; Richard A. Matthew et al. (eds), *Global Environmental Change and Human Security: Understanding Environmental Threats to Well-Being and Livelihoods* (Cambridge, MA: Massachusetts Institute of Technology Press, 2010).

7 Paul Gready and Jonathan Ensor (eds), *Reinventing Development? Translating Rights-based Approaches from Theory into Practice* (London: Zed Books, 2005).

8 United Nations General Assembly, *Report of the Office of the United Nations High Commissioner for Human Rights on the Relationship Between Climate Change and Human Rights*, Human Rights Council 10th sess., A/HRC/10/61, 15 January 2009, paras 17 and 18.

9 United Nations General Assembly, *Report of the Office of the United Nations High Commissioner for Human Rights*.

10 Wolfgang Sachs, 'Climate change and human rights', *Critical Currents*, 6: *Contours of Climate Justice – Ideas for Shaping New Climate and Energy Policies* (Uppsala: Dag Hammarskjöld Foundation, 2009), pp. 85–91.

11 See David Simon, 'Global change and urban risk: the challenge for African cities', *The Constitution*, 7(1), 2007, pp. 3–22; David Simon, 'The challenges of global environmental change for urban Africa', *Urban Forum*, 21(3), 2010, pp. 235–48; David Satterthwaite, 'The implications of population growth and urbanization for climate change', in José Miguel Guzmán et al. (eds), *Population Dynamics and Climate Change* (New York: UNFPA and IIED, 2009), pp. 45–63; Hania Zlotnik, 'Does population matter for climate change?', in Guzmán et al., *Population Dynamics and Climate Change*, pp. 31–44.

12 See Peter Utting (ed.), *The Greening of Business in Developing Countries: Rhetoric, Reality, and Prospects* (London: Zed Books in association with UNRISD, 2002).

13 Madagascar, Malawi, Mauritius, Seychelles, Swaziland, Zambia and Zimbabwe.

14 Ian H. Rowlands (ed.), *Climate Change Cooperation in Southern Africa* (London: Earthscan, 1998).

15 See David R. Black and Larry A. Swatuk (eds), *Bridging the Rift: The New South Africa in Africa* (Boulder, CO: Westview Press, 1997); David Simon (ed.), *South Africa in Southern Africa: Reconfiguring the Region* (Oxford: James Currey, 1998); Daniel C. Bach, *Regionalisation in Africa: Integration and Disintegration* (Oxford: James Currey, 1999); Christopher Clapham et al. (eds), *Regional Integration in Southern Africa: Comparative International Perspectives* (Johannesburg: South African Institute of International Affairs, 2001); Richard Gibb et al. (eds), *Charting a New Course: Globalisation, African Recovery, and the New Africa Initiative* (Johannesburg: South African Institute of International Affairs); J. Andrew Grant and Fredrik Söderbaum (eds), *New Regionalisms in Africa* (Aldershot: Ashgate); Hans van Ginkel, Julius Court and Luk Van Langenhove (eds), *Integrating Africa: Perspectives on Regional Integration and Development* (New York: United Nations University Press, 2003).

16 Deborah Potts and Tanya Bowyer-Bower (eds), *Eastern and Southern Africa: Development Challenges in a Volatile Region* (Harlow: Pearson/Prentice Hall, 2004).

17 See Michael H. Glantz, *The Role of Regional Organizations in the Context of Climate Change*, NATO ASI Series I, Global Environmental Change 14 (Berlin: Heidelberg, 1994).

18 Rowlands, *Climate Change Cooperation in Southern Africa*; Ian H. Rowlands, 'Regional approaches to global climate change policy in southern Africa', in Pak S. Low (ed.), *Climate Change and Africa* (Cambridge: Cambridge University Press, 2005), pp. 150–62.

19 Southern African Development Community (SADC), 'Programme of Action', www.sadc.int/index/print/63.

20 SADC, www.sadc.int/dmc/About DMC/operational_activities.htm.

21 SADC, *The Impact of Climate Change on the Poverty Situation in the SADC Region*, Background document (Gaborone: SADC Secretariat, 2008).

22 Ibid., p. 1.

23 Ibid., p. 3.

24 Alex Banda, SADC Secretariat, personal communication, 28 January 2010.

25 SADC, *The Impact of Climate Change*, pp. 38–9.

26 Ibid., pp. 41–2.

27 J. Mthetwa et al., 'Position paper: climate change, its impact on health, and policy responses in the SADC region', Unpublished paper (Gaborone: SADC Secretariat, n.d.).

28 SADC, 'Call: development of a SADC regional environmental mainstreaming instrument', Gaborone, August 2009, sec. 1.2.

29 Regional Climate Change Programme, www.rccp.org.za/index.php?option=com_content&view=article&id=68&Itemid=61&lang=en.

30 SADC, 'Final communiqué: SADC Summit of Heads of State and Government', Kinshasa, 8 September 2009.

31 Banda, personal communication, 28 January 2010, but see my earlier comments on the Kyoto process.

32 SADC, 'Final communiqué'.

33 Common Market for Eastern and Southern Africa (COMESA), 'Victoria Falls Town Declaration of the Second Joint Meeting of the COMESA Ministers of Agriculture, Environment, and Natural Resources', CS/PPSD/AGC/MAE/II/3 Annex II, Victoria Falls, Zimbabwe, 3/4 September 2009.

34 Ibid., p. 2.

35 Ibid.

36 Climate Change Initiative (CCI), programmes.comesa.int/index.php?option=com_content&view=article&id=163&Itemid=101&lang=en.

37 Ibid.

38 COMESA, 'The Sub-Regional Climate Change Initiative, 2009–2013', Lusaka, 2009, pp. 3, 13–14.

39 Ibid., p. 9.

40 COMESA, *COMESA Climate Change Initiative Annual Report 2009*, Lusaka, 2009, p. 2.

41 Ibid., p. 2.

42 Mclay Kanyangarara, COMESA CCU, personal communication, 17 February 2009.

43 COMESA, 'The Sub-Regional Climate Change Initiative'.

44 See United Nations Human Settlements Programme, *The State of African Cities 2008: A Framework for Addressing Urban Challenges in Africa*, Nairobi, 2008; David Simon and Hayley Leck, 'Urbanizing the global environmental change and human security agendas', *Climate and Development*, 2(3), 2010, pp. 263–75.

45 Alena Drieschova, Mark Giordano and Itay Fischhendler, 'Climate change, international cooperation, and adaptation in transboundary water management', in W. Neil Adger, Irene Lorenzoni and Karen O'Brien (eds), *Adapting to Climate Change: Thresholds, Values, Governance* (Cambridge: Cambridge University Press, 2009), pp. 384–98.

PART FIVE

External actors

14 | The European Union

Mzukisi Qobo

Relations between Europe and southern Africa have deep roots. Initially European interest was mainly focused on the sea route around Africa, and the need to service this route, but increasingly European colonial powers, especially Britain, came to see other reasons for involvement in the region, especially with the discovery of major mineral deposits on the Rand and elsewhere. As their economies developed, many southern African countries became heavily dependent on Europe as a market for their primary products. I argue here that this has acted to *limit* the region's sustained and beneficial integration into the global economy by perpetuating its dependence on the European market for both raw products and development aid.

In recent years, relations between Europe and southern Africa have undergone significant changes. This is in part a consequence of new developments within the European Union (EU) (for example, the Lisbon Treaty and Eurozone crisis), as well as the EU's economic partnership agreements (EPAs) with African, Caribbean and Pacific (ACP) regions. The EPAs aim at replacing existing non-reciprocal trade relations between the EU and the ACP countries with trading arrangements that are in line with the requirement of the World Trade Organization (WTO) that regional trade agreements, including the elimination of duties and other restrictive regulations of commerce, should cover 'substantially all trade' between the constituent territories. This chapter focuses mainly, though not exclusively, on developments in relations between the EU and the Southern African Development Community (SADC). To date, lack of political cohesiveness among SADC countries at the EPA negotiations has constrained the possibilities for a coordinated response that might shift the balance of power in favour of the region.

In order to assess critically the EU–SADC relationship, one needs to look at the wider historical context of the EU's relations with the African continent. In exploring the intricate client relationship between the EU and SADC, we see how the EU's economic hegemony over the region, entrenched through massive financial assistance, has effectively locked SADC into Brussels' sphere of influence. This chapter also briefly analyses the changing global geopolitical landscape and the challenges that this poses for the EU's long-term commercial strategy. I argue that the rise of emerging powers such as China, India and

Brazil has prompted the EU to consolidate its spheres of influence in order to gain a competitive advantage and increase its global market share relative to the rising powers. Finalizing an EPA with southern Africa is a key part of this calculation.

The EU's post-independence agreements with Africa

After most African states gained independence in the latter half of the twentieth century, the EU–Africa economic pattern continued on neocolonial terms, with Africa remaining dependent on its former colonial masters through asymmetrical trade relations.[1] During the negotiations leading up to the Treaty of Rome in 1957, which established the European Economic Community (EEC), European countries grappled with post-colonial Africa's status. France, for example, insisted that its Africa policy be acknowledged, so as to allow it to maintain a foothold on the continent. Similarly, when Britain acceded to the Lomé Convention in 1975, it insisted on the inclusion of its African, Caribbean and Pacific Commonwealth partners.[2] This marked the beginning of an institutionalized but complex aid and trade partnership between Africa and Europe at two levels: the multilateral Europe-wide level, and the bilateral level between influential countries in Europe and their former colonies in Africa. As Margaret Lee suggests, these relations nurtured structural dependence and ensured that Africa continued to export primary products to Europe, and import processed and manufactured goods.[3]

During the past five decades, in which Europe has clung to its position as Africa's pre-eminent trading partner, the dependency of the continent on the EU has deepened. Thirty-five years after the signing of the first Lomé Convention in 1975, African countries still export raw materials to Europe and import finished products derived from the same materials.[4]

SADC countries that are part of the Cotonou preferential trade scheme between the ACP and the EU have in the past experienced significant benefits through various protocols relating to trade in sugar, beef and textiles. These have been based on the provision of duty-free, quota-free access of such products from the former colonies into the EU market.[5] There are, in total, seventy-eight ACP countries that in 2000 signed the new Cotonou Partnership Agreement, which came into force in 2003. As noted before, the trading arrangement under the Lomé Convention did not promote diversification of African economies or reduce their dependence on income from the export of primary commodities. The favourable trade preferences extended by the EU to the ACP countries became a significant source of concern among other developing countries, especially those in Latin America, where banana producers felt competitively disadvantaged.[6] In addition to being a hindrance to structural diversification in developing economies, the preferences distorted global trade and made a mockery of free markets. Against the background of trade distortions generated by the EU–ACP scheme, some members of the WTO, especially in Latin America, intensified their calls for new forms of partnership between the EU and its former colonies. Furthermore, the EU's enlargement from fifteen to twenty-five member states in May 2004 necessitated the renegotiation of these special arrangements in order to provide significant reciprocal benefits for Europe. This was partly because new EU members in eastern Europe had far weaker historical ties with Africa, and were therefore less sympathetic to the preferential trade arrangements. For them, it was important that preferential trading relations with the ACP countries should generate concrete commercial benefits for EU member states.

The final waiver for continuing the preference mechanism under the Cotonou Agreement was obtained at the launch of the WTO's Doha round of trade negotiations in November 2001. This set the stage for the EU and its ACP partner countries to prepare to negotiate the EPAs. These differed from the preference scheme in one important respect: they were to be based on the notion of reciprocity, with a much larger threshold of tariff liberalization (with some asymmetry) for both sides.

The EPA negotiations between SADC countries and the EU commenced in 2004, with the deadline for completion set for 31 December 2007. But SADC and the EU failed to negotiate a full EPA by this date. A new deadline was then set for the end of 2010. Fears that this was an unrealistic time frame have now been realized, with the negotiations dragging into 2011. Apart from an agreement on the modalities for negotiating trade in goods, according to which SADC countries are expected to liberalize imports from the EU, there are several outstanding issues, including services, investment, competition, public procurement and intellectual property.

The EU's development policies: a hindrance to real development

Despite pro-development rhetoric concerning trade with Africa, the domestic trade policies of EU member states have hindered Africa's prospects for development. For example, while the trade preferences for ACP states have guaranteed access to EU markets for their products, helping African citizens to preserve livelihoods in the short to medium term, the tariff escalation for processed goods from Africa, along with other trade barriers, have retarded product and export diversification on the continent.[7]

The adverse effects of tariff escalations are clear: they limit African countries' prospects of graduating from being producers of a narrow range of commodities and exporters of raw materials, to being manufacturers of diverse and value-added products. According to a 2008 United Nations Conference on Trade and Development (UNCTAD) study, most tariff peaks and escalations have been applied to agriculture, with tariffs rising exponentially between raw and semi-finished as well as between semi-finished and finished products.[8]

For example, EU tariffs on imports of oil seeds are pegged at 0 per cent, but climb to 13 per cent on processed vegetable oils; raw tobacco carries a 14 per cent tariff, but tobacco products are levied at 38 per cent; the rate for live animals is 30 per cent, but prepared meat is pegged at 40 per cent.[9]

The EU has also retained higher tariffs for products from labour-intensive sectors, products for which most developing countries have a comparative advantage. These sectors include textiles and clothing, leather and footwear, and fish and fish products.[10] An econometric modelling exercise conducted by two WTO economists shows that a number of SADC countries will increase their specialization in agricultural products, especially beef and beef products for Zimbabwe and Botswana and processed food for Tanzania and Malawi, owing to further trade liberalizations foreseen in the EPAs with the EU.[11] This will not facilitate product and export diversification.

The EPAs are clearly a mechanism to consolidate the EU's pre-eminent place in African trade, and to open up new avenues of profitability in services, government procurement, intellectual property and investment. These are key areas in the EU's 'Global Europe Strategy', launched in 2006 to reinforce the EU's competitiveness by opening up more markets, creating opportunities for European business, and ensuring that the EU gets a 'fair share' of emerging markets. These external mechanisms are not accompanied by openness at the domestic level. Europe remains a fortress, and continues to protect its own agricultural sectors. The EPAs are essentially aimed at the pursuit of the EU's narrow commercial interests, particularly to manage the EU's internal dynamics associated with expansion. In addition, the EU intends to use the EPAs as a mechanism to respond to the changing geopolitical landscape characterized by the growth of emerging economies like China, India and Brazil. The common thread in the EU's strategic considerations in the EPA negotiations is its need to enhance its growth and external competitiveness.

The geopolitical challenges of the late twentieth century

The growing recognition of the central role of commerce in international relations in the late 1980s and early 1990s was accompanied by the consolidation of regional economic blocs. It was evident that competitive advantage rested on market expansion through greater regional integration and promotion of regional supply chains. Regionalism in much of the Western world took on a bifurcated shape expressed in what became known as 'New Regionalism'. This emphasized outward orientation and export-driven growth while protecting domestic industries. Accordingly, regionalism was to be used as an instrument to help develop competitive domestic industries, lending them advantage over their foreign rivals, with the purpose of ensuring the creation of large markets for domestic industries.[12] In the late 1980s the European Commission (EC) accelerated the pace of completion of the Single European Market and enlargement of the EU. By 1995 the EU had grown from six countries in the 1950s to fifteen. It further expanded to twenty-seven in 2007.

It took a while before the EU graduated from an inward-looking regional project to play a significant role as a global actor, elevating trade policy as a key component of foreign policy. The EU did not pay much attention to Asia until the early 2000s. Having recognized the shift in the locus of economic power from Western countries towards emerging powers such as Brazil, China and India, the EC observed that '[t]he changes in the global economic order we witness today are as significant for the world economy and international relations as the end of the Cold War'.[13] In its Global Europe Strategy, the EC further noted that '[i]n the second half of the twentieth century, OECD [Organisation for Economic Co-operation and Development] countries, in particular the United States, Europe and Japan, drove the global economy. In the first half of the twenty-first century they are being joined by new economic powers, in particular China and India, but also Brazil, Russia and others.'[14] The EU is concerned about losing global influence and trade advantages to these emerging powers as well as about being overtaken in productivity and innovation. The rise of China and India, in particular, threatens to hollow out low-cost activities from Europe, while posing a long-term challenge at the higher end of the production and services value chain.[15]

According to a 2010 UNCTAD report, China's growing economic activism in Africa has unsettled western European states, which traditionally viewed African countries as client states. China–Africa trade grew from US$8 billion in 2000 to US$90 billion in 2008.[16] China's engagement with Africa is comprehensive, including provision of funds, technology, infrastructure, social support and opening of the Chinese market to African products in order to facilitate Africa's development.[17] China's interests in Africa are not about benevolence or altruism, but largely about securing raw materials and markets for its growing economy. China's economic relationship with Africa, like the EU's with the continent, may also throttle Africa's structural diversification and transformation of export patterns.

The European Commission has insisted on the inclusion of a most favoured nation (MFN) clause in the EPAs in order to alleviate competitive disadvantages for the EU that might result from China's growing economic linkages with Africa. This controversial clause obliges EPA signatories to extend to the EU, on a line-by-line basis, any concession they offer to third parties under free trade agreements (FTAs). This clause, which is clearly targeted at the emerging powers, has frustrated South Africa's South–South strategy. South Africa seeks to diversify its trade relations away from traditional markets such as the European Union and the United States, and build deeper trade and investment relations with countries such as Brazil, India and China, which reflect the shifting balance of power in the global system and which are future engines of growth in the global economy. Recently this strategy has been markedly apparent in South African president Jacob Zuma's prioritization of bilateral state visits to Brazil, Russia, India and China (BRIC), as well as in South Africa's admission into the BRIC Forum.

Meanwhile, the EU's insistence on the prohibition of the use of export taxes by African countries is clearly aimed at ensuring that Europe's manufacturing sector continues to have access to Africa's unprocessed products. More recently, though, the EU has given some ground in this area, allowing SADC countries to use export taxes on the basis of infant industry protection subject to consultation with the EC.

South Africa and the European Commission

The EU–ACP Cotonou Agreement of February 2000 turned a new page in the relationship between the EU and the ACP countries. It accorded importance to a new regionalism based on fostering open and reciprocal trading arrangements – a far cry from the decades of preference-based mechanisms that existed under various Lomé agreements. The new regionalism, influenced more by a commercial impulse, is in stark contrast to the EU's earlier reluctance to sign up to preferential trade agreements. The preference-based mechanisms were, however, susceptible to rigorous scrutiny by the WTO and persistent pressure from Latin American countries being competitively disadvantaged in the product lines that were receiving preferential treatment. And the EU lost the appetite to defend these schemes at the WTO. Indeed, the Lomé (and later Cotonou) preference schemes were illiberal arrangements for both the recipients and the excluded. For the recipients, they constrained the option to diversify into the manufacturing of value-added products and so perpetuated Africa's state of underdevelopment.

The shortcomings of the EPAs as development instruments have also been highlighted by advocates of free trade. Patrick Messerlin, for example, argues that 'EPAs require the ACPs to eliminate their current tariffs on EC imports for the remaining (at most) 80 per cent of tariff lines. This will make it very easy for EC firms to compete with ACP producers in their own markets, and very hard for potential ACP producers to enter these markets'.[18] As Messerlin further asserts, the EPAs could generate high long-term economic costs for ACP countries without promoting economic diversification. Emily Jones and Darlan Marti note that 'EPAs can indeed aggravate existing developmental difficulties [in Africa], for instance, exacerbating balance of payment difficulties or reinforcing the reliance of ACP producers on the EU as an export market'.[19]

The failure of the EPAs to serve as credible vehicles for development and the serious risks they pose for deeper regional integration in southern Africa underlie the acute tension between the EU and South African negotiators. The EC and South Africa hold divergent views about economic development.

The former sees development as resulting from opening of markets and complemented by aid transfers. The latter, while recognizing the importance of open markets for deepening regional integration, sees this objective as secondary. South Africa prioritizes the improvement of infrastructure and supply-side capacity as a means to diversify.[20] This view is largely informed by its own domestic ideas on how to manage structural change, based on industrial and strategic trade policies.

Apart from the clear tensions that existed between the EC and South Africa, other smaller players in the EPA negotiations were not given much room to consider their options, particularly in terms of what signing up to the agreements could mean for their long-term economic development. The insistence by the EU on a narrow December 2007 deadline placed enormous pressure on smaller SADC countries, such as Botswana, Lesotho, Namibia and Swaziland (BLNS), leaving only nine months for negotiation of options, which began in March 2007. The EC's insistence on differentiating South Africa flew in the face of its earlier commitment to strengthen existing regional integration mechanisms. The multiplicity of agreements between SACU members and third parties inevitably threatened the rupture of the century-old customs union. (See Gibb in this volume.)

During the EPA negotiations, there were also marked differences around the following technical issues, revealing the EU's preoccupation with its own commercial interests:

- *Access to primary natural resources and export taxes.* Better access to primary resources such as energy, hides and skins, metals and scrap and other primary raw materials is important for the EU, as its manufacturing sector relies on imports from third countries to remain competitive. Scrap metals imported from Africa and Asia lie at the core of the competitiveness of the EU's metal industry. Export taxes, which developing countries use as part of their industrial policies to encourage diversification, can constrain other countries' access to inputs. This is particularly important for the EU given China's appetite for southern Africa's strategic resources for its expanding economy. The EU's measures to limit export taxes are meant to shore up its competitiveness vis-à-vis emerging powers such as China. The EC therefore effectively prioritized its commercial needs over the development interests of African countries that view these taxes as development tools.

- *Liberalization of services.* In 2009 the services sector accounted for over 75 per cent of gross domestic product and employment in Europe, a reality that has not changed much. Growth in exports from the EU's services sector is crucial for bolstering its economic growth and employment creation. The EU has aggressively pushed for the opening of service markets as part of negotiating the EPAs, largely for its own economic interests rather than to promote economic development in southern Africa. If the latter were the concern, unilateral liberalization of services by SADC countries negotiating the EPAs with the EU would have been sufficient. It is noteworthy that domestic service sectors such as banking and telecommunications in the EU were heavily protected and liberalized only in 1992.[21] Even after liberalization at the national levels, it took some time to facilitate internal regulatory harmonization within the EU. Yet the EU is pushing for SADC countries to open up their service markets without first harmonizing internal regulations. The appropriate route would have been to enter into a cooperative agreement in order to build southern Africa's capacity to manage internal regulatory harmonization, with the EU providing appropriate development support. There is hardly a development benefit for SADC in the EU's insistence on the liberalization of services under the EPAs. This could be better done under the MFN framework, outside of the EPAs, when countries in southern Africa are ready for such an undertaking.

- *Most favoured nation clause.* The EU's insistence on the MFN has emerged as one of the most divisive aspects of the EPA negotiations with SADC countries. It is also the most salient feature of the chasm that exists between the strategic perspectives of the EU and South Africa on the future of regionalism and the manner of integration into the global economy. The MFN framework demonstrates that the EU views itself as the only global pole that countries in southern Africa should trade with to realize their developmental goals. Having granted substantial amounts of aid to this region, the EU may feel it has a sense of entitlement to 'own' the region's trading options.

South Africa was very vocal in tackling the EU on some of these issues. Its position in the EPA negotiations was based on its strategic trade objectives, in particular the drive to diversify its exports and geographic destinations. Its view of economic development privileges production and export diversification, which cannot be fully addressed through extreme dependence on the EU market for commodities. Before the EPAs created difficulties for SACU, South Africa had viewed the customs union as a mechanism for managing regional integration using variable geometry, and as an instrument to be deployed in the service of its own external trade engagements on a diversified basis – that is, integration with both established and emerging powers. The developmental path that South Africa has chosen is centred on industrial policies whose main thrust is to diversify the production base, beneficiate natural resources and diversify exports. The signing of the interim economic partnership agreement (IEPA) by a handful of countries in the region – Botswana, Lesotho, Mozambique and Swaziland – in 2008 has effectively undercut South Africa's influence in the regional sphere. South Africa's main motivation for participating in the EPAs was to preserve the unity of the subregion, and to thwart the EU's increasing hegemonic encroachment.[22]

Lack of coherence in SADC

From the beginning of the EPA negotiations in 2002, SADC was not a coherent force. Three separate groups were constituted: the SADC EPA Group, comprising the BLNS countries, as well as Mozambique, Angola and Tanzania; the East African Community (EAC), comprising Kenya and Uganda (and later Tanzania, forced by the EC to participate); and the East and Southern African Group, comprising all the other SADC members. South Africa joined the SADC EPA Group in February 2006 in an attempt to resist the balkanization of the region. The key negotiating objective for South Africa was to align its separate trade arrangement with the EU, the Trade, Development and Cooperation Agreement (TDCA), with the SADC EPA arrangement, this in order to achieve its ultimate objective – consolidation of SACU as a formidable customs union arrangement relative to the EU.[23]

The TDCA, signed in 1999, is a bilateral agreement between the EU and South Africa that covers trade relations, development cooperation, economic cooperation and political dialogue. Its key aspect is the preferential trade arrangement. Accordingly, the main trade provision entails liberalization of 95 per cent of EU imports from South Africa within ten years, and 86 per cent of South African imports from the EU in twelve years, with certain exclusions for sensitive products for both countries.[24] However, SACU countries such as Botswana, Lesotho, Namibia and Swaziland objected to South Africa's negotiation approach, which excluded them. As such, they perceived South Africa to be more concerned about its own interests rather than those of the subregion, an accusation that is perhaps unfair given the weight of the revenue transfers that flow out of South Africa to support the national budgets of these countries.[25]

However, the EC exploited the divisions in SADC and individual countries' fear of losing preferential access to the EU market to thwart South Africa's objective. The EU instead pursued its own vision of regional integration. If the EC had been interested in promoting regional integration, at least via SACU, it would have agreed to a review of the TDCA, and to possible alignment of the interests of smaller countries with a TDCA that offers flexible time frames for tariff reductions. The main concern of the BLNS countries during the EPA negotiations was losing preferential market access, particularly for their agricultural products in the EU market. Botswana and Swaziland cited the fear of losing preferential access to the EU for their beef and sugar exports, respectively, as reasons for initialling the IEPA. Lesotho, for its part, argued that it sought new market opportunities for its clothing exports in the EU. Namibia, while recognizing profound difficulties with the IEPA, initialled with reservations in the face of losing preferential access to EU markets for

Namibian beef, fish and fruit. Angola and South Africa did not initial the IEPA. Angola indicated that it did not foresee any benefit from the IEPA, as it exports mainly oil and lacks an export-ready agriculture or industrial structure that could benefit from a trading arrangement with the EU.

A chronic asymmetry of power and capabilities as well as agenda-setting in favour of Europe has marked the EPA negotiations. The 'First Approximations' for the EPA negotiations, and the issues on the agenda, were largely defined according to a rigid template designed by the EU. The EU was careful not to include the important agriculture sector on the agenda, which it preferred to manage on its own terms. Yet the EU placed emphasis on issues such as services, investment, competition and government procurement. Another factor that underlines asymmetries of power (and skewed agenda-setting) is that the EPA provisions would be enforceable using EC standards in line with the EC Enforcement Directive, over which African countries have absolutely no influence.

The tensions that ensued in the context of the EPA negotiations within southern Africa boiled down to who could offer more market opportunities and aid. South Africa could not offer largesse to the scale of the EU's generosity. The reality of asymmetries of capabilities was probably the greatest factor that shaped the outcomes of the negotiations. In line with Amartya Sen's conception of development, looking at both the process and the outcomes, the EPAs can be regarded as anything but developmental. They constrain the policy space for, and economic sovereignty of, southern African countries, restricting the region to a relationship with only one pole of the global economy.

The EPAs have exposed the lack of a common SADC and SACU agenda and have resulted in the further weakening rather than strengthening of regional integration. In the wake of the EPA fallout, South Africa has signalled an intention to strengthen customs controls within SACU to avoid trans-shipment of EU exports to its market via the countries that signed up to the EPA. The common external tariff – a fundamental basis of a customs union – has been thoroughly vulgarized by the EPAs. SACU countries now have different obligations to a third party – the EU – via the TDCA for South Africa, and via the EPAs for the BLNS countries. Such a situation, in which various member states conclude trade agreements under different provisions dictated by an external actor, would be unimaginable in the EU.

Another substantive factor that undermined a regional buy-in to South Africa's proposed vision of integration is the normative chasm that exists between South Africa and the majority of SADC countries. There has not been a crystallization of norms tying the region to South Africa's leadership. South Africa's lack of a coherent narrative for regional leadership and appealing norms has also constrained the extension of its influence in both SADC and SACU. According to John Ikenberry and Charles Kupchan: 'Acquiescence is the result of the socialization of leaders in secondary nations. Elites in secondary nations buy into and internalize the norms that are articulated by the hegemon and therefore pursue policies consistent with the hegemon's notion of international order.'[26] This has not materialized in the region. The South African state has not yet developed a solid, consensual, normative platform through which to articulate its regional and multilateral trade interests.[27]

Conclusion

The relationship between the European Union and southern Africa spans many decades and has, from the outset, reflected asymmetrical power relations. These relations have reinforced the dependence of the region on the EU, and this dependence has largely come in the form of development aid and preference-based trading schemes. The external pressure arising from other developing countries that felt that the special preferences accorded to Europe's former colonies represented a serious disadvantage necessitated the renegotiation of the preferential arrangements in order to conform to the rules of the WTO, in particular Article XXIV, which sets out procedural guidelines to satisfy the 'substantially all trade' requirement. In essence, trade between parties should be sufficiently reciprocated.

The EU exploited this to push for a more comprehensive commercial approach that goes beyond the minimum requirements of the WTO, which would be satisfied by a narrow coverage of the goods sector. It pushed for a more comprehensive coverage, including services and the 'new generation' trade issues, in order to defend its long-term economic interests in Africa in general, and in southern Africa in particular, as this constitutes one of the important pillars of the EU's global role. This hard bargain did not create room for assessing the development impact of the EPAs on African countries and the extent to which the agreements could preserve existing regional integration mechanisms.

The growing role of emerging powers such as China and India in Africa, spanning trade, investment and development cooperation, threatens to undermine the EU's pre-eminent position in the region. Structuring partnerships that emphasize Brussels' commercial interests in areas such as services, investment, competition and government procurement is thus an important step for the EU in locking southern Africa into its sphere of influence. Furthermore, the insistence by the EU on the MFN clause is clearly directed at the emerging powers.

Tensions between the EU and the SADC countries in the EPA negotiations grew in the battle of ideas and influence between South Africa and the EC. South Africa and the EU have competing visions of regional integration and development. Both view southern Africa as part of their sphere of influence. Two things are clear. First, given the EU's economic weight, and the fact that historically it has offered Africa both aid and markets for the continent's agricultural products, it has an upper hand in influencing vulnerable countries in the region. Secondly, however, the main challenge to the EU's role in southern Africa is likely to be posed by emerging powers such as China, India and Brazil, which are fast increasing their trade and investment relationship with Africa, including southern Africa.

Notes

1 Margaret C. Lee, 'Trade relations between the European Union and sub-Saharan Africa under the Cotonou Agreement', in Roger Southall and Henning Melber (eds), *A New Scramble for Africa: Imperialism, Investment, and Development* (Scottsville: University of KwaZulu-Natal Press, 2009), p. 84.

2 Ibid., pp. 85–6.

3 Ibid., p. 85.

4 Dirk Kohnert, 'EU–African economic relations: continuing dominance, traded for aid?', in German Institute of Global and Area Studies and Institute of African Affairs, MPRA Paper no. 9434, 3 July 2008, p. 13.

5 Kym Anderson and Richard Blackhurst (eds), *Regional Integration and the Global Trading System* (New York: Harverster Wheatsheaf, 1993), pp. 1–2.

6 'Banana producers go to WTO over EU dispute', *Financial Times*, 7 March 2005.

7 Lee, 'Trade relations between sub-Saharan Africa and the European Union', p. 87.

8 United Nations Conference on Trade and Development (UNCTAD), *Economic Development in Africa: Trade Performance and Commodity Dependence*, Geneva, 2003, pp. 22–3.

9 Brigid Gavin, 'European perspective on trade', UNU-Comparative Regional Integration Studies, mimeo, January 2009.

10 Marc Bacchetta and Bijit Bora, 'Industrial tariff liberalization and the Doha development agenda', Working paper (Geneva: World Trade Organization, 2004).

11 Alexander Keck and Roberta Piermartini, 'The economic impact of EPAs in SADC countries', Discussion paper (Geneva: World Trade Organization, August 2005).

12 Helen Nesadurai, 'Globalisation and economic regionalism: a survey and critique of the literature', Working Paper no. 108/02, Centre for the Study of Globalisation and Regionalism, University of Warwick, November 2002, p. 22, www.csgr.org.

13 Commission of the European Communities, 'Annex to the Communication from the Commission to the Council, the European Parliament, the European Economic and Social Committee, and the Committee of the Regions: Global Europe: Competing in the World – A Contribution to the EU's Growth and Jobs Strategy', Brussels, 4 October 2006, p. 4.

14 Ibid.

15 European Commission, 'A Strategy for Smart, Sustainable, and Inclusive Growth', COM (2010) 2020, Brussels, 3 March 2010.

16 UNCTAD, *Economic Development in Africa: South–South Cooperation*, Geneva, 2010. See le Pere in this volume.

17 Ibid.

18 Patrick Messerlin, 'Economic partnership agreements: how to rebound?', in Emily Jones and Darlan F. Marti (eds), *Updating Economic Partnership Agreements to Today's Global Challenges*, Economic Policy Paper no. 9 (Washington, DC: German Marshall Foundation, 2009), p. 22.

19 Emily Jones and Darlan F. Marti, 'Updating EPAs: rising to the challenge', in Jones and Marti, *Updating Economic Partnership Agreements*, p. 9.

20 South African Department of Trade and Industry, *Trade Policy and Strategy Framework*, Pretoria, 2010.

21 Charlotte Bretherton and John Vogler, *The European Union as a Global Actor* (London: Routledge, 1999), p. 58.

22 This is based on discussions with officials at the Department of Trade and Industry in the course of 2008, when I worked in that organization.

23 Based on discussions with officials at the Department of Trade and Industry in the course of 2008.

24 European Commission, *Trade, Development and Cooperation Agreement*, europa.eu/legislation_summaries/development/south_africa/r12201_en.htm.

25 In the recent International Monetary Fund (IMF) Article IV Consultation with South Africa, transfers from South Africa to BLNS range from 0.6 per cent to 1.1 per cent of gross domestic product. See IMF, 'South Africa: Article IV Consultation – Staff Report; Staff Supplement; Public Information Notice on the Executive Board Discussion; and Statement by the Executive Director for South Africa; IMF Country Report no. 10/26', Washington, DC, September 2010.

26 John G. Ikenberry and Charles A. Kupchan, 'Socialization and hegemonic power', *International Organization*, 44(3), Summer 1990, p. 283. The two authors further argue that there are two ways in which power can be exercised by dominant nations: by manipulating material incentives, and by altering the substantive beliefs of leaders in other nations. This argument was an important innovation to approaches that emphasize structural sources of hegemony associated with the classical realist paradigm.

27 See Maxi Schoeman and Chris Alden, 'The hegemon that wasn't: South Africa's foreign policy towards Zimbabwe', *Strategic Review of Southern Africa*, 25(1), 2003.

15 | The United States

Nomfundo Xenia Ngwenya

The United States has a compelling concrete self-interest in the progress of
the SADC. ... [R]egional integration offers the promise of access to a large
commercial market sustained by politically stable member states. Realising
this trade potential rests on fostering a more secure environment – especially
ending [the] wars ... containing social tensions; and preventing them. (Jendayi
Frazer, former US assistant secretary of state for Africa)[1]

This chapter makes three central arguments. The first is that although the
global interests of the United States have remained consistent in the Cold War
and post-Cold War periods, the various nuances of different administrations
have affected US policies towards southern Africa. Secondly, South Africa has
always been central to US relations with the region, and thus these relations
have tended to prioritize and follow the bilateral US–South Africa trajectory.
Finally, given the emergence of Angola's importance to the USA, the relationship between the USA and the Southern African Development Community
(SADC) will have to be mindful of the potential and limitations of South Africa
and Angola in advancing regional cooperation.

Although events such as the United Nations (UN) debates on apartheid, the
Sharpeville massacre of 1960 and the activities of individuals like prominent
actor Paul Robeson placed South Africa on the US foreign policy agenda, it
was not until the 1970s that the debate on this agenda towards South Africa as
well as the southern African region as a whole intensified in the US Congress,
owing primarily to the unprecedented election of African-American representatives. The struggles against white minority rule in Namibia, Zimbabwe and
South Africa resonated with both black and white Americans who were active
in the civil rights movement. By 1976, TransAfrica had been established as a
human rights and global justice institution whose primary focus would be to
challenge the US government's unjust policies in Africa and the Caribbean.
The organization played a prominent role in the US anti-apartheid coalition
known as the Free South Africa Movement (FSAM). Frustrated by the lack of
US pressure on the South African government, the FSAM staged a successful
protest at the South African embassy in December 1984. That marked a significant shift of US interest in the country, from a minority of foreign-policy-aware
elites to the broader US public, including trade unions and religious groups.

In keeping with a general analysis of modern US foreign policy, one can distinguish two key periods for US policy towards southern Africa: the Cold War and post-Cold War eras. While styles have tended to differ from administration to administration, the central tenets of US foreign policy have remained the same in each period. During the Cold War, the main objective was to stop the spread of communism. The post-Cold War period has similarly seen the same interests across administrations: the spread of democracy around the world, the opening of markets for US goods, and the elimination of external physical threats to the USA (including the post-11 September 2001 anti-terrorism emphasis).

The pursuit of US Cold War interests in southern Africa

The late independence struggles of southern Africa coincided with the intensification of the Cold War. As a result, a number of southern Africa's leading liberation movements maintained close relations with Cuba and the Soviet Union (Angola, Namibia, Mozambique, South Africa) and China (Zimbabwe). The South African government positioned itself as a pro-Western capitalist stabilizer that would act as a deterrent to communist influence in the region. For this reason, South Africa became central to US foreign policy towards southern Africa, with the administrations of Richard Nixon, Gerald Ford, Jimmy Carter and Ronald Reagan focusing primarily on maintaining good relations with the country. The activities of Henry Kissinger, secretary of state under Nixon (1969–74), and Ford (1974–77) point to a policy of colluding with the apartheid regime as the Cold War intensified. The Carter administration (1977–81) employed a different strategy – trying to pursue a human-rights-based policy – but nevertheless maintained the same US interests and ultimately found it difficult to reconcile what it was saying in public with what it was doing to collaborate with South Africa and its destabilizing policies. Despite working for the independence of Namibia and Zimbabwe, the Carter administration continued to consider the apartheid regime as an insurance policy against Soviet domination in southern Africa and Cuban 'interference' in the region. Hence, '[w]hile its anti-apartheid rhetoric was strong, the Carter administration seemed reluctant to end all nuclear cooperation with South Africa, unclear about what it expected white South Africans to do and at what pace, unwilling to consider the threat of economic sanctions, and inclined to encourage US businesses to stay and play an active role in South Africa'.[2]

It was during Reagan's presidency (1981–89) that arguably the most devastating stance towards the southern African region was taken, through his policy of 'containment'. He was obstinate on the issue of South Africa, despite pressure from the growing domestic constituency as a result of the FSAM's sit-in at the South African embassy. He refused to consider sanctions until he was defeated in Congress. The most active individual on southern Africa policy was Chester Crocker, US assistant secretary of state for African affairs, who is sometimes accused of having been naive about the South African government's intentions in the region. He saw the Soviets as a real threat in Angola and Namibia, and possibly in Mozambique, and appeared to believe that South Africa was acting in self-defence.

After assessing that the Zimbabwe African National Union–Patriotic Front (ZANU-PF) was not aligned to the Soviet Union and that it did not allow African National Congress (ANC) bases on its territory, Crocker steered the Reagan administration towards supporting Zimbabwe, thus continuing the Carter administration's support of that country's independence. This was solidified by an aid package of US$225 million in 1981.[3] By the 1980s, Mozambique's socialist policies had failed and the country was increasingly turning towards the West. As the South African government escalated its cross-border attacks on Mozambique and Zimbabwe, the USA interceded at various times on behalf of the two countries, and thus good relations were maintained both with Samora Machel and his successor, Joaquim Chissano, as well as with Robert Mugabe. It was not until Zimbabwe escalated its verbal attacks on the USA and consistently voted against it at the UN that the Reagan administration ended its bilateral aid programme. Through its support for Zimbabwe the USA hoped to increase its influence in southern Africa, while countering criticism that it was against black rule and self-determination. The record of the USA in the region during the Cold War reflects consistent interests, which often had devastating economic effects that adversely affected the pace of development.

An aspect of US relations with southern Africa that is often ignored is the effect of historical memory on the way that the region views the USA. Given the historical nature of US involvement, the suspicion with which the region constantly views the USA should come as no surprise. Angola, Namibia, South Africa and Zimbabwe were all significantly bruised by US support for destabilizing policies. The USA must now conduct relations with southern African governments composed of the liberation movements that it previously undermined. This requires the USA to emphasize forums and initiatives that will promote dialogue and set US–southern Africa relations on a new footing of reduced suspicion.

Post-Cold War US interests in southern Africa

In her assessment of US interests in southern Africa, Jendayi Frazer, former US assistant secretary of state for Africa, wrote: 'Africa historically comes last in US geo-strategic regional priorities.'[4] Frazer provided a three-level analysis of how the USA executes its policies in Africa:

1 The overall approach to sub-Saharan Africa (low priority, low resources).
2 Distinct subregional strategies (southern Africa being the most integrated).

3 Individual policies towards specific African countries (South Africa and Nigeria prioritized as pivotal states in sub-Saharan Africa) and towards SADC members (the US focus being on South Africa, Botswana, Zimbabwe and Angola).

Frazer further argued that there are compelling reasons for the USA to take an interest in southern Africa. Key among these are socio-political stability through development and acceleration of regional integration in order to create a larger commercial market for US goods and services. Although Frazer served in the administration of George W. Bush, the interests she identifies are the same as those of the Bill Clinton and Barack Obama administrations.

Frazer's assessment was written in 2003, at a time when emerging powers had not made as significant progress in penetrating the African market as they have since. Once again, the broader challenges to US foreign policy come to play in southern Africa, particularly the current attempts by the USA to offer an effective response to the significant rise and influence within Africa of the emerging powers, especially China. During a congressional hearing on the Africa Command (AFRICOM), Kenyan academic Wafula Okumu testified that '[f]or a long time, the strategic thinking has been that the U.S. has no compelling interest in Africa and does not want anybody to have any, either. However, when a non-Western nation or idea made its way into Africa, the U.S. got very nervous.'[5] South African strategist Clem Sunter recounted that when he was invited to address the Central Party School of China's Communist Party in Beijing, a senior-ranking officer said that Africa was his 'continent of choice', since it was 'where they [the Chinese] did not have to bump into Americans'.[6]

Stating that the USA should pay attention to Africa in order to counter the emergence of China is not tantamount to calling for a reauctioning of the continent. Instead, it allows Africa to diversify its choices and gives it the opportunity to exploit different centres of global power in a more strategic way than it did during the Cold War. Southern Africa is of particular strategic significance because the region has become the playground of these emerging global powers. Because China has surpassed the USA as the major trading partner of South Africa, the region may not remain a low-level geo-strategic element of US foreign policy in the long term.

We now turn to an evaluation of the different US post-Cold War administrations and their interactions with southern Africa with respect to three main areas: the consistency of US interests in southern Africa; South Africa–US relations and their effects on US relations with the southern African region as a whole; and the role of Angola and South Africa as strategic partners.

In the post-Cold War period, the USA has sought to pursue its foreign policy objectives in developing countries through the identification of 'pivotal states', which have the capacity to influence developments in their respective regions while potentially affecting the stability of the international system.[7] Writing in 2001, Henry Kissinger emphasized the importance of leaving the resolution of Africa's security challenges to the continent's pivotal states.[8] Citing Kissinger and US foreign policy scholar John Stremlau, Chris Landsberg observed that South Africa and Nigeria appeared prominently in the US conceptualization of African pivotal states.[9] The Clinton administration combined political and economic tools to demonstrate the importance of South Africa to US policy towards SADC and the continent.

The Clinton years

In the immediate aftermath of the Cold War, the USA became the centre of a unipolar world. South Africa's first democratic government, of 1994, had therefore to develop strategies to forge a partnership with the USA. At that time, the USA was in the process of rethinking its international engagements, particularly in eastern Europe, where it sought to ensure that former Soviet states did not revert to communism. Within this process, the USA had to also rethink its geopolitical engagement with Africa. With the particular influence of the first US African-American secretary of commerce, Ronald H. Brown, South Africa occupied a prominent place on the US global strategic partnership agenda. Brown was of the conviction that South Africa's emergence from apartheid would mark the beginning of significant changes in southern Africa's and the rest of the continent's political and economic trajectory. He was the first in the USA to declare South Africa a 'big emerging market', thus elevating the level of attention and resources it would receive from the USA.[10] The USA immediately established the Bi-National Commission (BNC) with South Africa, chaired by Vice-Presidents Al Gore and Thabo Mbeki. This formalization of dialogue was extended to the regional level.

It should be recalled that the USA played an important role as one of the donors supporting the creation of SADC's predecessor, the Southern African Development Coordination Conference (SADCC). By the end of apartheid, the Clinton administration had identified the potential for SADC to act as a unified bloc, which would lead to greater political and economic integration. As part of that administration's initiative to show commitment to regionalism in SADC, the SADC–US Forum was born. According to Prega Ramsamy, a former Executive Secretary of SADC, the objective of the forum was to 'increase co-operation between the US and SADC to promote regional integration through increased trade and investment between the US and SADC; to co-ordinate US policy towards the region; to exchange ideas on economics, politics, crime, drug control, public health, the environment and technology; and to promote US technical input in areas of de-mining and disaster-preparedness'.[11] Some of the forum's deliberations were clearly targeted at addressing concerns that were directly linked to US interests, such as the protection of intellectual property rights. However, other projects focused on areas that were more directly important to the region's strategic interests and contributed to the building of goodwill, such as cooperation between SADC and the USA to establish a regional mechanism that would rapidly respond to disasters, an initiative that was triggered by the 2000 floods in Mozambique.[12] As will be discussed in more detail later, the SADC–US Forum was discontinued during the George W. Bush years.

The fall of apartheid in Africa's largest economy prompted the USA to seek a more organized manner of dealing with African trade and investment issues. Congress tasked President Clinton with developing a US trade policy for sub-Saharan Africa, and the deliberations, which started in 1998, culminated in congressional approval of the Africa Growth and Opportunity Act (AGOA) in May 2000.[13] The original expiry date of the act was 30 September 2008, but following the signing of the AGOA Acceleration Act of 2004, the expiry date was extended until 30 September 2015. Under the terms of AGOA, eligible African countries can export 6,000 product items duty-free into the USA.[14] Much of the implementation of AGOA took place during the administration of George W. Bush, and it has faced substantial criticism.

The George W. Bush years

The Bush administration's preoccupation with the 'war on terror' saw US foreign policy in Africa shift towards countries that were considered actual or potential terrorist threats. Secretary of State Condoleezza Rice, for example, visited a number of North African countries, including Algeria, Tunisia and Morocco. She also visited Ethiopia to attend a summit on the Great Lakes; Kenya in the wake of the 2008 post-election violence; and Ghana to attend an AGOA regional forum. None of her visits to the continent took her to southern Africa. Bush made two strategic miscalculations when it came to understanding the need for rebuilding confidence between the USA and southern Africa: ending the Bi-National Commission, and ending the SADC–US Forum.

Bush's first miscalculation was to instruct his secretary of state, Colin Powell, to terminate the US–South Africa Bi-National Commission. Although no official reason was made public, uncertainty about the future of the BNC emerged during the 2000 US presidential election. Writing about the election's implications for US–South Africa relations, Francis Kornegay noted that bi-national commissions were a product of each president's personal choices and of his political party's views of strategic relations between the USA and particular countries.[15] Indeed, shortly after assuming his role as Bush's secretary of state, Powell called for a review of all bi-national commissions in which the USA participated under the Clinton administration.[16] In an attempt to secure the continuation of the US–South Africa BNC, South African foreign affairs minister Nkosazana Dlamini-Zuma flew to Washington, DC, to meet Powell in April 2011. However, the lack of rapport between the ANC and the Republicans, whose most intense interaction had been acrimonious at the height of apartheid, was likely a key factor in the discontinuation of the BNC. The Republicans recognized the importance of South Africa as an economic and political actor in the region, but did not consider it necessary to invest additional resources into the relationship beyond the norms of bilateral engagement. While it is also possible that the USA may have had additional reasons to review its BNCs after September 2001, in order to focus money on pressing national security issues, it did not augur well for the USA to terminate a mechanism for communication between itself and the biggest economy in sub-Saharan Africa, which also happened to be the biggest contributor to peacemaking on the continent and was at that time actively engaged in drafting a new architecture for the reshaping of the Organization of African Unity (OAU) and the continent's institutional architecture. This absence of special dialogue made it more difficult to address tensions such as South Africa's opposition to the United States Africa Command (AFRICOM). Equally misguided was the Bush administration's decision to extend the termination of formal mechanisms for dialogue to the regional level, despite claiming that it was interested in fostering greater regional integration in Africa.

The Bush administration's non-committal stance on the SADC–US Forum is said to have been brought about primarily by disagreements between the USA and SADC on how to resolve the Zimbabwean crisis.[17] Given how close the Zimbabwe issue was to Britain's national politics and foreign policy, it may well be that Bush was under pressure to acquiesce to British demands for the USA to take a tougher approach to SADC for what the British perceived to be its 'soft' stance in handling Mugabe. Since Tony Blair was the one leader who most boldly came out in support of Bush in his 'war on terror', it may be the case that SADC and its forum with the USA became casualties of a more complex and broader US foreign policy dynamic. In 2006, when Bush's assistant secretary of state, Jendayi Frazer, and Clinton's former assistant secretary of state, Susan Rice, attempted to re-establish the forum, they did so on the basis of an acknowledgement that terminating the forum had 'harmed dialogue with other African countries'.[18]

Where Bush did succeed was in addressing an issue that is of primary human security concern to southern Africa, HIV/AIDS. (See Dzinesa in this volume.) Given the fact that southern Africa is the hardest-hit region on the continent, Bush's President's Emergency Plan for AIDS Relief (PEPFAR) was significant. At the end of Bush's second term in 2008, US$3.7 million, half of the total PEPFAR budget, was allocated to fifteen 'focus countries' around the world and a third of this allocation went to four southern African countries.[19]

This did not receive the positive publicity that it deserved, as the focus of attention was more on the abstinence programmes and on general perceptions of Bush's religious background influencing foreign policy. It was therefore ironic that it was with Bush's departure, particularly with President Obama's announcement that he would be cutting funding for antiretroviral treatment, that the real effects of Bush's PEPFAR were acknowledged.

An area in which the Bush administration received mixed reviews was trade. AGOA was intended to improve access to the US market for approximately six thousand goods from Africa. Statistics between 2000 and 2009, however, indicate that three sectors constitute 90 per cent of AGOA's products: energy-related products, textiles and transportation equipment. In southern Africa, Angola and South Africa form two of the continent's top five beneficiaries of AGOA (the other African countries are Nigeria, the Democratic Republic of the Congo and Chad).[20] With the exception of South Africa, these countries export oil and gas products.

Furthermore, countries within the Southern African Customs Union (SACU), such as Lesotho, Swaziland and to a lesser extent Botswana, have benefited from the apparel and textile exports, and Namibia has benefited from some agricultural exports. While Bush's implementation of AGOA was initially praised for increasing these countries' apparel exports, their inability to compete with Asian exports has led to more criticism that AGOA has failed to help countries diversify their economies and has failed to attract US foreign investment.[21] The other area in which implementation of AGOA undermines the USA's self-proclaimed principles of democracy promotion is the types of countries that appear on the list of beneficiaries. According to AGOA, the president can

> designate countries as eligible to receive the benefits of AGOA if they are determined to have established, or are making continual progress toward establishing the following: market-based economies; the rule of law and political pluralism; elimination of barriers to U.S. trade and investment; protection of intellectual property; efforts to combat corruption; policies to reduce poverty, increasing availability of health care and educational opportunities; protection of human rights and worker rights; and elimination of certain child labour practices.[22]

In southern Africa, Angola is one of the least democratic countries yet one of the top beneficiaries through its oil exports. The irony cannot escape any observer that Botswana, the one country that is hailed by the USA for its democratic values and promotion of good governance in the region, has benefited far less than some of the countries with the most dubious records in areas that AGOA claims to promote.

This also brings into question Bush's choice of Botswana as an ally. Although Bush presented Botswana as a model for southern African democracy and good governance, he did not sufficiently follow through by demonstrating the tangible value of that status for Botswana in its relationship with the USA, nor the benefits of that relationship for furthering the USA's democracy promotion objectives in the broader region. Instead, at the end of 2009 Botswana announced that a company employing 5,000 of the country's 8,500 textile and apparel industry workers would be retrenched as a result of their inability to compete with Asian exports.[23]

One might think that the USA would have partnered more closely with institutions like the Botswana Export and Development Agency, whose mandate it is to improve trade. This would have been a more effective public relations victory for the USA, if the region and continent were talking about Botswana and its great success with AGOA owing to concerted effort from its strategic ally the USA, rather than countries like Angola and Chad. While the USA did support Botswana in devising a diversification strategy, there is not much to show for it publicly. By the end of 2009, Botswana's exports to the USA under AGOA constituted only US$12 million of the approximately US$1.3 billion of its total exports to the USA.[24] Meanwhile, while Botswana realizes that AGOA is 'not enough', China is intensifying its relations with the country, including the granting of preferential loans, supply of agricultural technology, and improvement of road and rail infrastructure.[25]

Obama and southern Africa

Given that Obama has only just passed the midpoint of his presidential term, it would be premature to judge the impact of his policies on southern Africa. Nonetheless, there are some identifiable signs of the direction in which his administration is moving, especially on trade and HIV/AIDS. As it stands, he has not deviated much from Bush's policy towards Africa in terms of substance. He has not made any major changes to AGOA, although a new innovation has been to divide the AGOA Forum between Washington and the American heartland in an effort to improve the dialogue between US and African farmers.[26] Although there is no clarity yet on what Obama aims to achieve through these meetings, it remains difficult to see how such partnerships could be effectively beneficial for farmers in southern Africa, who must compete with US farming subsidies amounting to $20 billion annually.

The global economic crisis has had a particularly severe effect on the US economy since 2007, dictating that the Obama administration use fewer financial resources but still produce tangible outcomes. The first casualty of financial constraints in US–southern Africa relations has been the US provision of antiretroviral drugs for people living with HIV/AIDS. Under President Bush, PEPFAR was a critical source of these drugs and was a significant publicity success for that administration, especially since a number of southern African governments were either reluctant or unable to provide these drugs through their public health systems. If Obama is under pressure to reduce spending on PEPFAR, it would be more strategically significant for him to reduce support in areas that are well funded by other major donors, such as awareness and prevention campaigns, rather than halting the provision of antiretroviral drugs in a region that has the highest infection numbers on the continent. Because PEPFAR has faced minimal challenges on Capitol Hill and has enjoyed bipartisan support, it should therefore be one of Obama's strengths instead of the publicity disaster it has become, especially in South Africa, where people living with HIV/AIDS have protested and drawn public attention to the issue.

President Obama has added Angola as an additional pivotal state to the USA's strategic partnerships in Africa, bringing the number of such partnerships to two in southern Africa (South Africa and Angola) and one in West Africa (Nigeria). South Africa has played and continues to play a critical role in driving developments within southern Africa. A key factor in this has always been the centrality of the South African economy to those of its neighbours. The country accounts for 58 per cent of the region's gross domestic product (GDP).[27] Historically, the boom in the mining sector, particularly in gold and diamonds, created demand for labour from neighbouring countries, thus causing the economies of these countries to rely on South Africa. In the post-apartheid era, this reliance has extended beyond mining, as the country's diverse sectors require skills that the majority of the South African population could not acquire as a result of apartheid. This has attracted both skilled and unskilled workers from the region. World Bank statistics released in 2007 show that most of South Africa's migrants come from its immediate neighbours.[28]

South Africa is also in a customs union with four of its immediate neighbours – Botswana, Lesotho, Namibia and Swaziland. (See Gibb in this volume.) Furthermore, South Africa's substantial investments in the region in sectors as varied as mining, retail and communications have led to the revival of a number of southern Africa's economies. Writing in 2009, John Daniel and Mpume Bhengu argued that, seven years after the *New York Times* declared that the South Africans 'have arrived', South African companies remained a prominent feature of the African economy and were continuing to grow in number.[29] According to the *World Investment Report*, despite the emergence of new economic players in the form of China, India and other emerging powers, South Africa was the largest foreign direct investor in Africa between 2006 and 2008.[30] South Africa's innovations in regional development, as exemplified by projects such as the Spatial Development Initiatives (SDIs), have led to infrastructure and economic development, with Mozambique being an outstanding example. South Africa's state-created development finance institutions (DFIs) have also been critical sources of development funding for the region. Key among these are the Development Bank of Southern Africa, which funds infrastructure development projects in the region, and the Industrial Development Corporation, which funds the development of projects in a wide range of sectors. (See Monyae in this volume.)

At a regional political level, President Jacob Zuma appears to be paying much attention to the southern African region. For example, during Zuma's first year in office he visited a substantial number of southern African countries, including Angola, Mozambique, Namibia, Tanzania, Zambia and Zimbabwe. That Zuma was the head of the African National Congress's intelligence unit, headquartered in Lusaka, Zambia, means that he has alliances with the remaining ruling parties, whose past personal relations could be used to influence developments in the region. South Africa has also continued to play a critical role in resolving the war in the DRC, one of the countries visited by Secretary of State Hillary Clinton as part of the Obama administration's priority of resolving African conflicts.

It is clear that in order for Obama to achieve his four goals for southern Africa, he must prioritize relations with South Africa. In its 2010 National Security Strategy, the Obama administration identified South Africa as one of the emerging markets with which the USA ought to cooperate.[31] This was concretized by the signing of the US–South Africa Strategic Partnership Dialogue. As mentioned, the only other SADC country with which the USA has established such a structure is Angola. Its economy is the second biggest in SADC, accounting for 17 per cent of the region's total GDP. Although it trails South Africa's 58 per cent total, Angola's economy grew at an average of 20 per cent between 2004 and 2010. Despite having slowed owing to the global recession, Angola's economy is expected to remain among the fastest growing in the world, on the back of its oil reserves. Politically, Angola's historical role in assisting liberation movements in the region remains central to its legitimacy in southern Africa. The 1998 military intervention in the DRC, where Angola collaborated with Zimbabwe and Namibia while South Africa preferred a diplomatic and political solution, was a stark example of how much political influence Angola can wield and how it can become a source of discord within the region where its interests are at stake.

Angola is currently cultivating its own good relations with the USA. It was perhaps for this reason that, in 2003, Angola became the only SADC country to support the US invasion of Iraq. At a conference on Angola's post-war foreign policy at the Catholic University of Angola, Ambassador Nelson Cosme, the director-general for Africa and the Middle East in the Angolan Ministry for External Relations, identified the USA as one of Angola's strategic partners of the future.[32] As Angolan academic Assis Malaquias notes, Angola has reached out to China extensively in its period of reconstruction, and is likely to further reach out to the USA as it enters its period of development.[33] Though blame for the country's prolonged civil war can be laid at the door of the USA, Angola has demonstrated a pragmatism that probably dates back to the times of its founding father, Agostinho Neto, who supported non-alignment in order to derive maximum benefit from multiple relations.

Despite the much-publicized fact that Angola has been the playground of the Chinese since 2004, there is an increasing awareness within Angola that the country needs to open itself for business with other major powers, both established and old. To this end, as mentioned, Angola has accelerated its relations with the USA, with Hillary Clinton including Angola on her first official visit to Africa as secretary of state. But the USA needs to exercise caution that the relationship be seen as more than just unilateral in the interests of oil. The potentially important role that Angola can play in issues of peace-building in southern (as well as central) Africa should be part of this relationship.

Conscious of not wanting to be seen to be a pawn of the USA, Angola constantly emphasizes its pursuit of a pragmatic foreign policy that allows for partnership with multiple countries. It has also sought to emphasize that it is an equal partner that will not compromise its sovereignty for economic benefits. This was particularly evident when a press conference was held to mark the signing of the US–Angola Bilateral Partnership Agreement in Washington, DC. At the event, US Secretary of State Hillary Clinton concentrated her speech on statistics about US aid to and trade with Angola. In contrast, Angolan minister of external relations Assunção Afonso dos Anjos chose to focus on the importance of mutual respect among equals:

> Friendship and cooperation among men should not be based only in hard to grasp numbers and figures and commercial data. And cooperation should not just be aid and assistance from the developed countries to those countries in need. But however, cooperation through humanity and respect among men should be translated into proactive and dynamic actions that are undertaken together.[34]

The USA has also identified its own interests in Angola: security of US energy supplies and promotion of stability in southern Africa.[35] Although Angola remains limited in its ability to be a key regional military actor owing to the challenges of completing its demobilization process and enhancing its internal security,[36] it nonetheless has a significant role to play in conflict resolution, as it continues to boast one of the best-trained militaries on the continent. Indeed, in the past Angola has not hesitated to send its troops to manage conflicts where it has felt directly threatened, with the DRC being a specific case in point. What it lacks in diplomatic and negotiation capability it certainly makes up for in its ability to rapidly deploy troops in the event of crisis.

Furthermore, Angola is also looking to increasingly bolster its reputation as an important actor in SADC. With its latest acquisitions of several oil and gas interests across the region – notably in Namibia, Zambia, Mozambique and Botswana – it will find its economic interests becoming increasingly inter-twined with the region's political stability, which in turn may compel it to become more proactive in conflict prevention and resolution.

While it is understandable that the USA cannot elevate bilateral relations with every single state in southern Africa, or any other region of the world for that matter, it is important that it not cultivate these bilateral relations at the expense of structures that are aimed at accelerating regional integration.

Reviving the SADC–US Forum and promoting regional cooperation

As mentioned earlier, the SADC–US Forum ceased to exist primarily as a result of US opposition to SADC's position on Zimbabwe, which the USA considered too lenient on Robert Mugabe's ruling party. By 2003, during its presidency of SADC, Angola is alleged to have come under pressure from the USA not to invite Zimbabwe to the SADC–US Forum. But following the insist-ence of the region's members, Angola did extend the invitation to Mugabe.[37] This is a reminder of the importance of historical memory. Leaders in southern Africa continue to see their legitimacy as being anti-imperialist, and none would dare risk loss of credibility among their peers. While Angola broke ranks with SADC in supporting the Iraq War, this did not provoke the ire of its fellow SADC leaders. The USA's attempts to divide countries within the region is not forgotten among the former liberation fighters turned ruling elites. It is therefore in the USA's interests to continue engaging the collective, in addition to its more strategic bilateral engagements.

Various individuals and institutions within and outside the USA have called for a revival of the SADC–US Forum. They include former US assistant secre-taries of state Susan Rice and Jendayi Frazer and the US Council on Foreign Relations. South African-based American scholar Francis Kornegay has observed that the revival of a structured platform from which the USA can engage the region 'is an area in need of urgent revisiting, as the Obama administration evolves toward putting its own stamp on its approach to Africa'. He adds: 'Revisiting the SADC–US Forum, therefore, takes on added importance if the US is to re-establish itself as a leading player on the continent at a time when the economic diplomacies of the EU, China and other emerging powers are rapidly unfolding.'[38] It is at this forum that clear objectives and areas of cooperation can be defined and negotiated, providing Obama with the opportunity to break from the recent animosity between the USA and the southern African region.

It is the contention of this chapter that since the SADC–US Forum fell apart as a result of a misunderstanding on Zimbabwe, it is on the issue of Zimbabwe that the relationship should be reconstructed. Relations with Britain aside, the USA is squandering its political capital in southern Africa on a country that is not directly related to its regional interests. While of course resolution of the conflict in Zimbabwe is critical for progress in the region, it is more the message that the USA is sending in its handling of the situation which is detrimental. US action, particularly the continuation of targeted sanctions, is seen to undermine rather than strengthen the position of South Africa and Angola, the two countries with which the USA aims to prioritize relations. Angola and South Africa have both called for the USA to end sanctions against various members of ZANU-PF's leadership. This is especially the case because restrictive measures have been seen to be ineffective in bringing about change and have instead given ZANU-PF more reason to stall, while raising questions among African leaders about the real purpose of these measures.[39] If the Obama administration were to heed the call for a cancellation of sanctions, the USA could achieve the dual goal of averting accusations that it wants to impose its will on southern African countries that already have historical memory of US domination in the region, while indirectly placing pressure on its key regional strategic partners to deliver more tangible results in Zimbabwe. By claiming to have faith in African solutions, Angola and South Africa's leaders place their own political capital on the line and become more likely to cooperate in the push for a more effective regional effort. The year 2011 in particular presents an ideal time for Angola and South Africa to cooperate, as they both occupy important seats in SADC. Angola will chair SADC and South Africa will chair the SADC Organ on Politics, Defence and Security Cooperation (OPDSC) beginning in August 2011. Furthermore, with the strengthening of relations between the two countries during Angolan president José Eduardo Dos Santos's visit to South Africa in December 2010, there is an unprecedented opportunity for the two countries to explore cooperation on regional matters. Such an opportunity could be used strategically by the USA to re-engage the region through the leadership of its strategic partners in SADC.

Conclusion

Although this chapter has focused on how the USA engages southern Africa, it should also be noted that southern Africa needs to be more proactive in its engagement with the USA. As Gilbert Khadiagala observed about US–Africa relations in general: 'future US foreign policy needs to be secured on the principle of African reciprocity; Africa has to make a substantial contribution to the terms of engagement. But such an Africa must be one that is prepared to meet the world halfway, an Africa with national and continental sense of purpose.'[40] Indeed, these observations are applicable in the southern African context, where in the absence of an established forum for dialogue, SADC's expectations of the USA are not easily discernible. An official at the US embassy in Pretoria indicated that the USA has ongoing initiatives at the regional level, such as the Democracy and Governance Programme, the SADC Parliamentary Forum agreement on election observation in southern Africa, and the Southern

Africa Trade Hub.[41] What is not clear, however, is the extent to which these initiatives can be said to be unique to the southern African region. As Kaire Mbuende, a former Executive Secretary of SADC, notes, it is not enough for the region to complain about the USA prioritizing relations with key countries like South Africa; smaller countries would serve their interests better by leveraging the US–South Africa relationship in the context of SACU and SADC.[42]

In terms of how the USA engages southern Africa, the Obama administration can learn from the Clinton and Bush administrations which mistakes to avoid and which good practices to emulate in pursuit of US interests in the region. There are three key lessons for Obama. First, his foreign policy objectives do not differ much from those of his two predecessors. What will set him apart will be the extent to which he effectively manages bilateral relations with key regional partners to pursue broader regional objectives. Accordingly, he needs to invest in the building of trust through a forum that will seek regional consensus, namely the SADC–US Forum. Secondly, he must continue to improve relations with South Africa as the key economic anchor of the region, since failure to do so would inevitably lead to weak relations. Finally, Obama should ensure that Angola's new-found cooperation with the United States does not isolate Angola from the rest of the region. Instead, the United States should support a greater role for Angola in cooperation with South Africa and the rest of the region. Such action would lessen the concerns of each country about being a conduit of US foreign policy when it acts at a bilateral level with the USA. The southern African region is bound by many political, economic and social ties. By understanding these complexities and tailoring its approach to the region's historical and current dynamics, the Obama administration may find itself closer to achieving its four objectives: supporting strong, sustainable, democratic governments; fostering development that provides greater opportunity for the peoples of southern Africa; improving public health; and ending conflict.

Notes

1 Jendayi Frazer, 'The United States', in Mwesiga L. Baregu and Christopher Landsberg (eds), *From Cape to Congo: Southern Africa's Evolving Security Challenges* (Boulder, CO: Lynne Rienner, 2003), p. 278.

2 Pauline H. Baker, *The United States and South Africa: The Reagan Years* (Washington, DC: Ford Foundation, 1989), p. xiii.

3 Ibid., p. 21.

4 Frazer, 'The United States', p. 278.

5 Wafula Okumu, 'Africa Command: opportunity for enhanced engagement or the militarization of U.S.–Africa relations?', Testimony to the US House Committee on Foreign Affairs, Subcommittee on Africa and Global Health, 2007, www.internationalrelations.house.gov/110/oku080207.htm.

6 Clem Sunter, 'Mind of a fox', Speech at Valley Lodge, Magaliesburg, 26 January 2010.

7 Robert S. Chase, Emily Hill and Paul Kennedy, 'Pivotal states and US strategy', *Foreign Affairs*, 75(1), January/February 1996, p. 46.

8 Henry Kissinger, *Does the United States Need a Foreign Policy?* (New York: Simon and Schuster, 2001), p. 207.

9 Christopher Landsberg, 'The United States and Africa: malign neglect', in David Malone and Yuen Foong Khong (eds), *Unilateralism and US Foreign Policy* (London: Lynne Rienner, 2003), p. 351.

10 Harry Bodansky, 'In our international commercial relations, we must look like America: Secretary Brown makes outreach a part of the Commerce Department's new diversity policy', *Business America*, 1994, findarticles.com/p/articles/mi_m1052/is_n10_v115/ai_15902044/pg_3.

11 Quoted in Peter Fabricius, 'SADC, US create Disaster Reaction Forum', 2000, www.iol.co.za/index.php?sf=143&set_id=1&click_id=68&art_id=ct20000509210720531S320922,9.

12 Ibid.

13 Danielle Langton, 'U.S. trade and investment relationship with sub-Saharan Africa: the African Growth and Opportunity Act and beyond', Report no. RL31772 (Washington, DC: Congressional Research Service, 2008), p. 5.

14 Trade Law Centre for Southern Africa (Tralac), 'Botswana: 5000 workers lose jobs as textile factory closes down', 2009, www.agoa.co.za/index.php?view=.&story= news&subtext=1180.

15 Francis Kornegay, 'The United States presidential elections: implications for Africa and South Africa', *Global Insight*, 4, October 2000, p. 1.

16 Charles Cobb, 'Talks underway to re-evaluate US–South Africa link', 2001, allafrica.com/stories/200104180105.html.

17 Telephone interview with South African government official, 18 December 2010.

18 Francis Kornegay, 'United States–South African relations: exploring new directions in an ambivalent relationship', Unpublished paper, 2010, p. 7.

19 Avert, 'PEPFAR funding: how is the money spent?', 2011, /www.avert.org/pepfar-funding.htm.

20 US Trade Representative, 'Fact sheet on AGOA', 2009, www.ustr.gov/sites/default/files/AGOA%20Fact%20Sheet%2003.09.pdf.

21 Stephen Hayes, 'AGOA: a five-year assessment', Testimony by Stephen Hayes, president of the Corporate Council on Africa, to the US House Committee on International Relations, Subcommittee on Africa, Global Human Rights, and International Operations, 2005, p. 4, allafrica.com/download/resource/main/main/id atcs/00010164:84645f1d08050189ad540e4f6d463275.pdf.

22 African Growth and Opportunity Act, 'General Country Eligibility Provision', 2010, www.agoa.gov/eligibility/country_eligibility.html.

23 Tralac, 'Botswana'.

24 Tralac, 'Bilateral trade profile: US–Botswana', 2011, www.agoa.info/?view=country_info&country=bw&story=trade.

25 Chinese Embassy in Botswana, 'Bilateral relations', 2010, bw.chineseembassy.org/eng/sbgx.

26 Charles W. Corey, 'Obama administration committed to AGOA partnership with continent', 2010, allafrica.com/stories/201006030027.html.

27 Peter Draper, Sheila Kiratu and Cezanne Samuel, 'The role of South African FDI in southern Africa', 2007, p. 1, www.die-gdi.de/CMS-Homepage/openwebcms3.nsf/(ynDK_contentByKey)/ANES-882C6Q/$FILE/DP%208.2010.pdf.

28 Dilip Ratha and William Shaw, 'South–South migration and remittances', World Bank Working Paper no. 102, 2007.

29 John Daniel and Mpume Bhengu, 'South Africa in Africa', in Roger Southall and Henning Melber, *The New Scramble for Africa: Imperialism, Investment, and Development in Africa* (Durban: University of KwaZulu-Natal Press, 2009), p. 140.

30 Cited in Terence Creamer, 'SA confirmed as top developing country investor in Africa', 2010, www.polity.org.za/article/sa-confirmed-as-top-developing-country-investor-in-africa-2010-07-23.

31 White House, 'National Security Strategy', 2010, www.whitehouse.gov/sites/default/files/rss_viewer/national_security_strategy.pdf.

32 Nelson Cosme, Untitled speech delivered at a SAIIA-CEIC workshop on Angola's foreign policy, Catholic University of Angola, 3 March 2010.

33 Assis Malaquias, 'Angola's foreign policy: pragmatic recalibrations', Forthcoming occasional paper to be published by the South African Institute of International Affairs, Johannesburg, 2011; Kaire Mbuende, 'Southern African regional integration: the need for acceleration', Speech delivered at the South African Institute of International Affairs, Johannesburg, 22 February 2011.

34 US State Department, 'Clinton, Dos Anjos at signing of US–Angola strategic dialogue', 8 July 2010, www.america.gov/st/texttransenglish/2010/July/20100708190426i hecuoro.3388439.html&distid=ucs.

35 Council on Foreign Relations, *Toward an Angola Strategy: Prioritizing U.S.–Angola Relations*, New York, 2007, p. 8.

36 Ibid., pp. 26–7.

37 Telephone interview with South African government official, 18 December 2010.

38 Kornegay, 'United States–South African relations', p. 7.

39 Bryan M. Sims, Sydney Masamvu and Havi Mirell, 'Restrictive measures and Zimbabwe', 2010, p. 12, www.swradio africa.com/Documents/Idasa%20 Restrictive%20Measures%20Study%20 Zimbabwe.pdf.

40 Gilbert Khadiagala, 'The United States and Africa: beyond the Clinton administration', *SAIS Review*, 21(1), Winter–Spring 2001, p. 270.

41 US embassy in Pretoria, written response to questions from author, 6 April 2011.

42 Mbuende, 'Southern African regional integration'.

16 | China

Garth le Pere

Different manifestations of European settler colonialism, struggles for independence, and traditions of liberation have profoundly influenced the evolution of southern Africa. 'Colonialism of a special type' made the struggle for independence a particularly violent and protracted one in several countries. The particular character of settler oligarchies in southern Africa makes it the most Westernized of Africa's subregions, yet it suffers from the many scourges that afflict the rest of the continent: poverty, underdevelopment, poor governance, disease and food insecurity. All this influences China's approach to the region. The essential tenets of China's policy in Africa, namely the 'bilateralization' of these interests, are firmly embedded in the region. This goes to the heart of how China has developed its strategic framework and how countries have responded in shaping their own dynamics and bargains with China. In recent years, the Cold War ideological considerations that helped to define China's strategy in the region have been eclipsed by a new context, propelled by China's emergence as a global power and underpinned by its pursuit of its economic, political and military interests.

The cornerstones of the foreign policy of the People's Republic of China (PRC) in Africa are the pursuit of sources of raw materials, access to a largely untapped African market, and support for its global geopolitical ambitions.[1] These goals have been buttressed by Chinese offers of 'unconditional' aid, low-interest loans, investment packages and technical cooperation and trade agreements to boost the development prospects and productive capacities of African countries. China thus offers an alternative development model that most African countries find very attractive after a long history of Western colonial and neocolonial hegemony, exploitation and domination. According to one interpretation: 'China's capturing of markets through the combination of aggressive diplomacy, financial largesse and low costs, coupled with African aptitude in playing one suitor off the other, fuels this sense of impending relegation in Western capitals.'[2] This football metaphor means that China's premier-league presence could reduce the influence and power of Europe and the United States to that of secondary players on the continent.

China's relations with Africa have been given greater substance recently through deliberate policy innovations and institutional platforms. The Forum on China–Africa Cooperation (FOCAC), first convened in Beijing in 2000, and China's 2006 White Paper on Africa, are the primary expressions of the strategic importance and developmental and economic weight that China attaches to its Africa relations. The White Paper lays down the philosophical and normative markers meant to guide Sino-African relations: these are couched in the language of sincerity, friendship and equality; mutual benefit, reciprocity and common prosperity; and mutual support and close coordination.[3] To give effect to these principles, China recognizes the necessity of political agency in Africa as opposed to a Eurocentric and reductionist view of the continent simply as a subject of history and modernity.[4]

As Christopher Dent has argued, a range of economic security imperatives explain and motivate the closer relationship between China and Africa:[5]

- *Supply:* Ensuring that supply chains and their structures are maintained, especially with regard to strategic sources such as metal ores and oil.
- *Finance credit:* Helping African countries mitigate their financial solvency and debt relief predicaments.
- *Techno-industrial capability:* Improving the ability of African economies to generate growth and productivity, particularly in addressing their supply-side deficits and constraints.

These imperatives, together with the normative thrust of the White Paper and FOCAC's declaratory diplomacy, provide the vectors for China's relations with Africa, which in turn raise questions about the trajectory of development in Africa. In contrast to their increasingly ambivalent feelings about the West, African states are attracted to the Chinese model. One critical view holds that the West 'has not helped Africa overcome the structural obstacles to eradicating poverty and reversing its economic marginalization. Rather than develop, Africa is haemorrhaging while the rest of the world accumulates wealth at its expense through the unbalanced exploitation of its natural resources and the enforcement of a distorted international economic system.'[6] At the heart of the debate are Western world-views framed by the neoliberal orthodoxy on economic development and underpinned by various versions of market fundamentalism that are rooted in 'Washington Consensus' injunctions of good governance, privatization, deregulation, devaluation, market liberalization and export-led growth.[7] The Chinese paradigm challenges these beliefs, advancing a model that is based on enhancing development through promoting sovereign choice, political non-interference and policy autonomy, while maximizing social welfare and applying state-driven initiatives both to enable and restrain market forces. Rightly or wrongly, China bristles at any suggestion that it is complicit in a new 'scramble for Africa', that it has become a major player with the United States and the European Union (EU) in a 'divide and conquer' contest in Africa, that it is a rogue 'resource predator', that it has 'neoimperialist' designs, or that it provides succour to authoritarian and repressive regimes.[8]

China's (re-)entry into the region coincides with the forces unleashed by globalization and the region's ever-deepening incorporation into global circuits. Many of the region's countries experienced difficult moments of fiscal decline and had to resort to austerity measures dictated by the World Bank and the International Monetary Fund (IMF), fuelled in most instances by declining terms of trade in commodities, balance-of-payment problems and fiscal mismanagement. Conditional lending based on deregulation, fiscal prudence, privatization and trade liberalization imposed further social burdens on societies already bearing the brunt of structural underdevelopment and increasing poverty. Historical dependencies on the EU and latterly on the USA for trade, investment, debt relief and aid concessions lock the countries of the region into a North–South pattern of unequal relationships. This has, in a sense, been mitigated by China, which offers countries a different menu of options and fresh opportunities in terms of the overarching values of solidarity, friendship, sincerity and mutual benefit, as tendentious as these may be. These contrast with the neomercantilist inclinations of the West, exacerbated by its thinly disguised protectionist instrumentalities and retrenchment of aid commitments. Chris Alden has argued that 'China's rapid gains on the continent, far from being a sudden "scramble for Africa", could be more accurately described as pushing on an open door, one which in any case the West had left ajar as it scrambled eastward'.[9]

Historical dimensions

Chinese leaders rarely miss an opportunity to refer to their Africa policy by using historical antecedents and points of reference. These are important for how China projects itself on the continent and underpin the assertion of its self-identity as both a developing country and an emerging power. Indeed, 'a debate over China's use of history in Africa is one which touches on core concerns regarding both China's role and Africa's place in a changing international system'.[10]

The high-water mark of early Sino-African relations can be located in the Ming dynasty (1368–1644) and the great maritime adventures of the intrepid Admiral Zheng He, whose voyages took him to the eastern coast of Africa. In the contemporary period, the founding of the PRC in 1949 and the launching of its 'Five Principles of Peaceful Coexistence'[11] in the same year provided the impulse for a new and different relationship with Africa. At the Bandung Conference in 1955, Chinese premier Zhou Enlai sought out African leaders with whom he could create a sense of common purpose, and Egypt was the first African country to establish formal relations with the PRC, in 1956. By the 1960s there were fourteen African countries with such relations, by the

1970s there were twenty-two, and currently there are forty-nine with formal diplomatic relations with the PRC.[12]

In the 1950s, the PRC's policy in Africa closely mirrored that of the Soviet Union, on the basis of pro-liberation and anti-imperialism doctrines. The Soviet-dominated Afro-Asian People's Solidarity Organization (AAPSO), formed in 1957, became the main vehicle for promoting the PRC's influence in Africa. However, disenchanted with Soviet revisionism by 1960, the PRC adopted a more aggressive 'Third World' solidarity programme, in which Africa featured prominently. The PRC designated the Soviet Union as its principal enemy on the continent in order to 'discredit the Soviet Union as a revolutionary force by identifying her with "United States imperialism"'.[13] Following visits to Africa by Zhou in 1963 and 1964 (including Tanzania), relations were consolidated around the formal instruments of state-to-state interaction underpinned by friendship treaties, cultural projects, trade and payment agreements, economic aid and technical assistance. In the two decades from the 1950s to 1970s, the PRC gave almost US$2.5 billion to thirty-six African countries, with Tanzania and Zambia featuring prominently: they received US$362 million and US$307 million respectively.[14] (This level of aid is extremely generous considering, at the time, the PRC's per capita income was one fifteenth of Japan's and one fortieth of that of the USA.) The Tanzania–Zambia railway line, completed in 1976 at a cost of US$484 million, remains a symbol of Chinese engineering prowess, political commitment and economic sacrifice.

However, the PRC's relations with African liberation movements were to prove controversial. Its initial links to the Liberation Front of Mozambique (FRELIMO), the Popular Liberation Movement of Angola (MPLA), the National Liberation Front of Angola (FNLA) and others such as the National Liberation Front (FLN) in Algeria and the 'rebels' in Congo-Kinshasa were meant not only to enhance its prestige in the Organization of African Unity (OAU) and AAPSO, but also to counter Soviet 'hegemonism' in Africa.[15] When the MPLA's increasing pro-Soviet orientation started to erode China's influence, it switched its support to the FNLA in 1963, but then became disgruntled because Chinese representatives were not allowed into the Congo, where the FNLA was based. As a result, in the following year, China switched support to the National Union for the Total Independence of Angola (UNITA), which had split from the FNLA. UNITA's leader, Jonas Savimbi, had undergone military training in the PRC in 1964 and 1965 before UNITA was formally established in 1966 and had proclaimed Maoism as its formal doctrine. Even after the MPLA came to power in independent Angola in 1975, Beijing covertly supported UNITA and the FNLA, as part of an anti-Soviet strategy. In Mozambique a similar pattern unfolded: FRELIMO's pro-Soviet leanings saw China throwing its support behind RENAMO.[16] In Namibia, China also found itself on the wrong side of history by supporting the rival and politically insignificant South West Africa

National Union (SWANU) against the internationally recognized South West Africa People's Organization (SWAPO), which also boasted pro-Soviet credentials.[17] The same pattern repeated itself in South Africa and Zimbabwe: China supported the Pan-Africanist Congress (PAC) against the pro-Soviet African National Congress (ANC), and the Zimbabwe African National Union (ZANU)[18] against the pro-Soviet Zimbabwe African People's Union (ZAPU).

China learned valuable diplomatic lessons from its attempts at anti-Soviet radicalization and its wish to be the avatar of world socialist revolution in Africa during the 1960s. While it continued to provide political and material support to liberation movements in southern Africa, it moved to a more moderate diplomacy: promoting formal relations with African countries regardless of their ideological preferences, and extending economic assistance to them on the basis of the 'one China' policy. An immediate dividend and benefit was China's admission to the United Nations (UN) in 1971, gaining itself a permanent seat on the Security Council at the expense of Taiwan. This was made possible only by the support of twenty-six African countries, which constituted 34 per cent of the votes in the UN General Assembly at the time.[19] The PRC aggressively took its battle against Taiwan to Africa and by 1970 it had diplomatic ties with twenty African countries; by 1976 this number had risen to thirty-nine. When Premier Zhao Ziyang visited eleven African countries in 1982/83, including Tanzania, Zaire (now the Democratic Republic of the Congo, DRC), Zambia and Zimbabwe, he reaffirmed China's support for the liberation struggles in Namibia and South Africa, noted the importance of consolidating the gains of Africa's independence, and appealed for greater unity among developing countries to advance South–South cooperation. In the context of China's modernization drive, Zhao announced 'Four Principles on Sino-African Economic and Technical Cooperation' in Tanzania: mutual benefit, practical results, domestic development priorities, and common development. By the time Foreign Minister Qian Qichen visited fourteen African countries between 1989 and 1992, China's Africa aid amounted to US$375 million, spread among forty-three beneficiaries.[20] This level of aid gave China significant political purchase at a time when American interest in Africa was reduced and when the EU was reordering its priorities in trade and development cooperation through its economic partnership agreements (EPAs).[21]

This brief historical survey frames several implications in the ebb and flow of Sino-African relations. First, China's growing influence in Africa since the profound transformation of its domestic environment starting in 1978 is based on its economic profile and its multiplying commercial and trade interests. China's powerful economic engine generates opportunities and challenges for African countries because China is increasingly coming to occupy centre stage in international relations. Secondly, the Chinese impact on governance in Africa will continue to be contentious, especially when it is linked to categorical support for 'pariah' and autocratic regimes that abuse human rights or repress civic freedoms. Associated with this is a seeming insensitivity to environmental and labour standards. China will, willy-nilly, have to confront calls for greater accountability and transparency in its Africa diplomacy. And thirdly, African leaders will have to take account of shifts in China's policy and geopolitical priorities on the continent. They have moved from a focus on the primary acquisition of raw materials and natural resources to a deepening economic engagement exemplified by fast-expanding financial services, large-scale infrastructure development, a burgeoning demographic and commercial presence, and agriculture and commercial farming (including so-called land grabbing). This will require more prudential regulation and oversight on the part of African governments to ensure welfare gains, better growth opportunities and development spin-offs that are of benefit to both China and African partners.[22]

Post-apartheid political relations

Turning to China's relations with South Africa, we notice that the close ties that the apartheid government had with Taiwan persisted into South Africa's democratic transition. Fearing a change in posture in favour of Beijing after the 1994 elections, Taipei went as far as making a substantial contribution to the ANC's electoral war chest, estimated at US$25 million.[23] Taiwan's anxieties were further allayed by the fact that it had investments in South Africa worth US$1.6 billion, which provided 40,000 jobs; furthermore, bilateral trade stood at a healthy US$1.8 billion.[24] Indeed, it was often said that in Africa, South Africa was considered to be the jewel in Taiwan's diplomatic crown.[25]

On the other hand, there was greater potential for trade and investment with the PRC, a rising global power. Since formal diplomatic ties were established between the PRC and South Africa in early 1998, there has been a remarkable growth in economic ties and closer political cooperation.[26] Several other factors propelled the change in relations: South Africa's ambition to play an active role in international affairs could be greatly assisted by relations with China, especially given its veto power on the UN Security Council; South Africa accepted the correctness of the 'one China' policy; the PRC had supported Africa's liberation struggles and there was a long historical friendship between the Chinese Communist Party and its South African counterpart.[27]

One of the important building blocks for enhanced engagement was President Jiang Zemin's state visit to South Africa in April 2000, during which he signed the 'Pretoria Declaration on the Partnership between the People's Republic of China and the Republic of South Africa' with President Thabo Mbeki. The most important outcome of this visit was the establishment of the Bi-National Commission (BNC), the only one of its kind between China and an African country. This was indicative of the readiness on both sides to elevate relations to a broader strategic and systemic level. The BNC would provide a forum for coordinating government-to-government business, as well as for constructive dialogue for expanding economic ties and assisting the two countries to advance peace, security and development in Africa. Deepening and extending relations to broader areas of cooperation would include a commitment to ameliorating the negative effects of globalization, opposing unilateralism in international affairs in the interests of restructuring the global economic architecture, and ensuring a more consequential South–South cooperation. Furthermore, China recognized the importance of a recalibrated role for South Africa in the region and in Africa, and hence the need for the countries to strengthen cooperation.[28]

The formal launch of the BNC took place during President Mbeki's state visit to Beijing in December 2001. Operational and policy discussions also took place at ministerial and senior official levels involving delegates from the departments of foreign affairs, economics and trade, public security, the judiciary, science and technology, energy, and tourism. Four sectoral committees were established, dealing with foreign affairs, economy and trade, science and technology, and national defence. Subsequently, the BNC platform has been strengthened by frequent exchanges of high-level visits between the countries. The final version of the Pretoria Declaration, concluded in April 2002, suggested a framework for a broad strategic partnership that was grounded in the same principles that historically had defined Sino-African relations: friendship, equality and sovereignty, common development and mutual benefit, and consultation on international affairs in the spirit of South–South cooperation.

At the conclusion of the BNC meeting in Pretoria in 2004, then deputy president Jacob Zuma noted the broadening interaction in trade, culture, education, science and technology, and cooperation on international issues. Adding to the agreements signed in April 2000 (covering police cooperation, maritime transport, arts and culture, animal health and quarantine, and avoidance of double taxation), there were now further undertakings on human resource development, formal recognition of China's market economy status, increasing agricultural exports to China, and strengthening the role of developing countries in the World Trade Organization's (WTO) Doha negotiations. This meeting also recognized the importance of China–South Africa relations in promoting peace, stability and development in Africa through the FOCAC process.

Critically for the region there was also a commitment to begin free trade negotiations between the Southern African Customs Union (SACU) and China, though a major stumbling block was, and remains, SACU member Swaziland's ongoing diplomatic ties with Taiwan.[29] In June 2006, President Mbeki and Premier Wen Jiabao signed an agreement to help protect the South African textile industry from the influx of cheap Chinese textiles. A further thirteen agreements were signed to include cooperation in agriculture, minerals and energy, technical matters, investment and trade promotion, customs and nuclear non-proliferation. This was followed by another visit by President Hu Jintao in early 2007 as part of an eight-nation tour to give effect to the 2006 FOCAC commitments.[30] To date, there are thirty-two agreements between China and South Africa covering political, social and economic issues.

With South Africa firmly ensconced in China's political and diplomatic orbit, the stage was set for China to consolidate and accelerate its influence across the region in the post-apartheid era. Malawi, the other holdout besides Swaziland, severed ties with Taiwan in January 2008 and established formal relations with the PRC. This brought the majority of countries of the region under China's diplomatic umbrella. The post-Cold War context of globalization, the nature of the region's enfeebled and fragile interstate system, and the advantages of China's bilateral chemistry at the state-to-state level, all give it unparalleled leverage to craft a strategic symbiosis, but one nevertheless subject to the asymmetric dictates of the realpolitik of its own interests, objectives and priorities.[31] This raises questions about whether China can provide a developmental stimulus for the region and its complex integration agenda. Particularly, and as part of the wider Africa debate,[32] will China undermine or help sustain the progress that is necessary for macroeconomic reform, including measures to promote efficiency in prices and markets, promote exports and foreign investment, and provide essential social services? Will it assist with reinvigorating public institutions and strengthening state capacity and legitimacy, or be complicit in their erosion? As China's outward foreign direct investment (FDI) seems to be attracted to large markets and countries with large natural resources and poor institutions, it may not.[33]

Assessing China's economic role

In February 2009, prior to another critically important visit to Africa by President Hu, Assistant Foreign Minister Zhai Jun was quite clear that, notwithstanding the effects of the global financial crisis, 'China will honour its commitment to support the development of African countries and continue to encourage Chinese companies to invest and establish businesses in Africa'.[34] These remarks were a prelude to fresh commitments China made at the November 2009 FOCAC meeting in Egypt, despite being faced by an adverse domestic situation: first, the yuan was allowed to appreciate over 20 per cent, from US$8.28 in June 2005 to US$6.83 in August 2009; secondly, increased market-based wages were becoming a concern, since a new labour law that took effect in January 2008 drastically raised labour costs; and thirdly, incipient inflationary pressures were magnified by the collapse of global demand. The negative impact on China's domestic economy was immediate: foreign companies fled China in droves and nearly twenty million Chinese workers lost their jobs amid rising social protests and popular demonstrations. Beijing's response, however, was decisive: the announcement on 9 November 2008 of a US$586 billion fiscal stimulus package, focused mainly on improving deteriorating physical infrastructure, whereas the equivalent US package concentrated on healthcare, education and alternative energy. The stimulation effects on the Chinese economy were remarkable: fixed asset investment in the first half of 2009 rose 33.5 per cent over the same period in 2008; national retail spending in the first half of 2009 grew 15 per cent; in August 2009, real estate investment was up 14.7 per cent over August 2008; and in early 2009, China overtook the USA for the first time in total car sales, anticipated to be 10–12 million units for the year.[35] Most tellingly, from a gross domestic product (GDP) growth of 7.9 per cent in the second quarter, China ended 2009 with an incredible 10.7 per cent, the fastest growth spurt since 2007 and one that exceeded World Bank and other forecasts of an aggregate 8.7 per cent.[36]

What are the implications for Africa? Beijing has already mobilized the disbursement of aid packages, and while aid remains small as a share of China's GDP, it is valued for strengthening political relations and leveraging economic opportunities. China's trade with Africa dropped from US$107 billion in 2008 to US$91 billion in 2009.[37] However, China's inelastic demand for Africa's natural resources, combined with its infrastructure-focused stimulus package, will guarantee demand for key commodities in the face of otherwise falling global prices and deteriorating terms of trade. While Africa's imports from China dropped nearly 38 per cent, demand for Chinese light industrial products, electrical appliances, footwear, clothing and other consumer products will not be seriously affected. As far as investment is concerned, there is unlikely to be a reduction in public and private investments; indeed, the investment potential of the US$5 billion China–Africa Development Fund has yet to be fully harnessed. Africa also provides alternative markets against falling demand for Chinese exports to Europe and the USA.[38] But while Beijing spoke of engaging with African institutions on a multilateral basis – and for southern Africa that would primarily be the Southern African Development Community (SADC) – its Africa policy was mostly conducted on a bilateral basis, which some observers saw as a 'divide and rule' tactic.

Chinese spending helped keep South Africa's economy from sinking into deeper recession as its exports to the EU and the USA declined. In 2009 China overtook the USA to become South Africa's biggest market, with exports of R41.2 billion (US$5.5 billion) and imports of R59.1 billion (US$7.9 billion), compared to R33.2 billion (US$4.4 billion) and R35.4 billion (US$4.7 billion) with the USA.[39] Altogether, South African exports to the USA, the United Kingdom, Japan and Germany shrank more than 40 per cent for the period. (While South Africa's trade deficit with China is a source of political tension, it fell from R36 billion [US$4.8 billion] to R18 billion [US$2.4 billion] in 2008.)[40] Chinese investments in South Africa total around US$750 million in over a hundred projects covering agriculture, textiles, electronics, mining, banking, transportation and communications. China's bold entry into financial services is best captured by the Industrial and Commercial Bank of China's US$5.4 billion purchase of 20 per cent of South Africa's Standard Bank in November 2007, intended to expand its reach into Africa.[41] South Africa has also increasingly become a base for Chinese exports into the region; for example, Hi-Sense produces high-tech electronic goods that are exported to Botswana, Lesotho, Mozambique and Namibia.

South Africa is the only African country with a significant investment profile in China, estimated at US$1.2–1.5 billion and covering manufacturing (Metspan), mining (AngloGold and AngloCoal), financial services (Standard Bank), energy (Sasol), beverages (SABMiller), media (Naspers) and engineering (Bateman and Landpac).[42] Tourism is also becoming increasingly important, with over 45,000 Chinese visiting South Africa in 2007/08 out of a total of close to one million tourists.[43] A major development has been the announcement that South Africa and China would start negotiations to conclude a free trade agreement in order to enhance market access, remove regulatory restrictions, improve trade and investment opportunities, and remove tariff and non-tariff barriers. Provided that the Swaziland conundrum can be resolved, this will have positive spin-offs for South Africa and its partners in SACU, since such an agreement would reflect the unprecedented WTO commitments China has made in its own trade, market access and economic liberalization agenda.[44]

Trade reflects the unequally distributed geography of resources. Five oil- and mineral-exporting countries account for 85 per cent of Africa's exports to China.[45] Let us examine some indicative examples from the region:

- *Angola:* By 2008, oil accounted for almost 100 per cent of Angola's exports to China, amounting to 500,000 barrels per day or 18 per cent of China's total imports.[46] This makes Angola China's third-largest source of oil, after Saudi Arabia and Iran. In 2006, with bilateral trade amounting to US$12 billion, Angola was China's largest trading partner in Africa. Fuelled by record high international oil prices and robust growth in both the oil and non-oil sectors, Angola's real GDP growth reached 18.6 per cent in 2006, 23.4 per cent in 2007, and 26.6 per cent in 2008.[47] Chinese financial and technical assistance has helped over a hundred projects get off the ground in areas as diverse as energy, water, health, education, telecommunications, fisheries and public works. In March 2004, China's Export-Import Bank approved a US$2 billion oil-backed loan to finance the country's shattered infrastructure. In 2005, the China International Fund extended an additional credit facility of US$2.9 billion to assist with Angola's post-war reconstruction effort; this was followed by another oil-backed loan of US$2 billion signed in September 2007.[48] Both packages have been designed to rehabilitate highways, railways, airports and housing. China has provided funding for strategic post-conflict projects that Western donors were hesitant or unwilling to fund, offering better conditions than commercial loans, lower interest rates, and longer repayment schedules.[49] China has also provided military equipment to Angola: eight SU-27 fighter aircraft were ordered in 2007 and it is likely that further arms-for-oil deals will take place.[50]

- *Zimbabwe:* Since an official 'look east policy' was declared in 2003, significant bilateral visits have taken place, including President Robert Mugabe's state visit in July 2005. This politically motivated approach aimed to help Zimbabwe out of its dire economic straits. After South Africa, China has become the second-largest investor in Zimbabwe, its investment estimated at US$600 million. This is a direct consequence of the deterioration of relations with the EU and the World Bank and the IMF following the country's decline into hyperinflation and political instability. This decline explains the low levels of trade: in the first half of 2007, Chinese exports were worth US$187 million and imports from Zimbabwe a meagre US$16 million.[51] However, signs of improving economic and political stability in Zimbabwe led China to offer it a US$8 billion gold deal in exchange for rail and urban development in October 2009.[52] Other activities worth noting include a credit facility of US$200 million to improve agricultural inputs; an agreement to upgrade the fixed-line network with Tel One for US$288 million; and investment of US$300 million by the Shanghai Baosteel group in chrome, platinum, nickel and copper mining. Controversially, military relations also form part of the 'look east policy'. Besides personnel exchanges, there have been arms procurement agreements resulting in a US$200 million purchase of fighter jets and military vehicles by Zimbabwe. The most controversial of these exchanges was the delivery of Chinese military equipment to Zimbabwe in May 2008.[53]

- *Zambia:* After Egypt, Zambia was one of the first African countries to establish relations with China, in 1964. China's relations with Zambia therefore go back to the liberation era, during which Lusaka played a prominent role in the 'Frontline States', with the construction of the Tanzania–Zambia railway further solidifying relations. Currently, nearly two hundred Chinese companies are active in Zambia in mining, construction, banking and agriculture. From a low of US$20 million in the 1990s, trade grew to US$300 million in 2006.[54] Chinese companies have also become the largest investor in rehabilitating Zambia's ailing copper industry, although occupational accidents at the Chambishi copper mine have tarnished its image; in 2006, forty-six miners were killed in one of the worst mining disasters in Zambia. The 2006 agreement to set up the Zambia–China Chambishi Trade and Economic Zone is expected to generate US$800 million in Chinese investment, anchored by a US$250 million copper smelter.[55] Zambia's energy shortages and increased demand are being addressed through a US$250 million agreement in 2006 between the Zambia Electricity Supply Corporation and Sinohydro Corporation. However, the large presence of Chinese people in Zambia has become a political issue; during the 2006 presidential elections, an opposition leader campaigned on an anti-China platform, going as far as threatening to expel the Chinese and establish diplomatic relations with Taiwan.[56] The Chinese ambassador threatened to withdraw all Chinese assistance to Zambia should Michael Sata be elected president.[57]

- *Tanzania:* Like Zambia, Tanzania has been one of China's strongest historical allies in Africa. The PRC supported its *ujamaa* socialist programme and role in the liberation struggles of southern Africa. As early as 1965, Tanzania's president Julius Nyerere signed a 'Friendship Treaty' in Beijing. This ideological convergence resulted in Tanzania becoming the largest recipient of Chinese aid, including aid for building the Tan-Zam railway. With the Cultural Revolution, China significantly scaled down its support, resulting in severe economic hardship for Tanzania, which was forced to adopt the austerity measures of the IMF and World Bank as part of efforts to keep its economy afloat. However, with ties resuscitated in the 1990s, Sino-Tanzania relations entered a new phase. No longer grounded in ideological affinities, relations were driven by investment, trade in raw materials, manufacturing and infrastructure development such that by 2006 there were 134 projects worth US$833 million.[58] As part of an effort to revive the ailing Tan-Zam railway, China invested in the Dar es Salaam Special Economic Zone as a trans-shipment hub for commodities mined in the Zambian copper belt. Trade has also grown rapidly, although it has reflected the typical imbalances of non-oil exporters. In 2005, Chinese exports to Tanzania totalled US$303 million, in the form of foodstuffs, vehicles, textiles, light industrial products, chemical products, mechanical equipment, electrical appliances and steel, while Chinese imports from Tanzania totalled US$171 million, mostly comprising seafood, raw leather, coarse copper, handicrafts, cotton, timber, iron and fruit.[59]

- *Namibia:* Diplomatic ties between China and Namibia were established soon after SWAPO led the country to independence in March 1990. Between 1992 and 2004, President Sam Nujoma visited China five times, while President Jiang Zemin visited Namibia in 1996, Foreign Minister Tang Jiaxuan in 2000, and President Hu twice in recent years. Total trade between China and Namibia has grown from a low base of US$12 million in 2000 to US$100 million in 2004 to US$150 million in 2010.[60] China's exports are predominantly manufactured goods, while it imports mostly fish, live animals and non-ferrous metals. Total investment is around US$30 million, mostly in construction and real estate development. Development assistance amounts to about US$60 million, covering low-cost housing, buildings for government, medical facilities and upgrades for railways. The Export-Import Bank of China also provided a loan of US$28 million to finance sixteen locomotives for the TransNamib railway line.[61] As has been the case in so many other African countries, Namibia has seen mounting anti-Chinese sentiment as the numbers of Chinese have swelled, a consequence of the growing presence of Chinese firms and their success in winning public tenders and private contracts backed by soft loans and grants from the Chinese government. Chinese market share of private building contracts is estimated to be 15 per cent and growing, while local firms find themselves unable to compete effectively or go out of business, thereby fuelling resentment against the Chinese firms, which typically do not employ indigenous labour.[62]

- *Botswana, Mozambique and the DRC:* In Botswana, Chinese firms have won about 80 per cent of all government procurement contracts, especially in construction.[63] In Mozambique, China's Export-Import Bank has provided a US$2.3 billion loan to construct the Mepanda Nkua dam and hydroelectric plant.[64] In the DRC in September 2007, China provided a US$5 billion investment package, including US$3 billion for infrastructure rehabilitation, and US$2 billion to develop mines in Katanga, Ituri and the Kivus.[65]

Conclusion

There can be no denying that China has had a remarkable impact on southern Africa's history and subsequent development. China's involvement in the region was first determined by the ideological prism of the Cold War, which resulted in egregious strategic and tactical errors of judgement. Its post-Cold War posture has become much more pragmatic and flexible. China has used its bilateral-centred foreign policy template to good effect in the region by establishing strong political and trade ties with countries in a hierarchy that conforms to its own national interests and potential for generating positive development outcomes. As a consequence, China offers an alternative template for trade and development at a time when both the EU and the USA have proved to be less than willing to meet their own aid pledges, and when countries face increasing impediments to trade in the form of onerous tariff and non-tariff barriers. China offers a different configuration of trade, aid and development opportunities in a global political economy in which African countries, especially the seven least-developing countries in southern Africa, face the spectre of ongoing marginalization and impoverishment. No wonder that China's policies of 'non-interference' and 'no political strings' have resonated so powerfully among African countries wearied by those sanctimonious clichés about democracy, human rights and good governance originating in the West. In contrast to European-style imperialism, the Chinese make no attempt to convert Africans to any ideology. China has no 'civilizing mission' other than trying to spread its rhetoric of sincerity, friendship, mutual benefit, partnership and the like. As has been argued, 'What one sees in relations between China and Africa is more reminiscent of a "tributary state system" which, through the use of "soft power", caused kingdoms to emulate Chinese civilization.'[66] In addition, China respects the sovereignty of African countries, and seeks 'win-win' outcomes, even though these sometimes smack of paternalism and raise questions about China's support for undemocratic regimes.

Notes

1 Garth Shelton, 'Afro-Chinese relations in an era of globalisation', in K. K. Prah, *Afro-Chinese Relations: Past, Present, and Future* (Rondebosch, Cape Town: CASAS, 2007), pp. 238–9.

2 Chris Alden, Daniel Large and Ricardo Soares de Oliveira (eds), Introduction to *China Returns to Africa: A Rising Power and a Continent Embrace* (London: Hurst, 2008), p. 23.

3 Piet J. Konings, 'China and Africa: building a strategic partnership', *Journal of Developing Societies*, 23(3), 2007, pp. 341–67.

4 Li Xing, 'Paradigm shift: from "Washington Consensus" to "Beijing Consensus"', in Prah, *Afro-Chinese Relations*, pp. 101–25.

5 Christopher M. Dent, 'China and Africa: towards a conceptualisation of "development relations"', Unpublished paper presented at the seminar 'China/ Africa Development Relations', University of Leeds, 27 February 2009, pp. 5–8.

6 Firoz Manji and Simon Marks (eds), *African Perspectives on China in Africa* (Cape Town: Fahamu and Pambazuka, 2007), p. 17.

7 Denis M. Tull, 'The political consequences of China's return to Africa', in Alden, Large and de Oliveira, *China Returns to Africa*, pp. 135–41.

8 See Chris Alden, *China in Africa* (London: Zed Books, 2007).

9 Alden, Large and de Oliveira, Introduction to *China Returns to Africa*, p. 21.

10 Chris Alden and Ana Cristina Alves, 'History & identity in the construction of China's Africa policy', *Review of African Political Economy*, 115(35), March 2008, p. 43.

11 These were: mutual respect for territorial integrity and sovereignty, mutual non-aggression, mutual non-interference in internal affairs, equality, and mutual benefit.

12 Only four African countries maintain diplomatic relations with Taiwan in 2011: Burkina Faso, the Gambia, São Tomé and Príncipe, and Swaziland.

13 George T. Yu, 'Sino-African relations: a survey', *Asian Survey*, 5(7), 1966, p. 464.

14 George T. Yu, 'The Tanzania–Zambia railway: a case study in Chinese economic aid to Africa', in W. Weinstein and T. H. Henriksen (eds), *Soviet and Chinese Aid to African Nations* (New York: Praeger, 1980), p. 121.

15 George T. Yu, 'China's failure in Africa', *Asian Survey*, 6(8), 1968, p. 1026.

16 See Steven Jackson, 'China's Third World foreign policy: the case of Angola and Mozambique, 1961–93', *China Quarterly* 14(2), 1995, pp. 389–422.

17 Robin Sherbourne, 'China's growing presence in Namibia', in Garth le Pere, *China in Africa: Mercantilist Predator, or Partner in Development?* (Johannesburg: Institute for Global Dialogue and the South African Institute of International Affairs, 2007), pp. 161–2.

18 Mugabe and ZANU's exclusive reliance on Chinese military support during the liberation struggle helps to explain their strong affinity to China today. See Gilbert Khadiagala, *Allies in Adversity: The Frontline States in Southern Africa, 1975–1993* (Lanham, MD: University Press of America, 2007), p. 63.

19 Garth le Pere and Garth Shelton,

China, Africa, and South Africa: South–South Co-operation in a Global Era (Midrand: Institute for Global Dialogue, 2007), pp. 73–6.

20 Li Xing, 'Paradigm shift: From "Washington Consensus" to "Beijing Consensus"', in Prah, *Afro-Chinese Relations*, p. 120.

21 Ian Taylor, 'The "all weather friend"? Sino-African interaction in the 21st century', in I. Taylor and P. Williams (eds), *Africa in International Politics: External Involvement on the Continent* (London: Routledge, 2004), p. 87.

22 See Denis Tull, 'China in Africa: scope, significance, and consequences', *Journal of Modern African Studies*, 44(3), 2006, pp. 459–79.

23 Deon Geldenhuys, 'The politics of South Africa's China switch', *Issues and Studies*, 33(7), 1997, p. 98.

24 Le Pere and Shelton, *China, Africa, and South Africa*, p. 161.

25 South Africa had established diplomatic relations with Taiwan at consular level in 1962; these were upgraded to ambassadorial level in 1976.

26 See Geldenhuys, 'The politics of South Africa's China switch', pp. 93–131.

27 Le Pere and Shelton, *China, Africa, and South Africa*, p. 162.

28 Garth Shelton, 'China's Africa policy and South Africa: building new economic partnerships', *SA Yearbook of International Affairs* (Johannesburg: SAIIA, 2001), pp. 390–2.

29 Sanusha Naidu, 'Balancing a strategic partnership? South Africa–China relations', in Kweku Ampiah and Sanusha Naidu (eds), *Crouching Tiger, Hidden Dragon: Africa and China* (Scottsville, South Africa: University of KwaZulu-Natal Press, 2008), p. 172.

30 Ibid., p. 173.

31 See Francis A. Kornegay, 'Africa's strategic diplomatic engagement with China', and Adam Habib, 'Seeing the "new scramble" for what it really is: reflections on the United States and China', in H. Edinger, H. Herman and J. Jansson (eds), *New Impulses from the South: China's Engagement of Africa* (Stellenbosch, South Africa: Centre for Chinese Studies), pp. 3–12 and 24–7 respectively.

32 Peter Lewis, 'Economic reform and political transition in Africa: the quest for a politics of development', *World Politics*, 49(1), 1996, pp. 92–129.

33 Ivar Kolstad and Arne Wigg, 'Chinese investment in SADC: a global perspective?', in FOPRISA Report no. 7, *Furthering Southern African Integration*, 2009, pp. 194–5. See also Roger Southall and Henning Melber (eds), *A New Scramble for Africa: Imperialism, Investment, and Development* (Scottsville, South Africa: University of KwaZulu-Natal Press, 2009), p. 73.

34 *Business Day*, 19 January 2010.

35 William H. Overholt, 'China in the global financial crisis: rising influence, rising challenges', *Washington Quarterly*, 33(1), January 2010, p. 29.

36 *Business Day*, 19 January 2010.

37 Centre for Chinese Studies, 'Weekly briefing', University of Stellenbosch, January 2010.

38 Africa has been called the best 'refuge for preventing sunstroke during the financial crisis'. See Institute for Development Studies, 'China and the global financial crisis: implications for low-income countries', Briefing no. 7 (Brighton: University of Sussex, March 2009), p. 3.

39 Ethel Hazelhurst, 'China is SA's biggest market', *Star: Business Report*, 14 January 2010, p. 13.

40 Ibid., p. 13.

41 Department of International Relations and Cooperation, *Annual Report 2009–10*, Pretoria, 2010, p. 59.

42 Kobus van der Wath, *Doing Business in China* (Beijing: Beijing Axis, 2004), p. 154.

43 See Naidu, 'Balancing a strategic partnership?', pp. 177–82; and le Pere and Shelton, *China, Africa, and South Africa*, pp. 170–9.

44 Peter Draper and Garth le Pere, *Enter the Dragon: Towards a Free Trade Agreement between China and the Southern African Customs Union* (Johannesburg:

Institute for Global Dialogue and South African Institute of International Affairs, 2005), pp. 21–3.

45 Harry Broadman, *Africa's Silk Road: China and India's New Economic Frontier* (Washington, DC: World Bank, 2007), p. 12.

46 Manuel E. Ferreira, 'China in Angola: just a passion for oil', in Alden, Large, and de Oliveira, *China Returns to Africa*, p. 302.

47 Ibid., pp. 303–4.

48 Lucy Corkin, 'All's fair in loans and war: the development of China–Angola relations', in Ampiah and Naidu, *Crouching Tiger, Hidden Dragon*, pp. 109–10.

49 See generally Indira Campos and Alex Vines, 'Angola and China: a pragmatic partnership', Working paper (London: Centre for Strategic and International Studies, March 2008), pp. 5–13; and Corkin, 'All's fair in loans and war', pp. 108–23.

50 See Martin Rupiya and Roger Southall, 'The militarisation of the new scramble in Africa', in Southall and Melber, *A New Scramble for Africa*, p. 180.

51 *Business Day*, 9 October 2009.

52 Ibid.

53 The so-called ship of shame could not offload its cargo in South Africa, Namibia and Mozambique, and thus did so via the Congolese port of Ponta Negra. See, for example, Southall and Melber, *A New Scramble for Africa*, p. 74. See also Sven Schwersensky, 'Harare's "look east" policy now focuses on China', in le Pere, *China in Africa*, pp. 186–200; and Lloyd Sachikonye, 'Crouching tiger, hidden agenda? Zimbabwe–China relations', in Ampiah and Naidu, *Crouching Tiger, Hidden Dragon*, pp. 124–37.

54 Muna Ndulo, 'Chinese investments in Africa: a case study of Zambia', in Ampiah and Naidu, *Crouching Tiger, Hidden Dragon*, p. 142.

55 Ibid., p. 142.

56 Ibid., pp. 138–51.

57 Southall and Melber, *A New Scramble for Africa*, p. 72.

58 Mwesiga Baregu, 'The three faces of the dragon: Tanzania–China relations in historical perspective', in Ampiah and Naidu, *Crouching Tiger, Hidden Dragon*, p. 158.

59 Baregu, 'The three faces of the dragon', pp. 152–66. For a very engaging account, see also Jamie Monson, 'Liberating labour? Constructing anti-hegemony on the TAZARA railway in Tanzania, 1965–76', in Alden, Large and de Oliveira, *China Returns to Africa*, pp. 197–219.

60 'Namibia trade with China up by 600 per cent', *The Namibian*, 13 August 2010.

61 Sherbourne, 'China's growing presence in Namibia', pp. 160–71.

62 See Gregor Dobler, 'Solidarity, xenophobia, and the regulation of Chinese businesses in Namibia', in Alden, Large and de Oliveira, *China Returns to Africa*, pp. 237–55.

63 Botswana Ministry of Trade and Industry, 'Botswana–China trade strengthens', 3 September 2009, www.mti.gov.bw.

64 'China–Mozambique bilateral relations', *China Daily*, 26 January 2007.

65 Wenran Jiang, 'A Chinese "Marshall Plan" or business', *Asia Times* (online), 14 January 2009, atimes.com.

66 Chris Alden, 'Africa without Europeans', in Alden, Large and de Oliveira, *China Returns to Africa,* p. 355.

Conclusion

Dawn Nagar, Chris Saunders
and Gwinyayi A. Dzinesa

Region-building in southern Africa is, as we have seen, a work in progress, one that has taken particular forms, shaped in part by the history of colonialism and apartheid and the struggle to overcome those legacies from the past. From the formation of the Front Line States (FLS) in 1975, and its successor organization, the Southern African Development Coordination Conference (SADCC) of 1980, the Southern African Development Community (SADC) was born in 1992, as an organization to promote the development of the region, in the belief that peace and security are essential prerequisites for economic development. The Southern African Customs Union (SACU) is now the world's oldest such body, having been created in 1910. To date, region-building has been very much a top-down process, in which attempts at economic integration have gone along with security integration. The last section of this book has shown how region-building in this part of Africa has also been shaped by external actors in significant ways, just as regional integration in Europe was influenced by the United States in particular. In 2011, the exemplar for region-building, the European model that has taken that continent from the European Economic Community of 1957 to the European Union of today, was facing new challenges, with some predicting in 2011 that the crisis over sovereign debt in some of its constituent states would undermine it, while others suggested that a distinction between an inner core and an outer periphery of states was growing, raising the prospect of a 'two speed' Europe.[1] Ironically in the last few years Europe has produced much dissent in the southern African region by trying to conclude economic partnership agreements (EPAs) with individual states in the region, necessary because preferential treatment in earlier arrangements now runs contrary to World Trade Organization rules. That southern African countries have adopted different responses to the proposed EPAs has threatened the very survival of SACU. Whatever happens in Europe, and however the EPA issue is finalized, most will agree that in southern Africa, with its relatively weak economies, widespread poverty and great inequalities, region-building remains a goal progressively to be aimed at, one that can help promote economic development and ensure continued political and social stability.

If this is agreed, how then to accelerate region-building in this case? As this volume – which has examined challenges at three interdependent levels, domestic, regional and external – has shown, region-building in southern Africa has to date been half-hearted, and has proceeded by fits and starts. But the potential is great for a region of 257 million people, with an estimated gross domestic product (GDP) of US$471 billion in 2010. Region-building in the south of the continent is, moreover, part of a broader project of continental unity, with SADC one of the eight key building blocks identified by the African Union (AU). But there are many questions to ponder about region-building in southern Africa. The region has not followed Europe and required conditions for membership of the main regional organizations. Though SADC is unwieldy, there are ongoing attempts, within it, to create a larger customs union, a free trade area and even a common monetary zone, along with efforts to link SADC's integration efforts to those of the Common Market for Eastern and Southern Africa (COMESA) and the East African Community (EAC). Some have argued that the emphasis should rather be placed on smaller units, such as SACU. Though SACU is not recognized as a building block for the AU, it includes among its members the key regional hegemon, South Africa. Another issue is what the role of civil society organizations should be in promoting region-building in a part of the continent that has no common identity or even a set of shared values.

However it is defined, and whatever the ultimate goal, there is a strong argument that region-building in southern Africa should be tackled holistically. The sixteen chapters in this book have addressed particular aspects, but many of these closely interrelate to each other. Perhaps most obviously, significant climate change will affect everything else, from food security to institutional architecture, but the general point is valid for other challenges facing the region as well. Because of this, a properly integrated plan of action should be drawn up, one that identifies priorities and places greater emphasis than at present on a regional approach to key issues related to development and security. To this end, the main regional institutions should be strengthened, with more staff and funding given, for example, to the SADC Secretariat, and these institutions should move from rhetoric to action and speedily implement the region-building goals expressed in SADC's more than forty protocols. A clearer system is needed to take more effective decisions between the annual summits of SADC heads of state, and the role of the SADC Executive Secretary should be strengthened so that policies can be implemented more effectively. Regional policies should become coherent programmes of action, which should be closely monitored to ensure that they are effectively carried out.[2] Historically, in southern Africa, efforts to achieve democratic governance have been hampered by a lack of strong political parties, parties that can provide the backbone for strengthening governance in the subregion. Political parties, in turn, should work more closely with civil society actors, and actively engage the media to promote region-building. To date, the goals set by SADC, SACU and other regional institutions have not been communicated effectively to the broader public in southern Africa. The more people become part of the process, the less elite-driven will regional integration be, and the more likely that its goals, which are often not communicated beyond national leaderships, will be realised. Communication between political elites and ordinary citizens should urgently be improved and SADC's work should be more widely publicized across the region.

Region-building in southern Africa cannot be carried out in isolation from broader considerations. As we have seen from several of the chapters in this volume, aspects of region-building in southern Africa are part of continental designs, and, as a regional economic community (REC) under the AU, SADC needs to work closely with that body to achieve its core functions, as enshrined in the Strategic Indicative Plan of the Organ (SIPO) of 2004, and the Regional Indicative Strategic Development Plan (RISDP) that SADC launched in 2003. And southern Africa can learn from other regions on the continent. Closer collaboration should thus be fostered with other African subregional organizations such as the Economic Community of West African States (ECOWAS) and the Intergovernmental Authority on Development (IGAD), to benefit from their experiences.

Climate change, which often affects the most vulnerable members of society, should be a priority for action, and early warning systems and strategies should be established to mitigate its negative impacts. Common policies on managing natural resources such as water are needed, in order to avoid future conflicts. Despite southern Africa's regional integration efforts, and support for the idea of the free movement of capital and labour, tighter controls are being imposed on the free movement of people across the subregion. SADC and SACU should introduce robust policies that filter down to the national level in order to maximize the free movement of people regionally, and prevent future xenophobic violence.[3]

Peace-building in one country cannot take place in isolation, and regional considerations often have a major bearing on whether or not peace-building efforts succeed. The adoption of a new strategy for Africa entitled 'The European Union and Africa: Towards a Strategic Partnership' in December 2005 provided EU leaders with a comprehensive, integrated and long-term framework for managing Europe's relations with Africa. This approach was designed to guide interaction between Brussels and pan-African institutions such as the AU and subregional organizations such as SADC. The plan was built on four pillars – 'good governance'; peace and security; trade; and health, education and a safe environment – and sought to support Africa's efforts to reach the UN Millennium Development Goals' (MDGs) aim of halving poverty by 2015.

Though the EU has supported SADC's peacekeeping efforts through a €300 million Africa–EU Peace and Security Partnership, unequal trade relations between Africa and the EU persist. Brussels continues to pay European farmers large production subsidies of €50 million annually, and to apply import tariffs. The huge disparity between the EU's economy of $8 trillion, in contrast to South Africa's $276 billion, reduces the impact of the EU/South Africa Trade Development and Cooperation Agreement of 1999 and hampers regional integration efforts. The agreement has caused large revenue losses to other SADC states. Non-SACU southern African countries have argued that this accord undermines SADC and SACU's regional integration agenda. Common policies across the subregion towards the EU, and more equitable trade deals with Brussels, have therefore been identified as important areas of policy concern.

While regional integration in southern Africa has been pursued for more than three decades, market integration still lags. Eight SADC member states – the Democratic Republic of the Congo (DRC), Madagascar, Malawi, Mauritius, Seychelles, Swaziland, Zambia and Zimbabwe – are also members of COMESA. A southern African free trade area has been implemented to promote regional industrial development and integration within SADC, but South Africa remains dominant, accounting for more than 70 per cent of the subregional economy. The idea of introducing a monetary union in southern Africa would, *inter alia*, result in a reduction in the transaction costs associated with trading goods and services between countries using different currencies, but there is much work to be done if the southern African subregion is to realize even a common market by 2015.

Peace and security throughout the subregion will help attract greater foreign direct investment. Southern Africa has experienced a great deal of armed conflict over recent decades, with conflict of various kinds in Angola, the DRC, Lesotho, Madagascar, Mozambique, Swaziland and Zimbabwe. Democratic governance is a prerequisite for peace-building efforts to succeed. Several SADC members are seeking to establish 'liberal democracies', but elections alone are insufficient to entrench democracy. A key component of democratic governance is the strengthening of public institutions for the effective delivery of social services to citizens in southern Africa. Public sector reform and institutional capacity-building, particularly within national civil services, are vital to achieving this goal. National parliaments should be empowered, the independence of judiciaries strengthened, and the autonomy of oversight institutions such as anti-corruption commissions, human rights bodies, auditing institutions and ombudsmen must be safeguarded.

A SADC Brigade (SADCBRIG) is being established as part of the African Stand-by Force (ASF) and training for the brigade is being organized by SADC's Organ on Politics, Defence and Security Cooperation (OPDSC), and through its Regional Peacekeeping Training Centre and the Southern African Regional

Police Chiefs Coordinating Organization, both based in Zimbabwe. However, many details about the effective functioning of SADCBRIG remain unclear. The effective operationalization of the brigade should be spelt out, for member states need to take collective decisions relating to issues such as the procurement of equipment and the interoperability of armies and equipment. The United Nations (UN) should retain a central role in peacekeeping efforts, and in operationalizing the SADC Brigade lessons should be learned from the UN missions in Namibia, Mozambique, Angola and the DRC.

Several of the principal challenges for women in this region pertain directly to violent conflict and its consequences. Women constitute the majority of southern Africa's estimated 470,000 refugees, internally displaced persons (IDPs) and asylum seekers, and are increasingly subjected to xenophobia and discrimination in their host countries. Furthermore, as in many patriarchal and conservative post-conflict settings, women in Zimbabwe, Mozambique and Namibia in particular have experienced rejection of their wartime freedoms from both national governments and local communities, and been compelled to return to the domestic arena. Women, who comprise the majority of the poor in the region, have limited access to resources such as credit finance, land or livestock. Gender equality will benefit women, men and children, but will only be possible through joint concerted efforts at international, regional and grassroots levels. Sustainable peace across the region will help address *all* structural inequalities, including race, class and gender.

Human security and traditional state security are now increasingly viewed as complementary and mutually dependent. Southern African countries face a number of significant challenges in order to ensure food security in the subregion. For example, years of drought have crippled agricultural production in Lesotho, while a number of people died in riots over increases in food prices in Mozambique in 2010. The agriculture sector in the subregion generally remains underfunded and underdeveloped. SADC's strategy to tackle food insecurity includes improving access to food through promoting employment and developing safety nets for vulnerable groups; increasing general nutrition; developing effective forecasting and early warning systems for disasters such as droughts and floods; building capacity to implement food security programmes; and taking account of gender issues in this sector.[4] Southern Africa's natural resources such as water, fisheries, forest and wildlife should be much better utilized for the benefit of its citizens. In addition, food security cannot be isolated from the land question. Land reform and land redistribution may help to eliminate poverty in countries such as Zimbabwe, Namibia and South Africa.[5]

The HIV/AIDS pandemic has affected southern Africa more severely than any other subregion in the world, for over 14 million of the 40 million people worldwide living with the disease are in southern Africa. Mobile populations, such as migrant workers, facilitate the spread of HIV/AIDS, which exacerbates poverty. The accelerated economic integration of southern Africa could, paradoxically, extend the reach of the virus. Acute poverty among child-headed or elderly-headed households in southern Africa is increasing owing to the pandemic. HIV/AIDS may lead to resource competition between civil and military institutions, adversely affecting the economy and potentially depleting the capacity of key sectors such as health and education. Weakened militaries may compromise the territorial integrity of states, and drain resources for care, support and treatment of the rank and file. A number of southern African militaries have implemented a broad range of HIV/AIDS prevention and treatment programmes, which could form the basis for a common SADC policy on HIV/AIDS management and care. A comprehensive policy to deal with communicable diseases such as HIV/AIDS, malaria and tuberculosis on a subregional basis is urgently needed, and common policies on responding to HIV/AIDS should be developed into coherent programmes of action.

The movement of people across southern Africa has a long history. South Africa's mines, farms and industry attracted hundreds of thousands of workers from neighbouring countries, and migrant labour became a major source of revenue for Mozambique, Malawi and Lesotho. These workers were not offered permanent residence in South Africa, despite contributing to building the country for decades, until amnesties in 1995–97 granted about 124,000 foreigners South African citizenship. By 1999, an estimated 55 per cent of mineworkers in South Africa came from neighbouring countries. South African farms also employed workers from Lesotho, Mozambique and Zimbabwe, often on seasonal contracts.[6] Free movement of people remains an important issue for SADC, which adopted a Protocol on the Free Movement of Persons in 1995. Horrific xenophobic attacks in South Africa against citizens from neighbouring countries in May 2008 resulted in at least sixty-two deaths and about 100,000 displaced people, and the issue of xenophobia has not been fully resolved, as attacks against foreigners continue in 2011. While coping with migration in a rapidly globalizing environment is a policy challenge facing many governments, the free movement of people and steps to counter future xenophobic violence constitute important and urgent issues for SADC and SACU to address.

As evidence has mounted of climate change negatively affecting southern Africa, a consensus has increasingly emerged about the need to tackle climate change challenges with coherent and effective policies. The UN Framework Convention on Climate Change, agreed in 1994, has served as a platform for talks to promote climate change, and the 1997 Kyoto Protocol set binding targets for rich and developing countries to reduce greenhouse gas (GHG) emissions. Industrialized countries are now being held to account for more than 150 years of industrial activity, which has resulted in high levels of GHG emissions and made it possible for these countries to become wealthy. Climate change is already posing threats to agricultural production in southern Africa through droughts and water scarcity. Early warning systems and strategies should be established to mitigate the negative impacts of climate change. SADC needs to develop common polices on managing natural resources such as water in order to avoid future conflicts.

Development finance institutions (DFIs) play an important role in region-building. The post-apartheid South African government after 1994 radically transformed the agendas of the Development Bank of Southern Africa (DBSA) and the Industrial Development Corporation (IDC), in a bid to meet the sub-region's infrastructural and developmental objectives. The DBSA has granted financial assistance to development projects in Angola, Botswana, Lesotho, Malawi, Mauritius, Mozambique, Namibia, Swaziland, Tanzania and Zambia, seeking to foster human and institutional capacity, broad-based economic growth and job creation. The DBSA also promotes tourism, energy, telecommunications, transport and mining. However, the institution faces financial constraints and would need a vastly increased budget to fulfil its key objectives adequately. The IDC has played a major role in promoting industrial development in Mozambique in particular.

Finally, key external actors can also contribute to region-building in southern Africa. By 2011 China had become the third-largest foreign investor in Africa after Europe and the United States and the world's second-largest economy after the USA. Beijing has signified its intention to play a greater role in peace and security issues on the continent, recently contributing 1,700 troops to seven UN peacekeeping missions in Africa. China's most lucrative trade relations in Africa are with Angola and South Africa, while Beijing also has important interests in Zimbabwe, Zambia and the DRC. China has, however, been criticized for selling arms to African governments, condoning autocratic regimes and destroying African textile sectors through the export of cheap Chinese goods – South Africa and Lesotho have been particularly adversely affected.[7] The United States' Africa Growth and Opportunity Act (AGOA) of 2000, which has boosted trade between Africa and the USA, shows how external actors can potentially play a critical role in supporting SADC's development and security efforts. Realizing the potential benefits of this relationship will depend on continued stability in southern Africa. Investing in African national armies and subregional organizations to prevent, manage and resolve conflicts can reduce the need for the deployment of external peacekeepers. American military goals in Africa will be pursued in future through the controversial US Africa Command (AFRICOM). While AFRICOM aims to build partnership capacity in the security field, some SADC governments and civil society activists view the new initiative as a form of American military expansionism, launched in the name of the 'war on terror' under the administration of US president George W. Bush (2001–08). Though Washington has provided bilateral and multilateral security assistance to African militaries and supported the development of an African Stand-by Force, its major focus has been anti-terrorism activities. The United Nations (UN) has played a critical role in relation to southern Africa's peacekeeping challenges in SADC countries such as Namibia, Angola and Mozambique. Since 2000, the UN has deployed a 20,000-strong mission to the DRC.

What, then, of the future of the region-building project in southern Africa? The challenges are many. They include rebuilding the political, security and socio-economic dimensions of societies emerging from conflict; addressing the root causes of conflicts, while promoting social and economic justice; and putting in place political structures of governance and the rule of law to consolidate peace, to promote reconciliation, and to further the development of the subregion. In setting out such challenges, and crafting concrete recommendations to address them, it is hoped that this volume may help in a modest way to secure the necessary policy responses that will help build a more effective southern African region.

Notes

1 See especially Perry Anderson's magisterial 2009 book *The New Old World* (London: Verso) and David Phinnemore and Alex Warleigh-Lack, *Reflections on European Integration. 50 Years of the Treaty of Rome* (Basingstoke: Palgrave Macmillan, 2009).

2 Since 2000 a useful set of yearly publications have been produced on this: the most recent yearbook, the ninth, appeared in 2009: Anton Bosl et al. (eds), *Monitoring Regional Integration in Southern Africa* (Stellenbosch and Windhoek: Trade and Law Centre for Southern Africa and Konrad-Adenauer-Stiftung).

3 Similar recommendations were made in a report that became available as this Conclusion was being written: African Development Bank/African Development Fund, 'Southern Africa. Regional Integration Strategy Paper 2011–2015' (n.p., March 2011).

4 Scott Drimie and Sithabiso Gandure, 'Hunger and food insecurity: an ongoing threat to human security in southern Africa', Paper presented at the CCR seminar 'Peacebuilding in Southern Africa', Cape Town, South Africa, 25/26 February 2010, p. 30.

5 Sam Moyo and Ruth Hall, 'Conflict and land reform in southern Africa: how exceptional is South Africa?', in Adekeye Adebajo, Adebayo Adedeji and Christopher Landsberg (eds), *South Africa in Africa: The Post-Apartheid Era* (Scottsville, South Africa: University of KwaZulu-Natal Press, 2007), pp. 150–76.

6 See Jonathan Crush and David A. McDonald, 'Introduction to special issue: evaluating South African immigration policy after apartheid', *Africa Today*, 48(1) (Autumn 2001), pp. 1–13; Zimitri Erasmus, 'Race and identity in the nation', in John Daniel, Roger Southall and Jessica Lutchman (eds), *State of the Nation: South Africa 2004–2005* (Cape Town: Human Sciences Research Council, 2005), pp. 15–19; and Audie Klotz, 'Migration after apartheid: deracialising South African foreign policy', *Third World Quarterly*, 21(5), 2001, pp. 831–47. See also, for example, Francis B. Nyamnjoh, *Insiders and Outsiders: Citizenship and Xenophobia in Contemporary Southern Africa* (London: Zed Books, 2006); Human Sciences Research Council (HSRC), *A Research Review of the Policies Surrounding the Issue of the Free Movement of People across International Borders with*

Specific Reference to Southern Africa and the Particular Effect Thereof on South Africa, (Tshwane: HSRC, 2005); Francis Nyamnjoh and Patience Mususa, 'Migration and xenophobia in southern Africa', Paper presented at the CCR seminar 'Peacebuilding in Southern Africa', 25/26 February 2010.

7 Adekeye Adebajo, 'An axis of evil? China, the United States, and France in Africa', in Adebajo, The Curse of Berlin: Africa After the Cold War (Scottsville, South Africa: University of KwaZulu-Natal Press, 2010), pp. 163–89.

About the contributors

Scott Drimie is a research fellow with the International Food Policy Research Institute, where he coordinates the Regional Network on AIDS, Livelihoods and Food Security. He holds a PhD on the political economy of land reform in South Africa from the University of Cambridge.

Gwinyayi A. Dzinesa was a senior researcher at the Centre for Conflict Resolution, in Cape Town. He has co-edited a book on *Peacebuilding in Africa* and has published several articles on peace and security issues in Africa.

Sithabiso Gandure, who works for the Wahenga Institute, Johannesburg, South Africa, is a livelihood specialist who holds a doctorate in climate change and livelihoods from the University of the Witwatersrand, South Africa.

Richard Gibb is Pro Vice-Chancellor and Dean in the Faculty of Science and Technology at the University of Plymouth.

Gilbert M. Khadiagala is the Jan Smuts Professor of International Relations and head of the Department of International Relations at the University of the Witwatersrand, Johannesburg, South Africa. His research focuses on security and politics in eastern Africa, southern Africa and the Great Lakes region.

Chris Landsberg served as director of the Centre for Policy Studies in Johannesburg, South Africa, between 2001 and 2006, before becoming a research professor at the University of Johannesburg. He was a co-founder of the Centre for Africa's International Relations (CAIR) at the University of the Witwatersrand, where he lectured for several years.

Garth le Pere was executive director of the Institute for Global Dialogue for fifteen years until he joined DAJO Associates as a senior partner in January 2010. An Extraordinary Professor of Political Science at the University of Pretoria, his research interests include China's role in Africa, state–society dynamics in Africa, EU–Africa relations, theories of international relations, South African foreign policy, multilateral trade, global conflict, regional integration and South–South cooperation.

Khabele Matlosa worked for the Electoral Institute of Southern Africa (EISA) until he became governance adviser for the United Nations Development Programme (UNDP) based in Addis Ababa, Ethiopia, from March 2010. He has researched and written widely on various aspects of democratization and conflicts in Africa.

Kaire M. Mbuende was until recently ambassador and Permanent Representative of Namibia to the United Nations. He served as the Executive Secretary of the Southern African Development Community (SADC) from 1994 to 1999.

David Monyae is a senior policy analyst in the Development Planning Division (DPD) at the Development Bank of Southern Africa (DBSA). He is also a member of the Higher Education Ministerial Task Team reviewing the National Student Financial Aid Scheme (NSFAS). Before joining DBSA, Monyae was a lecturer in the Department of International Relations at the University of the Witwatersrand.

Patience Mususa is currently completing her PhD in the Department of Social Anthropology at the University of Cape Town on the experiences of miners on the Zambian Copperbelt who lost their jobs because of the privatization of the mines.

Dawn Nagar is a researcher in the Policy Development and Research cluster at the Centre for Conflict Resolution, Cape Town. Her main field of research is regional integration in southern Africa.

Nomfundo Xenia Ngwenya is head of the South African Foreign Policy and African Drivers Programme at the South African Institute of International Affairs (SAIIA) in Johannesburg, South Africa. She was previously a specialist on African affairs in the South African Secret Service and has taught International and African Politics at the University of South Africa.

Francis Nyamnjoh is Professor of Social Anthropology at the University of Cape Town. He was Head of Publications at the Council for the Development of Social Science Research in Africa (CODESRIA) from July 2003 to July 2009. He has published widely on globalization, citizenship, media and the politics of identity in Africa.

Elizabeth Otitodun is a researcher in the Policy Development and Research cluster at the Centre for Conflict Resolution, Cape Town. She has attended training programmes on International Civilian Peacekeeping and Peacebuilding at the Austrian Study Centre for Peace and Conflict Resolution (ASPR).

Antonia Porter is a researcher at the Centre for Conflict Resolution, Cape Town. She was previously Project Officer in the Conflict Intervention and Peacebuilding Support programme at the Centre for Conflict Resolution, University of California, Berkeley.

Mzukisi Qobo is head of the Emerging Powers and Global Challenges programme at the South African Institute of International Affairs (SAIIA) in Johannesburg, South Africa. He was formerly Chief Director responsible for trade policy development at the Department of Trade and Industry, Pretoria.

Chris Saunders is an emeritus professor at the University of Cape Town and a research associate at the Centre for Conflict Resolution, Cape Town. He has written widely on southern Africa.

David Simon is head of department and Professor of Development Geography at Royal Holloway, University of London, UK. He is a specialist on sub-Saharan Africa and has extensive experience in Namibia, South Africa (his home country), Ghana and Kenya. He serves on the Scientific Steering Committee of the Urbanization and Global Environmental Change core project of the International Human Dimensions Programme on Global Environmental Change (IHDP).

Bibliography

Abi-Saab, G. (1978) *The United Nations Operation in the Congo, 1960–1964*, Oxford: Oxford University Press

Adar, K. G. and R. Ajulu (eds) (2002) *Globalization and Emerging Trends in African States' Foreign Policy-making Process: A Comparative Perspective of Southern Africa*, Aldershot: Ashgate.

Adebajo, A. (2004) 'Rethinking a continent: from Kwame Nkrumah to Thabo Mbeki', *Mail and Guardian*, 30 April–6 May, www.ccr.org.za.

— (2006) 'Chronicle of a death foretold: the rise and fall of UN reform: ending global apartheid: sustainable development, aid, and trade', in A. Adebajo and H. Scanlon (eds), *A Dialogue of the Deaf: Essays on Africa and the United Nations*, Auckland Park, Johannesburg: Jacana.

— (2010a) 'An axis of evil? China, the United States, and France in Africa', in A. Adebajo, *The Curse of Berlin: Africa After the Cold War*, Scottsville, South Africa: University of KwaZulu-Natal Press.

— (2010b) *The Curse of Berlin: Africa After the Cold War*, Scottsville, South Africa: University of KwaZulu-Natal Press.

Adedeji, A. (1999) 'Comparative strategies of economic decolonization in Africa', in A. Mazrui and C. Wondji (eds), *General History of Africa*, vol. 8: *Africa Since 1935*, Oxford: James Currey.

— (2004) 'ECOWAS: a retrospective journey', in A. Adebajo and I. Rashid (eds), *West Africa's Security Challenges: Building Peace in a Troubled Region*, Boulder, CO: Lynne Rienner.

Adepoju, A (1995) 'Migration in Africa: an overview', in J. Baker and T. A. Aina (eds), *The Migration Experience in Africa*, Uppsala: Nordiska Afrikaninstitutet.

AfDevInfo (2008) 'SADC Standing Committee of Officials, SADC Council of Ministers', www.sadc.int/English/about/struct ...; www.afdevinfo.com/htmlreports/org/org_48953.html, 28 April.

Africa News/Mmegi (2009) 'Foreigners take our jobs – artisans', 16 February.

Africa News/Times of Zambia (2008) 'Zambia protest by 360 workers should serve as a lesson', 23 April.

— (2009) 'Businessman narrates beating ordeal', 22 June.

African Development Bank (AfDB) (1993) 'Economic integration in southern Africa', Oxford.

African Development Bank/African Development Fund, Southern Africa (2011) *Regional Integration Strategy Paper 2011–2015*, n.p., March.

African Growth and Opportunity Act (AGOA) (n.d.) www.agoa.gov.

— (2010) 'General Country Eligibility Provision', www.agoa.gov/eligibility/country_eligibility.html.

African National Congress (ANC) (1994) *The Reconstruction and Development Programme: A Policy Framework*, www.anc.org.za.

African Peer Review Mechanism (APRM) Secretariat (2007) 'Country Review Report of South Africa', 19 October.

— (2010) 'Country Review Report no. 12: Kingdom of Lesotho', Mimeo, Midrand, South Africa.

African Union (AU) (2000) *Constitutive Act*, Articles 4(h) and 4(j).

— (2002) *Protocol Relating to the Establishment of the Peace and Security Council of the African Union*, Article 13, Durban, December 2003.

— (2004) 'Common African Defence and Security Policy', para. 6, www.

africa-union.org/News_Events/2ND%20
EX%20ASSEMBLY/Declaration%20on
%20a%20Comm.Af%20Def%20Sec.pdf.

— (2005) 'Roadmap for the Operationalisation of the African Standby Force',
Experts' Meeting on the Relationship
between the AU and the Regional
Mechanisms for Conflict Prevention, Management, and Resolution,
EXP/AU-Recs/ASF/4(I), Addis Ababa,
22–23 March.

— (2007) 'Audit Report', europafrica.net/
key-documents.

— (2009a) 'AU Assembly Decision on the
African Common Position on Climate
Change', Assembly/AU/Dec.236(XII),
www.africa-union.org/root/ua/confer-
ences/2009/jan/summit_jan_2009/
doc/conference/assembly%20au%20
dec%20%20208-240%20(xii).pdf.

— (2009b) 'Gender policy', www.africa-
union.org/.../african%20union%20
gender%20policy.doc, February.

— (2010a) 'Briefing note: mitigating vulnerabilities of women and children in
armed conflict', PSC/PR/3 (CCXXIII).

— (2010b) Press release no. 150, www.
globalsecurity.org/military/library/
news/2010/10/mil-101022-voa05.htm.

African Women Decade Promises Greater
Gender Parity (2010) www.allvoices.
com/contributed-news/7031937-african-
women-decade-officially-launched.

Akokpari, J. (2008) 'Dilemmas of regional
integration and development in Africa',
in J. Akokpari, A. Ndinga-Muvumba
and T. Murithi (eds), The African Union
and Its Institutions, Johannesburg:
Jacana.

Ala, J. (1998) 'AIDS as a new security
threat' in M. Baregu et al. (eds), From
Cape to Congo, pp. 131–58.

Alden, C. (2008) 'Africa without Europeans', in C. Alden, D. Large and R. S.
de Oliveira, China Returns to Africa: A
Rising Power and a Continent Embrace,
London: Hurst, p. 355.

Alden, C. and A. C. Alves (2008) 'History
and identity in the construction of
China's Africa policy', Review of African
Political Economy, 115(35): 43.

Alden, C. and G. le Pere (2004) 'South
Africa's post-apartheid foreign policy:
from reconciliation to ambiguity',
Review of the African Political Economy,
31(100): 284.

Allais, C. et al. (2010) Tsireledzani:
Understanding the Dimensions of
Human Trafficking in Southern Africa,
Pretoria: National Prosecuting Author-
ity of South Africa, www.hsrc.ac.za/
Research_Publication-21609.phtml.

Ampiah, K. and S. Naidu (eds) (2008)
Crouching Tiger, Hidden Dragon? Africa
and China, Scottsville: University of
KwaZulu-Natal Press.

Anderson, K. and R. Blackhurst (eds)
(1993) Regional Integration and the
Global Trading System, New York:
Harverster Wheatsheaf.

Anderson, P. (2009) The New Old World,
London: Verso.

Annan, K. (2000) 'Secretary-General
salutes international workshop on
human security in Mongolia', Press
release SG/SM/7382, Ulan Bator,
8–10 May, www.un.org/News/Press/
docs/2000/20000508.sgsm7382.doc.
html.

Anstee, M. (1996) Orphan of the Cold War:
The Inside Story of the Collapse of the
Angolan Peace Process, 1992–93, Basing-
stoke: Macmillan.

Asante, S. K. B. (1997) Regionalism
and Africa's Development, London:
Macmillan.

Asante, S. K. B. in collaboration with
D. Chanaiwa (1999) 'Pan-Africanism
and regional integration', in A. Mazrui
et al. (eds), General History of Africa,
pp. 725–7.

Asplund, B. (2010a) 'Africa: African elections put fewer women in parliament',
Mail and Guardian Online, 9 December,
mg.co.za/article/2010-12-09-un-
african-elections-put-fewer-women-in-
parliament.

— (2010b) 'Elections in the region have
shown regression with regard to
women's representation in parliament',
Mail and Guardian Online, 9 December.

Avert (2011) 'PEPFAR funding: how is the

money spent?', www.avert.org/pepfar-funding.htm.

Bacchetta, M. and B. Bora (2004) 'Industrial tariff liberalization and the Doha development agenda', Working paper, Geneva: World Trade Organization.

Bach, D. C. (1999) *Regionalisation in Africa: Integration and Disintegration*, Oxford: James Currey.

— (2008) 'The AU and the EU', in J. Akokpari, A. Ndinga-Muvumba and T. Murithi (eds), *The African Union and Its Institutions*, Johannesburg: Jacana.

Baker, D. P. and S. Maeresera (2009) 'SADCBRIG intervention in SADC member states: reasons to doubt', *African Security Review*, 18(1).

Baker, P. H. (1989) *The United States and South Africa: The Reagan Years*, Washington, DC: Ford Foundation.

Balassa, B. (1961) *The Theory of Economic Integration*, Baltimore, MD: Johns Hopkins University Press.

Baregu, M. (2006) 'Congo in the Great Lakes region', in G. Khadiagala (ed.), *Security Dynamics in the Africa's Great Lakes Region*, New York: International Peace Academy.

— (2008) 'The three faces of the dragon: Tanzania–China relations in historical perspective', in K. Ampiah and S. Naidu, *Crouching Tiger, Hidden Dragon? Africa and China*, Scottsville: University of KwaZulu-Natal Press, p. 158.

Baregu, M. and C. Landsberg (eds) (2003) *From Cape to Congo: Southern Africa's Evolving Security Challenges*, Boulder, CO: Lynne Rienner.

Barnett, J. (2006) 'Climate change, insecurity, and injustice', in W. N. Adger et al. (eds), *Fairness in Adaptation to Climate Change*, Cambridge, MA, and London: Massachusetts Institute of Technology Press, pp. 115–29.

Bertelmann-Scott, T. (2003) 'The European Union', in M. Baregu et al. (eds), *From Cape to Congo: Southern Africa's Evolving Security Challenges*, Boulder, CO: Lynne Rienner, p. 314.

— (2010) 'SACU – one hundred not out: what future for the Customs Union?', SAIIA Occasional Paper no. 68, September.

Black, D. R. and L. A. Swatuk (eds) (1997) *Bridging the Rift: The New South Africa in Africa*, Boulder, CO: Westview Press.

Bodansky, H. (1994) 'In our international commercial relations, we must look like America: Secretary Brown makes outreach a part of the Commerce Department's new diversity policy', *Business America*, findarticles.com/p/articles/mi_m1052/is_n10_v115/ai_15902044/pg_3.

Bond, P. (2010) 'First class failure', *BBC Focus on Africa*, October–December, p. 26.

Bösl, A. et al. (eds) (2009) *Monitoring Regional Integration in Southern Africa*, vol. 9, Stellenbosch: Trade Law Centre for Southern Africa.

Bösl, A., G. Erasmus, T. Hartzenberg and C. McCarthy (2010) 'Introduction: monitoring the process of regional integration in southern Africa in 2009', *Monitoring Regional Integration in Southern Africa Yearbook 2009*, Stellenbosch, South Africa: Trade Law Centre for Southern Africa, Konrad-Adenauer-Stiftung.

Botswana Ministry of Trade and Industry (2009), 'Botswana–China trade strengthens', 3 September, www.mti.gov.bw.

Bradshaw, Y. and S. N. Ndegwa (eds) (n.d.) *The Uncertain Promise of Southern Africa*, Bloomington: Indiana University Press.

Bretherton, C. and J. Vogler (1999) *The European Union as a Global Actor*, London: Routledge.

Breytenbach, W. (2007) 'Failure of security cooperation in SADC: the suspension of the Organ for Politics, Defence, and Security', *South African Journal of International Affairs*, 7(1): 7.

Broadman, H. (2007) *Africa's Silk Road: China and India's New Economic Frontier*, Washington, DC: World Bank.

Buanews (2009) 'SA's Burundi mission accomplished', 31 July, www.

southafrica.info/news/international/burundi-310709.htm.

Bunwaree, S. (2008) 'Achieving human security in insecure southern Africa: a gender perspective', *New Agenda*, 4th quarter, pp. 68–71.

— (2008) 'NEPAD and its discontents' in J. Akokpari et al. (eds), *The African Union and Its Institutions*, Johannesburg: Jacana.

— (2009) 'Gender, human rights, and peacebuilding in Africa', Paper presented at the Centre for Conflict Resolution 'Peacebuilding in Africa' research and policy seminar, Gaborone, 25–28 August.

Business Report (2011) 'Why China invited SA to join BRIC', January, www.iol.co.za/business/business-news/why-china-invited-sa-to-join-bric-1.1017796.

Caholo, J. C. (2010) 'Status of regional integration in the SADC region', 18 October, www.un.org/africa/osaa/speeches/SADC_Presentation_18Oct2010.pdf.

Calcaterra, M., J. Kirsten and D. Poonyth (2001) 'Is agricultural sector growth a precondition for economic growth? The case of South Africa', Working paper, Pretoria: Department of Agricultural Economics, Extension, and Rural Development, University of Pretoria.

Campbell, E. K. and J. Oucho (2003) 'Changing attitudes to immigration and refugee policy in Botswana', Migration Policy Series no. 28, Cape Town: SAMP.

Campos, I. and A. Vines (2008) 'Angola and China: a pragmatic partnership', Working paper, London: Centre for Strategic and International Studies, March.

Carim, X. (2009) 'Keynote address from the Sixth Southern African Forum on Trade', *From Cape to Cairo: Exploring the COMESA–EAC–SADC Tripartite FTA*, 3/4 August.

Centre for Chinese Studies (2010) 'Weekly briefing', University of Stellenbosch, January.

Centre for Civil Society (2006) 'Civil society guide: deliberative policy, civil society, and Africa's continental mechanisms and programmes', Durban, November.

Centre for Conflict Resolution (CCR) (2005a) 'Whither SADC? An agenda for southern Africa's post-apartheid security', Seminar report, Cape Town, 18/19 June.

— (2005b) 'The peacebuilding role of civil society in southern Africa', Seminar report, Maseru, Lesotho, 14/15 October.

— (2006a) 'HIV/AIDS and militaries in southern Africa', Seminar report, Windhoek, Namibia, 9/10 July.

— (2006b) 'Women in post-conflict societies in Africa', Seminar report, Johannesburg, 6/7 November.

— (2007a) 'Eurafrique? Africa and Europe in a new century', Seminar report, 31 October/1 November.

— (2007b) 'HIV/AIDS and militaries in Africa', Seminar report, Addis Ababa, Ethiopia, November.

— (2008a) 'From Eurafrique to Afro-Europa', Seminar report, Stellenbosch, 11–13 September.

— (2008b) 'SADC: building an effective security and governance architecture for the 21st century', Seminar report, Dar es Salaam, Tanzania, 29/30 May, www.ccr.uct.ac.za.

— (2008c) 'Security and development in southern Africa', Seminar report, Johannesburg, 8–10 June, www.ccr.uct.ac.za.

— (2009) 'Peacebuilding in post-Cold War Africa: problems, progress, and prospects', Seminar report, Gaborone, 25–28 August.

— (2010a) 'Stabilising Sudan: domestic, sub-regional, and extra-regional challenges', Seminar report, Cape Town, 23/24 August.

— (2010b) *HIV/AIDS in Integrated Peace Support Operations in Africa: A Training Manual*, Cape Town.

— (2010c) *Building Peace in Southern Africa*, Policy seminar report, Vineyard Hotel, Cape Town, South Africa, 25/26 February.

— (2011a) 'Adedeji at 80: moving Africa from rhetoric to action', Policy brief, Ijebu-Ode, Nigeria, 18–20 December.

— (2011b) 'Building peace in southern Africa', Seminar report, Cape Town, 25/26 February.

Chase, R. S., E. Hill and P. Kennedy (1996) 'Pivotal states and US Strategy', *Foreign Affairs*, 75(1): 46.

Cheru, F. (2002) *African Renaissance: Road-maps to the Challenge of Globalization*, London: Zed Books.

Chikova, A. (2009) 'Energy trading in the Southern African Power Pool', www.sapp.co.zw.

China Daily (2007) 'China–Mozambique bilateral relations', 26 January.

Chirwa, M. C. and C. A. D. Namangale (2008) 'SADC training needs for peace support operations: the case for a wider future role of the RPTC', Paper for Foprisa conference, Centurion, South Africa, November.

Cilliers, J. and J. Potgieter (2010) 'The African Standby Force', in U. Engel and J. G. Portes (eds), *Africa's New Peace and Security Architecture: Promoting Norms, Institutionalizing Solutions*, Farnham: Ashgate.

Clapham, C. (2001) 'The changing world of regional integration in Africa', in C. Clapham, G. Mills, A. Morner and E. Sidiropoulos (eds), *Regional Integration in Southern Africa*, Johannesburg: South African Institute of International Affairs, p. 62.

Clapham, C., G. Mills, A. Morner and E. Sidiropoulos (eds) (2001) *Regional Integration in Southern Africa*, Johannesburg: South African Institute of International Affairs.

Clarke, Y. (2008) 'Security sector reform in Africa: a lost opportunity to deconstruct militarised masculinities?', *Feminist Africa*, 10: 49–66.

Clover, J. (2003) 'Food security in sub-Saharan Africa', *African Security Review*, 12(1), www.iss.co.za/pubs/ASR/12No1/Clover.pdf.

Cobb, C. (2001) 'Talks underway to re-evaluate US–South Africa link', allafrica.com/stories/200104180105.html.

Cockburn, C. (2002) 'Gender, armed conflict, and political violence', www.genderandpeacekeeping.com.

Coleman, K. P. (2007) *International Organisations and Peace Enforcement: The Politics of International Legitimacy*, Cambridge: Cambridge University Press.

Collier, P. (2009) *Wars, Guns, and Votes: Democracy in Dangerous Places*, London: Bodley Head.

Commission of the European Communities (2006) 'Annex to the Communication from the Commission to the Council, the European Parliament, the European Economic and Social Committee, and the Committee of the Regions: Global Europe: Competing in the World – a Contribution to the EU's Growth and Jobs Strategy', Brussels, 4 October.

Common Market for Eastern and Southern Africa (COMESA) (n.d.) Treaty chapter (24), about.comesa.int/attachments/comesa_treaty_en.pdf.

— (2009a) 'Victoria Falls Town Declaration of the Second Joint Meeting of the COMESA Ministers of Agriculture, Environment, and Natural Resources', CS/PPSD/AGC/MAE/II/3 Annex II, Victoria Falls, Zimbabwe, 3/4 September.

— (2009b) *COMESA Climate Change Initiative Annual Report 2009*, Lusaka.

Conflict Transformation and Peacebuilding in Southern Africa (2008) Seminar report, Johannesburg, 19/20 May.

Construction for Development Magazine (2009) October, www.isiza.co.za/features/bric-nations/303573.htm.

Corey, C. W. (2010) 'Obama administration committed to AGOA partnership with continent', allafrica.com/stories/201006030027.html.

Corkin, L. (2008) 'All's fair in loans and war: the development of China–Angola relations', in K. Ampiah and S. Naidu, *Crouching Tiger, Hidden Dragon? Africa and China*, Scottsville: University of KwaZulu-Natal Press, pp. 109–10.

Cosme, N. (2010) Untitled speech delivered at a SAIIA-CEIC workshop on Angola's foreign policy, Catholic University of Angola, 3 March.

Cotula, L. et al. (2009) *Land Grab or Development Opportunity? Agricultural Investment and International Land Deals in Africa*, International Institute for Environment and Development (IIED), Food and Agriculture Organization (FAO) and International Fund for Agricultural Development (IFAD).

Council of the European Union (2005) 'The EU and Africa: towards a strategic partnership', Brussels, December, www.consilium.europa.eu/ueDocs/cms_Data/docs/pressData/en/er/87673.pdf.

Creamer, T. (2010) 'SA confirmed as top developing country investor in Africa', www.polity.org.za/article/sa-confirmed-as-top-developing-country-investor-in-africa-2010-07-23.

Cronje, J. B. (2010) 'Possible changes to the SACU revenue sharing formula', Tralac, www.tralac.org.

Crush, J. (2008) *The Perfect Storm: The Realities of Xenophobia in Contemporary South Africa*, Cape Town: SAMP.

Crush, J. and D. A. McDonald (2001) 'Introduction to special issue: evaluating South African immigration policy after apartheid', *Africa Today*, 48(1): 1–13.

Crush J. and W. Pendleton (2004) 'Regionalizing xenophobia? Citizen attitudes to immigration and refugee policy in southern Africa', Migration Policy Series no. 30, Cape Town: South African Migration Project (SAMP).

Crush, J., B. Frayne and M. Grant (2006) 'Linking migration, HIV/AIDS, and urban food security in southern and eastern Africa', programs.ifpri.org/renewal/pdf/urbanrural.pdf.

Crush, J., V. Williams and S. Peberdy (2005) 'Migration in southern Africa', Paper prepared for the Policy and Research Programme of the Global Commission on International Migration.

Curtis, D. (2007) 'South Africa: exporting peace to the Great Lakes region?', in A. Adebajo et al. (eds), *South Africa in Africa: The Post-Apartheid Era*, Scottsville: University of KwaZulu-Natal Press.

Daniel, J. and M. Bhengu (2009) 'South Africa in Africa', in R. Southall and H. Melber, *The New Scramble for Africa: Imperialism, Investment, and Development in Africa*, Durban: University of KwaZulu-Natal Press, p. 140.

Davies, R. (2008) 'Bridging the divide: the SADC EPA', *Trade Negotiations Insights*, 7(4): 1, trade.ec.europa.eu/doclib/docs/2009/july/tradoc_143981.pdf.

De Beer, G. (2001) 'Regional development corridors and Spatial Development Initiatives: some current perspectives and potentials on progress', Paper presented at the conference 'Transport Challenges in Southern Africa', July, available at repository.up.ac.za/upspace/bitstream/2263/8129/1/3a11.pdf.

De Lombaerde, P. (2005) 'Regional integration and peace', *Peace and Conflict Monitor*, May, www.monitor.upeace.org/innerpg.cfm?id_article=268.

De Schutter, O. (2009) 'Large-scale land acquisitions and leases: a set of core principles and measures to address the human rights challenges', United Nations Special Rapporteur on the Right to Food (UN/SRRF), 11 June.

De Waal, A. (2000) 'Democratic political process and the fight against famine', Working Paper no. 107, London: IDS.

— (2007) 'AIDS, hunger, and destitution: theory and evidence for the "new variant famines" hypothesis in Africa', in S. Devereux, *The New Famines: Why Famines Persist in an Era of Globalisation*, London: Routledge.

De Waal, A. and A. Whiteside (2003) 'New variant famine: AIDS and food crisis in southern Africa', *The Lancet*, 362(9391): 1234–7.

De Wit, M. (2009) 'Hunger in SADC with specific reference to climate change: a longer-term, regional analysis', Unpublished paper, Cape Town: One World Sustainable Investments.

Deighton, A. (1998) 'The remaking of Europe', in M. Howard and William R. Louis (eds), *The Oxford History of the Twentieth Century*, Oxford: Oxford University Press.

Denning, G. et al. (2009) 'Input subsidies to improve smallholder maize productivity in Malawi: toward an African green revolution', *PLoS Biol*, 7(1).

Dent, C. M. (2009) 'China and Africa: towards a conceptualisation of "development relations"', Unpublished paper presented at the seminar 'China/Africa Development Relations', University of Leeds, 27 February.

Department for International Development (DfID) (2006) 'Reducing the risk of disasters: helping to achieve sustainable poverty reduction in a vulnerable world – a DfID policy paper', London.

Department of Foreign Affairs (DFA) (2003) 'Developments relating to SADC, African Union, and NEPAD', Pretoria, 31 March.

Development Bank of Southern Africa (DBSA) (2010) 'The evolution of the Development Bank of Southern Africa 2010: development activism through development finance'.

— (2011) 'DBSA and Zambian RDFA sign a historic road development loan', Press release, 26 January.

Devereux, S. (2007) 'From "old famines" to "new famines"', in S. Devereux (ed.), *The New Famines: Why Famines Persist in an Era of Globalisation*, London: Routledge.

— (2008) 'Innovations in the design and delivery of social transfers: lessons learned from Malawi', Brighton: Institute of Development Studies.

Devereux, S. and S. Maxwell (2001) *Food Security in Sub-Saharan Africa*, London: Intermediate Technology Development Group.

Dier, A. (2010) 'The African Standby Force put to the test', *CSS Analysis in Security Policy*, 84: 3; 'New African Standby Force faces first test', VOA News.com, 22 October.

Dlamini-Zuma, N. (2009) 'Post-Council media briefing' by South African minister of foreign affairs and chair of the SADC Council of Ministers, Cape Town, 27 February.

Dobler, G. (2008) 'Solidarity, xenophobia, and the regulation of Chinese businesses in Namibia', in C. Alden, D. Large and R. S. de Oliveira, *China Returns to Africa: A Rising Power and a Continent Embrace*, London: Hurst, pp. 237–55.

Dokubo, C. (2005) 'Nigeria's international peacekeeping and peacebuilding efforts in Africa, 1960–2005', in B. Akinterinwa (ed.), *Nigeria and the United Nations Security Council*, Ibadan: Vantage.

Donnelly, L. (2010) 'Eskom's early Xmas gift', *Mail and Guardian*, 29 October, p. 11.

Dorward, A. et al. (2008) 'Towards "smart" subsidies in agriculture? Lessons from recent experience in Malawi', *Natural Resource Perspectives*, 116, September.

Draper, P. and G. le Pere (2005) *Enter the Dragon: Towards a Free Trade Agreement Between China and the Southern African Customs Union*, Johannesburg: Institute for Global Dialogue and South African Institute of International Affairs.

Draper, P., S. Kiratu and C. Samuel (2007) 'The role of South African FDI in southern Africa', www.die-gdi.de/CMS-Homepage/openwebcms3.nsf/(ynDK_contentByKey)/ANES-882C6Q/$FILE/DP%208.2010.pdf, p. 1.

Drieschova, A., M. Giordano and I. Fischhendler (2009) 'Climate change, international cooperation, and adaptation in transboundary water management', in W. N. Adger, I. Lorenzoni and K. O'Brien (eds), *Adapting to Climate Change: Thresholds, Values, Governance*, Cambridge: Cambridge University Press, pp. 384–98.

Drimie, S. (2004) 'The underlying causes of the food crisis in the southern Africa region: Malawi, Mozambique, Zambia, and Zimbabwe', Policy research paper, Oxford: Oxfam Great Britain.

Drimie, S. and M. Casale (2009) 'Multiple stressors in southern Africa: the link between HIV/AIDS, food insecurity, poverty, and children's vulnerability now and in the future', *AIDS Care*, 21(S1): 21–6.

Drimie, S. and S. Gandure (2010) 'Hunger and food insecurity: an ongoing threat to human security in southern Africa', Paper presented at the CCR seminar 'Peacebuilding in Southern Africa', Cape Town, South Africa, 25/26 February.

Dugger, C. W. (2008) 'Mbeki's resignation risks Zimbabwe deal', *New York Times*, 23 September.

Duvvury, N. and R. Strickland (2003) 'Gender equity and peacebuilding: from rhetoric to reality – finding the way', Discussion paper, Washington, DC: International Center for Research on Women (ICRW).

Dzinesa, G. (2004) 'A comparative perspective of UN peacekeeping in Angola and Namibia', *International Peacekeeping*, 11(4).

Ecobank Transnational Incorporated (n.d.) www.firstglobalselect.com/scripts/cgiip.wsc/globalone/htm/quote_and_news.r?pisharetype-id=17780.

Economist (2009) 23 May.

El-Agraa, A. M. (ed.) (1997) *Economic Integration Worldwide*, New York: St Martin's Press, discussed in Margaret C. Lee (2003), *The Political Economy of Regionalism in Southern Africa*, Lansdowne: University of Cape Town Press, p. 20.

Electoral Institute of Southern Africa (EISA) (2003) 'The 2003 EISA/ECF Principles for Election Management, Monitoring, and Observation (PEMMO) in the SADC region', Mimeo, Johannesburg, South Africa.

— (2009) 'South Africa: women's representation quotas', www.eisa.org.za/WEP/souquotas.htm.

Embassy of China in Botswana (2010) 'Bilateral relations', available at bw.chineseembassy.org/eng/sbgx.

Erasmus, G. (2004) 'New SACU institutions: prospects for regional integration', Working paper, Stellenbosch, South Africa: Trade Law Centre for Southern Africa.

Erasmus, Z. (2005) 'Race and identity in the nation', in J. Daniel, R. Southall and J. Lutchman (eds), *State of the Nation: South Africa 2004–2005*, Cape Town: Human Sciences Research Council (HSRC), pp. 15–19.

Esplen, E. (2006) *Engaging Men in Gender Equality: Positive Strategies and Approaches – Overview and Annotated Bibliography*, BRIDGE Bibliography No. 15, Brighton: Institute of Development Studies,

European Commission (2008) 'What will an economic partnership agreement do?', *Trade Policy in Practice: Global Europe*, Brussels: Commission of the European Communities, External Trade.

— (2010) 'A strategy for smart, sustainable, and inclusive growth', COM (2010) 2020, Brussels, 3 March.

Fabricius, P. (2000) 'SADC, US create disaster reaction forum', www.iol.co.za/index.php?sf=143&set_id=1&click_id=68&art_id=ct20000509210720531S320922,9.

Fan, S., B. Omilola and M. Lambert (2009) 'Public spending for agriculture in Africa: trends and composition', Regional Strategic Analysis and Knowledge Support System (ReSAKKS) Working Paper no. 28, IFPRI, April, www.ifpri.org.

Ferreira, M. E. (2008) 'China in Angola: just a passion for oil', in C. Alden, D. Large and R. S. de Oliveira, *China Returns to Africa: A Rising Power and a Continent Embrace*, London: Hurst, p. 302.

Financial Mail (South Africa) (2008) 'Xenophobia: what lies beneath?', 30 May.

Financial Times (2005) 'Banana producers go to WTO over EU dispute', 7 March.

Fine, J. and W. Bird (2006) *Shades of Prejudice: An Investigation into the South Africa's Media's Coverage of Racial Violence and Xenophobia*, Johannesburg:

Centre for the Study of Violence and Reconciliation.

Fisher, L. M. (2008) 'Peace support operations: UN/AU implications for SADC', www.foprisa.net/publications/documents/PeaceSupportOperations-UN-AU.pdf;

— (n.d.) 'The Southern African Development Community in the continental security architecture', Unpublished paper.

Flak, A. (2011) 'South Africa says coal for power a priority', Reuters, 2 February, www.reuters.com/article/2011/02/02/mining-safrica-idUSLDE7110IC20110202.

Food and Agriculture Organization (FAO) and World Food Programme (WFP) (2009) *The State of Food Insecurity in the World 2009: Economic Crises – Impacts and Lessons Learnt*, Rome, ftp.fao.org/docrep/fao/012/i0876e/i0876e.pdf.

Fourie, P. and M. Schönteich (2001) 'Africa's new security threat: HIV/AIDS and human security in southern Africa', *African Security Review*, 10(4): 29–42.

Fowale, T. J. (2001) 'The Zimbabwe factor in Thabo Mbeki's fall: silent diplomacy', Suite 101.com, 19 July 2009.

Francis, D. (2004) *Culture, Power Asymmetries, and Gender in Conflict Transformation*, Berlin: Berghof Research Centre for Constructive Conflict Management.

Franke, B. (2008) 'Africa's evolving security architecture and the concept of multilayered security communities', *Cooperation and Conflict*, 43: 317, quoting *Communist Review* (1922).

— (2010) 'Steady but uneven progress: the operationalization of the African Standby Force', in H. Besada (ed.), *Crafting an African Security Architecture*, Farnham: Ashgate.

Frayne, B. and W. Pendleton (2002) 'Mobile Namibia: migration trends and attitudes', Migration Policy Series no. 27, Cape Town: SAMP.

Frazer, J. (2003) 'The United States', in M. Baregu and C. Landsberg (eds), *From Cape to Congo: Southern Africa's Evolv-*ing *Security Challenges*, Boulder, CO: Lynne Rienner, p. 278.

Friedmann, J. (1972) *A General Theory of Polarized Development*, cited in R. Gilpin, *The Political Economy of International Relations*, Princeton, NJ: Princeton University Press, p. 21.

Gambari, I. A. (2003) 'The United Nations', in M. Baregu and C. Landsberg (eds), *From Cape to Congo: Southern Africa's Evolving Security Challenges*, Boulder, CO: Lynne Rienner.

Gandure, S. (2008) 'High food prices in eastern, central, and southern Africa: assessing impact and tracking progress towards meeting the CFA objectives', WFP, home.wfp.org/stellent/groups/public/documents/ena/wfp197247.pdf.

Gavin, B. (2009) 'European perspective on trade', Mimeo, UNU-Comparative Regional Integration Studies, January.

Geldenhuys, D. (1997) 'The politics of South Africa's China switch', *Issues and Studies*, 33(7): 98.

Gibb, D. (2000) 'The United Nations: international peacekeeping and the question of "impartiality" – revisiting the Congo operation of 1960', *Journal of Modern African Studies*, 38(3).

Gibb, R. (1997) 'Regional integration in post-apartheid southern Africa: the case of renegotiating the Southern African Customs Union', *Journal of Southern African Studies*, 23(1): 67–86.

— (2003) 'Globalisation and Africa's economic recovery: a case study of the European Union–South Africa post-apartheid trading regime', *Journal of Southern African Studies*, 29(4): 885–901.

Gibb, R. et al. (eds) (2002) *Charting a New Course: Globalisation, African Recovery, and the New Africa Initiative*, Johannesburg: South African Institute of International Affairs.

Gillespie, S. et al. (eds) (2007) 'Poverty, HIV, and AIDS: vulnerability and impact in southern Africa', *AIDS*, 21(7) (special issue).

— (2009) 'Food prices and the HIV response: findings from rapid regional assessments in eastern and southern Africa', *Food Security: The Science, Sociology, and Economics of Food Preparation and Access to Food*, 10 July, www.springerlink.com/content/9557g3121t5x202r/.

Gilpin, R. (1987) *The Political Economy of International Relations*, Princeton, NJ: Princeton University Press.

Glantz, M. H. (1994) *The Role of Regional Organizations in the Context of Climate Change*, NATO ASI Series I, Global Environmental Change 14, Berlin: Heidelberg.

Global Environmental Change and Human Security project (n.d.) www.gechs.org.

Grant, J. A. and F. Söderbaum (eds) (n.d.) *New Regionalisms in Africa*, Aldershot: Ashgate.

Gready, P. and J. Ensor (eds) (2005) *Reinventing Development? Translating Rights-based Approaches from Theory into Practice*, London: Zed Books.

Green, R. and K. Green (1967) *Economic Cooperation in Africa: Retrospect and Prospects*, London: Oxford University Press.

Green, R. H. (1988) 'The SADCC on the frontline: breakdown or breakthrough?', in C. Legum (ed.), *Africa Contemporary Record: Annual Survey and Documents, 1986–1987*, New York: Africana Publishing House, pp. A33–34.

Green, R. H. and C. B. Thompson (1986) 'Political economies in conflict: SADCC, South Africa, and sanctions', in P. Johnson and D. Martin, *Destructive Engagement: Southern Africa at War*, Harare: Zimbabwe Publishing House, pp. 245–80.

Griffith-Jones, S., D. Griffith-Jones and D. Hertova (2008) 'Enhancing the role of regional development banks', G24 Discussion Paper no. 50, July.

Guardian (2011) 'Fukushima radiation from Japan's stricken plant detected across UK', 29 March, www.guardian.co.uk/uk/2011/mar/29/fukushima-raditation-found-across-uk.

Gumbi, L. (1995) 'Instability in Lesotho: a search for alternatives', *African Security Review*, 4(4).

Gyimah-Boadi, E. (1996) 'Civil society in Africa', *Journal of Democracy*, 7(2): 118.

Haarlov, J. (1997) *Regional Cooperation and Integration within Industry and Trade in Southern Africa: General Approaches, SADCC, and the World Bank*, Aldershot: Avebury.

Habib, A. (2008) 'Seeing the "new scramble" for what it really is: reflections on the United States and China', in H. Edinger, H. Herman and J. Jansson (eds), *New Impulses from the South: China's Engagement of Africa*, Stellenbosch, South Africa: Centre for Chinese Studies, pp. 24–7.

Haddad, L. and L. C. Smith (2000) *Explaining Child Malnutrition in Developing Countries: A Cross-Country Analysis*, Washington, DC: IFPRI.

Harper, C., R. Marcus and K. Moore (2003) 'Enduring poverty and the conditions of childhood: lifecourse and intergenerational poverty transmissions', *World Development*, 31(3): 535–54.

Hartzenberg, T. (2001) 'South African regional industrial policy: from border industries to Spatial Development Initiatives', *Journal of International Development*, 13: 771.

Havnevik, K. (2009) 'Outsourcing of African lands for energy and food: challenges for smallholders', Paper presented to IPD's African Task Force, Pretoria, South Africa, July.

Hayes, S. (2005) 'AGOA: a five-year assessment', Testimony by Stephen Hayes, president of the Corporate Council on Africa, to the US House Committee on International Relations, Subcommittee on Africa, Global Human Rights, and International Operations, allafrica.com/download/resource/main/main/id atcs/00010164:84645f1d08050189ad540e4 f6d463275.pdf.

Hazelhurst, E. (2010) 'China is SA's biggest market', *Star: Business Report*, 14 January, p. 13.

Hearn, R. (1999) *UN Peacekeeping in Action: The Namibian Experience*, Commack, NY: Nova Science.

Hecker, H. (2009) 'Effects of the global

economic crisis: examining the impact on HIV and AIDS funding', www.sangonet.org.za/category/defined-tags/health/hiv-and-aids?page=.

Hentz, J. J. (2005) *South Africa and the Logic of Regional Cooperation*, Bloomington: Indiana University Press.

Hill, C. and M. Smith (2005) *International Relations and the European Union*, Oxford: Oxford University Press.

Hirch, A. (2005) *Season of Hope: Economic Reform Under Mandela and Mbeki*, Scottsville: University of KwaZulu-Natal Press.

Horvei, T. (1998) 'Powering the region: South Africa in the Southern Africa Power Pool', in D. Simon, *South Africa in Southern Africa: Reconfiguring the Region*, Oxford: James Currey.

Howard, A. A. and W. M. El-Sadr (2010) 'Integration of tuberculosis and HIV services in sub-Saharan Africa: lessons learned', *Clinical Infectious Diseases*, 50(supp. 3): S238–44, programmes. comesa.int/index.php?option=com_content&view=article&id=163&Itemid=101&lang=en.

Hudson, H. (2009) 'When feminist theory meets peacebuilding policy: implications of gender mainstreaming and National Action Plans', Paper presented at the annual conference of the International Studies Association, New York, 15–18 February.

Hudson, J. (2007) 'Economic expansion into Africa', in A. Adebajo, A. Adedeji and C. Landsberg (eds), *South Africa in Africa: The Post-Apartheid Era*, Scottsville: University of KwaZulu-Natal Press.

Hull, C. and M. Derblom (2009) *Abandoning Frontline Trenches? Capabilities for Peace and Security in the SADC Region*, Stockholm: Swedish Defence Research Agency.

Human Sciences Research Council (HSRC) (1995) 'A research review of the policies surrounding the issue of the free movement of people across international borders with specific reference to southern Africa and the particular effect thereof on South Africa', Tshwane: Human Sciences Research Council.

Ikenberry, J. G. and C. A. Kupchan (1990) 'Socialization and hegemonic power', *International Organization*, 44(3): 283.

Independent Online (2011) 'Why China invited SA to join BRIC', January, www.iol.co.za/business/business-news.

Industrial Development Corporation (IDC) (2006) *Annual Report*, www.idc.co.za/Conference%20Papers/2006/Africa%20Development%20Finance%20Week/LumkileMondi.pdf.

— (2009) 'IDC pushes for more support for local SMMEs', *Business Report*, 17 June.

— (2010) *Annual Report: Towards a New Developmental Growth Path*, www.idc.co.za.

Institute for Development Studies (2009) 'China and the global financial crisis: implications for low-income countries', Briefing no. 7, Brighton: University of Sussex, March.

Intergovernmental Panel on Climate Change (IPCC) (2007) *Climate Change 2007: Impacts, Adaptation, and Vulnerability – Working Group II Contribution to the Fourth Assessment Report of the Climate Change Intergovernmental Panel on Climate Change*, Cambridge: Cambridge University Press.

International AIDS Society (2010) 'Advancing evidence and equity: report on the XVIII International AIDS Conference (AIDS 2010)', Vienna, 18–23 July.

International Monetary Fund (IMF) (2010) 'South Africa: Article IV Consultation – Staff Report; Staff Supplement; Public Information Notice on the Executive Board Discussion'.

International Organization for Migration (2004) 'Partnership on HIV/AIDS and mobile populations in southern Africa', Pamphlet, April. See also SADC, 'SADC HIV prevention meeting'.

International Peace Academy (IPA) (2000) 'Southern Africa's evolving security architecture: problems and prospects', Seminar report, Gaborone, December.

International Rivers, People, Water, Life (2010) 'African dams briefing', Report, Berkeley, CA: International Rivers Africa Program.

International Union for Conservation of Nature (IUCN) (2010) 'The World Conservation Union: 2010 scoping paper', Pretoria, South Africa, www.countdown2010.net/2010/wp-content/uploads/Scoping-paper-Final.doc.

Interview (2009a) Personal communication with Mclay Kanyangarara, COMESA CCU, 17 February.

— (2009b) 'Perspectives on DFIs and on the DBSA's role in regional economic development', Interview with Tomaz Salomão, SADC Executive Secretary and former Mozambican planning minister.

— (2009c) L. Bottoman, email to the author, 14 December.

— (2010a) Personal communication with Alex Banda, SADC Secretariat, 28 January.

— (2010b) L. Bottoman, telephone conversation, 1 February.

— (2010c) Telephone interview with Lieutenant Colonel T. Mothae, 4 February.

— (2010d) Telephone interview with South African government official, 18 December.

— (2010e) Personal communication with K. Mudambo, SADC Secretariat, 5 August.

Jackson, S. (1995) 'China's Third World foreign policy: the case of Angola and Mozambique, 1961–93', *China Quarterly*, 142: 389–422.

Jeong, H. (2005) *Peacebuilding in Post-conflict Societies: Strategies and Process*, London: Lynne Rienner.

Jiang, W. (2009) 'A Chinese "Marshall Plan" or business', *Asia Times* (online), 14 January, atimes.com.

Johnson, P. and D. Martin (eds) (1986) *Destructive Engagement: Southern Africa at War*, Harare: Zimbabwe Publishing House.

Joint United Nations Programme on HIV/AIDS (UNAIDS) (2005) *Operational Guide on Gender and HIV/AIDS: A Rights-based Approach*, Amsterdam: UNAIDS Inter-Agency Task Team on Gender and HIV/AIDS and KIT Publishers, www.genderandaids.org/downloads/events/Operational%20Guide.pdf.

— (2006) 'Report on the global AIDS epidemic', May.

— (2008a) 'Achieving the MDGs: why the AIDS response counts', www.unaids.org/en/KnowledgeCentre/Resources/FeatureStories/archive/2008/20080925_Achieving_MDG.asp.

— (2008b) 'Fact sheet: AIDS funding', data.unaids.org/pub/FactSheet/2009/20090209_fs_available funding_en.pdf.

— (2010a) 'AIDS epidemic update: December 1998', data.unaids.org/publications/irc-pub06/epiupdate98_en.pdf.

— (2010b) 'Sub-Saharan Africa: latest epidemiological trends', www.unaids.org/en/media/unaids/contentassets/dataimport/pub/factsheet/2009/20091124_fs_ssa_en.pdf.

— (2010c) 'Swaziland: HIV and AIDS estimates', www.unaids.org/en/regions-countries/countries/swaziland.

Joint United Nations Programme on HIV/AIDS (UNAIDS) and World Bank (2009) 'The global economic crisis and HIV prevention and treatment programmes: vulnerabilities and impact', June, data.unaids.org/pub/Report/2009/jc1734_econ_crisis_hiv_response_en.pdf.

Jones, E. and D. F. Marti (2009) 'Updating EPAs: rising to the challenge', in E. Jones and D. F. Marti, *Updating Economic Partnership Agreements to Today's Global Challenges*, Economic Policy Paper no. 9, Washington, DC: German Marshall Foundation, p. 9.

Jones, P. G. and P. K. Thornton (2003) 'The potential impacts of climate change on maize production in Africa and Latin America in 2055', *Global Environment Change – Human and Policy Dimensions*, 13(1): 51–9.

Jones, R. (2005) *Rising Up in Response: Women's Rights Activism in Conflict*, Urgent Action Fund, AWID, 4 March.

Jusu-Sheriff, Y. (2004) 'Civil society', in A. Adebajo and I. Rashid (eds), *West Africa's Security Challenges: Building Peace in a Troubled Region*, Boulder, CO: Lynne Rienner, p. 265.

Kadzandira, J. M. (2007) *Regional Evidence Building Agenda (REBA) Case-Study on the Input Subsidy Program, Malawi*, Report prepared for REBA of the Regional Hunger and Vulnerability Programme (RHVP), June.

Kandji, S. T. and L. Verchot (2006) *Climate Change and Climate Variability in Southern Africa: Impacts and Adaptation in the Agricultural Sector*, Nairobi: United Nations Environment Programme and World Agro-Forestry Centre.

Kaunda, J. M. and F. Zizhou (2009) 'Furthering Southern African integration', in *Proceedings of the 2008 FOPRISA Annual Conference*, Gaborone: Botswana Institute for Development Policy Analysis, pp. 33–4.

Keck, A. and R. Piermartini (2005) 'The economic impact of EPAs in SADC countries', Discussion paper, Geneva: World Trade Organization, August.

Keepin, W. (2007) *Divine Duality: The Power of Reconciliation Between Women and Men*, Arizona: Hohm.

Kegley, C. W., Jr (2007) *World Politics: Trend and Transformation*, 11th edn, Belmont, CA: Wadsworth Publishing.

Keohane, R. and R. Gilpin (2006) 'Two-level games and the Africa dilemma', Discussed in H. Stephan et al., *The Scramble for Africa in the 21st Century: A View from the South*, Cape Town: Renaissance, p. 225.

Kesselman, B. (2009) 'Human security in the SADC region', *Pax-Africa: Africa Peace and Security Agenda*, 5(1), March.

Khadiagala, G. M. (1994) *Allies in Adversity: The Frontline States in Southern African Security, 1975–1993*, Athens: University of Ohio Press.

— (2001) 'The United States and Africa: beyond the Clinton administration', *SAIS Review*, 21(1): 270.

— (2007) *Allies in Adversity: The Frontline States in Southern Africa, 1975–1993*, Lanham, MD: University Press of America.

Khoza, R. (2003) 'Eskom's new focus and outward looking policies', Chairperson's report, in H. Stephan et al., *The Scramble for Africa in the 21st Century: A View from the South*, Cape Town: Renaissance, p. 315.

Kirk, R. and M. Stern (2003) 'The new Southern African Customs Union Agreement', Africa Working Paper no. AWPS57, Washington, DC: World Bank.

Kissinger, H. (2001) *Does the United States Need a Foreign Policy?*, New York: Simon and Schuster.

Klot, J. (2007) 'Women and peacebuilding', Independent expert paper commissioned by the United Nations Development Fund for Women (UNIFEM) and the UN's Peacebuilding Support Office (PBSO).

Klotz, A. (2000) 'Migration after apartheid: deracialising South African foreign policy', *Third World Quarterly*, 21(5): 831–47.

Kohnert, D. (2008) 'EU–African economic relations: continuing dominance, traded for aid?', in German Institute of Global and Area Studies and Institute of African Affairs, MPRA Paper no. 9434, 3 July, p. 13.

Kolstad, I. and A. Wigg (2009) 'Chinese investment in SADC: a global perspective?', in FOPRISA Report no. 7, *Furthering Southern African Integration*, pp. 194–5.

Konings, P. J. (2007) 'China and Africa: building a strategic partnership', *Journal of Developing Societies*, 23(3): 341–67.

Koops, J. and J. Varwick (2008) *Ten Years of SHIRBRIG: Lessons Learned, Development Prospects, and Strategic Opportunities for Germany*, Berlin: Global Public Policy Institute.

Kornegay, F. (2000) 'The United States presidential elections: implications for Africa and South Africa', *Global Insight*, 4: 1.

— (2008) 'Africa's strategic diplomatic engagement with China', in H. Edinger,

H. Herman and J. Jansson (eds), *New Impulses from the South: China's Engagement of Africa*, Stellenbosch, South Africa: Centre for Chinese Studies, pp. 3–12.

— (2010) 'United States–South African relations: exploring new directions in an ambivalent relationship', Unpublished paper.

Kynoch, G. and T. Ulicki (2001) 'Cross-border raiding and community conflict in the Lesotho–South African border zone', Migration Policy Series no. 21, Cape Town: SAMP.

Laker, J. (2010) 'Gender and democracy in Africa', Paper presented at the biannual conference of the South African Association of Political Studies (SAAPS), Stellenbosch, 1–4 September.

Landsberg, C. (2003) 'The United States and Africa: malign neglect', in D. Malone and Y. Foong Khong (eds), *Unilateralism and US Foreign Policy*, London: Lynne Rienner, p. 351.

— (2004) *The Quiet Diplomacy of Liberation: International Politics and South Africa's Transition*, Johannesburg: Jacana.

— (2007) 'The Making of the AU and NEPAD', in A. Adebajo et al. (eds), *South Africa in Africa: The Post-Apartheid Era*, Scottsville: University of KwaZulu-Natal Press.

Landsberg, C. and D. Monyae (2006) 'South Africa's foreign policy: carving a global niche', *South African Journal of International Affairs*, 13(2): 131–45.

Langton, D. (2008) 'U.S. trade and investment relationship with sub-Saharan Africa: the African Growth and Opportunity Act and beyond', Report no. RL31772, Washington, DC: Congressional Research Service.

Le Pere, G. and G. Shelton (2007) *China, Africa, and South Africa: South–South Co-operation in a Global Era*, Midrand: Institute for Global Dialogue.

Lee, M. C. (1989) *SADCC: The Political Economy of Development in Southern Africa*, Nashville, TN: Winston-Derek.

— (2003) *The Political Economy of Regionalism in Southern Africa*, Lansdowne, South Africa: University of Cape Town Press.

— (2009) 'Trade relations between the European Union and sub-Saharan Africa under the Cotonou Agreement', in R. Southall and H. Melber (eds), *A New Scramble for Africa: Imperialism, Investment, and Development*, Scottsville: University of KwaZulu-Natal Press, p. 84.

Lefko-Everett, K. (2009) 'We cannot afford a fresh outbreak of xenophobia', *Pretoria News*, 5 August.

Legum, C. (ed.) (1981) *Africa Contemporary Record: Annual Survey and Documents, 1979–1980*, New York: Africana Publishing House.

Lerner, G. (1986) *The Creation of Patriarchy*, New York: Oxford University Press.

Lesotho Ministry of Finance (2010) Minister of finance, 'Budget Speech to Parliament', www.lesotho.gov.ls/documents/speeches.php.

Lewis, P. (1996) 'Economic reform and political transition in Africa: the quest for a politics of development', *World Politics*, 49(1): 92–129.

Links, E. (1998) 'The European Union and southern Africa: between Lomé and a free trade agreement', in G. Mills, *Southern Africa into the Next Millennium*, Johannesburg: South African Institute of International Affairs (SAIIA).

Long, S. (2003) *More than a Name: State-sponsored Homophobia and Its Consequences in Southern Africa*, New York: Human Rights Watch and International Gay and Lesbian Human Rights Commission.

Lopi, B. (n.d.) 'Is gender-based violence adequately addressed in SADC?', *Southern African News Features (SANF)*, www.sardc.net/editorial/newsfeature/gender.htm.

Lucas, R. (1987) 'Emigration to South Africa's mines', *American Economic Review*, 77(3): 317.

Lynes, K. and G. Torry (eds) (2005) *From Local to Global: Making Peace Work for Women*, New York: Working Group on Women, Peace, and Security.

Madakufamba, M. (2007) 'SADC in the 21st century', *Open Space*, 2(1): 90.

Magongo, T. (2010) 'Umbutfo Swaziland Defence Force (USDF) HIV/AIDS programme', Presentation at the SADC Military HIV and AIDS Technical Committee Workshop, Victoria Falls, Zimbabwe, 2–4 August.

Mahmud, T. (1997) 'Migration, identity, and the colonial encounter', *Oregon Law Review*, 77: 636–7.

Makoni, S. (1981) 'SADCC's new strategies', *Africa Report*, 32(3): 31–2.

— (1990) 'SADDC in a post-apartheid environment', *Africa Report*, 35(5): 35.

Malaquias, A. (2002) 'Dysfunctional foreign policy: Angola's unsuccessful quest for security since independence', in K. G. Adar and R. Ajulu (eds), *Globalization and Emerging Trends in African States' Foreign Policy-making Process: A Comparative Perspective of Southern Africa*, Aldershot: Ashgate, pp. 19–31.

— (2011) 'Angola's foreign policy: pragmatic recalibrations', Forthcoming occasional paper to be published by the South African Institute of International Affairs, Johannesburg.

Malawi Government Vulnerability Assessment Committee (2009) 'Vulnerability forecast', *Bulletin*, 5(1), July.

Mandaza, I. (1987) 'Perspectives on economic cooperation and autonomous development in southern Africa', in S. Amin, D. Chitala and I. Mandaza (eds), *SADCC: Prospects for Disengagement and Development in Southern Africa*, London: Zed Books.

Mandaza, I. and A. Tostensen (1994) *Southern Africa: In Search of a Common Future*, Gaborone: Southern African Development Community.

Mandrup, T. (2009) 'South Africa and the SADC Stand-by Force', *Scientia Militaria: South African Journal of Military Studies*, 37(2): 4, 10.

Manji, F. and S. Marks (eds) (2007) *African Perspectives on China in Africa*, Cape Town: Fahamu and Pambazuka.

Martin, C. (1997) *Unconsummated Union*, Manchester: Manchester University Press.

Martin, G. (2002) 'African regional cooperation and integration', in G. Martin, *African World Politics: A Pan-African Perspective*, Trenton, NJ: Africa World Press.

Martin, W. G. (2008) 'South Africa's imperial futures: Washington Consensus, Bandung Consensus, or People's Consensus', *African Sociological Review*, 12(1): 131.

Matlosa, K. (1999) 'The Lesotho conflict: major causes and management', in K. Lambrechts (ed.), *Crisis in Lesotho: The Challenge of Managing Conflict in Southern Africa*, Johannesburg: Foundation for Global Dialogue, pp. 6–10.

— (2007a) 'Regional integration and civil society engagement in southern Africa: can SADC-CNGO make a difference?', *Open Space*, 2(1): 97.

— (2007b) 'Regional security in southern Africa', in A. Adebajo, A. Adedeji and C. Landsberg (eds), *South Africa in Africa: The Post-Apartheid Era*, Scottsville: University of KwaZulu-Natal Press.

— (2008) 'Elections and conflict in southern Africa', in A. Nhema and P. Zeleza (eds), *The Resolution of African Conflicts: The Management of Conflict Resolution and Post-Conflict Reconstruction*, Oxford: James Currey.

Matlosa, K. and K. Lotshwao (2009) *Political Integration and Democratization in Southern Africa: Progress, Problems, and Prospects*, Johannesburg: Electoral Institute of Southern Africa, 18 December.

Matlosa, K., G. Khadiagala and V. Shale (eds) (2010) *When Elephants Fight: Preventing and Resolving Election-related Conflicts in Africa*, Johannesburg: EISA Books.

Matthew, R. A. et al. (eds) (2010) *Global Environmental Change and Human Security: Understanding Environmental Threats to Well-being and Livelihoods*, Cambridge: Massachusetts Institute of Technology Press.

Maunder, N. (2006) Cited in A. Witteveen, 'Chronic food insecurity and vulnerable livelihoods in southern Africa: exploring the issues and reflecting on a role for Oxfam GB', Unpublished paper, Pretoria.

Maunder, N. and S. Wiggins (2006) *Food Security in Southern Africa: Changing the Trend? Review of Lessons Learnt on Recent Responses to Chronic and Transitory Hunger and Vulnerability*, Oxford: Oxfam Great Britain, World Vision International, CARE, RHVP and OCHA.

Mbeki, T. (2005) 'Speech at the Second Joint Sitting of the Third Democratic Parliament', Cape Town, 11 February, www.info.gov.za/speeches/2005/05021110501001.htm.

Mbuende, K. (2011) 'Southern African regional integration: the need for acceleration', Speech delivered at the South African Institute of International Affairs, Johannesburg, 22 February.

McAskie, C. (2008) 'Women's equal participation in conflict prevention, management, and conflict resolution and in post-conflict peacebuilding', UN Commission on the Status of Women, 52nd session, www.un.org/peace/peacebuilding/Statements/ASG%20Carolyn%20McAskie/ASG%20MCAskie%20CSW%20SPEECH%2029.02.08.pdf.

McCarthy, C. (2003) 'The Southern African Customs Union in transition', *African Affairs*, 102.

— (2008) 'The challenge of reconciling revenue distribution and industrial development in SACU', in B. Vickers (ed.), *Industrial Policy in the Southern African Customs Union: Past Experiences, Future Plans*, Midrand, South Africa: Institute for Global Dialogue (IGD), p. 30.

— (2009) 'Perspectives on the Southern African Customs Union', TRALAC: Trade Law Centre for Southern Africa, 29 July, www.tralac.org/cgi-bin/giga.cgi?cmd=cause_dir_news_item&news_id=70726&cause_id=1694.

Mead, D. C. (1969) 'Economic cooperation in East Africa', *Journal of Modern African Studies*, 7(2).

Mehra, R. and G. R. Gupta (2006) *Gender Mainstreaming: Making It Happen*, February, siteresources.worldbank.org/INTGENDER/Resources/MehraGuptaGenderMainstreamingMakingItHappen.pdf.

Menon, A. (2008) *Europe: The State of the Union*, London: Atlantic.

Messerlin, P. (2009) 'Economic partnership agreements: how to rebound?', in E. Jones and D. F. Marti (eds), *Updating Economic Partnership Agreements to Today's Global Challenges*, Economic Policy Paper no. 9, Washington, DC: German Marshall Foundation, p. 22.

Meyns, P. (2002) 'Strengthening regional institutions: politics and governance in the SADC region', in D. Hansohm, C. Peters-Berries, W. Breyten Bach and P. Meyns (eds), *Monitoring Regional Integration in Southern Africa*, Windhoek: Gamsberg Macmillan.

Michal, E., G. Häfner, R. Huber and P. Vogel (2009) *Europe: 'Not Without the People!'*, Hamburg: VSA.

Michalak, W. and R. Gibb (1997) 'Trading blocs and multilateralism in the world economy', *Annals of the Association of American Geographers*, 87(2): 264–79.

Millennium Ecosystem Assessment (2005) *Ecosystems and Human Well-being: Synthesis*, Report of the Millennium Ecosystem Assessment, Washington, DC: Island.

Miller E. (2009) *The Inability of Peacekeeping to Address the Security Dilemma: A Case Study of the Rwandan–Congolese Security Dilemma and the United Nation's Mission in the Congo*, Saarbrucken: Lambert Academic.

Mkapa, B. (2004) Foreword to Southern African Development Community (SADC), *Regional Indicative Strategic Plan*, Gaborone.

Mmegi/The Reporter (2009) 'Zimbabwe immigrants claim abuse', 16 February.

Modisaotsile, I. (n.d.) 'HIV and AIDS in the SADC region: responses and challenges', www.uneca.org/tap/InterAgency/HIV-AIDS-SADC-Region.ppt.

Mohamudally, P. A. (2005) *Regional Indica-*

tive Strategic Development Plan (RISDP), Mauritius.

Mohanty, R. (2010) 'The infinite agenda of social justice: Dalit mobilization in the institutions of local governance', in V. Schattan, P. Coelho and B. von Lieres (eds), *Mobilising for Democracy: Citizen Action and the Politics of Public Participation*, London: Zed Books, p. 97.

Monson, J. (2008) 'Liberating labour? Constructing anti-hegemony on the TAZARA railway in Tanzania, 1965–76', in C. Alden, D. Large and R. S. de Oliveira, *China Returns to Africa: A Rising Power and a Continent Embrace*, London: Hurst, pp. 197–219.

Monyae, D. (2010) 'South Africa's foreign policy and the United Nations in Africa', Paper written for the United Nations Development Programme.

Morna, C. L. and L. J. Nyakujarah (eds) (2010) *SADC Gender Protocol 2010 Barometer*, Johannesburg: Southern Africa Gender Protocol Alliance.

Morna, C. L. and D. Walter (eds) (2009) *SADC Gender Protocol Baseline Barometer*, Johannesburg: Gender Links.

Moser, C. (1999) 'Violence and poverty in South Africa: their impact on household relations and social capital', Poverty and Inequality Informal Discussion Paper Series, Washington, DC: World Bank.

Moyo, S. and R. Hall (2007) 'Conflict and land reform in southern Africa: how exceptional is South Africa?', in A. Adebajo et al. (eds.), *South Africa in Africa: The Post-Apartheid Era*, Scottsville: University of KwaZulu-Natal Press, pp. 150–76.

Mthetwa, J. et al. (n.d.) 'Position paper: climate change, its impact on health, and policy responses in the SADC region', Unpublished paper, Gaborone: SADC Secretariat.

Mugomba, A. T. (1978) 'Regional organizations and African underdevelopment: the collapse of the East African Community', *Journal of Modern African Studies*, 2(2).

Mulama, J. (2010) 'Women leaders ask where is our money', ipsnews.net/Africa/nota.asp?idnews=42914.

Murray, R. (2004) *Human Rights in Africa: From the OAU to the African Union*, Cambridge: Cambridge University Press.

Musaba, L. (2010) 'South Africa country seminar on cross border trading and SAPP day ahead market', www.sapp.co.zw.

Mutambara, T. E. (2009) 'Regional transport challenges within the Southern African Development Community and their implications for economic integration and development', *Journal of Contemporary African Studies*, 27(4), October.

Mwaniki, D. (2009) 'Supporting the peace in the DRC', *Pax-Africa: African Peace and Security Agenda*, 5(1), March.

Mwapachu, J. (2011) 'Southern Africa: region moves to set up free trade area', *All Africa*, 25 January.

Myataza, T. (2009) 'Towards security co-operation between African sub-regional organisations and the African Union: the case of Southern African Development Community and the AU', Unpublished paper, Grahamstown, November.

Nagar, D. I. (2010a) 'Towards a Pax Africana: southern Africa's development community's architecture and evolving peacekeeping efforts, 1996–2010', Master's thesis, University of Cape Town, South Africa.

— (2010b) 'Africa's peace efforts at risk from HIV/AIDS', *Business Day* (South Africa), 26 November.

Naidu, S. (2008) 'Balancing a strategic partnership? South Africa–China relations', in K. Ampiah and S. Naidu (eds), *Crouching Tiger, Hidden Dragon? Africa and China*, Scottsville, South Africa: University of KwaZulu-Natal Press, p. 172.

Namibian (2010) 'Namibia trade with China up by 600 percent', 13 August.

Nathan, L. (2009a) 'The AU and regional organisations in Africa: security communities or communities of insecurity?', *African Studies Review*, December.

— (2009b) 'The failure of the SADC Organ: regional security arrangements in southern Africa, 1992–2003', Unpublished PhD thesis, Cape Town: University of Cape Town.

Naysmith, S., A. De Waal and A. Whiteside (2010) 'Revisiting new variant famine: the case of Swaziland', *Food Security*, 1(3): 251–60.

Ndinga-Muvumba, A. and R. Pharoah (eds) (2008) *HIV/AIDS and Society in South Africa*, Scottsville, South Africa: University of KwaZulu-Natal Press.

Ndulo, M. (2008) 'Chinese investments in Africa: a case study of Zambia', in K. Ampiah and S. Naidu, *Crouching Tiger, Hidden Dragon? Africa and China*, Scottsville, South Africa: University of KwaZulu-Natal Press, p. 142.

Neocosmos, M. (2006) 'From "foreign natives" to "native foreigners": explaining xenophobia in post-apartheid South Africa', in Council for the Development of Social Science Research in Africa, *Citizenship and Nationalism, Identity and Politics*, Dakar.

Nesadurai, H. (2002) 'Globalisation and economic regionalism: a survey and critique of the literature', Working Paper no. 108/02, Centre for the Study of Globalisation and Regionalism, University of Warwick, November, www.csgr.org.

New Partnership for Africa's Development (NEPAD) (2009) *CAADP Pillar III Framework for African Food Security (FAFS)*, n.p.: African Union and NEPAD.

Ngoma, N. (2003) 'SADC: towards a security community?', *African Studies Review*, 12(3).

— (2005) 'The Organ on Politics, Defence, and Security: the rise and fall of a security model?' in N. Ngoma, *Prospects for a Security Community in Southern Africa: An Analysis of Regional Security in the Southern African Development Community*, Pretoria: Institute for Security Studies.

Nolutshungu, S. C. (1982) 'Sceptical notes on "constructive engagement"', *Issue: A Journal of Opinion*, 12(3/4): 8.

Nsekela, A. (1981) *Southern Africa: Toward Economic Liberation*, London: Rex Collings.

Nyambe, J. and K. Schade (2009) 'Progress towards the SADC free trade area: the challenges', in J. Mayuyuka Kaunda and F. Zizhou, *Furthering Southern African Integration: Proceedings of the 2008 FOPRISA Annual Conference*, Gaborone: Botswana Institute for Development Policy Analysis and Lightbooks, pp. 33–51.

Nyamnjoh, F. B. (2006) *Insiders and Outsiders: Citizenship and Xenophobia in Contemporary Southern Africa*, London: Zed Books.

— (2007) 'Ever diminishing circles: the paradoxes of belonging in Botswana', in M. de la Cadena and O. Starn (eds), *Indigenous Today*, Oxford: Berg, p. 306.

Nyamnjoh, F. and P. Mususa (2010) 'Migration and xenophobia in southern Africa', Paper presented at the CCR seminar 'Peacebuilding in Southern Africa'.

Nyerere, J. (1984) 'North–South dialogue', *Third World Quarterly*, 6(4): 836.

O'Brien, K. (2006) 'Are we missing the point? Global environmental change as an issue of human security', *Global Environmental Change*, 16(1): 1–3.

O'Brien, K. and R. Leichenko (2007) 'Human security, vulnerability, and sustainable adaptation', in United Nations Development Programme (UNDP), *Human Development Report 2007/2008: Fighting Climate Change: Human Solidarity in a Divided World*, Human Development Report Office Occasional Paper 2007/9.

Odera, J. and I. Zirimwabagabo (2009) 'The UN Development Fund for Women', in A. Adebajo (ed.), *From Global Apartheid to Global Village: Africa and the United Nations*, Pietermaritzburg: University of KwaZulu-Natal Press.

O'Grady, V. (1987) 'Corridors of commerce', *African Review of Commerce and Technology*, 1: 8357.

Ohlson, T. and S. Stedman (1994) *The New is Not Yet Born: Conflict Resolution in Southern Africa*, Washington, DC: Brookings Institution.

Okumu, W. (2007) 'Africa Command: opportunity for enhanced engagement or the militarization of U.S.–Africa relations?', Testimony to the US House Committee on Foreign Affairs, Subcommittee on Africa and Global Health, www.internationalrelations. house.gov/110/oku080207.htm.

Oman, C. (1994) *Globalisation and Regionalisation: The Challenge for Developing Countries*, Paris: Organisation for Economic Co-operation and Development.

Omari, A. H. and P. Macaringue (2007) 'Southern African security in historical perspective', in G. Cawthra, A. du Pisani and A. Omari, *Security and Democracy in Southern Africa*, Johannesburg: Wits University Press.

Oosthuizen, G. (2006) *The Southern African Development Community: The Organisation, Its Policies and Prospects*, Johannesburg: Institute for Global Dialogue.

Osei-Hwedie, B. Z. (1983) 'The Frontline States: cooperation for the liberation of southern Africa', *Journal of African Studies*, 10(4).

Oucho, J. (2007) 'Migration in southern Africa: migration management initiatives for SADC member states', Paper Series no. 157, Pretoria: Institute for Security Studies, December.

Oucho, J. and J. Crush (2001) 'Contra free movement: South Africa and the SADC migration protocols', *Africa Today*, 48(3): 146.

Overholt, W. H. (2010) 'China in the global financial crisis: rising influence, rising challenges', *Washington Quarterly*, 33(1): 29.

Overseas Development Institute (ODI) '1997 global hunger and food security after the World Food Summit', Briefing paper, www.odi.org.uk/publications/briefing-papers/1997/1-global-hunger-food-security-world-food-summit.pdf.

Oxfam International (2006) 'Causing hunger: an overview of the food crisis', Oxfam Briefing Paper 91.

Paavola, J. (2008) 'Science and social justice in the governance of adaptation to climate change', *Environmental Politics*, 17(4): 644–59.

Palmer, R. (2010) 'An annotated guide to the bibliographies on biofuels, land rights in Africa, and global land grabbing', September, www.oxfam. org.uk/resources/learning/landrights/downloads/annotated_guide_to_bibliogs_biofuels_africanlandrights_global_land_grabbing_sept_2010.pdf.

Pankhurst, D. (2000) 'Women, gender, and peacebuilding', Working Paper no. 5, Bradford: Centre for Conflict Resolution, University of Bradford.

Paulo, M. J. (2004) 'The role of the United Nations in the Angolan peace process', www.c-r.org/our-work/accord/angola/un-role.php.

Pax Africa (2009) 'SADC and Pax Africa host conference on human security', *Africa Peace and Security Agenda*, 5(1): 32.

Peace Women (2010) 'Southern Africa: regional consultation on the Africa UNiTE campaign', www.peace women.org/news_article.php?id=825&type=news.

Peberdy, S. (2002) 'Hurdles to trade? South Africa's immigration policy and informal sector cross-border traders in the SADC', Paper presented at a training course for the United Kingdom's Department for International Development, March.

Phinnemore, D. and A. Warleigh-Lack (2009) *Reflections on European Integration. 50 Years of the Treaty of Rome*, Basingstoke: Palgrave Macmillan.

Pillay, S. (2008) *Citizenship, Violence, and Xenophobia: Perceptions from South African Communities*, Pretoria: Human Sciences Research Council, Democracy and Governance Programme.

Pinder, J. and S. Usherwood (2007) *The European Union: A Very Short Introduction*, Oxford: Oxford University Press.

Potts, D. and T. Bowyer-Bower (eds) (2004)

Eastern and Southern Africa: Development Challenges in a Volatile Region, Harlow: Pearson/Prentice Hall.

Pretoria News (2008a) 'Flames and mobs' fury', 21 February.

— (2008b) 'Xenophobia the result of a broken African psyche', 15 May.

Qhena, G. (2006) 'DFI positioning', IDC case study, 23 November, www.idc.co.za/Conference%20Papers/2006/Africa%20Development%20Finance%20Week/GeoffreyQhena.pdf.

Ramdas, K. (2010) 'It ain't what you do, it's the way that you do it', *Responsive Philanthropy: NCRP's Quarterly Journal*, Summer, pp. 1, 11–14.

Ramsamy, P. (2000) *Poverty Reduction: A Top Priority in SADC's Integration Agenda*, Gaborone: SADC Review.

— (2009) 'African regional integration', Paper presented at the Department of International Relations and Cooperation conference 'Closing the Gap Between Domestic and Foreign Policies', Pretoria, 5/6 November.

Rao, A. (2008) Cited in J. Jaquette and A. Rao, 'Setting the context: approaches to promoting gender equity', in E. Bryan and J. Varat (eds), *Strategies for Promoting Equity in Developing Countries: Lessons, Challenges, and Opportunities*, Washington, DC: Woodrow Wilson International Center for Scholars.

Rapoo, T. (2007) *Gender and the New Africa Agenda: Examining Progress towards Gender Equality in SADC*, Policy Brief no. 49, Johannesburg: Centre for Policy Studies.

Ratha, D. and W. Shaw (2007) 'South–South migration and remittances', World Bank Working Paper no. 102.

Ravenhill, J. (1985) 'The future of regionalism in Africa', in R. I. Onwuka and A. Sesay, *The Future of Regionalism in Africa*, London: Macmillan.

Redi, O. (2010) 'Women's Decade: greater attention to implementation', Inter Press Service News Online, ipsnews.net/news.asp?idnews=50419.

Regional Climate Change Programme

(n.d.) www.rccp.org.za/index.php?option=com_content&view=article&id=68&Itemid=61&lang=en.

Reuters (2010) 'BHP seeks Congo power project to replace Westcor', 26 February, www.reuters.com/article/2010/02/26/congo-democratic-ingax-idUSLDE61O2QK20100226.

Reyntiens, F. (2009) *The Great African War: Congo and Regional Geopolitics, 1996–2006*, Cambridge: Cambridge University Press.

Richter, L., G. Foster and L. Sherr (2006) *Where the Heart is: Meeting the Psychosocial Needs of Young Children in the Context of HIV/AIDS*, The Hague: Bernard van Leer.

Robson, P. (1967) 'Economic integration in southern Africa', *Journal of Modern African Studies*, 5(4).

— (1980) *The Economics of International Integration*, London: Allen and Unwin.

— (1998) *The Economics of International Integration*, London: Routledge.

Rocha, J. (2009) 'The implementation of NEPAD in the SADC region', *Pax-Africa: African Peace and Security Agenda*, 5(1), March.

Rogerson, C. M. (2000) 'Spatial Development Initiatives in southern Africa: the Maputo Development Corridor', *Tijdschrift voor economische en Sociale Geografie*, 92(3): 324–46.

Rohmer-Heitman, H. (2009) 'A400M – R30 billion saved? Not really', *Weekend Argus*, 11 November.

Roland, J. (1967) 'The experience of integration in French-speaking Africa', in A. Hazelwood (ed.), *African Integration and Disintegration*, New York: Oxford University Press.

Ronald, H. (1972) *The Failure of South African Expansion, 1908–1948*, London: Macmillan.

Rotberg, R. (2000) *Peacekeeping and Peace Enforcement in Africa*, Washington, DC: Brookings Institution.

Rowlands, I. H. (ed.) (1998) *Climate Change Cooperation in Southern Africa*, London: Earthscan.

— (2005) 'Regional approaches to global

climate change policy in southern Africa', in Pak S. Low (ed.), *Climate Change and Africa*, Cambridge: Cambridge University Press, pp. 150–62.

Rupiya, M. (ed.) (2006) *The Enemy Within: Southern African Militaries' Quarter-century Battle with HIV and AIDS*, Pretoria: Institute for Security Studies.

Sachikonye, L. (1995) 'Civil society, social movements, and democracy in southern Africa', *Innovation*, 8(4).

— (2008) 'Crouching tiger, hidden agenda? Zimbabwe–China relations', in K. Ampiah and S. Naidu, *Crouching Tiger, Hidden Dragon? Africa and China*, Scottsville: University of KwaZulu-Natal Press, pp. 124–37.

Sachs, W. (2009) 'Climate change and human rights', in *Critical Currents, 6: Contours of Climate Justice – Ideas for Shaping New Climate and Energy Policies*, Uppsala: Dag Hammarskjöld Foundation, pp. 85–91.

SADC (1992) *Declaration, Treaty, and Protocol of Southern African Development Community*, Gaborone.

— (2003a) *SADC HIV and AIDS Strategic Framework and Programme of Action: 2003–2007.*

— (2003b) *The Regional Indicative Strategic Development Plan.*

— (2004a) *Strategic Indicative Plan for the Organ on Politics, Defence and Security Cooperation*, www.sadc.int.

— (2004b) *Institutional Framework for the SADC HIV and AIDS Programme*, Gaborone: SADC HIV and AIDS Unit.

— (2005) *Feasibility Study for the Production and Use of Biofuel in the SADC Region*, Gaborone.

— (2006) 'Expert think tank meeting on HIV prevention in high-prevalence countries in southern Africa', Meeting report, Maseru, Lesotho, 10–12 May.

— (2007a) 'SADC member states HIV and AIDS epidemic update: proposed report format', July, www.sadc.int.

— (2007b) *African Conference of (Staff College) Commandants*, www.acoc-Africa.org/docs/28JuneCJACInstruction.pdf.

— (2007c) *Establishing the SADC Land Reform Support Facility and Inception Activities*, Final report, September.

— (2008a) *Protocol on Gender and Development*, www.genderlinks.org.za/page/sadc-protocol-policy.

— (2008b) *Protocol on Politics, Defence, and Security Cooperation.*

— (2008c) *SADC HIV and AIDS Epidemic Report*, Gaborone: SADC HIV and AIDS Unit.

— (2008d) *The Impact of Climate Change on the Poverty Situation in the SADC Region*, Background document, Gaborone: SADC Secretariat.

— (2008e) 'SADC Secretariat Capacity Development Framework', SADC/CM/2/2008/3.5, Gaborone, March.

— (2009a) 'Call: development of a SADC regional environmental mainstreaming instrument', Gaborone, August.

— (2009b) 'Final communiqué: SADC Summit of Heads of State and Government', Kinshasa, 8 September.

— (2009c) 'SADC Infrastructure Development Status Report for Council and Summit', September, www.sadc.int/cms/uploads/K-7543%20RTFP%20SADC%20Infrastructure%20brochure_English_V11_LR.pdf.

— (2010a) 'SADC pushes free trade, Customs Union', 18 August, www.southafrica.info/africa/sadc-180810.htm.

— (2010b) *Southern Africa Today*, 12(6), October.

— (2010c) 'Investment Promotion Strategy to Promote Sustainable Investment into the SADC Region During the 2010 CAF Africa Cup of nations [10–31 January 2010] and the 2010 FIFA World Cup [11 June–11 July 2010]', Strategy document, www.sadc.int/cms/SADC%202010%20strategy(2).pdf.

SADC Parliamentary Forum (2001) 'Norms and standards for elections in the SADC region', Mimeo, Windhoek, Namibia.

— (2007) *Strategic Plan for SADC-PF on HIV and AIDS, 2007–2011*, www.sadcpf.org.

SADC Secretariat (2004) 'Principles and guidelines governing democratic elections in the SADC region', Mimeo, Gaborone.

SADC Treaty (n.d.) www.sadc.int/index/browse/page/119.

Sagala, J. K. (2006) 'HIV/AIDS and the military in sub-Saharan Africa: impact on military organizational effectiveness', *Africa Today*, 53(1): 53–77.

Salmi, J. (2000) 'Violence, democracy, and education: an analytical framework', LCSHD Paper Series no. 56, Washington, DC: World Bank.

Sanger, N. (2008) 'Foreigners know how to treat a woman: our South African brothers are players, abuse physically and emotionally; you can't depend on them – interrogating the links between xenophobic attitudes, gender, and male violence in Du Noon', Cape Town, www.boell.org.za/downloads/Report_on_Xenophobia_and_Gender.pdf.

Saunders, C. (2009) 'UN peacekeeping in southern Africa: Namibia, Angola, and Mozambique', in A. Adebajo (ed.), *From Global Apartheid to Global Village: Africa and the United Nations*, Pietermaritzburg: University of KwaZulu-Natal Press.

Schoeman, M. and C. Alden (2003) 'The hegemon that wasn't: South Africa's foreign policy towards Zimbabwe', *Strategic Review of Southern Africa*, 25(1).

Schönteich, M. (2001) 'HIV/AIDS and security', Regional Governance and AIDS Forum, Institute for Democracy in Africa (IDASA)/United Nations Development Programme (UNDP), HIV Development Project for Southern Africa, 2–4 April.

Schulze, R. E. (2005) 'Climate change and water assessments and analysis in SADC region, through the SADC Regional Vulnerability Assessment Committee: a five year programme (2005–09)', Gaborone.

Schwersensky, S. (2007) 'Harare's "look east" policy now focuses on China', in G. le Pere, *China in Africa: Mercantilist Predator, or Partner in Development?*, Johannesburg: Institute for Global Dialogue and the South African

Institute of International Affairs, pp. 186–200.

Sen, A. (1981) *Poverty and Famines: An Essay on Entitlement and Deprivation*, Oxford: Clarendon Press.

— (1999) *Development as Freedom*, Oxford: Oxford University Press.

Sharp, J. (2008) '"Fortress SA": xenophobic violence in South Africa', *Anthropology Today*, 24(4): 1–3.

Shell, R. (2000) 'Halfway to the holocaust: the economic demographic and social implication of the AIDS pandemic to the year 2010 in the southern African region', in *HIV/AIDS: A Threat to the African Renaissance*, Occasional Paper Series, Johannesburg: Konrad Adenauer Foundation.

Shelton, G. (2001) 'China's Africa policy and South Africa: building new economic partnerships', in *SA Yearbook of International Affairs*, Johannesburg: SAIIA, pp. 390–92.

— (2007) 'Afro-Chinese relations in an era of globalisation', in K. Prah, *Afro-Chinese Relations: Past, Present, and Future*, Rondebosch, Cape Town: CASAS, pp. 238–9.

Sherbourne, R. (2007) 'China's growing presence in Namibia', in G. le Pere, *China in Africa: Mercantilist Predator, or Partner in Development?*, Johannesburg: Institute for Global Dialogue and the South African Institute of International Affairs, pp. 161–2.

Short, H. W. (2006) 'Revitalizing the SADC economic development and integration agenda', Commandant's research paper, South African National Defence College, 31 October.

Sibanda, P. (1999) 'Lessons from UN peacekeeping in africa: from UNAVEM to MONUA', in J. Cilliers and G. Mills (eds), *From Peacekeeping to Complex Emergencies*, Johannesburg: South African Institute of International Affairs.

Sichone, O. (2008) 'Xenophobia and xenophilia in South Africa: African migrants in Cape Town', in P. Werbner (ed.), *Anthropology and the New Cosmopolitanism: Rooted, Feminist, and*

Vernacular Perspectives, Oxford: Berg, pp. 309–32.

Sidaway, J. and R. Gibb (1988) 'SADC, COMESA, SACU: contradictory formats for regional integration', in D. Simon (ed.), *South Africa in Southern Africa: Reconfiguring the Region*, Oxford: James Currey, ch. 10, pp. 164–84.

Sigsworth, R. (2008) 'Gender-based violence in transition', Concept paper produced for the Centre for the Study of Violence and Reconciliation's 'Violence and Transition' project roundtable, 7–9 May, Johannesburg.

Simapuka, L. F. (2010) 'Challenges of management of HIV infection in the Zambia Defence Force (ZDF)', Presentation at the SADC Military HIV and AIDS Technical Committee Workshop, Victoria Falls, Zimbabwe, 2–4 August.

Simelane, H. and J. Crush (2004) 'Swaziland moves: perceptions and patterns of modern migration', Migration Policy Series no. 2, Cape Town: SAMP.

Simon, D. (1998a) 'Shedding the past, shaping the future', in D. Simon (ed.), *South Africa in Southern Africa: Reconfiguring the Region*, Oxford: James Currey.

— (1998b) *South Africa in Southern Africa: Reconfiguring the Region*, Oxford: James Currey.

— (2007) 'Global change and urban risk: the challenge for African cities', *The Constitution*, 7(1): 3–22.

— (2010) 'The challenges of global environmental change for urban Africa', *Urban Forum*, 21(3): 235–48.

Simon, D. and H. Leck (2010) 'Urbanizing the global environmental change and human security agendas', *Climate and Development*, 2(3): 263–75.

Sims, B. M., S. Masamvu and H. Mirell (2010) 'Restrictive measures and Zimbabwe', www.swradioafrica.com/Documents/Idasa%20Restrictive%20Measures%20Study%20Zimbabwe.pdf.

Sisk, T. and A. Reynolds (eds) (1998) *Elections and Conflict Management in Africa*, Washington, DC: US Institute of Peace Press.

Söderbaum, F. (1996) *The New Regionalism and the Quest for Development Cooperation and Integration in Southern Africa*, Minor Field Study Series no. 73, Lund: Department of Economics, University of the Lund.

South Africa (1969) 'Customs Union Agreement between the Governments of the Republic of South Africa, the Republic of Botswana, the Kingdom of Lesotho, and the Kingdom of Swaziland', *Government Gazette*, 54(1212): 1–16, Pretoria: Government Printer.

South Africa Department of Health (2010) 'Universal access: treatment and prevention scale-up – the South African experience', Speech by Aaron Motsoaledi, South African minister of health, at the XVIIIth International AIDS Conference, 20 July, www.doh.gov.za/search/index.html.

South Africa Info (2004) 'Africa's biggest water project', 17 March, www.safrica.info/business/economy/infrastructure/sa-lesothowaterproject.htm.

South African Department of Defence (2004) *Bulletin*, 71, 15 September, www.dcc.mil.za/bulletins/Files/2004/71bulletin2004.htm.

South African Department of Economic Development (2010) *The New Growth Path*.

South African Department of Foreign Affairs (DFA) (2003) 'Developments relating to SADC, African Union, and NEPAD', Pretoria, 31 March.

— (2006) 'Revitalising the SADC economic development and integration agenda', Draft discussion paper prepared by the Inter-Departmental Task Team, Pretoria, June.

— (2008) 'Developments in the SADC region', Briefing to the diplomatic trainees, Pretoria: Foreign Service Institute, 16 April.

South African Department of International Relations and Cooperation (2010) *Annual Report 2009–10*, Pretoria.

South African Department of Trade and Industry (DTI) (2010) 'A South African trade policy and strategy framework', May, www.dti.gov.za/TPSF.pdf.

South African Institute of International Affairs (SAIIA) (2004) *SADC Barometer*, 5, April.

— (2010) 'One hundred years and not out: what future for SACU', Conference held by SAIIA, Pretoria, June, www.saiia.org.za/component/registrationpro/event/198/One-Hundred-Not-Out--What-Future-For-SACU.

South African Institute of Race Relations (2009/10) 'South Africa survey report', Johannesburg.

South Africa's Foreign Policy Discussion Document (2006) South African Department of Foreign Affairs.

Southall, R. and H. Melber (eds) (2009) *A New Scramble for Africa: Imperialism, Investment, and Development*, Scottsville, South Africa: University of KwaZulu-Natal Press, p. 73.

Southern Africa HIV and AIDS Information Dissemination Service (2011) 'About us', www.safaids.net/content/about-us.

Southern African Catholic Bishops Conference (2009) 'Human trafficking in South Africa: 2010 and beyond', www.sacbc.org.za/Site/index.php?option=com_content&view=article &id=286& Itemid=111.

Southern African Customs Union (SACU) Secretariat (2003) *Southern African Customs Union Agreement 2002*, Windhoek.

Southern African Development Community (SADC) (1993) 'Southern Africa: a framework and strategy for building the community', Gaborone.

— (2004) 'Dar es Salaam Declaration on Agriculture and Food Security in the SADC Region', 15 May, www.sadc.int/index/browse/page/173.

— (2007) *Today*, 10(2), August.

— (2009a) 'SADC HIV prevention meeting: achieving prevention targets', Meeting report, Johannesburg, 7–9 June.

— (2009b) *Food Agriculture and Natural Resources Directorate Annual Report, April 2008–March 2009*, Gaborone.

— (n.d.) 'Programme of action', www.sadc.int/index/print/63.

— (n.d.) *Declaration on Gender and Development*, www.sadc.int/index/browse/page/174.

Southern African Power Pool (SAPP) (n.d.) www.dme.gov.za/energy/electricity.stm#5.

Stephan, H. and A. F. Hervey (2008) 'New regionalism in southern Africa: functional developmentalism and the Southern African Power Pool', *Politeia*, 27(3).

Stephan, H., M. Power, A. Fane Hervey and R. Steenkamp Fonseca (2006) 'Regional theory and southern African regional solutions', in H. Stephan et al., *The Scramble for Africa in the 21st Century: A View from the South*, Cape Town: Renaissance.

Stern, N. (2007) *The Economics of Climate Change: The Stern Review*, Cambridge: Cambridge University Press.

Stiglitz, J. (2006) *Globalisation and Its Discontents*, London: Penguin.

Stolcke, V. (1995) 'Talking culture: new boundaries, new rhetorics of exclusion in Europe', *Current Anthropology*, 36(1): 12.

Sunter, C. (2010) 'Mind of a fox', Speech at Valley Lodge, Magaliesburg, 26 January.

Sy, E. (2001) 'Gender, HIV/AIDS, and human security', www.un.org/womenwatch/daw/csw/Sy2001.htm.

Synge, R. (1997) *Mozambique: UN Peacekeeping in Action, 1992–1994*, Washington, DC: United States Institute for Peace.

Taylor, I. (2004), 'The "all weather friend"? Sino-African interaction in the 21st century', in I. Taylor and P. Williams (eds), *Africa in International Politics: External Involvement on the Continent*, London: Routledge, p. 87.

Teriba, Y. (2007) 'The AU Solemn Declaration on Gender Equality in Africa', Paper presented at the conference 'Popularization and Implementation of the Solemn Declaration on Gender Equality in Africa: The Role of Parliament', Addis Ababa, Ethiopia, 10–12 October.

Thabede, M. S. H. (2008) *The IDC in SADC*,

ujdigispace.uj.ac.za:8080/dspace/
bitstream/.../IDCinSADCreport.pdf.
Thomas, P. (n.d.) 'Women and gender
mainstreaming', in *Women, Gender, and
Development in the Pacific: Key Issues*,
Canberra: Australian National University, Development Studies Network,
pp. 1–7.
Thomas, R. H. (2002) 'SDIs in southern
Africa as a strategy for attracting FDIS
into the SADC region: origins and
future prospects', Gaborone: SADC.
— (2009) 'Development corridors and
Spatial Development Initiatives in
Africa', Mintek Research Report, Johan-
nesburg, January.
Thompson, C. (1985) *Challenge to Imperial-
ism: The Frontline States in the Libera-
tion of Zimbabwe*, Harare: Zimbabwe
Publishing House.
Thornberry, C. (2004) *A Nation is Born: The
Inside Story of Namibia's Independence*,
Windhoek: Gamsberg Macmillan.
Timaeus, I. M. (2008) 'Deaths in the family: AIDS, demography, and poverty
in Africa', Inaugural lecture delivered
to the London School of Hygiene and
Tropical Medicine, London, 26 February.
Trade Law Centre for Southern Africa
(Tralac) (2009) 'Botswana: 5000 workers lose jobs as textile factory closes
down', www.agoa.co.za/index.php?view
=.&story=news&subtext=1180.
— (2011) 'Bilateral trade profile: US–Bot-
swana', www.agoa.info/?view=country_
info&country=bw&story=trade.
Tripp, A. M. (2003) 'The changing face
of Africa's legislatures: women and
quotas', Paper presented at the
Parliamentary Forum conference 'The
Implementation of Quotas: African
Experiences', International Institute for
Democracy and Electoral Assistance
(IDEA), Electoral Institute of Southern
Africa (EISA) and Southern African
Development Community (SADC),
Pretoria, South Africa, 11/12 November.
Tull, D. (2006) 'China in Africa: scope, sig-
nificance, and consequences', *Journal
of Modern African Studies*, 44(3): 459–79.

— (2008) 'The political consequences of
China's return to Africa', in C. Alden,
D. Large and R. S. de Oliveira, *China
Returns to Africa: A Rising Power and
a Continent Embrace*, London: Hurst,
pp. 135–41.
United Kingdom Department for Inter-
national Development (DfID) (2010)
*The Neglected Crisis of Undernutrition:
DFID's Strategy*, www.dfid.gov.uk/.../
The-neglected-crisis-of-undernutrition-
DFIDs-strategy.
United Nations (1996) *Promotion and
Protection of the Rights of Children:
Impact of Armed Conflict on Children*,
A/51/306, www.unhchr.ch/huridocda/
huridoca.nsf/(Symbol)/A.51.306.En?
Opendocument.
— (2002) *Report of the Secretary General on
Women, Peace, and Security*, S/2002/1154,
16 October.
— (2006) Working Group on Women,
Peace, and Security, *Security Council
Resolution 1325 on Women, Peace, and
Security: Six Years On Report – SCR 1325
and the Peacebuilding Commission*, New
York.
— (2007) *Twenty-third Report of the
Secretary-General on the United Nations
Organization Mission in the Democratic Republic of the Congo*, S/2007/156,
20 March.
— (2008) *Mixed Record on Millennium
Development Goals Underlines Need for
Sustained Push*, New York: Department
of Public Information, News and
Media Division, 1 April, www.un.org/
News/Press/docs/2008/sgsm11487.doc.
htm.
— (2009) *Human Development Report* (lists
SADC countries in the 'Low Develop-
ment' index category).
— (2010) *Implementation of the Recom-
mendations Contained in the Report of
the Secretary-General on the Causes of
Conflict and the Promotion of Durable
Peace and Sustainable Development in
Africa*, A/65/152, 20 July.
United Nations and African Union (AU)
Commission (2010) 'Report on climate
change and development in Africa',

www.uneca.org/cfm/2010/documents/
English/Report-onClimateChange-
andDevelopment-inAfrica.pdf.

United Nations Children's Fund (UNICEF)
(2008) *The State of the World's Children:
Maternal and Newborn Health*, New
York, December.

United Nations Conference on Trade
and Development (UNCTAD) (2003)
*Economic Development in Africa: Trade
Performance and Commodity Dependence*, Geneva.

United Nations Department of Peacekeeping Operations (DPKO) (n.d.) www.
un.org/depts/DPKO/Missions/unavem1/
unavemi.htm.

United Nations Development Report
(UNDP) (1994) *Human Development Re-
port 1994*, New York: Oxford University
Press.

— (2010) 'Elections and conflict prevention: a guide to analysis, planning, and
programming', Mimeo, New York.

United Nations Economic and Social
Council (ECOSOC) (1999) 'Substantive
Issues Arising in the Implementation
of the International Covenant on
Economic, Social, and Cultural Rights:
International Code of Conduct on the
Human Right to Adequate Food', 20th
session, Geneva, 26 April–14 May, www.
unhchr.ch/tbs/doc.nsf/0/3d02758c707031
d58025677f003b73b9.

— (2011a) 'Overview of economic and
social conditions in Africa in 2010', E/
ECA/COE/30/2 & AU/CAMEF/EXP/2(VI),
March, www.uneca.org/cfm/2011/
documents/English/Overview-of-
economic-and-social-conditions-
inAfrica-in2010%20_11.pdf.

— (2011b) *UN Economic and Social Council
Resolution 1997/2: Agreed Conclusions*,
1997/2, 18 July 1997, www.unhcr.org/
refworld/docid/4652c9fc2.html.

United Nations Economic Commission for
Africa (2005) 'Institutions and regional
integration in Africa', www.uneca.org/
aria2/chap2.pdf.

United Nations Framework Convention on
Climate Change (2009) *The Copenhagen
Accord*, advance unedited version,

18 December, unfccc.int/files/meetings/
cop_15/application/pdf/cop15_cph_auv.
pdf.

United Nations General Assembly (2009)
*Report of the Office of the United Nations
High Commissioner for Human Rights on
the Relationship between Climate Change
and Human Rights*, Human Rights
Council 10th session, A/HRC/10/61,
15 January.

United Nations Human Settlements
Programme (2008) *The State of African
Cities 2008: A Framework for Addressing
Urban Challenges in Africa*, Nairobi.

United Nations Refugee Agency (2011)
'Southern Africa', www.unhcr.org/
pages/49e45abb6.html.

United States (2010) White House,
'National Security Strategy', www.
whitehouse.gov/sites/default/files/rss_
viewer/national_security_strategy.pdf.

United States Trade Representative (2009)
'Fact sheet on AGOA', www.ustr.gov/
sites/default/files/AGOA%20Fact%20
Sheet%2003.09.pdf.

US Agency for International Development (USAID) (2011) 'HIV/AIDS health
profile: southern Africa region', www.
usaid.gov/our_work/global_health/
aids/Countries/africa/southernafrica_
profile.pdf.

Utting, P. (ed.) (2002) *The Greening of Busi-
ness in Developing Countries: Rhetoric,
Reality, and Prospects*, London: Zed
Books in association with UNRISD.

Vale, P. (2003) *Security and Politics in South
Africa: The Regional Dimension*, Boulder,
CO: Lynne Rienner.

Van der Wath, K. (2004) *Doing Business in
China*, Beijing: Beijing Axis.

Van der Westhuizen, C. (ed.) (2005) *Gender
Instruments in Africa: Critical Perspec-
tives, Future Strategies*, Midrand, South
Africa: Institute for Global Dialogue.

Van Ginkel, H. J. Court and L. Van Lan-
genhove (eds) (2003) *Integrating Africa:
Perspectives on Regional Integration and
Development*, New York: United Nations
University Press.

Van Nieuwkerk, A. (2009) 'Overview of the
SADC Strategic Indicative Plan for the

Organ (SIPO): achievements and challenges', *Pax-Africa*, 5(1): 9.

Vickers, B. (2010) 'SADC's international trade relations', in C. Harvey (ed.), *Proceedings of the 2009 FOPRISA Annual Conference*, Gaborone: Botswana Institute for Development Policy Analysis.

Vigneswaran, D. (2007) 'Free movement and the movement's forgotten freedoms: South African representation of undocumented migrants', Working Paper no. 41, Oxford: Refugee Studies Centre, July.

Viner, J. (1950) *The Customs Union Issue*, New York: Carnegie Endowment for International Peace.

Vogt, J. (2007) *Die regionale Integration des südlichen Afrikas: unter besonderer Betrachtung der Southern African development community (SADC) (Schriften zur Europäischen Integration und internationalen Wirtschaftsordnung)*, Baden-Baden: Nomos, 2007.

Voice of Africa's LGBTI Community (2010) 'Is the African Commission dictated to by religious and political leaders on sexual minorities?', www.mask.org.za/is-the-african-commission-dictated-to-by-religious-and-political-leaders-on-sexual-minorities/#more-3076.

Von Braun, J. (2008) 'The food crisis isn't over (commentary)', *Nature*, 456(701).

Von Grebmer, K. et al. (2009) *Global Hunger Index: The Challenge of Hunger – Focus on Financial Crisis and Gender Inequality*, Washington, DC: International Food Policy Research Institute (IFPRI), www.ifpri.org/sites/default/files/publications/ghi09.pdf.

Wagle, U. (1999) 'The civil society sector in the developing world', *Public Administration and Management: An Interactive Journal*, 4(4).

Wallerstein, I. (2005) 'Regional unity and African unity' in I. Wallerstein, *Africa: The Politics of Independence and Unity*, Lincoln: University of Nebraska Press.

Wiig, A. and T. B. Seleka (2008) 'Will intraregional trade liberalisation within SADC reduce poverty? The case of Malawi', in G. Cawthra and J. M. Kaunda,

Towards Political and Economic Integration in Southern Africa: Prospects of the 2007 FOPRISA (the Formative Process Research on Integration in Southern Africa) Annual Conference, Gaborone: Lightbooks.

Williams, P. D. (2009) 'The Peace and Security Council of the African Union: evaluating an embryonic international institution', *Journal of Modern African Studies*, 47(41): 604, 618.

Wilson, S., A. Sengupta and K. Evans (eds) (2005) *Defending Our Dreams: Global Feminist Voices for a New Generation*, London: Zed Books in association with the Association for Women in Development (AWID).

Wisner, B. et al. (2007) 'Climate change and human security', www.radixonline.org/cchs.html and www.radixonline.org/cchs.doc.

World Food Programme (WFP) (2002) 'WFP issues global alert at UN Security Council', Press release, one.wfp.org/english/?ModuleID=137&Key=581.

World Health Organization (WHO) (2006) 'Report from the Expert Consultation on Drug-Resistant Tuberculosis', www.sahealthinfo.org/tb/expert.htm.

World Trade Organization (WTO) (2003) *Trade Policy Review: Southern African Customs Union*, Report no. WT/TPR/S/114, Geneva.

Wright, S. (1998) 'The Politicization of Culture', *Anthropology Today*, 14(1).

Xing, L. (2007) 'Paradigm shift: from "Washington Consensus" to "Beijing Consensus"', in K. Prah, *Afro-Chinese Relations: Past, Present, and Future*, Rondebosch, Cape Town: CASAS, pp. 101–25.

Xinhua General News (2009) 'Malawi expels foreign tobacco buyers', 8 September.

Yu, G. T. (1966) 'Sino-African relations: a survey', *Asian Survey*, 5(7): 464.

— (1968) 'China's failure in Africa', *Asian Survey*, 6(8): 1026.

— (1980) 'The Tanzania–Zambia railway: a case study in Chinese economic aid to Africa', in W. Weinstein and T. H. Henriksen (eds), *Soviet and Chinese Aid to African Nations*, New York: Praeger, p. 121.

Zartman, W. I. (1971) *The Politics of Trade Negotiations Between Africa and the Economic Community: The Weak Confront the Strong*, Princeton, NJ: Princeton University Press.

Ziervogel, G. et al. (2006) 'Climate variability and change: implications for household food security', Assessments of Impacts and Adaptations to Climate Change (AIACC) Working Paper no. 20.

Zlotnik, H. (2009) 'Does population matter for climate change?', in J. M. Guzmán et al., *Population Dynamics and Climate Change*, New York: UNFPA and IIED, pp. 31–44.

Zondi, S. (2008) 'The State of the Southern African Development Community: A Critical Assessment – State of Regional Integration Project of the Development of Southern Africa', Paper prepared for the Southern African Development Bank, Midrand.

Index

Clinton, Hillary, 275; visit to Africa, 274
Coalition of African Lesbians (CAL), 115
cobalt, 172
Cold War, 281, 293
colonialism, 217–18, 225; struggles against, 4, 17
Common African Defence Act, 199
common currency, 7
common market, 3, 26, 39, 40
Common Market for Eastern and Southern Africa (COMESA), 3, 4, 7, 9, 15, 40, 49, 51, 133, 138, 141, 164, 165, 236, 298, 300; and climate change, 230, 232, 237; Climate Change Initiative, 242–3, 244; Climate Change Unit (CCU), 243; membership overlap with SADC, 245
common monetary area (CMA) agreement, 7
common monetary zone, 26
communitarian nationalism, 218
Community of Sahel-Saharan States (CENSAD), 4
Comoros, peacekeeping in, 97, 99
Comprehensive Africa Agricultural Development Programme (CAADP), 188
Conference of Berlin (1884), 223
conflict management in southern Africa, 78–91
Congress of South African Trade Unions (COSATU), 167
Constellation of Southern African States (CONSAS), 5, 28, 29
Continental Customs Union, 66
Convention on the Elimination of All Forms of Discrimination against Women (CEDAW), 110
Copenhagen Climate Summit (2009), 231
copper production, 172; in Zambia, 291–2
corridors of development, 144; HIV infection in, 202
Cosme, Nelson, 274
Côte d'Ivoire, peacekeeping in, 97
Cotonou trade scheme, 252–3, 256
credit, access to, 110
Crocker, Chester, 266
cross-border trade: of the poor, 216; of women, 224
Crush, Jonathan, 220
Cuba, 265; troops in Angola, 30, 93
customs, within SACU, 155

customs union, 2, 3, 7, 26, 39, 258, 260

dams: Cahora Bassa, 170, 173; Grand Inga Dam, 137, 142; Katse, 175; Mohale, 175
Daniel, John, 273
Dar es Salaam Declaration on Agriculture and Food Security, 189
Dar es Salaam Special Economic Zone, 292
Darfur: peacekeeping in, 101; UN mission in, 99
de-mining, 269
decision-making, processes of, 156–61
decolonization, 28, 32, 36
democracy, 78, 85; 'democracy fever', 43; promotion of, 271–2
Democracy and Governance Programme, 277
democratic governance, 71
Democratic Party (Botswana), 78
Democratic Republic of the Congo (DRC), 5, 27, 67, 79, 94, 107, 137–8, 142, 199, 224, 271, 274, 300; abandonment of electricity project, 13; hydroelectric resources of, 135; joins SADC, 45–6; land issues in, 192; relations with China, 143, 293; SADC intervention in, 96; UN mission in, 92, 99
democratization, 156–61
Dent, Christopher, 282
Department for International Development (DfID) (UK), 182
deregulation, 283
desertification, 232
Development Bank of Southern Africa (DBSA), 14, 17, 18, 34, 144, 164, 171, 273–4, 303; in SADC region, 171–6
Development Bank of Southern Africa Act (1997) (South Africa), 171
development finance institutions (DFIs), 14, 164–77
Devereux, Stephen, 183
diamonds, 174
disaster risk reduction (DRR), 238
distribution of wealth, in South Africa, 144
Dlamini-Zuma, Nkosazana, 270
Dos Santos, José Eduardo, 277
drought, 181; early warning of, 238; mitigation of, 49
Duvvury, Nata, 116

free trade areas, 3, 6, 26, 39, 49, 50, 66
Frontline States (FLS), 5, 25, 27, 29, 32, 35, 42, 43–4, 57, 71, 297
Fund for African Women, 111

G8 Africa Action Plan, 166
Galtung, Johan, 107
Garvey, Marcus, 97
gender, 74, 184–5; and peace-building, 107–27; mainstreaming of, 109
gender equality, 120, 121, 301; achievement of, 118–20; in decision-making, 117
gender fatigue, 115–18, 119
General Agreement on Tariffs and Trade (GATT), 40, 160
General Peace Agreement (Mozambique, 1992), 81
Germany, SADC relations with, 55
Ghana–Guinea–Mali Union, 3
girls, withdrawn from education, 201
Global Aids Alliance, 206
global environmental change (GEC), 230; and human security and human rights, 233–6; mainstreaming of policies, 235, 241
global financial crisis, 187
global warming, 235–6
globalization, responding to, 65
Gore, Al, 268
governance, 13; good, 8; see also democratic governance
'governmental politics', 63
governments, role of, in regional integration, 52–3
grassroots women's groups: financial support of, 119; importance of, 118–20
Green Revolution, 190
green technologies, transfer of, 241
greenhouse gas emissions, 134, 231–2; reduction of, 302
Growth, Employment and Redistribution Policy (GEAR) (South Africa), 142
Gyimah-Boadi, Emmanuel, 88

Haas, Ernst, 2
Hammarskjöld, Dag, 92
harmonization: of migration laws, 215; of policies, 1, 41
Havnevik, Kjell, 192
He, Zheng, 283
healthcare, 10, 176

Hi-Sense company, 290
highly indebted poor countries (HIPC), 174
HIV/AIDS, 6, 8, 16, 66, 74, 112, 120, 185, 186, 236, 241, 270–1, 272, 301–2; 3 Ones Principle on HIV/AIDS, 204; and military security, 207–9; and human security, 198–214; control of, 15; prevention of, 204, 207, 210, 302; statistics for, 198; threat to region-building, 9–10
HIV/AIDS in Integrated Peace Support Operations in Africa, 208–9
homophobia, 114
homosexuality, banning of, 114
hospitals, 176
Houphouët-Boigny, Félix, 3
Hu Jintao: visits to Namibia, 292; visit to southern Africa, 288
Human Development Report, 199
human rights, 286; related to climate change, 233–6
Human Sciences Research Council, 216
human security, 198–214, 301; and HIV/AIDS, 207–9
hunger, freedom from, 181–3 see also food insecurity

identity politics, 216
Ikenberry, John, 260
immigrants: harassment of, 202; 'illegal', 218, 220, 222, 224; Zimbabwean, abusive treatment of, in Botswana, 221
Impact of Armed Conflict on Children report, 114
independence, struggle for, 3
India, 251, 255, 273; involvement in Africa, 261, 262
Indian Ocean Commission (IOC), 138
Industrial and Commercial Bank of China, 290
Industrial Development Act (1997) (South Africa), 168
Industrial Development Corporation (IDC) (South Africa), 14, 17, 18, 164, 167–9, 274, 303; role of, in Mozambique, 169–70
inequality, 152–3 see also gender equality
informal settlements, growth of, 222
infrastructure, 175, 190, 257; in transport (development of, 48; sabotage of, 31); problems of, 164, 166

Makoni, Simba, 29, 84

Malaquias, Assis, 274

Malawi, 29, 30, 41, 49, 80, 114, 188, 219, 254, 300; agriculture in, 190–1; cereal production of, 184; cuts relations with Taiwan, 288; deportation of tobacco buyers from, 224; electricity supply in, 133; US aid for, 32; women's political representation in, 117

malnutrition *see* food insecurity *and* hunger

Mandela, Nelson, 5, 35, 45, 95, 166, 173, 220

manufacturing sector, 143

Maputo Development Corridor (MDC), 34, 48, 132, 170, 173

Maputo Port Development Company, 174

markets, integration of, 49

Marti, Darlan, 256

masculinity, 120

Mauritius, 6, 80, 98, 143, 300

Mbeki, Thabo, 5, 17, 46, 83, 133, 175, 220, 268, 286; visit to China, 287

Mbuende, Kaire, 12–13, 278

Messerlin, Patrick, 256

Mfecane, 218

migrant workers, 302

migration: and xenophobia, 215–29; cross-border, 219; issues of, planning for, 215; related to HIV/AIDS, 201–2

military, and HIV/AIDS transmission, 207–9

military force, regional, 95–7

Millennium Development Goals (MDG), 11, 74, 110, 115, 181, 182, 203, 299

Millennium Summit Declaration, 142

Ming dynasty, 283

mining, 135, 174, 273; informal, 224

Mitsubishi Corporation, 169

mobility of labour, 219, 224, 302

Mobutu Sese Seko, 94

monetary union, 7, 300

Monterrey Consensus (2002), 115

mortality, maternal, 113

most favoured nation status, 255, 258

Mothae, Tanki, 209

Movement for Democratic Change (MDC) (Zimbabwe), 46, 82, 83

Moyo, Jonathan, 83

Mozal Community Development Trust (MCDT), 170

Mozambique, 7, 30, 31, 32, 41, 80, 81, 84, 108, 170, 171, 199, 219, 258, 259, 265, 266, 273, 284; DBSA operations in, 173–4; effects of HIV/AIDS on education in, 200; elections in, 90; floods in, 269; food riots in, 301; independence of, 27; investment in, 140; relations with China, 293; role of Industrial Development Corporation in, 169–7

Mozambique Aluminium Smelter (Mozal), 169–70

Mozambique National Resistance (RENAMO), 31

MTN company, 139

Mugabe, Robert, 35, 45, 82, 84, 95, 266, 270, 276, 291

Multilateral Investments Guarantee Agency (MIGA), 51

multinational corporations, 6, 139; hiring of foreign labour, 224

Mulungushi Club, 27

Mutambara, Arthur, 82

Mutual Defence Pact, 65

Namibia, 7, 14, 27, 42, 45, 80, 94, 96, 108, 114, 139, 148, 149, 153–6, 172, 219, 257, 265, 266, 271, 273, 274; attitude to EPAs, 12; control of migration in, 215; dispute with Botswana, 58; elections in, 90; presence of Chinese people in, 293; relations with China, 292–3; xenophobia in, 219–20

nation state, formation of, 217

National Gender Equality Funds, 111

National Liberation Front (FLN) (Algeria), 284

National Union for the Total Independence of Angola (UNITA), 30, 58, 93–4, 284

natural disasters, 174

neo-functionalism, 2

neocolonialism, 252

Neocosmos, Michael, 217

neoliberalism, 222

Netcare company, 175

Neto, Agostinho, 275

New Partnership for Africa's Development (NEPAD), 110, 142, 166, 168, 203, 245; e-Africa commission, 169; High-Level Subcommittee on Infrastructure, 164; ICT Broadband Infrastructure for Eastern and Southern Africa, 169

Nigeria, 268, 271; relations with USA, 273

operations in, 172; dispute with
Angola, 58; HIV/AIDS incidence in, 201,
204; land issues in, 192; presence of
Chinese people in, 292; relations with
China, 284, 291–2; TB rates in, 200; US
aid for, 32; xenophobia in, 221

Zambia–China Chambishi Trade and
Economic Zone, 291

Zambia Electricity Supply Corporation,
292

Zanzibar, 114

Zhai, Jun, 288

Zhao, Ziyang, visits Africa, 285

Zhou, Enlai, 283; visits Africa, 284

Zimbabwe, 5, 6, 27, 28, 30, 35, 41, 45,
46, 49, 67, 79, 81, 94, 95, 96, 108, 114,
186, 188, 219, 224, 254, 265, 267, 270,
274, 276–7, 300; China's provision of
military equipment to, 291; elections
in, 82–4, 89; environmental rights in,
236; peacekeeping in, 96; relations with
China, 291; US support for, 266

Zimbabwe African National Union–
Patriotic Front (ZANU-PF), 27, 46, 82–4,
101, 266, 285; sanctions against, 277

Zimbabwe African People's Union (ZAPU),
27, 285

Zimbabwe Election Support Network
(ZESN), 83

Zimbabwe–Zambia–Botswana–Namibia
electricity project (ZIZABONA), 133, 135

Zuma, Jacob, 5, 7, 141, 164, 256, 274, 287

About Zed Books

Zed Books is a critical and dynamic publisher, committed to increasing awareness of important international issues and to promoting diversity, alternative voices and progressive social change. We publish on politics, development, gender, the environment and economics for a global audience of students, academics, activists and general readers. Run as a co-operative, Zed Books aims to operate in an ethical and environmentally sustainable way.

Find out more at:

www.zedbooks.co.uk

For up-to-date news, articles, reviews and events information visit:

http://zed-books.blogspot.com

To subscribe to the monthly Zed Books e-newsletter, send an email headed 'subscribe' to:

marketing@zedbooks.net

We can also be found on **Facebook**, **ZNet**, **Twitter** and **Library Thing**.